CAROLINA FAMILIES

A Bibliography of Books About North and South Carolina Families

by **Donald M. Hehir**

HERITAGE BOOKS, INC.

Other Heritage Books from
Donald M. Hehir:

Georgia Families: A Bibliographic Listing of Books About Georgia Families

Kentucky Families: A Bibliographic Listing of Books About Kentucky Families

Ohio Families: A Bibliography of Books About Ohio Families

Published 1994 by

HERITAGE BOOKS, INC.
1540-E Pointer Ridge Place,
Bowie, Maryland 20716
(301) 390-7709

ISBN 0-7884-0036-3

Dedication:

To Jeanne McAdam Hehir

ACKNOWLEDGEMENTS

Particular thanks are due to Karen Ackermann at Heritage Books for her very helpful advice on putting together this and previous works and to Donald Odell Virdin for his always helpful suggestions and encouragement.

TABLE OF CONTENTS

INTRODUCTION

The works in this bibliography, covering over 1400 family names, deal with families who have some connection to the Carolinas. A separate section lists family histories and genealogies on microfilm at the Library of Congress as of mid-1992. A brief introduction to that section of this book may be found on page 285.

By far the largest portion of the works covered in this book can be found at the Library of Congress in Washington, D.C., the National Genealogical Society (NGS) Library Arlington, Virginia, or in the Daughters of the American Revolution (DAR) Library in Washington, D.C.

Also included are a significant number of books from more than 15 historical association and public libraries from Massachusetts to California, including the New York Public Library, the Allen County Public Library (Fort Wayne, Indiana), and the San Francisco Public Library.

The reader should remember that no work of this kind can ever be complete. Many family histories are privately printed and never make their way into large collections. Similarly, many newer works will not have been published, or cataloged, in time for inclusion in this book. It is neither possible, nor practicable, to review individual bibliographies and family histories. For this reason, family names included here may, or may not, be primarily or exclusively associated with the Carolinas and some works, published in the Carolinas and included here, may occasionally refer to non-Carolina families, with the only reference to the State being the fact that the bibliography or history was published there. They have been included in order to cast as wide a net as practicable to include all possible references to families with some association with the Carolinas. By the same token, there may be other published material on Carolina families in works relating to other areas of the country, but they are not included here, because there was no way to identify a relationship to the Carolinas. Many of the books cited here include references to other states and countries.

This work follows primarily the Library of Congress system for cataloging names, so, for example, a work on "Cline" might be shown under the Library of Congress Family Name Index of "Kline" even when "Kline" is not mentioned in the title or the description of the book.

Similarly, since different libraries catalog publications with slightly differing classification systems, family names may have different spellings, depending on the system being used. As a result, there are listings in this book, which may in some cases be duplicative of other listings, since it was not always possible to determine if references were to the same book, to different editions, or to different books.

In compiling the bibliographies and family histories listed, I have attempted to err on the side of including, rather than excluding, works with similar titles and publication dates where the possibility exists that the books are, at least, different editions of the same work. The Cross-Reference Index will show the page location in this book of all families mentioned in the descriptions in the original source documents.

Among the various sources , the use of the terms "pages" and "leaves" is not always consistent from library to library, so that the same book in different libraries may be shown as having "n" leaves, or "n" pages. Similarly, different catalogers may use different styles to indicate pagination, e. g. 47 pages in one source may appear as 2, 1, 44 pages in a different source, yet both are indicating a total of 47 pages. This adds to the problem of determining whether different catalogers were reporting on the same, or different, editions, of the same book. In the interests of simplicity, I have shortened some lengthy pagination descriptions so that, for example, a pagination description of 5p., 1., 145, (1)p,, 1 l., is generally rendered here as 5, 145, 1p.

Another area, which may present difficulty to the reader, occurs when catalogers indicate the pagination as, for example, 160 [i.e.326]p. Usually this means that there are 160 numbered pages with data on one side only, with the added possibility of additional blank pages and some sheets numbered on both sides. In such cases, the bracketed figure generally indicates the total number of pages in the volume. This, fortunately, does not often occur.

Where different library catalogers have used different descriptions for the same work, the more detailed description has generally been followed, and in some cases, differing descriptions have been combined to provide the user with as much information possible about the content of an individual work.

FORMAT: The description of bibliographies and family histories contained in this volume generally follows the format indicated below:

FAMILY NAME -- Author (Compiler or Editor). *Title. Subtitle.* Place of Publication, Date of Publication. Number of pages or leaves. Additional Descriptive Material, if any. [Source abbreviation. Library catalog or page number in that source for the referenced work may also be given, e. g. L600 shows that the genealogy is listed as item 600 in Genealogies in the Library of Congress].

Note that in the Section dealing with Histories and Genealogies on Microfilm at the Library of Congress, the last item will be the catalog number for the Microfilm which contains the book, chart, or other document cited.

ABBREVIATIONS FOR SOURCES

Each source cited and its abbreviations used in this work are as follows:

A - Appendices to KAMINKOW, Marion J. Genealogies In The Library of Congress. Baltimore, Maryland, 1972.

C - KAMINKOW, Marion J. Genealogies In The Library of Congress, Second Supplement 1976 - 1986. Baltimore, Maryland, 1987.

D - MICHAELS, Carolyn Leopold and Kathryn S. Scott. DAR Library Catalog, Volume One, Second Revised Edition, Family Histories and Genealogies. Washington, DC, 1983.

DC - GRUNDSET, Eric B. & Bebe METZ. DAR Library Catalog, Volume Three Centennial Supplement: Acquisitions 1985-1991. Washington, DC, 1992.

DS - MICHAELS, Carolyn Leopold and Kathryn S. SCOTT. DAR Library Catalog, Volume One - Supplement - Family Histories and Genealogies. Washington, DC, 1984.

G - GENEALOGIES Cataloged in the Library of Congress Since 1986. Washington, DC, 1992.

L - KAMINKOW, Marion J. Genealogies In The Library of Congress. Baltimore, 1972. 2. v. A-L and M-Z.

NG - National Genealogical Society Library Book List, 5th Edition. Arlington, Virginia, 1988.

NGS - National Genealogical Society Library Book List, 5th Edition Supplement. Arlington, Virginia, 1989.

NGN - National Genealogical Society, Library Acquisitions, December 1989 through December 1992. Arlington, Virginia, National Genealogical Society, 1993.

S - KAMINKOW, Marion J. Genealogies In The Library of Congress Supplement 1972-76. Baltimore, 1976.

VV - VIRDIN, Donald O. Virginia Genealogies and Family Histories. Bowie, Maryland, Heritage Books, Inc., 1990.

VP - VIRDIN, Donald O. Pennsylvania Genealogies and Family Histories. Bowie, Maryland, Heritage Books, Inc., 1992.

X - KAMINKOW, Marion J. A Complement To Genealogies In The Library of Congress. Baltimore, 1981.

XA - Appendix to KAMINKOW, Marion J. A Complement To Genealogies In The Library of Congress. Baltimore, Maryland, 1981.

In the above sources the numbers following the entry in the text refer to the number assigned to the entry in the source publication and not to a page number:

A - C - G - S - D - DC - DS - L

In other sources, the number refers to the page number where the genealogy or family history is located in that source, e. g. NG123 shows that the genealogy is located on page 123 of the National Genealogical Society Library Book List. The exception being the works listed as NGN, which indicates the volume, the number, and the year in which the items was listed in the NGS Newsletter. e.g. NGN17-1-92 indicates newsletter issue: volume 17, no. 1, 1992. Unfortunately the NGS Newsletter entries do not indicate the place or date of publication, or the pagination. These works are for the most part available through the NGS Library Loan Service.

NG - NGS - VP - VV - X - XA

While most citations are to specific library collections, the Virdin Virginia (VV) and Pennsylvania (VP) genealogies are not contained in any specific library. Library collections for entries followed solely by [VV] or [VP] may be in some of the other library collections cited, but the user is advised to consult other libraries and historical and genealogical societies in the states concerned. All other source references are to libraries and genealogical societies located in the Metropolitan Washington, DC area, except those marked "X-____ or XA-____".

Note that the entries for the <u>Complement to the Genealogies in the Library of Congress</u>, "X" and "XA", are for genealogies and family histories <u>not</u> in the Library of Congress at the time "A Complement... " was written and many are not in the Library of Congress collection to this date. The coding, at the end of each entry, will indicate if any particular "X" or "XA" entry is also shown as being in the Library of Congress collection. The X is followed, by the initials of the Library, or Libraries, where the genealogy or family history is located, e.g.

[X-FW] Allen County Public Library, Fort Wayne, Indiana

[X-NY/SL] New York Public Library and St. Louis Public Library.

Library Designators used with the "X" (and "XA") entries are:

AH	Alaska Historical Society
BA	Boston Athenaeum
CH	Cincinnati Historical Society

DP	Denver Public Library
FW	Allen County Public Library, Fort Wayne, Indiana
GF	Genealogical Forum of Portland, Oregon
IG	Idaho Historical Genealogical Library, Boise
KY	Kansas State Historical Society, Topeka
LA	Los Angeles Public Library
LI	Long Island Historical Society, Brooklyn, N. Y.
MH	Minnesota Historical Society, St. Paul
NJ	Gloucester County Historical Society, Woodbury, N. J.
NY	New York Public Library
OH	Ohio Historical Society, Columbus
OL	The State Library of Ohio, Columbus
OS	Oregon State Library, Salem
PH	The Historical Society of Pennsylvania, Philadelphia
PP	Library Association of Portland, Oregon
SF	San Francisco Public Library
SP	Seattle Public Library
SL	St. Louis Public Library
SU	Sutro Branch of the California State Library, San Francisco

SW Spokane Washington, Public Library

WR Western Reserve Historical Society, Cleveland, Ohio

GLOSSARY

? - Indicates a doubt by the compiler of this work as to the accuracy of the material shown in the original source; Also, indicates a conflict in the data shown in different sources when referring apparently to an identical work.

! - Indicates a doubt by the compiler of the source document as to the accuracy of the material shown in the referenced work.

c. - Circa. (Also, ca.)

ed. - Edition.

enl. - Enlarged,

l. - Leaf (Leaves).

NAS - No Author or Compiler shown in the source listing.

NP - No Place of Publication indicated.

n.d. - No Date of Publication indicated.

numb. - Numbered.

p. - Page(s).

pni - Pagination Not Indicated

rep. - Reprint.

rev. - Revised, Revision.

sic _ Used to indicate that the previous word or phrase has been copied precisely from the original source even though apparently misspelled or incorrect.

unp. - Unpaged.

v. - Volume or Volumes.

A

ABRAMS -- Abrams, George Carter. *The Abrams Family Genealogy, 1745-1979.* Newberry, SC, Abrams, 1979. ix, 416p. [D19].

ACKER -- Acker, George H. *Descendants of Peter Acker and Wife Jane Sutherland, Settlers of 1787 in the Pendleton District of South Carolina.* Cleveland, OH, 1966, 75 l. X gives 74 leaves. [NG14; X3-FW].

ADAMS -- Adams, Macie Marie. *The Adams Family of Pendleton.* Buda, TX, D.F. Forsythe, 1988- v. <1 >. Contents: v. 1. The Generation of Rev Nathaniel A. Adams and Catherine Winiford Barker. 1. Adams Genealogy. 2. South Carolina-Genealogy. [G3].

ADAMS -- Baldwin, Emma. *An Adams - Goolsby Genealogy, Some Descendants of Robert Adams of Virginia, Georgia and Texas, 1624-1982, and a Shirley Genealogy: Some Descendants of Thomas Shirley of Virginia, South Carolina, Georgia, and Texas, 1612-1982.* Tenaha, TX, E. G. Baldwin, 1983. vii, 272p. [C3; VV1].

ADAMS -- Bivins Caroline Pasteur Holmes. *Pedigree Chart of Caro Meriwether Adams (1870-1962) John Jefferson Adams (1880-1964) Robert Hammond Adams (1883), Agnes Adams (1885), Olivia Orme Adams (1888), Leroy Hammond Adams (1894).* Greensboro, NC, 1970. 3 l. [A5].

ADAMS -- Brockman, Charles Raven. *<u>Adams, Caruthers, Clancy, Neely, and Townsend Descendants</u> Composing the Adams, Legerton, Wakefield, Brockman and Other Twentiety Century Families of the Carolinas.* Charlotte, NC, Brockman, 1950. 118 leaves. D gives underscored part of title. [L120; D52].

ADAMS -- Kunkle, James M. *The Adams Family of Wilkes County, North Carolina.* Charlotte,

NC, Kunkle, 1977. ca. 155p. in various pagings. Part of illustrative matter in pocket. 1. Adams family. [G4].

ADAMSON -- Dixon, Ben F. and Alice L. (Dwelle) Dixon. *The Adamson Source Book, A Genealogy of the Descendants of Rachel Williams Adamson (1775-1850) of Surry County, NC, Jefferson County, Tenn, and Lawrence County, Indiana.* Washington, DC 1942. 56 leaves. [NG14].

ADAMSON -- Dixon, Ben F. and Alice L. (Dwelle) Dixon. *The Adamson Source Book, A Genealogy of the Descendants of Rachel Williams Adamson (1775-1850) of Surry County, NC, Jefferson County, Tenn, and Lawrence County, Indiana.* Washington, DC 1942-1961. 2 vols. Benjamin Franklin Junior Historical Series, no. 1-4. Part 2 has title: Rachael Williams Adamson and her Hoosier Clan & Imprint: San Diego, CA. [X6-FW/NY/SU].

ADDERTON -- Walser, Richard. *Jerimiah Adderton and Some of His Descendants.* Raleigh, NC, Wolf's Head Press, 1979. 46p. [D76].

ADDINGTON -- Patterson, Naomi Louise Addington. *Addington: A Directory of the Descendants of Henry and Sarah Addington of Union County, South Carolina. 1st ed.* Bowie, MD, Heritage Books, 1989. xvi, 431p. 1. Addington family. 2. Addington, Henry, 1720-1789-Family. 3. South Carolina-Genealogy. [G5; NGN17-1-91; DC29].

ADGER -- Law, John Adger. *Adger - Law Ancestral Note-book.* Spartanburg, SC, Jacobs Graphic Arts Co., 1936. 4, 170, 4p. [L139].

ADGER -- Stevenson, Mary. *The Diary of Clarissa Adger Bowen, Ashtabula Plantation, 1865 with Excerpts from Other Family Diaries and Comments by Her Granddaughter, Clarissa Walton Taylor, and Many Other Accounts of the*

Pendleton Clemson Area, South Carolina, 1776-1889. Pendleton, SC, Research and Publication Committee, Foundation for Historic Restoration in Pendleton Area, 1973. 128p. 1. Pendleton (S.C.)-History-Sources. 2. Adger family-Diaries. [G5].

AKERS -- NAS. *The Akers Family of Franklin County, Virginia; Combined with the Boone, Cannaday, Hickman, and Pridgin Families.* Roanoke Rapids, NC, Akers, 1953. xvi, 159p. D gives underscored title. [L160; D89; VV1].

ALBRIGHT -- Albright, A. G... *Some Data on the Albright Family.* Memphis, TN, Press of S.C. Tool & Co., 1915. 83p. [L171].

ALBRIGHT -- McClain, Clarabel Albright. *Some Records of the Albright Family.* St. Joseph, MO, 1941. 35p. -- Additional findings on North Carolina Albright lineage: A supplement to "Some Records of the Albright Family" published in 1941. St. Joseph, MO, 1950. 18p. Bound with the main work. [L172].

ALDERMAN -- Alderman, J. T.? *Daniel Alderman, Abagail Harris; Removed to North Carolina in 1775 from Salem Co., N.J. (Southern Branch of Aldermans by J. T. Alderman)* Hendersonville, NC, 1917. Chart. [X10-LI].

ALDERMAN -- Parker, William Alderman. *Aldermans in America.* Raleigh, NC, Parker, 1957. xv, 714p. [L202; D124].

ALDRICH -- Aldrich, James. *A Short Sketch of the Lives of James Aldrich, Esq. and His Wife, Mrs. Isabel Coroneus Aldrich, with Genealogical Data.* Aiken, SC, 1903. 40p. X adds underscored part of title. [DC47; X10-LI].

ALDRIDGE -- Sausaman, William A. *Nathan Aldridge (1739-1826) of North Carolina and*

Tennessee and His Descendants. Springfield, IL, 1971. 129p. [X11-FW].

ALEXANDER -- NAS. *Sketches of North Carolina, Historical and Biographical Illustrative of the Principles of a Portion of Her Early Settlers.* New York, NY, R. Carter, 1846. Raleigh, NC, Published by H.J. Dudley for the Committee on Historical Matters of the Synod of North Carolina, Presbyterian Church in the U.S.A., 1965. 593p. "Third Edition, 1965" A reproduction of the 1st ed. 1846, with new preface, bibliography and index. [L212].

ALEXANDER -- NAS. *Biographical Sketches of the Early Settlers of the Hopewell Section and Reminiscences of the Pioneers and Their Descendants by Families...* Charlotte, NC, Observer Printing and Publishing House, 1897. 104p. [L216].

ALEXANDER -- Alexander, Henry Aaron. *Notes on the Alexander Family of South Carolina and Georgia, and Connections.* Atlanta, GA, Alexander, 1954. 142p. D gives 143 pages. [L227; D132; NGN18-2-92].

ALEXANDER -- Alexander, Charles C. and Virginia W. *Alexander Kin.* (Columbia, TN), The Authors, Greenville, SC, Southern Historical Press, 1965, 1980. 2 v. [DC48].

ALEXANDER -- Davidson, Theo F. & Foster A. Sundley. *Alexander - Davidson Reunion, Swannanoa, N. C., Aug. 26, 1911. Addresses by Foster A. Sundley... and Hon. Theo F. Davidson.* Swannanoa, NC, 1911. 53p. [X11-FW/LI/NY].

ALEXANDER -- Ingram, Annie K. Blythe. *The Six Alexanders Who Signed the Mecklenburg Declaration of Independence.* Wadesboro, NC, Liberty Hall Chapter, NC, DAR, 1952. 3, 9, ix, 81 leaves. [D146].

ALEXANDER -- Perry, S. *Alexander Family Records*. Camden, SC, 19__, 38p. [X11-DP].

ALEXANDER -- Peterson, Ruth S. *Descendants of Captain William Alexander and Elizabeth King of Lancaster County, Pennsylvania, Guilford and Roncolph sic Counties, North Carolina, Green County, Tennessee.* NP, 1952. 94 leaves. [D151].

ALEXANDER -- Rich, Peggy Burton. *Alexander Families of Upper South Carolina.* Clemson, SC, P.B. Rich, 1988. x, 1086p. 1. Alexander family. 2. South Carolina-Genealogy. DC gives author as Jerry L. Alexander. [G8; DC49].

ALEXANDER -- Sondley, F.A. LL.D. *Descent of the Scottish Ancestors; A Genealogical Sketch, with Discussion of Some Historic Matters and with Several Rare Tables....* Asheville, NC, Hackney and Moole Co., 1912. 73p. [L222].

ALLDREDGE -- Lester, Memory Aldridge. *Alldredge - Aldridge - Bracken - Nesmith Families and Their Kin.* Chapel Hill, NC, Lester, 1957. 223p. [D160].

ALLDREDGE -- Sausaman, William Amel. *Nathan Alldredge (1739-1862) of North Carolina and Tennessee and His Descendants.* Springfield, IL, Sausaman, 1971. 113p. [D161].

ALLEN -- Allen, Clarence B. *William Benjamin and Theodosia Allen Family.* Latta, SC, Herald Pub., Co. 1973. 23p. [D166].

ALLEN -- Allen, Lester M. *The Allen Family: Descendants of John and Amy Cox Allen with Allied Lines.* Greensboro, NC, L.M. Allen, 1987. xi, 524p. 1. Allen family. 2. Allen, John, 1694-1771-Family. [G9].

ALLEN -- Allen, Maude Bliss. *Samuel Allin Revolutionary War Soldier, 1756-1841, of North*

Carolina and Kentucky. NP, Allen, 1966. 456, 51p. [D175].

ALLEN -- Allen, Maude Bliss. *Samuel Allin Revolutionary War Soldier, 1756-1841, of North Carolina and Kentucky.* Salt Lake City, UT, R.R. Robins, 1969. 456, 51p. [X15-NW/NY].

ALLEN -- Barekman, June B. *Allens of Early Rowan County, N.C. Abstracted from the Records in the McCubbins Files and Court House, Salisbury, N.C.* Chicago, IL, 11 leaves. [S44].

ALLEN -- Carpenter, Reva Nance. *The Allens of Cribbs Creek in Burnsville, Township, Anson County...* Charlotte, NC, The Authors, 1979. 91p. [DC62].

ALLEN -- Dunn, Doris Allen O'Neal. *Allen and Allied Families.* Greenville, SC, Dunn, 1978. 117p. [D183].

ALLEN -- Goddard, Margaret E. *Annals of an Allen Family in Maryland, North Carolina, Tennessee, Indiana, Minnesota, and Iowa.* Cottonwood, AZ, The Author, 1985. 2 v. [DC3].

ALLEN -- Kelly, Jeannette H. *My Stewart and Other Kin of Iredell County, N.C. Allen, Stikeleather, Wallace, Brown, Lawson, and Tolbert Families.* York, SC, J.H. Kelly, 1986. xiv, 893p., 30p. of plates. 1. Stuart family. 2. Allen family. 3. Stikeleather family. 4. Iredell County (N.C.)-Genealogy. 5. North Carolina-Genealogy. [G9].

ALLEN -- McFarland, Wilbur Galloway. *Turner Allen's Forebears.* Duke University, NC, McFarland, 1946. 104 leaves. [D192].

ALLEN -- Miller, Norma Carter. *Allens of the Southern States.* Baltimore, MD, Gateway Press, 1989. xiii, 495p. 1. Allen family. 2. Southern States-Genealogy. [G9].

ALLGOOD -- Wigington, Elizabeth Allgood. *Allgood Genealogy.* Greenville, SC, Poinsett Printing Co., 1963. 159, 6p. [D205; X16-FW].

ALLISON -- Allison, Charles Walter. *The Reverend Thomas Johnston Allison Family History, Including Tillett History (and) Wyche History.* Charlotte, NC, 1955. 64, 195, 171p. [L313].

ALLRED -- Bennett, Archibald F. *Lineage of the Allred Family in North Carolina.* NP, 1954. 7 leaves. [X17-FW].

ALLSTON -- Allston, Elizabeth Deas. *The Allstons and Alstons of Waccamaw.* Charleston, SC, Walker, Evans & Cogswell Co., 1936. 99p. [L321].

ALLSTON -- Allston, Susan Lowndes. *Brookgreen, Waccamaw, in the Carolina Low Country.* NP, Allston, 1935. 32p. [L320; D215].

ALLSTON -- Easterby, James, Ed. *South Carolina Rice Plantation... Papers of Robert F. W. Allston.* Chicago, IL, University of Chicago Press, 1945. pni. Published under direction of American Historical Assoc. [X17-PP].

ALLSTON -- Groves, Joseph A. *The Alstons and Allstons of North and South Carolina; Compiled from English, Colonial, and Family Records, with Personal Reminiscences also Notes of Some Allied Families.* Atlanta, GA, The Franklin Printing and Publishing Co., 1901. 5, 55p. [See below: ALSTON -- Groves, Joseph A. [L318; D225].

ALSTON -- NAS. *Society and Family Book.* Rocky Mount, NC, Alston-Williams-Boddie-Hilliard Society. 1961- v. DAR library has v. I(1958-1961). [D224].

ALSTON -- NAS. *The Alstons and Allstons of North and South Carolina.* Reprint of the 1901

Ed. Reprint: Easley, SC, Southern Historical Press, 1976. 534p. [X18-FW/NY].

ALSTON -- Groves, Joseph A. *Supplemental Notes to The Alstons and Allstons of North and South Carolina, Atlanta, GA, 1901.* Supplemental Notes, 1903. 20 l. [X18-NY].

ALSTON -- Groves, Joseph A. *The Alstons and Allstons of North and South Carolina.* Atlanta, GA, Franklin Printing and Publishing Co., 1957. 367p. [D225; NGN17-4-91].

ALSTON -- Mason, Olivia G. *The James Alston Line: Son of Col. Phillip Alston of the House in the Horseshoe, Moore County, North Carolina.* Ft. Worth, TX, O.G. Mason, 1986. 14, 2 leaves. [DC76].

AMIS -- Hodges, Alice Amis. *Ancestors and Descendants of John Woodson Amis of Granville Co., N.C. and Scott Co., Miss.* Pendleton, SC, Hodges, 1978. 30, 1p. [D242].

ANDERSON -- NAS. *William Anderson and Rebecca Denny and Their Descendants.* Columbia, SC, R.L. Bryan, 1914. 287p. [D262].

ANDERSON -- Anderson, Edward Lee. *A History of the Anderson Family, 1706-1955, through the Descendants of James Mason Anderson and His Wife, Mary "Polly" Miller* Columbia, SC, Anderson, 1955. Columbia, SC, R.L. Bryan Co. 1955. 250p. D gives underscored part of title. [D253; X21-FW/NY].

ANDERSON -- Anderson, Francis I. *Anderson & Irving of Rockingham County, North Carolina; Cox & Bryan of Onslow County.* Greensboro, NC, The Author, 1980. 325p. [DC82].

ANDERSON -- Anderson, Katie Weatherford. *Standing in the Doorway of a Day Long Ago; History of Some Families: Anderson, Berry, Dew, Hampton, Weatherford, Wise.* Hartsville,

SC, Anderson, 1963. 145p. D gives underscored part of title. [L397; D257].

ANDERSON -- Goodlett, Mildred Wilson. *Waterloo, A History of the Anderson Family of old Laurens District of South Carolina.* Greenville, SC, Hiatt Press, 1961. 239p. [L396].

ANDERSON -- McNees, Lucien L. *Descendants of Capt. Henry Anderson, Sr., of Newberry County, South Carolina.* Ebenezer, MS, McNees, 1972. 165p. [D276].

ANDREWS -- Ruth, Lawrence W. *The Andrews Family of Orange & Chatham Counties of North Carolina.* Greensboro, NC, L.W. Routh, 1980. 227p. [DC90].

ANGLE -- Robertson, Irma Matthews. *Neighbors and Us.* East Bend, NC, I.M. Robertson, 1990. 165p. 1. Matthews family. 2. Angle family. 3. Blakely family. 4 Davis family. 5. North Carolina-Genealogy. [G15].

ANTLEY -- Antley, Eugene Brevard. *Southern Families: One Man's Search for Roots.* __, SC, E.B. Antley, 1988. 146, 4p. 1. Antley family. 2. Brevard family. 3. Brewton family. 4. Southern States-Genealogy. [G16].

APPLEWHITE -- Norris, Mary Applewhite. *A History of the Ancestors and Descendants of Robert Council Applewhite and Viola Felt.* Delco, NC, Norris, 1956. 36, 1p. [D337; X26-FW].

ARCHIBALD -- Bell, Jessie Lynn. *Archibald: A History and Genealogy of Descendants of William Archibald Immigrant and Settler of Rowan County, North Carolina.* Archibald, LA, 1969. 121, 208p. [L502].

ARCHIBALD -- Bell, Jessie Lynn. *Archibald: A History and Genealogy of Descendants of*

William Archibald Immigrant and Settler of Rowan County, North Carolina. NP, The Authors, 1979. 1 v. [DC102].

ARDERY -- Ardery, Julia A. *Ardery (Ardrey) Chart*, Lexington, KY, The Keystone Printery, 1930. Genealogical Tables of the Kentucky, North Carolina, South Carolina, Pennsylvania, and Ohio branches of the Ardery (Ardrey) family. [L503].

AREY -- Davidson, Harriet Arey. *Palatine Progeny: The Arey Family of Rowan County North Carolina and Related Families, 1749-1983.* Davidson, NC, Briarpatch, 1983. 324p. [DC103].

ARLINE -- Wynn, Louise Tomkins & Charles Arthur Wynn, Jr., with the Kittrell Family. *Jeremiah Arline of Nansemond Co., Va., 1695, and Descendants in North Carolina, Georgia, and Florida: Including a Short Account of the Kittrell Family*. Decorah, Iowa, Anundsen Pub. Co., 1983. xvi, 149p. [C19; NG16; VV5].

ARMSTRONG -- Armstrong, T. W. *Armstrongs, with a Brief Genealogy of One Branch of the Clan.* Raleigh, NC, Spocks, Pr., 1970. 28p. [X29-FW].

ARNOLD -- Arnold, Howard L. *Arnel's[sic] / Arnold's of North Carolina and Virginia; Family Histories.* Milan, TN, H.L. Arnold, 1988. vi, xx, 319p. 1. Arnold family. 2. North Carolina-Genealogy. 3. Virginia-Genealogy. [G19; DC110].

ARNOLD -- MacIvor, Hazel A. *Some Ancestors and Descendants of Benjamin Arnold, King William County, Virginia and Greenville, S.C.* Lake Grion, MI, 1974. 165p. [NG16; VV6].

ARRINGTON -- Linn, Jo White. *Drake - Arrington - White - Turner, Linn - Brown, and Two Dozen Related Southern Lines: Treadwell, Slade, Lacey, Harrison, Cathey, Redwine,*

Krider, Wood, McNair, Peden, Sandefer, Tompkins, Bennett, Hodges, Goodrich, Bechinoe, Williams, Bustin, Outlaw, Fox, Smith, George, Doll, and Stahle. Salisbury, NC, J. W. Linn, 1984. xii, 469p. 1. Drake family. 2. Arrington family. 3. White family. 4. North Carolina-Genealogy. 5. Georgia-Genealogy. DC gives underscored part of title. [G20; DC1093].

ASH -- Ashe, John R. *Ash, Ashe, Stillwell.* Greensboro, NC, Ashe, 1977. 239p. [D375].

ASHFORD -- Ashford, Charlie Rabb. *Some of the Ancestors and Descendants of James and George Ashford, Jr. of Fairfield County, S.C.* Starkville, MS, Ashford, 1956. 3, 123 leaves. [L565; D384].

ASHLEY -- Ashley, Allen Lane. *The Ashley Family: The Descendants of Thomas Ashley, 1781-1830, a Veteran of the War of 1812, Revolutionary War Soldier.* Honea Path, SC, A.L. and J.R. Ashley, 1985. x, 370p. 1. Ashley-family. 2. Ashley, Thomas, 1771-1830-Family. [G21].

ASKEW -- Askew, Alice Ann. *Josiah Askew of Edgecombe County, North Carolina: Ancestors and Descendants.* Bartlesville, OK, A.A. Askew, 1988. vii, 200p. 1. Askew family. 2. Askew, Josiah, ca. 1740-1818-Family. [G22; DC126].

ASKEW -- Eskew, John Daniel. *The Eskew Story: The David Bryant Eskew Family, Ancestors and Descendants, and Other Eskew's of South Carolina and Georgia.* West Chester, OH, J. D. Eskew, 1986. v, 60p. 1. Askew family. 2. Eskew, David Bryant, 1851-1915-Family. [G22].

ATCHINSON -- Barekman, June Beverly. *History of Edmund Etchison, Revolutionary Soldier of NC and His Descendants Including Atchisons, VA, MD, KY, Records of Atchison,*

Atchinson, Autchersin, Etcheson, Etchison, Ethinson, Eytchison Kin Throughout America. Chicago, IL, 1980. 264p. [NG16].

ATHEY -- Athey, Thomas Whitfield. *The Descendants of Henry Athey of Maryland, South Carolina, and Alabama.* Luverne, AL, Luverne Journal Press, 1972. 59, 1p. [D398; X33-LA].

AULD -- Auld, James. *The Journal of James Auld, 1765-1770. In Southern Historical Association Publications,* Washington, DC, 1904. v. 8, p.253-268. Introductory sketch by R. T. Bennett. Diary of a journey from Dorchester County, Md., to North Carolina in 1765, with accounts and personal notes. [L627].

AUMAN -- Auman, Mae Caudill, et al comp. *The Genealogy of the Andrew Auman Family.* Seagrove, NC, Andrew Auman Family Reunion, Asheboro, NC. 1985. 245p. 1. Auman family. 2. Auman, Andrew, ca. 1759-ca. 1839-Family. [G24].

AUSTIN -- Austin, Aurelia. *Captain Nathaniel (Nathan) Austin of Gilder Plantation, S.C. and His Sons in the American Revolution: Includes Other Revolutionary War Soldiers in Allied Lines, Wm. Allen... et al.* Decatur, GA, D.R. Benbow, 1986. 277p. 1. Austin family. 2. Austin, Nathaniel ca. 1720-1798-Family. 3. United States-History-Revolution, 1775-1783-Biography. [G24; DC136].

AVANT -- Avant, David A. Jr. *Florida Pioneers and Their Alabama, Georgia, Carolina, Maryland and Virginia Ancestors.* Tallahassee, FL, 1974. 500p. [X-GF].

AVINGER -- Orvin, Ella Veronica Milings. *The Avinger and Related Families; A Genealogical Survey.* Charleston, SC, Maxwell Clayton Orvin, 1961. 144p. D gives underscored part of title. [L666; D446].

AYERS -- White, Paul Richard. *Taproots, a Virginia & Carolina Legacy. 2nd ed.* Nashville, TN, P.R. White, 1986. xv, 860p. 1. Ayers family. 2. Blackwell family. 3. Virginia-Genealogy. [G26; DC143].

B

BABB -- Babb, Robert E., Jr. *Babb Family.* Charleston, SC, Babb, 1978. 30 l. [D462].

BABYLON -- Duttera, Rev. William Babylon and Maurice Clayton Duttera. *Babylon, Ba-bil-on Family History.* Salisbury, NC, 1936. 2p., 21 numb. leaves, 22-55 numb. leaves, 4 plates. Typed. Loose-leaf. [L704].

BAGBY -- Bagby, George K. *Genealogy of the Bagby Family.* Durham, NC, L.D. Baker, 1973. 33p. Typed. [X411-FW].

BAGLEY -- Bagley, Ernest Griffen. *The Bagley Family, 1066-1958.* Raleigh, NC, Bagley, 1958. v, 111 leaves. D gives underscored title. [L735; D496; VV8].

BAILEY -- Haun, Weynette P. *James A. (Jr.) and Anna (Shufflebarger) Bailey of Pope County, Illinois, and Descendant.* Durham, NC, 1975. 71 leaves. [X43-FW].

BAILEY -- Holcomb, Brent. *Ancestors and Descendants of Mercer Silas Bailey (1841-1926), 1767-1988* Columbia, SC, B.H. Holcomb, 1988. viii, 105p. 1. Bailey family. 2. Bailey, Mercer Silas, 1841-1926-Family. 3. North Carolina-Genealogy. 4. South Carolina-Genealogy. [G29].

BAILEY -- Lambeth, Mary Weeks. *Memories and Records of Eastern North Carolina.* Nashville, TN, 1957. 252p. [L757].

BAILEY -- Willis, Betsy Lawson and Martha Barksdale Craddock. *Sketches and Genealogy of* *the Bailey - Craddock - Lawson Families of Virginia and North Carolina; With Notes on the Families of Coleman, DuVal, Scott, Easley, Madison, Lanier, Allen, Hunt, Wimbish, Traynham, Ragland, and Barksdale.* Alexandria, VA, Willis, 1974. iii, 218p. D gives underscored title. [D510; VV8].

BAKER -- Epps, Evelyn Baker. *The Baker Family: the Ancestors and Descendants of Harvey and Jane Coker Baker.* Clemson, SC, E.B. Epps, 1985. 31 leaves. Binders title: The Baker family. [DC160].

BAKER -- Shipp, Ralph D. *A Baker Family Genealogy: Pioneers of North Carolina, Kentucky, Indiana, Missouri, and Iowa and Allied Families, Dunn, Gourley, Russell.* Baltimore, MD, Gateway Press, xiv, 324p, 1 plate leaf. [C31].

BAKER -- Walker, Alica A. *A Walker Family History: with an Allied Baker Line: Descendants of Samuel Walker, b 1749, and His Seven Children, from North Carolina to Henry Country (sic) Kentucky, to Central Indiana, and Elsewhere.* Blue Mound, KS, A.A. Walker, 1985. 192p. 1. Walker family. 2. Baker family. 3. Walker, Samuel, 1749-1823-Family. [G31].

BALDWIN -- Baldwin, Ralph E. *Theophilus Baldwin, 1792-1851, and His Descendants, North Carolina-Indiana.* Speedway, IN, 1988. v, 206p. [NGS3; DC167].

BALDWIN -- Horne, Mary Virginia. *Descendants of Jesse Baldwin of Richmond County, North Carolina, and Baldwin Family History in New Jersey and Connecticut.* 1975. 97 leaves. [D552].

BALL -- Ball, Nan S. *Ball Family of Stoke-in-Teignhead, Devon, England.* Charleston, SC, 1944. 30p. [L833].

BALL -- Deas, Anne Simons. *Recollections of the Ball Family of South Carolina and the Comingtee Plantation.* Summerville, SC, Deas, 1909. 189P. D gives 191p. [L873; D566].

BALLARD -- Wooden, Russell B. *Ballardiana.* Asheville, NC, 1962. 206 l. [X49-NY].

BALLENGER -- Knox, John Ballenger. *The Ballenger Family of Oconee County, South Carolina.* Seneca, SC, Grady Woodfin Ballenger, 1956. 32p. [L905; D580].

BALTHROP -- Bumpus, Anne Shirley. *The Balthrop Family from Bute County & Warren County, North Carolina.* Columbia, TN, Bumpus, 1978. 48p. [D588].

BANDY -- Bandy, Allen H. *The History of the Bandy Clan.* Hickory, NC, AlphA Omega Pub. Co., 1980. 220p. [DS32].

BARBEE -- Shields, Ruth Herndon. *A Study of the Barbee Families of Chatham, Orange and Wake Counties in North Carolina.* Boulder, CO, Stone, 1971. 2 v. in 1. [S gives iii, 254p]: Bound with: A Supplement to a study of the Barbee families... consisting of corrections and additions including a study of the Virginia ancestors / compiled by Kathryn Crossley Stone, 1976. (See just below). [S135; D604].

BARBEE -- Stone, Kathryn Crossley. *Supplement to: A Study of the Barbee Families of Chathan, etc.,* Boulder, CO, 1976. 1 v. (various paging). Corrections and additions, including: A study of the Virginia ancestors of the Barbee families of Chatham, Orange and Wake Counties in North Carolina. [X51-FW/NY; VV9].

BARBER -- Barber, Eva Bell. *The R. N. Barber Family.* Waynesville, NC, Barber, 196_. 87 leaves. [D606].

BARENTINE -- Stone, Fay Campbell. *Alexander Barentine, 1817-1890, and His Wife, Tabitha Eleanor Overton, 1818-1864, Silas Monroe Barentine, 1821-????, and His Wife, Emily Morris, 1821-1888.* Canby, OR, F.C. Stone, 1987. vi, 461p. Cover title: "South Carolina and Georgia to Arkansas, with related families of Campbell, Brewer, Sorrels, Griffin, Orrick, Henderson, Overton, Cash, Riggins, Watkins, Hight, Self, Tedder, Smith. Limited ed. 125 copies. 1. Barrentine family. 2. Barrentine, Alexander, 1817-1890-Family. 3. Barrentine, Silas Monroe, b. 1821-Family. 4. Brewer family. 5. Campbell family. DC gives title as underscored but lists as BAKENTINE[?]. [G34; DC158].

BARNES -- NAS. *Geneology (sic) of Shadrack Barnes of Rowan County, North Carolina, a Soldier in the Revolutionary War 1957 ed with Supplements for Chapters vi, vii, x, and xi added to the Geneology (sic).* Washington, DC, McElwee, 1957. 147p. [L1044].

BARNES -- Lambeth, Mary Weeks. [L1045]. See above: BAILEY. [L757].

BARNES -- McElwee, Pickney G. *Genealogy of Shadrack Barnes of Rowan County, North Carolina, a Soldier in the Revolutionary War.* Washington, DC, McElwee, 1951. 1 v. (Unpaged). [L1041].

BARNES -- McElwee, Pickney G. *Genealogy of Shadrack Barnes of Rowan County, North Carolina, a Soldier in the Revolutionary War.* Washington, DC, McElwee, 1952. 131p. See also: (just below) Genealogy of Shadrack Barnes of Rowan County, North Carolina, who was a soldier in the Revolutionary War/ by Pinckney G. McElwee, 1858 ed.
[L1042; D656].

BARNES -- McElwee, Pickney G. *Geneology (sic) of Shadrack Barnes of Rowan County,*

North Carolina. Washington, DC, 1958. 197p. [L1048; NG18].

BARNETT -- Barnett, John J. *Barnett Family of the Carolinas, Georgia and Alabama.* Nashville, TN, Barnett, 1952. 42 leaves. [D661].

BARNWELL -- Barnwell, Joseph W. and Stephen B. *Barnwell of South Carolina: Originally Compiled to 1901 by Joseph Barnwell... Rev. to 1946 by Stephen Barnwell.* Berkeley, CA, Priv. Print, 1946. 43, vii, p. 'The original was published in vol. II of the S.C. historical and genealogical magazine' (Jan. 1901). [X56-NY/SU].

BARNWELL -- Howard, Barnwell Rhett. *Genealogical Chart, Barnwell of South Carolina.* Albany, NY, 1898. [L1068; NG18].

BARR -- Anderson, Annie Marie Barr. *The Barr Family of South Carolina.* St. Petersburg, Fl, Anderson, 1951. 40 leaves. [D679].

BARR -- Barr, James T. *From Whence We Came: The Family History Book: Bowles, Ray, Barr, Grider: A Genealogical Record.* Lexington, SC, J.T. Barr, 1982. 85 leaves, 1 leaf of plates. 1. Barr family. 2. Grider family. 3. Bowles family. [G36].

BARRINGER -- Barringer, Sheridan Reid. *Our Family Tree, the Barringer Branch: Ancestors of the Sheridan Reid Barringer Family.* Newport News, VA, S.R. Barringer. 1986. 1 v. (various pagings). 1. Barringer family. 2. North Carolina-Genealogy. [G36].

BARRINGER -- Barringer, Sheridan Reid. *John Paul Barringer, 1721-1807 of Mecklenburg and Cabarrus, North Carolina.* Newport News, VA, S.R. Barringer, 1990. 1 v. (various foliations). D gives 114 leaves in various foliations. 1. Barringer, John Paul, 1721-1807. 2. Mecklenburg County (N.C.)-Biography. 3. Cabarrus County, (N.C.)-Biography. 4. Barringer family. 5. North Carolina-Genealogy. [G36; D206].

BARROW -- NAS. *Barrow: An Early Southern Family.* Summerfield, NC, Barrow Family Association, 1987- v. Quarterly Index in each volume. See library shelflist for DAR holdings. [DC207].

BARROW -- North, Mae Belle Barrow. *The Barrow Family of Virginia, 1620-1972.* Summerfield, NC, North, 1972. 204 p. S & VV list as BARROWS.
[S150; D697; X58-FW; VV11].

BARTON -- Barton, William Baynard. *A Genealogy Study of the Descendants of Anthony Barton; the First American Barton of This Record, an Emigrant from England to America 1825.* Stonega, VA, 1956. 1 v. (various pagings). Cover title: The Bartons of Carolina. Half title: The Bartons of Charleston, South Carolina and Orangeburg, South Carolina. This primary edition limited to 30 copies. LC copy replaced by Microfilm. 1. Barton family. [G37].

BARTON -- Steadman, Joseph Earle. *Barton and Stedman: Also Steedman and Steadman Families.* West Columbia, SC, J.E. Steadman, 1987. v, 139p. 1. Barton family. 2. Steadman family. 3. Southern States-Genealogy. DC lists as STEEDMAN.
[G38; DC3463].

BASKIN -- Bell, Raymond M. *The Baskins - Baskin Family, Pennyslvania, Virginia, South Carolina.* Washington, PA, 1957-58. 70p. NG gives 1957 publication date. X gives 102p. (in 2 vols) & Supplement (p. 71-102) issued in 1958 with special title page and index to the whole. X notes NY has 70p. only. [Same ed.

as NG].
[NG18; X61-FW/MH/NY/PH; VP14; VV12].

BASKIN -- Bell, Raymond Martin. *The Baskins-Baskin Family, Pennyslvania, Virginia, South Virginia, South Carolina. rev.* Washington, PA, 1963. 85. VP omits "rev." [L1144; NG19: VP14].

BASKIN -- Bell, Raymond M. *Andrew Baskin, Esq.; Kershaw and Lancaster Counties, South Carolina and Other Baskin Notes.* Washington, PA, 1965. 12 leaves. [X61-LA/SL].

BASKIN -- Bell, Raymond M. *The Baskin(s) Family, South Carolina - Pennyslvania, with Stephens and Martin Notes.* Washington, PA, 1975. 49p. [NG19; X61-LA/NY/SL; VP14].

BASS -- Bell, Albert Dehner. *Bass Families of the South; A Collection of Historic and Genalogical Source Materials from Public and Private Records.* Rocky Mount, NC, Bell, 1961. Limited ed. 1 vol. D gives 386, 84p and underscored part of title. [L1152; D744].

BATES -- Lanphere, Edward Everett. *The Bates Family in America and Corrections and Additions to the Lanphere and Related Families Genealogy, 1970 Revised Edition.* Chapel Hill, NC, Lanphere, 1972. ii, 41 i.e. 24 leaves. [D767; X61-SL/NY].

BATES -- Lanphere, Edward Everett. *Descendants of Bates Ancestors Who Lived in Virginia.* Chapel Hill, NC, Lanphere, 1973. xii, 104 leaves. [S157; D768; VV12].

BATSON -- Bornemann, Vivian Davis. *The Batson Family in Virginia, North Carolina, and Georgia, Mississippi, Louisiana, and Texas. Related Families: Dale, Hatten, Culpepper, Price, Smith, Lott, Longino, Daughdrill, Davis, Terrell. Memorabilia and Biography.* New Orleans, 1959. x, 170p. D gives

underscored title.
[L1181; NG19; D769; VV13].

BAUM -- Hanbury, Elizabeth Baum. *Currituck Legacy: The Baum Family of North Carolina.* Chesapeake, VA, E.B. Hanbury, 1985. 261p. D gives 259p. 1. Baum Family. 2. North Carolina-Genealogy. [G41; DC224].

BAXTER -- Baxter, Lionel Francis. *A Baxter Family from South Carolina: Scotch Irish Pioneers from Ulster.* St. Petersburg, FL, Genealogy Pub. Service, 1989. xii, 514p. 1. Baxter family. 2. South Carolina-Genealogy. 3. Scotch-Irish-United States-Genealogy. 4. Ulster(Northern Ireland and Ireland)-Genealogy. D gives underscored title. [G41; NGN17-3-91; DC225].

BAXTER -- Baxter, Miss Frances. *The Baxter Family, Descendants of George and Thomas Baxter of Westchester County, New York, as well as Some West Virginia and South Carolina Lines.* New York, NY, T.A. Wright. 1913. 3p, 157p, [L1208; VV13].

BAYNARD -- Hassell, Annie Baynard Simmons. *Baynard. An Ancient Family Bearing Arms.* Columbia, SC, R. L. Bryan Co., 1972. xxiv, 251p. S gives: vii, 252p. DS gives underscored title. [S166; DS35].

BEAL -- Adams, Katherine Beall. *Maryland Heritage: A Family History.* Hillsborough, NC, K.B. Adams, 1983. 421p., 15 p. of plates. 1. Beal Family. 2. Maryland-Genealogy. [G42].

BEAL -- Beal, John Russell. *Reflections: The Beals as I Remember.* Greensboro, NC, March Street Press, 1990. vi, 245p. 1. Beal family. 2. Beal, John Russell-Family. 3. Ontario-Biography. 4. Ontario-Genealogy. 5. Michigan-Biography. 6. Michigan-Genealogy. [G42].

BEAL -- Lowe, Blanch Beal. *William Beal, Bucks County, Pa.; An Incomplete Chronicle of One Family Line Descending From William Beal, Yeoman, Presumably From Ross, Herefordshire England.* Durham, NC, Printed by the Seeman Printery, 1961. 134p. [L1255].

BEAM -- Beam, L. Carl. *A History of John Teeter Beam's Generations.* Crause, NC, 105p. "Sketches of the life of J. T. Beam and his fifteen children up to the third generation from 1742-1897, by A. R. Beam... 1898": p. 1-13. [L1259].

BEAM -- Conley, Katherine Logan. *A Branch of the Beam Family Tree.* Rutherford, NC, Conley, 1978. 104 leaves. [D830].

BEASLEY -- Manship, Louise Beasley. *William Jesse Beasley, M.D., Hartsville, S.C.* Hartsville, SC, 1965. 4p. In verticle file. Ask librarian. [L1281].

BEATTY -- Barnhill, Edward Stanley. *The Beatys of Kingston.* Mt. Pleasant, SC, Barnhill, 1958, iii, 143p. D lists under BEATY. [11287; D854].

BECKHAM -- Beckham, Annie L. *Beckham Family of Virginia, North Carolina, Georgia and Texas.* Dallas, TX, 1957. 10p. [X70-FW; VV14].

BEDENBAUGH -- Holcomb, Brent H. *The Bedenbaugh - Betenbaugh Family of South Carolina.* Easley, SC, Southern Historical Press, 1978. 46, 21p. [DS38].

BEEMAN -- Beeman, Ray. *The Beeman, Beaman, Beemon Family of North Carolina and Mississippi, Especially the Ivy Beeman Line.* Memphis, TN, Beeman, Searcy, AK, Browning, 1977, 62 leaves. [D891].

BEERS -- Rhodes, Raymond C. *Blocks From Whence The Chip Came, or My Ancestry and* *possibly Some of Yours.* Raleigh, NC, R.C. Rhodes, 1988. viii, 64p., 2 folded leaves of plates. 1. Rhodes family. 2. Rhodes, Raymond C.-Family. 3. Beers family. 4. Blosser family. [G45].

BEESON -- Beeson, Margaret Ailene. *A Genealogy of the Beeson Family.* Greensboro, NC, Beeson, 1973. 56 leaves. S gives date as 1974. [S188; D898].

BELL -- Bell, Frank Frederick. *Bell - Sharpe; A Collection of Genealogical and Biographical Notes on Beuttelspach(er) - Bidelspacher - Bell, Laugenstein, Edwards, Attmore, Stull, Strope, George, Lassatt, Sharpe, Reese, Polk, Green(e), Tumlin and Attendant Families of Pennsylvania, North Carolina, and Georgia.* NP, 1951. 194 l. [L1393; VP18].

BELL -- Bell, Frank Frederick. *Bell - Sharpe; the Biedelspach(er) and Bell Families of the United States of America and Their Origin, the Beutelsbach - Beutelspacher Family in Germany.* Dallas, 1959. 209p. [L1395].

BELL -- Bell, Frank Frederick. *Bell - Sharpe. Final Revision Containing Genealogical and Some Biographical Sketches and Illustrations of the Bidelspach(er) - Bell Families in America and Their Origin, the Beutelsbach - Beutelsbach - Beut(t)slspacher Families in Germany with Allied Families of Langstein (German and American) and Sharpe and Allied Families in America. Allied Families to Bell: Attmore, Edwards, George, Lausatt, Rakestraw, Stroop, Stull, Zane. Allied families to Sharpe: Green, Polk, Reese, Tumlin, and others.* Dallas, 1960. 209 p. [L1396].

BELL -- Bell, Marie L. *The Bells and Allied Families.* Columbia, SC, 1953. 78 leaves. [X75-FW/NY/SU].

BELL -- Delmar, Marybelle. *Colonial James Bell of Cateret County and Some of His Descendants.* Raleigh, NC, 1946. 37 leaves. [X74-SP].

BELLAH -- Bellah, Lovick Pierce. *Register of the Bellah Family, Descendants of William Ballagh of Charles Town, S. C.* Nashville, TN, Bellah, 1945. 185p. [D931].

BELLUNE -- Ashford, Elizabeth Jeannette. *The Bellune Family.* Pawley's Island, SC, 1982. 54p. [NG20].

BELSER -- Belser, William G. *The Belser Family of South Carolina.* NP, 1941. 67p. [X76-MH/NY].

BENNEHAN -- Anderson, Jean Bradley. *Piedmont Plantation: The Bennehan - Cameron Family and Lands in North Carolina.* Durham, NC, Historic Preservation Society of Durham, 1985. xix, 227p., 10p. of plates. 1. Fairntosh Plantation (N.C.) 2. Stagville Plantation (N.C.) 3. Bennehan family. 4. Cameron family. 5. Plantation Life-North Carolina-History. 6. North Carolina-Biography. [G48; DC272].

BENNETT -- Bennett, Benjamin Hugh. *A History of Richard Bennett Family of Westmoreland County, Virginia and Iredell County, N. C.* Washington, DC, 1960. 21 leaves. [L1458; D954; VV15].

BENNETT -- Bennett, H. L. *Bennett Family..* Greensboro, NC, 1960. 23p. [X78-FW].

BENSON -- Benson, John T., Jr. *Bensons: Early Settlers from North Carolina to Middle Tennessee, 1796-1820 - 2nd ed.* Gallatin, TN, J.T. Benson, Jr., 1980. 414p. [DC280].

BENTON -- Redden, Alma Check. *A Chronicle of Two Pioneer Families, the Bentons and the*

Taylors of North Carolina Back County. Hillsborough, NC, Redden, 1969. 60p. X gives Greensboro, NC, Acme Print & 58p. [D990; X80-FW].

BERGEN -- Silvers, Peggy. *Echoes in the Mist: The Burgin Family, 1677-1989.* Nebo, NC, P. Silvers, 1989. viii, 393, xxx, 17p.1. Bergen family. 2. North Carolina-Genealogy. [G51].

BERRY -- Berry, Lloyd E. *Hudson Berry and His Descendants.* Pelzer. SC. The Berry - Gaines - Harrison Reunion, 1956. 6, 106p. [L1526; D1003].

BERRY -- Still, Samuel Hutchins... *Notes on the Berry Family of South Carolina with Special Reference to Those Families in Charleston and Orangeburg Districts.* Washington, DC, 1936. 3p., 2-10 numb. leaves. [L1525].

BESSELLIEU -- Johnson, Charles Owen. *Bessellieu, Cheche, Frazer, and Allied Families of Charleston, South Carolina.* Monroe, LA, 1959. 2 v. [L1534].

BESSENT -- Hayman, Carol Bessent. *The Bessent Story.* Jacksonville, NC, Hayman, 1976. 3, 30, 27 leaves. [D10015].

BEST -- Hoffman, Laban Miles. *Our Kin: Being a History of the Hoffman, Rhyne, Costner, Rudisill, Best, Hovis, Hoyle, Wills, Shetley, Jenkins, Holland, Hambright, Gaston, Withers, Cansler, Clemmer, and Lineberger Families.* Baltimore, MD, Gateway Press, 1984. 585p. Reprint. Originally published: Charlotte, NC, Press of Queen City Print Co., 1915. 1. Hoffman family. 2 Costner family. 3. Best family. 4. Wills family. [G54].

BETHEA -- Cooper, John Purley, Jr. *Sketches of John Purley Cooper and Wife, Ethel Mae*

Bethea: with Notes on Their Ancestry, Descendants, Some Kindred, and Random Recollections. Baltimore, MD, Gateway Press, v, 184p., 15 p. of plates. 1. Cooper family. 2. Bethea family. 3. Cooper, John Purley, 1881-1963-Family. 4. Cooper, Ethel Mae, 1881-1947-Family. [G54].

BEVERLEY -- McGill, John. *The Beverley Family of Virginia, Descendants of Major Robert Beverley, 1641-1687, and Allied Families.* Columbia, SC, R.L. Bryan Co., 1956. vi, 1117p. D gives underscored title. [L1553; D1024; DC298; VV16].

BEVILLE -- Lichliter, Asselia Strobhar. *Pioneering with Beville and Related Families in South Carolina, Georgia, and Florida: Their Lives, Times, and Descendants. Also Candler, Colson, Daly, Garnett, King, Matthews, McRae, Oliver, Parrish, Pearce, Peace, Porter Families.* Washington, DC, 1982. 791p. DS gives underscored title and xii, 791 leaves. [NG21; DS49].

BIGHAM -- Boling, Katharine Boling. *A Piece of the Fox's Hide - 1st ed.* Columbia, SC, Sandlapper Press. 1972. xiv, 361p. [S221].

BILLINGS -- Gordon, Naomi B. *The Billings Family of North Carolina and Virginia.* [NGN18-6-92].

BINGHAM -- Tifft, Susan E. *The Patriarch: The Rise and Fall of the Bingham Dynasty.* New York, NY, Summit Books, 1991. 574p., 16p. of plates. 1. Bingham family. 2. Bingham, Barry, 1906-1988-Family. 3.Publishers and publishing -Kentucky-Biography. 4. Educators-North Carolina-Biography. 5. Kentucky-Genealogy. 6. North Carolina-Genealogy. [G57].

BISSELL -- Sluby, Paul E. *Genealogy of the Collins - Bizzell Families.* Washington, DC,

W.K. Collins, Sr. <1985-1988 >. v. <2-3 >. "First... second publication compiled by Wm. K. Collins, Sr." V. 2. t.p." Third publication compiled by Paul E. Sluby Sr. and William K. Collins, Sr. 1. Collins family. 2. Bissell family. 3. North Carolina-Genealogy. [G58].

BLACKWELDER -- Williams, Deward Charles. *The Blackwelder and Allied Families of North Carolina and Illinois.* Mt. Carmel, IL, Williams. 1964. 1 v. (various pagings). See also: The Blackwelder and allied families from Cabarrus to the land of the Illini: A genealogy of the descendants of Caleb Blackwelder, 1722-1794, and his wife Betsy Phifer/by Deward C. Williams (below). X gives: "1947, (Reprinted 1963)". [D1138; X94-SL].

BLACKWELDER -- Williams, Deward Charles. *The Blackwelder Family of Germany and America, 1556-1969.* Mt. Carmel, IL, Williams. 1964. 239p. Bound with The Bicentennial edition, 1776-1976. [D1139].

BLACKWELDER -- Williams, Deward Charles. *The Blackwelder and Allied Families of Cabarrus to the Land of the Illini; A Genealogy of the Descendants of Caleb Blackwelder, 1722-1794 and His Wife, Betsy Phifer.* Edwardsville, IL, Williams, 1947. vi, 104, 21p. See also: The Blackwelder and allied families of North Carolina and Illinois/by Deward Charles Walker, 1964 (just above). D gives underscored part of title. [D1140; X94-FW/SL].

BLACKWELL -- Blackwell, Nancy Neckers. *Ancestors, Descendants and Connections of Carle Gratz Blackwell and Goldie Blanche Hill; Virginia, North Carolina, Tennessee...* Zionsville, ?, Blackwell, 1986, 210p. [DC328].

BLACKWELL -- White, Paul Richard. [G60]. See above: AYERS. [G26].

BLAIR -- NAS. *The Blair Family: A Genealogical Study of the Blair Family from the Time of Samuel Blair of County Tyrone, Ireland, 1768 Who Settled in York County, South Carolina to the Time of His Descendants of the Present Day, 1989.* Valdese, NC, H.W. Blair, 1989. 1 v. (various foliations). 1. Blair family. 2. Blair, Samuel, 1768-1834-Family. 3. Ireland-Genealogy. 4. South Carolina-Genealogy. [G60].

BLAIR -- Blair, John Clyde. *The Blair Families Originating in Ireland, South Carolina, Georgia, and Alabama.* [NGN17-6-91].

BLAKELY -- Robertson, Irma Matthews. [G61]. See above: ANGLE. [G15].

BLALOCK -- Blalock, Delton D. *Blalock and Related Families: Pioneers in Virginia, the Carolinas, Georgia, Alabama, and Texas, 1597-1988.* Montgomery, AL, D. D. Blalock, 1988, viii, 273, 31p., 13 p. of plates. 1. Blalock family. 2. Southern States-Genealogy. [G61].

BLAND -- Gottschalk, Katherine Cox. *Bland Family of Pitt County, North Carolina and of Shelby County, Tennessee.* NP, 1940. 52 leaves. [D1185].

BLANDING -- Blanding, A. L. *Blanding - McFaddin, 1553-1906.* Fountain Inn, SC, Blanding, 1927. 62p. [D1188].

BLAYLOCK -- Blaylock, Frederick R. *The Blaylock Family.* Lexington, NC, Blaylock, 1953. 35 leaves. [D1199].

BLEDSOE -- NAS. *Bledsoe Family Quarterly.* Dallas, TX, Banks, McLaurin, 1985- v. Published Irregularly. See DAR shelflist for library holdings. [DC341].

BLEWETT -- Blewett, George Edgar. *William Blewett, Who Settled in North Carolina in*

1746; A History and Genealogy of Him and His Descendants. Ft. Worth, TX, 1954. 220p. [L1740].

BLOSSER -- Rhodes, Raymond C. [G62]. See above: BEERS. [G45].

BLOUNT -- Blount, Virginia Lightle. *The Blount Family of England, North Carolina and South Carolina, A.D. 935 to 1936.* NP, Blount, 1969. 105 leaves. Bound with the Lines Family, Midway District, Georgia, 1725-1956 and the Allied Chisolm Family; Descendants of Edda Dale Chisolm and William Augustus Blount of Barnwell County, Georgia. [D1228].

BLOUNT -- Lambeth, Mary Weeks. [L1771]. See above: BAILEY. [L757].

BLOYD -- Nichols, Edna Bloyd. *William Bloyd-Bloyed of Maryland, Virginia, North Carolina and and Green County, Kentucky and His Descendants.* Baltimore, Gateway Press, 1980. xiii, 333p. [C68; DC347; VV18].

BLUE -- Blu, Elmer F. *The Descendants of John Blue of Lancaster Co., Pa., South Carolina, Fleming Co., Kentucky, Ohio, Illinois and Indiana.* 1944. 20, 2 l. [D1230].

BLUNT -- Green, C. Sylvester. *Blounts of Pitt County, North Carolina.* Greenville, NC, Pitt County Historical Society, Distributed by Book Barn, 1978. 147p. 1. Blunt family. 2. Pitt County (N.C.)-Genealogy. [G63].

BLUNT -- Overlander, Rufus M. *Blount Family of North Carolina and Allied Families Miller, Dyer, Gray.* Seabrook, TX, Rufus M. Overlander, III, 1987. 32, 2, 13, 1 leaves. 1. Blunt family. 2. Miller family. 3. Dyer family. 4. Gray family. 5. Southern States-Genealogy. [G63].

BLYTHE -- Ingram, Annie Blythe. *Notes on the Pedigree of the Family of Blyth or Blythe* *of Mecklenburg County, North Carolina.* Wadesboro, NC, Ingram, 1959. 37 leaves. [D1238].

BOBBS -- Ralph L. *Bobbs and Related Families.* Winnsboro, SC, Winnsboro Press, 1976. 369 leaves. [X101-NY].

BODENHAMER -- Heuss, Lois Ione Hotchkiss. *Christian Bodenhamer (Bodenheimer - Bodenhammer) of Rowan County, North Carolina and His Descendants.* Charlotte, NC, Herb Eaton, 1979. xiv, 605p. [DC353].

BOGUE -- Deming, Flora Bogue. *Bogue Genealogy; Descendants of John Bogue of East Haddam, Conn., and Wife, Rebecca Walkley; Also, the North Carolina Bogues and Miscellaneous Bogue Records; Ancestors of James Hubbard Bogue and Wife, Polley Adelaide Phillips, Their Royal Lines.* Rutland, VT, The Tuttle Publishing Co., Inc., 1944. xxix, 2, 322, 6p. [L1823].

BOGUE -- Zoellner, L. R. *Bogue Family of North Carolina.* NP, 1945. 59 l. [X103-LA].

BOND -- Garrett, Samuel Bond. *Bond Genealogy, A History of the Descendants of Joseph Bond, Born 1704, in Wiltshire, England; Died 175_, in North Carolina.* Muncie, IN, Garrett, 1913. 268p. [D1286].

BONITZ -- Bonits, John H., Jr. *Some Bonitz Families, A Genealogical Survey - 1st ed.* Greensboro, NC, 1973. 1 v. (various pagings). [S250].

BONNER -- Smallwood, Marilu Burch. *Some Colonial and Revolutionary Families of North Carolina, Vol. 1. Biggs, Bonner, Gaylord, Grist (Grice) Harding, Heather, Burbage, Holstein, Hughed (sic), Lucas, Nicholson, O'Brien, O'Cain, Peyton, Pope, Respess, Satchwell, Smaw.* Macon, GA., 1964. 532p. [NG22].

BOOHER -- Phillips, Mary Palmer. *The Family Record of David Lehman Booher and His Wife Elizabeth Nutts.* Pinnacle, NC, Phillips, 1956. 98p. [L1885; D1312].

BOOZER -- Boozer, Mary Elizabeth. *The Boozer Family of South Carolina.* [NGN17-1-91].

BORUM -- Buchanan, Paul C. *Boring / Boren / Boram Families of Colonial Virginia, Maryland, and North Carolina.* Springfield, VA, P.C. Buchanan, 1989. 32p. 1. Borum family. 2. Virginia-Genealogy. 3. Maryland-Genealogy. 4. North Carolina-Genealogy. [G71].

BOST -- NAS. *Dedication of Memorial Honouring Pioneer William Bost, Oct. 12. 1975.* Newton, NC, Hickory Tavern Chapter, DAR, 1975. 4p. [X112-PH].

BOSTIAN -- Bostian, Frank K. *Our Bostian Family from Christopher and Ann Bastian.* Salisbury, NC, Salisbury Printing Co., 1970. iv, 87p. [D1360].

BOSTIAN -- Jorgensen, Ada Petrea. *One Line of the Bostian Family of Rowan County, North Carolina.* 1982. 61 leaves. [NG19].

BOSTON -- Wise, M. *The Boston Family of Maryland. 2nd rev. ed. with suppl.* Charlotte, NC, Delmar Co., 1986. xii, 661p. 1. Boston family. 2. Maryland-Genealogy. [G72].

BOSWELL -- Pippenger, Jean Boswell. *Descendants of Edward Boswell: Prince William County, Virginia and Orange County, North Carolina.* Baltimore, MD, Gateway Press, 1986. vi, 294p. 1. Boswell family. 2. Boswell, Edward, ca. 1750-1830-Family. [G72; VV20].

BOURQUIN -- Davis, Harry Alexander. *Some Huguenot Families of South Carolina and Georgia; Supplement 3: Bourquin Family, 2nd* *ed. rev.* Washington, DC, 1940. 3p., iv, 94 numb. leaves. [L1980; NG23].

BOWEN -- NAS. *The Bowen Family, with McGowan and Brooks Lineage, of George's Creek, Pickens County, South Carolina.* Atlanta, GA, 1962. 115p. [L2013].

BOWEN -- Field, Nora Deniza Nimmons. *Genealogy and History.* Seneca, SC, Field, 1960. 351p. [D1394].

BOWERS -- Bowers, Ralph L. *Ancestors and Descendants of Levi and Elizabeth Ann Young Bowers.* Greenville, SC, 1968. 30p. [X116-FW].

BOWIE -- NAS. *A History of the Ancestors of Duncan McFarland Buie, Highland Scotch and Mary Jane McKay, Lowlander Scotch-Irish and Dutch, Married in North Carolina in 1857: Buie (McFarland)-McKay (Bozeman).* NP, 197_. 28 leaves. 1. Bowie family. [G78].

BOWLBY -- Barekman, June B. *Some New Jersey Families Found in Early Rowan County, North Carolina; Bowlby, Palmer, Dailey, Todd, Stevens.* Chicago, IL, Barekman, 1970. 59p. [X116-FW].

BOWLES -- Barr, James T. [G79]. See above: BARR. [G36].

BOWMAN -- Bowman, Charles Harwood. *Bowman and Related Families.* Greenville, NC, Wiggins and Bowman, 1968. vi, 124 leaves. [L2045].

BOYD -- Boyd, John Wright. *A Family History: Boyds and Connected Families: Early Settlers, Central Savannah River Area of Georgia and South Carolina.* Tignall, GA, J. W. Boyd, 1980. xv, 788p. NG omits "A Family History" in title. [C81; NG23; DC404].

BOYD -- DeHuff, Elizabeth Willis. *The Family of Reuben Boyd (1769-1827), of Barnwell*

County, South Carolina. Augusta, GA, DeHuff, 1963. 55p. [D1439].

BOYD -- Johnson, Catherine Boyd. *Boyd Family History: Archibald Boyd of Pennsylvania and South Carolina, 1758-1802, Related Families: Young, Fair, Jones, Crow, Dickson, Goss.* Roanoke, AL, Yarbrough Commercial Printing, 105p. 1. Boyd family. 2. Dickinson family. 3. Crowe family. [G79].

BOYD -- Lambeth, Mary Weeks. [L2070]. See above: BAILEY. [L757].

BOYD -- Perry, Max. *The Descendants of the Robert Boyd and the Charles Boyd Families of Chester County, South Carolina.* Midland, TX, M. Perry, 1987. 116 leaves. Spine title: Boyd, Drennan, Lewis, Perry. 1. Boyd family. 2. Boyd, Robert, ca. 1705-ca. 1761-Family. 3. Boyd, Charles, 1759-1844-Family. 4. South Carolina-Genealogy. [G79; DC405].

BOYKIN -- Boykin, Edward M. *History of the Boykin Family, from Their First Settlement in Virginia, 1685, and in South Carolina, Georgia, and Alabama, to the Present Time.* Camden, SC, Colin Macrea, 1876. 27p. [D1452; X118-FW; VV21].

BRABHAM -- Brabham, Angus McKay. *Mizpah.* Bamberg, SC, Mizpah Family Book Committee, 1978. xiii, 302p. p. 1-144 are a reprint of: A family sketch, and else, or Buford's Bridge and its people/ by M.M. Brabham, 1923. [D1461].

BRADFORD -- Gottschalk, Kathrine Cox. *Descendants of John Bradford Sr. of Sumter District, South Carolina.* NP, 1974. 64 leaves. [D1476].

BRADFORD -- McDowell, Grace Bradford. *Descendants of David Bradford, Mecklenburg, Cabarrus, Iredell Counties.* NP, McDowell, 1971. 61p. [D1480].

BRADLEY -- Ensworth, Sarah Isabelle Bradley. *The Bradleys and Allied Families of South Carolina. Also Wilson Family.* Medina, OH, Emsworth Printing Co., 1969. 428p. [A76; NG24; D1491].

BRADHAM -- Brewster, Janet Bradham. *A Bradham Family History and Genealogy.* Manning, SC, J.B. Brewster, 1986. xvii, 661p. 1. Bradham family. 2. South Carolina-Genealogy. [G81].

BRADY -- Phillips, Lois Smith. *The Brady Family of Moore and Chatham Counties.* Charlotte, NC, Herb Eaton Historical Publications, 1987. 1 v. (various pagings). 1. Brady family. 2. North Carolina-Genealogy. [G82].

BRADY -- Reynolds, June Cooper. *Notes on a Brady Family.* Greenville, SC, 1985. 84, 2p, 1 folded leaf of plates. 1. Brady family. NG gives 84p.; DC gives 84, 4p. [G82; NG24; DC426].

BRAGG -- NAS. *Bragg Family of North Carolina.* NP, 1978. ca. 78 leaves. [D1507].

BRAKE -- Edwards, David D. *Brake: A Family, a Tradition, a Contribution, and a Legacy.* Baltimore, MD, Gateway Press, 1990. 225p. 1. Brake family. 2. Germany-Genealogy. 3. North Carolina-Genealogy. 4. Virginia-Genealogy. [G83].

BRANDON -- Betts, Arlie Brandon. *The Brandons of Halifax County, Virginia, Gaston County, North Carolina & York County, South Carolina.* Deerfield, MA, A. Brandon Betts, 1987. 192p. 1. Brandon family. 2. Southern States-Genealogy. [G83].

BRANSON -- Branson, Rev. Levi, Ed. *Branson Magazine of Genealogies... V. 1 (no. 1-2); June 1898-June, 1899.* Raleigh, NC, L. Branson, 1898-1899. 57p. [L2186].

BRASWELL -- Kiker, Irene Braswell. *The Braswell Family.* Sumter, SC, L.B. Kiker, Hopkins, SC, W.W. Braswell, 1985. 176p. in various pagings. 1. Braswell family. 2. North Carolina-Genealogy. [G84].

BRAY -- Reece, Edna B. *The Brays of Fish River.* Jonesville, NC, Reece, 1970, 1982. 2 v. Supplement, 1982. [DS77].

BREVARD -- Antley, Eugene Brevard. [G86]. See above: ANTLEY. [G16].

BREWER -- Stone, Fay Campbell. [G87]. See above: BARANTINE. [G34].

BREWER -- Brewer, Warren H. *History of Brewer Family of North Carolina, Tennessee, Indiana, and Illinois, and McKnight, Galyean (Gallion) Barr, Hutton, Bloxom, Lamb, Lewis, and Related Families, also Woodworth, Newkirk, Crossland, Finley, Hatch, Hubbard and Carter.* Terre Haute, IN, Brewer, 1935. 50p., 70 numb. leaves. D gives 69 1 (sic) leaves. [L2244; D1564].

BREWSTER -- Brewster, Marcus V. *Mark Brewster of Hull, England and Allied Families in America: Including Atkey, Carpenter, Dare, Fowler, Hiscock, Hewitt, Potter, and Yelf.* Manning, SC, M.V. Brewster, 1990. xvi, 336p. 1. Brewster family. 2. Brewster, Mark, 1822-1917-Family. 3. England-Genealogy. 4. Illinois-Genealogy. [G87].

BREWTON -- Antley, Eugene Brevard. [G88]. See above: ANTLEY. [G16].

BRICKHOUSE -- Brickhouse, Grady Gordon. *The Brickhouse Family History.* Black Hawk, SD, G.G. Brickhouse, 1987. 348 leaves. 1. Brickhouse family. 2. Virginia-Genealogy. 3. North Carolina-Genealogy. [G88].

BRIGHT -- Bright, C. Emmert. *The Life Adventures of Aldeba Klepinger Bright and*

Hamilton Garver Bright. Clemmons, NC, Bright, 1988. 1 v. (various paginations). [DC457].

BRIGHT -- Creasy, William Murlin. *Bright and Allied Families.* Wilmington, NC, Creasy, 1937. 2, 19 leaves. [D1602].

BRIGHT -- Jernigan, Rupert W. *The Ancestors and Descendants of J. Wesley Bright (1873-1938), Frederick M. Hopkins (1864-1948), Watson M. Jernigan (1848-1905), Henry E. Marsh (1855-1922).* Charleston, SC?, Jernigan, 1967. 56p. [D1604].

BRISTOW -- Bristow, Emmett Albion. *Descendants of John Bristow of Middlesex County, Va., & William Bristow of Orange and Randolph Counties, N.C., 1650-1919.* Bel Air, MD, 1971. pni. [VV23].

BRITT -- Lipkey, Cora Lee Britt. *The Britts of Robeson County, North Carolina.* NP, Lipkey, 1958. 43 leaves. [D1621].

BROADNAX -- Lawson, Percy Bethel. *From Slaveryship through Hardship to Ownership: A History of American [i.e. America] Wesson Broadnax's Family from Slavery to 1920.* Greensboro, NC, P.B. Lawson, 1985. 65p., 1 l. of plates. 1. Broadnax family. 2. Wesson family. 3. Hamlin family. 4. Broadnax, America Wesson-Family. 5 Rockingham County (N.C.)-Genealogy. 6. Afro-Americans-North Carolina-Rockingham County-Genealogy. [G90].

BROCKMANN -- Brockmann, Charles Raven. *Brockmann - Raven - Zucker Biographical Geleaology (sic).* Charlotte, NC, Brockmann, 1966. 75 leaves. [A90; D1635].

BROOKS -- Kellam, Ida (Brooks). *Brooks and Kindred Families.* Wilmington, NC, 1950. 384p. [L2389; NG24].

BROOKS -- Longmire, Norma Lee. *John Brooks and Some of His Descendants.* Raleigh, NC,

Longmire, 1962. 60 leaves. See also 1977 edition (next below). [D1661].

BROOKS -- Longmire, Norma Lee. *John Brooks and Some of His Descendants.* Henderson, NC, Longmire, 1977. 123p. [D1660; DC473].

BROOKSHIRE -- Brookshire, William F. *Genealogy: De(s)cendants of Joel and Nancy Brookshire, Western North Carolina.* Lenoir, NC, Smith Print Co., 1969. 82p. [A93].

BROWDER -- Browder, Blanche Penland. *Notes on the Browder Family of Tidewater Virginia, 1695-1850. Rev. ed., 2nd ed.* Raleigh, NC, B.P. Browder, 1984. xiv, 221p. Rev. ed. of Notes on the Browder family of Tidewater, Virginia, 1704-1850 by Nathaniel C. and Blanche Browder, 1970. 1. Browder family. 2. Virginia-Genealogy. [G98].

BROWDER -- Browder, Nathaniel C. and Blanche, *Notes on the Browder Family of Tidewater, Virginia, 1704-1850.* Hayesville, NC, 1970. vii, 153 leaves. 1. Browder family. 2. Genealogy-Virginia. [G98; S335; D1675; x133-FW].

BROWER -- Butler, James M. *Some Descendants of Christian Browder and Allied Families.* Greensboro, NC, J.M. Butler, 1984. iii, 172, 72p. [DC478].

BROWER -- Butler, James M. *Your Family and Mine.* Greensboro, NC, J.M. Butler, 1986. xii leaves, 562p. 1. Butler family. 2. Carver family. 3. Brower family. [G98].

BROWN -- NAS. *Brown and Related Families Records, Tennessee, North Carolina, South Carolina, Maryland.* NP, 1975. 40 leaves. [X137-LA].

BROWN -- Brown, Channing Bolton. *Book of Brown; The History of a Family.* Charlotte, NC, 1967. 72p. [L2495].

BROWN -- Brown, J. Parsons. *Brown (Browne) and Their Descendants in Carolina Today.* Kingston, NC, Brown?/Jarrett? 1965. 239p. X gives: Editor, Alice D. Southerland, Jarrett. [D1689; X136-NY].

BROWN -- Brown, Rev. Richard L. *A History of the Michael Brown Family of Rowan County, North Carolina, Tracing Its Ancestry from the Original Michael Brown to the Present Generation and giving something of the Times One Hundred Years Ago Together with Many Historic Facts of Local and National Interest.* Granite Quarry, NC, Michael Brown Family Association, 1921. 190p. D gives underscored part of title; no place of publication. [L2452; D1694].

BROWN -- Brown, Richard L. and Robert E. *A Brown Family of Spartanburg and Greenville Counties, South Carolina.* Maplewood, NJ, 1963. 35 leaves. "The material was collected between 1934 and 1937 and no attempt has been made to bring it up to date." [L2490].

BROWN -- Brown, Richard L. and Robert E. *Cobb and Kindred Families of Abbeville (Greenwood) and Spartanburg Counties, South Carolina.* Maplewood, NJ, 1964. 24 leaves. [L2492].

BROWN -- DeHuff, Elizabeth Willis. *Brown Family of Virginia and South Carolina.* NP, 1964. 24p. [D1708; VV25].

BROWN -- Fisher, Roscoe Brown. *Michael Braun (Brown) of the Old Stone House.* Charlotte, NC, Delmar Publishers and Printers, 1975. xxi, 201p.. [D1712].

BROWN -- Langston, Eula Belle Driggers. *Our Brown Family.* Hartsville, SC, 1971. 20 l. 1. Brown family. [G100; S341].

BROWNE -- Hollowell, Lucy Elliott. *The Descendants of Dr. Samuel Browne of Bertie,*

Northampton, Hertford Counties, North Carolina. Woodland, NC, 1971. 136 leaves. X gives 138p. [NG25; X137-FW].

BROWNLEE -- Holman, Mrs. Olive Hariet Brownlee. *German-Swiss and Scotch-Irish Settlements in South Carolina. Brownlee - Holman and Collaterals.* Anderson, SC, 1937. 87p. Includes Padgett, Caldwell, Acker, Brown, Hubbard, Waddell, Wannamaker, and Rumph Families. [L2506].

BROWNLEE -- Thies, Lynn Walker. *The Brownlees*. Charlotte, NC, Thies, 1973. 26p., 13 leaves. [D1751].

BRUTON -- Bruton, Eric H. *Descendants of George Bruton, 1744-1811 and Wife Susan Wilson, 1747-1807*. High Point, NC, Bruton, Bruton, 1984. 339p. [DC502].

BRUTON -- Stewart, Albert. *John Calvin Bruton, 1856-1931*. Fayetteville, NC, Stewart, 1978. iv, 65 leaves. [D1780].

BRYANT -- Bryant, Lawrence C. *A Historical and Genealogical Record of Lawrence Bryant and Pattie Sessom's Five Other Sons of Nash County, North Carolina*. Orangeburg, SC, 1968. iv, 144p. [L2552].

BRYANT -- Kendrick, Mattie Bryant. *My Dearest One*. Greenville, SC, 1955. 126p. [L2551].

BUGG -- Bugg, William Emmanuel. *Journals of William Emmanuel Bugg, 1848-1935, Mecklenburg, County, Virginia and Warren County, North Carolina with Bugg, Davis, Hudgins, Nicholson, Smith, Walker*. New Orleans, LA, B. FFyliaid [or Fflaid] Publications, 1986. 381p. 1. Bugg, William Emmanuel, 1848-1935-Diaries. 2. Mecklenburg County (Va.)-Biography. 3. Warren County (N.C.)-Biography. 4. Pioneers-Virginia -Mecklenburg County-Diaries. 5. Pioneers-North Carolina-Warren County-Diaries. 6.

Bugg family. 7. Davis family. 8. Hutchins family. DC gives underscored title. [G105; DC521].

BULL -- Bull, Henry DeSaussure. *The Family of Stephen Bull of Kinghurst Hall, County Warwick, England and Ashley Hall, South Carolina, 1600-1960.* Georgetown, SC, Winyah Press, 1961. xii, 161p. [D1836; X145-FW/NY].

BULL -- Bull, Kinloch. *The Oligarchs in Colonial and Revolutionary Charleston: Lieutenant Governor William Bull II and His Family.* Columbia, SC, University of South Carolina Press, 1991. xvi, 415p., 16p. of plates. 1. Bull, William, 1710-1791. 2. South Carolina-Politics and Government-Colonial Period, ca. 1600-1775. 3. South Carolina-Politics and Government-Revolution, 1775-1783. 4. Charleston (S.C.)-History-Colonial Period, ca. 1600-1775. 5. Charleston (S.C.)-History-Revolution, 1775-1783. 6. Bull family. 7. Lieutenant Governors-South Carolina-Biography. [G105].

BULLEN -- Gosnold, Flora B. *Genealogy and Works of Rev. Joseph Bullen, Jr., and Some Associated Families.* Hickory, NC, F.B. Gosnold,1968. 215p. [X145-FW/NY].

BULLOCH -- Bullock, Lewis T. *Bullock Family; Abstract of Tax Lists of Granville County, N. C., 1765-1935.* Los Angeles, CA, 1967. 16, 74 leaves. [L2639].

BULLOCK -- Bullock, James Garland. *Families of Bullock - Roebuck.* Greensboro, NC, Bullock, 1977. 203, 57 leaves. [D1851].

BULLOCK -- Ray, Worth Stickley. *Colonial Granville County and Its People. Loose Leaves from "The Last Tribes of North Carolina."* Austin, TX, 1945. 193-312p. [L2640].

BUMPASS -- Bumpus, Anne Shirley. *The Bumpass Family from Pearson County, North*

Carolina. Columbia, TN, Bumpus, Durham, NC, Townsend, 1972. 157p. [D1857].

BUNDY -- Bundy, V. Mayo. *The Descendants of William and Elizabeth Bundy of Rhode Island and North Carolina.* Charleston, NC, Herb Eaton Historical Publications, 1986. xii, 512p. "Supplement No. 1 to the Descendants of William and Elizabeth Bundy of Rhode Island and North Carolina." - Cover. 1. Bundy family. 2. Bundy, William, ca. 1630-1692-Family. [G106].

BURBAGE -- Clark, Joliene Byrd. *Pamticoe Cousins of Beaufort County, N.C.* Baltimore, MD, Gateway Press, 1988. vi, 775p. 1. Burbage family. 2. Burnett family. 3. Clark family. 4. North Carolina-Genealogy. [G106].

BURGESS -- Burgess, Michael. *The House of Burgesses. 2nd ed.* San Bernardino, CA, Borgo Press, 1989. pni. "Being a genealogical history of Edward Burges of King George Co., Virginia, with the Descendants in the Male Line of His Sons, Garner Burges of Fauquier Co., Virginia, William Burgess of Staff Co., Virginia, Edward Burgess, Jr. of Fauquier Co., Virginia, Moses Burgess of Orange Co., Virginia, and Reuben Burgess of Rowan (later Davie)Co. North Carolina." 1. Burgess family. [G107].

BURGESS -- Clarkson, Francis O. *Genealogies of the Burgess and Stukes Families.* Charlotte, NC, Clarkson, 1981. 60 leaves. [D1897].

BURGESS -- Trimble, Eugene E. *The Burgess Family of Camden (formerly Pasquotank) County, N.C.* Kensington, MD, Trimble, 1960. 23p. [D1898].

BURGIN -- Silvers, Peggy. *Echoes in the Mist: The Burgin Family, 1677-1989.* Nebo, NC, Silvers, 1989. 393, xxx, 17p. [DC536].

BURGWIN -- Jones, Walter Burgwyn. *John Burgwin, Carolinian; John Jones, Virginian; Their Ancestors and Descendants.* Montgomery, AL, Priv. Print. 1913. 199p.. [L2681].

BURNETT -- Clark, Joliene Byrd. [G108]. See above: BURBAGE. [G106].

BURNETT -- Gass, Francis. *A Burnett Family of the South: Thomas , 1755-1780, of Virginia and North Carolina and His Descendants.* Washington, DC, National Pub. Co., 1964. xv, 250p. [L2703; VV28].

BURNS -- Stewart, Estelle M. Burns. *The Burns Family and Allied Lines of North Carolina, Alabama, and Texas.* Huntsville, TX, 1969, 31, 6 leaves, 7p. [X149-FW/NY].

BURNS -- Burns, James Calhoun. *Burns Family, Old 96 District, South Carolina.* Greenwood, SC, Burns, 1954. 16, 35, 2 leaves. [D1928].

BURROWS -- Burough, Howard Duane. *The Burrow Family: Descendants of Henry and Lucy Burrow, from Virginia to North Carolina and Beyond: Allison, Amick, Bowman, Buckles, Burough, Burrough, Burroughs, Burrow, Embler, Gombie, Goodman, Lane, McCarry, Moore, Robinson, Stout, Warren, Yergin, York and Related Families.* Augusta, GA, H . D . Burrows. 1981. 1 v. various pagings. [C103; VV28].

BURROWS -- Burroughs, Franklin. *Horry and the Waccamaw.* New York, Norton, 1992. pni. 1. Waccamaw River (N.C. and S.C.)-Description and travel. 2. Canoes and Canoeing-Waccamaw River (N.C. and S.C.). 3. Horry County (S.C.)-Descriptions and travel. 4. Burroughs, Franklin-Journeys-Waccamaw River(N.C. and S.C.). 5. Burrows family. [G109].

BUSH -- DeHugg, Elizabeth Willis. *The Bush Family as Descended from John and Mary Bryan*

Bush of North Carolina. Augusta, GA, DeHuff, 1967. 169, 4p. [D1967].

BUSH -- Edwards, Katharine Bush. *The Bush and Foster Families.* Greenville, SC, Edwards, 1976. 6, 5 leaves. [D1968].

BUTLER -- Bell, Malcolm. *Major Butler's Legacy: Five Generations of a Slave Holding Family.* Athens, GA, The University of Georgia, 1987. xxiv, 673p. 1. Butler, Pierce, 1744-1822. 2. Butler Family. 3. Plantation owners-Georgia-Biography. 4. Plantation owners-South Carolina-Biography. 5. Plantation life-Georgia-History-19th century. 6. Plantation life-South Carolina-History-19th century. [G111; DC553].

BUTLER -- Butler, Ermon Mrs. (Marilee Gerrell). *A Book of Butlers: Jacob Butler (1812-1853) of Sampson County, North Carolina and Decatur (now Grady) County, Georgia and Some of His Antecedents and Descendants. Also Some Related Lines.* Calvary, GA, M. G. Butler, 1985. 178p. [C105].

BUTLER -- Butler, Mary Louise. <u>*A Butler Family History*</u>*. William Butler, John W. Butler (of Sampson County, North Carolina), and Their Descendants* Charlotte, NC, Delmar Printers, 1972. xx, 256p. D gives underscored title. [S385; D1985].

BUTLER -- Butler, James M. [G111]. See above: BROWER. [G98].

BYERLY -- Byerly, Wesley Grimes, Jr. *The Byerlys of Carolina.* Hickory, NC, 1960. 69p. [NG27].

BYERLY -- Byerly, Wesley G. Jr. *The Byerlys of Carolina.* Hickory, NC, 1960-65. 2 vos. (171p.) PH has 1 vol. [X154-FW/NY/PH/SP].

BYERLY -- Byerly, Wesley Grimes, Jr. *The Byerlys of Carolina.* Hickory, NC, Economy

Print Co., 1960-1976. 3 v. (424p.) [D2004; X155-FW/NY].

BYLERLY -- Treadway, William E. *Byerlys from North Carolina.* Topeka, KS, Treadway, 1965. 140p. [D2005].

BYLER -- Byler, Roger Louis. *Jacob Byler of North Carolina Who Died in 1804 and His Descendants.* Sweeny, TX, 1985. 609p. 1. Byler family. 2. Byler, Jacob, ca. 1740-1804-Family. 3. North Carolina-Genealogy. [G111].

BYRD -- Hardin, Vera. *The Ironmasters Kin: The Genealogy of William and Mark Bird, 1621-1985.* Blacksburg, SC, V. Hardin, 1985. 60p. 1. Byrd family. 2. Bird, William, 1707 or 7-1761-Family. 3. Bird, Mark, 1739-1812-Family. [G113].

BYRD -- Skeen, A. T. *Coveys of Birds.* Troutman, NC, A.T. Skeen, 1989. xiv, 447p. 1. Byrd family. 2. Tennessee Genealogy. [G113].

BYROM -- Keller, Velma Byrum. *The Sons of Isaac; (A Genealogy of the Byroms of North Carolina and Indiana).* Allentown, PA, National Advertising Manufacturing Co., 1969. viii, 379p. [L282].

C

CABE -- Browning, Hugh Conway. *More Orange County, North Carolina Families; Breeze, Brown, Cabe, Johnson, Latta, Lockhart, McCown, Patterson, Piper, Shields, Strayhorn, etc.* Chapel Hill, NC, Browning, 1968. 78 leaves. [D2019].

CABE -- Wheatcroft, Elsie Cabe. *The Genealogy of 1500 Descendants of Amos, Samuel, Stephen, and Zachariah Cabe.* Franklin, NC, Wheatcroft, 1983. X, 144p. [DC565].

CAFFEY -- Reed, Beatrice M Caffey. *Genealogies of the Caffey, Iseley & Ireland Families of Rockingham, Guilford, & Alamance Counties in North Carolina.* High Point, NC, B.M.C. Reed, 1981. xi, 141p. [D2032].

CAIN -- Blackmore, Eleanor Cain. *Family Connections: Ferebec 1642, Hutchins 1645, Harbin 1787, Naylor 1780...* Winston-Salem, NC, 1983. 210p. [DC569].

CALDWELL -- Arnett, Ethel Stephens. *David Caldwell.* Greensboro, NC, Media, 1946. xiii, 106p. [D2039].

CALDWELL -- Caldwell, Ray Von. *The Genealogy of James Caldwell and His Descendants, 1750-1968.* Newton, NC, Caldwell, Epps Pringting Co., 1968. 3977p. [D2044].

CALDWELL -- Foote, William Henry. *Sketches of North Carolina, Historical and Biographical, Illustrations of Her Early Settlers.* New York, NY, R. Carter, 1846. Raleigh, NC, H.J. Dudley of the Committee on Historical Matters of the Synod of North Carolina, Presbyterian Church in the U.S., 1965. 593p. "Third editions, 1965." A reproduction of the 1st ed., 1846 with a new preface, bibliography and index. [L2857].

CALDWELL -- Peoples, David Stuart. *Cook, Caldwell, Peoples, Stuart, and Other Families.* Baltimore, MD, Gateway Press, Winston-Salem, NC, D.S. Peoples [distributor], 1990. 84p. 1. Cook family. 2. Caldwell family. 3. Peoples family. 4. Stuart family. [G115].

CALDWELL -- Weede, Fred Lewis. *The James Caldwell Family of Eire, Penna. and Chillicothe, Ill; Geneological (sic) Tabulation of Their Descendants, Including Data of Forebears of Caldwell, Booth, Hay, Armstrong, and Other Allied Families in France, England, Scotland, Ireland, and America.* Asheville, NC, Weede, 1959. 37p. D gives underscored part of title. [L2873; D2049].

CALHOUN -- Calhoun, Robert D. *The Calhouns of Ninety-Six, South Carolina and Their Descendants.* NP, 1922. 33, 12 leaves. [X159-DP].

CALHOUN -- Dundas, F. de S. *Calhoun Settlement, District of Abbeville, South Carolina.* Staunton, VA, 1949. 24p. [L2879].

CALHOUN -- Dundas, F. de S. *Calhoun Settlement, District of Abbeville, South Carolina.* Staunton, VA, 1949. 60p. VV & X give date as 1950. 2nd ed. [L2880; NG27; X159-FW; VV31].

CALHOUN -- Hollifield, Mary Ann. *John Calhoun and Sara Jane Scott Martin and Their Descendants.* __, NC, M.A. Hollifield and B.M. Martin, 1987. 327p. 1. Calhoun family. 2. Martin, John Calhoun, ca. 1830-1909-Family. [G115].

CALHOUN -- Polson, Lois N. *William Calhoun of Guilford County, North Carolina.* Victorville, CA, L.N. Polson, 1970. 57 leaves. [X159-FW/NY].

CALHOUN -- Wick, Mildred Calhoun. *Living With Love.* Newport, DE, Serendipity Press, 1986. xi, 167p. 1. Calhoun family. 2. South Carolina-Biography. 3. United States-Biography. [G115].

CALLAHAN -- Callahan, Anna Deihls. *A History of the Callahan and Carwile Families.* Charlotte, NC, 1976. 493p. [NG27].

CAMERON -- Anderson, Jean Bradley. [G116]. See above: BENNEHAN. [G48].

CAMP -- Carter, Nell Jones. *Camp, Jones and Related Families of Connecticut, Illinois, Missouri, Virginia, Carolina, Georgia,*

Alabama, Mississippi, Louisiana, Texas and Points West. Tallahassee, FL, Carter, 1977. vii, 430p. [C111; D2085; VV31].

CAMPBELL -- Lee, Henry. *History of the Campbell Family.* Charleston, SC, Garnier & Co., 1920. Reprinted 1968. 156p. [X162-FW/NJ].

CAMPBELL -- Stone, Fay Campbell. [G118]. See above. BARENTINE. [G34].

CAMPBELL -- Temple, Sarah E. *Our Campbell Ancestors, 1742-1937. Tradition and History of the Family of Five Campbell Brothers and Sisters; John, James Douglas, Hester, Mary and Samuel: Including What is Known of Them in New Jersey, York County, Pennsylvania, Union County, South Carolina and in Ohio. A Genealogy of the Known Descendants of John Campbell through His Son James, and Samuel Campbell through His Son Ralph, also Brief Ancestral Notes on Families Connected by Marriage with the Foregoing; viz. Parnell, Clark, Spray, Wilson, Haskett, Mendenhall, and Underhill.* Burbank, CA, I. Deash, Jr., 1939. 225p. [L2955; VP39].

CAMPBELL -- Campbell, Thomas. *Descendants of Capt. Angus Campbell of Laurens, South Carolina.* Charlottesville, VA, 1955. 1 v. (various pagings). 100 copies printed. Addenda and errata sheet inserted. [L2960].

CAMERON -- Cameron, J. B. *History of the Cameron Family; Descendants of Allen Cameron and His Wife, Mary Stewart.* Broadway, NC, J.B. Cameron, 1967. 41p. [XA1069-FW].

CANTEY -- Ames, Joseph S.... *Six Generations of the Cantey Family of South Carolina.* Charleston, SC, Walker, Evans & Cogswell, co., 1910. 1, 56p. "Reprinted from the South Carolina historical and genealogical magazine. [L2981].

CAPERS -- MacDowell, Dorothy Kelly. *Descendants of William Capers and Richard Capers and Related Families.* Aiken, SC, McDowell, S gives: Columbia, SC, R.L. Bryan Co., 1973. xiii, 134p. [S409; NG27; D2137].

CARLTON -- NAS. *Some Records of the Descendants of William Carlton, Son of John and Nancy Ann Alderman Carlton, Son of Thomas and Martha Carleton of Duplin County, N. C.* Athens, GA, 1959. 2 parts in 1 vol. (Part 2 is Descendants of Stephen Carlton). [X166-FW].

CARLTON -- Carleton, Luther Findley. *History of the Carlton Family of Wilkes County, North Carolina.* Phoenix, AZ, 1974. 133p. [NG28; X165-FW/LA].

CARPENTER -- McKoy, Henry Bacon. *The Carpenter - Weir Family of Upper South Carolina, and Other Ancestors, Including Benson, Berry, Blassingame, Caldwell, Maxwell, Richey, Sloan, Stewart, Wilson.* Greenville, SC, 1959. 305p. [L3403; NG28].

CARR -- Carr, James Ozborn. *The Carr Family of Duplin County.* Wilmington, NC, Wilmington Stamp & Printing Co., 1939. 65p. X gives: written about 1920. [D2180; X168-FW/LA/MH/NY].

CARRINGTON -- Tilley, Mary Ethel. *Carrington.* Rougemont, NC, Tilley, 1943. 88p. [D2192].

CARRUTH -- Carson, Arlie Aaron. *Carruth to Carson: A Genealogy.* Columbia, SC, A.B. Carson, 1990. iv, 126p., 4 p. of plates. 1, Carson family. 2. Carruth family. [G124].

CARSON -- Carson, Arlie Aaron. [G124]. See just above: CARRUTH. [G124].

CARTER -- Foster, Carolyn Agnes (Mrs. Edgar M. Marbourg). *Carter Family of North*

<u>*Carolina*</u>*; Descendants of Robert Carter of Bertie County.* Richmond, VA, Foster, (Whittet & Shepperson, Printer), 1914. 40p. D gives underscored part of title. [L3095; D2214; VV33].

CARTER -- Holland, Mary Ketus Dean. *A Genealogy of the Descendants of Jacob Carter of South Carolina.* Sanford, FL, Holland, 1974. viii, 100 leaves. D gives: "See also: V. 1. Miles, Kemp, Hall; v. 2. Holland genealogy; v. 4. A geneal. of the descendants of John Miles." [S428; NG28; D2216].

CARTER -- McGhee, Acie. *The little Lights of Mine: the William and Sallie Carter Family.* Kernersville, NC, McGhee, [c1980-c1986]. 2 v. 1. Carter family. 2. Magee family. 3. Afro-Americans-Genealogy. [G125].

CARTWRIGHT -- Walter, Alice G. *Cartwright and Shipp Families of Lower Norfolk, Princess Anne & Surry Counties, Virginia and North Carolina.* Lawrence, NY, 1968. 1 Sheet (Genealogical Chart). [X171-NY].

CARVER -- Butler, James M. [G126]. See above: BROWER. [G98].

CASSAT -- Cassat, Rowena Wilson. *A Long Far View: The Story of My First Ninety Years. - 2nd ed.* Asheville, NC, 1981. 112p., 51 leaves. [DC640].

CASSELL -- Cassels, Louis & Charlotte. *An Inquiry into the Origins of the Cassels Family of Ellenton, S.C.* Bethesda, MD, 1971. 6, 2 leaves. [S448].

CASTON -- Floyd, Viola Caston. <u>*Caston and Related Families*</u>*; Descendants of Glass Caston of Lancaster County, South Carolina.* Lancaster, SC, Floyd, 1972. 204p + 8 leaves of corrections. D gives underscored title. [D2259; X173-FW/LA/NY].

CATHEY -- NAS. *Cathey Kith and Kin. 1951-* Gastonia, NC, Annual vol. for 1963 not published. Publ. by Cathey Family Association (1951-70 under variant forms of name). Title varies. [X174-NY].

CATHEY -- NAS. *The Cathey Family.* NP, William Gaston Chapter, North Carolina, DAR, G.R.C., 1954. 55 leaves. [DC651].

CATLETT -- Baer, Mabel Van Dyke. *Catlett - Taliaferro Families of Virginia, and Farr - Stribling Families of South Carolina and Mississippi.* NP, 1973. 119 leaves. [D2269].

CATLETT -- Fisher, Sunie Garrett Talbert Elliott. *Garrett, Catlett, Ware and Related Families.* Cullman, AL, Cregath Co., North August, SC, 326p., 4p. of plates. 1. Garrett family. 2. Catlett family. 3. Ware family. 4. Southern States-Genealogy. [G128].

CAWOOD -- Caywood, James Alexander, II. *Cawood and Related Families.* Fripp Island, SC, 1982, 31p. [NG29].

CAWOOD -- Keith, Arthur Leslie. *The Cawood Family.* Also by James C. Presgraves. Fripp Island, SC, 1985. 194p. [NG29].

CHADWICK -- McGuinn, M. S., Ed. *Chadwick Chat. Mar. 1938-1956 (Incomplete).* Spartanburg, SC,. __ vols. Monthly. Began Publ. Oct. 1937. Ceased Dec. 1956. [X175-NY].

CHADWICKS -- Muse, Amy. *Grandpa Was a Whaler; A Story of the Carteret Chadwicks.* New Bern, NC, Owen G. Dunn Co., 1961. v, 126p. X lists as CHADWICK. [D2292; NG29; X176-FW/NY].

CHAMBERLAIN -- NAS. *Record of One Line of Descendants of Edmund Chamberlain, (- 1696) English Emigrant.* Charleston, SC, 1920. 12p. [X176-FW].

CHAMBERS -- Chambers, Mamie. *The Chambers Family of Duplin County, North Carolina.* Elizabeth City, NC, 1969. iv, 182 leaves. [A121].

CHAMBERS -- Horlacher, Gary T. *Chambers and Moad Families.* Orem, UT, Horlacher, 1987. vi, 110p. 1. Chambers family. 2. Moad family. 3. North Carolina-Genealogy. 4. Tennessee-Genealogy. 5. Missouri-Genealogy. [G131].

CHAMBERS -- Sawyer, Mamie Chambers. *The Chambers Family of Duplin County, N.C.* Elizabeth City, NC, Sawyer, 1969. 182p. [D2316].

CHANCE -- Chance, Hilda. *Chance of Ohio, Virginia, North Carolina, Georgia, Texas, Tennessee, Kentucky, Delaware, Maryland, Pennsylvania, Michigan, California, Indiana, New Jersey.* Liberty, PA, 1970. 19 leaves. [A122; VV36].

CHANCE -- *Supplement to Chance of Ohio, Virginia, etc.* Liberty, PA, 1970. 19 leaves. [A122; VV36].

CHAPLIN -- Chaplin, Ellen P. *The Chaplins and Allied Families.* Neeses, SC, 1964.1 v. (unpaged). [L3285].

CHAPMAN -- Edmonds, Elsie Chapman. *John Chapman of Spottsylvania County, Virginia, Thomas Powe of Cheraw, South Carolina, and Related Families.* Newton, MS, Edmonds, 1971. ii, 421p. D gives underscored part of title. [S472; D2354; VV36].

CHASE -- Florance, Chris. *Up from Mount Misery: The Blossoming of North Carolina's Sandhills.* Asheboro, NC, Down Home Press, 1990. xviii, 211p. 1. Sandhills (Ga.-N.C.)-History. 2. Sandhills (Ga.-N.C.)-Biography. 3. Farm life-Sandhills (Ga.-N.C.)-History-20th century. 4. Chase family. [G133].

CHESBROUGH -- Wrigley, Harold Chandler. *Genealogy of the Descendants of Avery, Chesbrough, Palmer, and Miner Families.* Arden, NC, Wrigley, 1983. 326p. [DS118].

CHESTNUT -- Chestnutt, Joseph H. *Voices From the Past: Chestnutt, A Southern Colonial Family.* Wilmington, NC, C. Perdue, 1987. iv, 152p. 1. Chestnut family. 2. Southern States-Genealogy. [G135].

CHEWNING -- Watts, Dorothy Chambers. *Chewnings of South Carolina: Descendants of Theophilus and Peter Chewning, and Allied Families of Sanders, Corbitt, Felder, Ragin, Joye, and McLeod.* Albuquerque, NM, Watts Publishers, 1986. xiv, 126p. 1. Chewning family. 2. Chewning, Theophilus, b. ca. 1784-Family. 3. Chewning, Peter, 1796-1880-Family. 4. South Carolina-Genealogy. [G135].

CHILTON -- Harbour, Lizora Powell. *Gibbs - Chilton - Evans: Families of Rockingham County, N. C.* Ruffin, NC, L.P. Harbour, 1989. 179p. 1. Chilton family. 2. Gibbs family. 3. Evans family. 4. Rockingham County (N.C.)-Genealogy. 5. North Carolina-Genealogy. [G136].

CHIPMAN -- Chipman, Bert Lee. *The Chipman Family.* Winston-Salem, NC, Chipman, 1920. 321p. D gives: Bound with Chipmans of America / by Alberto Lee Chipman, 1904. [L3401; D2409].

CHISHOLM -- Chism, John D. *The Chisz: A History of the Chisholme / Chism Family.* Clemson, SC, J.D. Chism, Jr., 1989. 911, 63p. 1. Chisholm family. 2. Texas-Genealogy. [G136].

CHRISTIAN -- Christian, Bickham. *A Genealogical Study of James Christian, ca. 1750 - 11 Oct. 1826, Sergt. Cook's Co. N.C. Continental Line ... and His Ancestors and Descendants.* NP, 1958. 185 l. [D2424].

CHRISTIAN -- Puterbaugh, John C. *The Life Journey of Lydia Dohner and Samuel Christian.* Clemons, NC, C. Emmert Bright, 1983. 146p. [DS121].

CHRISTOPHER -- Whitehurst, Anna Holleman. *Genealogy of the Haylander Family to the Ninth Generation, 1742-1988: Inside - Including Ridges, Christophers, Hollemans, and Whitehursts.* Williamsburg, VA, A.H. Whitehurst, 1988. 170 leaves. "Revised ed. of: Genealogy of the Haylander family to the fifth generation." 1. Haylander family. 2. Ridge family. 3. Christopher family. 4. Holleman family. 5. North Carolina-Genealogy. [G138].

CLAPP -- Whitsett, William Thornton. *History of the Brick Church and the Clapp Family.* Greensboro, NC, Whitsett, Harrison Printing Co., 1925. 28p. [L3458; D2463].

CLARK -- NAS. *Clark Family of North Carolina; Edward E. & Daisy Carolina.* NP, North Carolina DAR, 1946. 69 leaves. D gives underscored title. [D2502; DC729].

CLARK -- Bobbitt, Addie Clark. *The Branches From Roots.* __, NC, A.C. Bottitt, 19__, 32 leaves, 2 leaves of plates. Errata slip inserted. 1. Clark family. 2. Afro-American-Genealogy. [G141].

CLARK -- Clark, Alexander Wilbur. *Ancestry and Descendants of Neill Alexander Clark (c1822/23-1864) of Cumberland County, North Carolina.* NP, 1958. 15p. [L3525].

CLARK -- Clark, A. Wilbur. *Ancestry and Descendants of Neill Alexander Clark (c1822/23-1864) of Cumberland County, North Carolina.* __, NC, 1987, 1986 (Fayetteville, NC, Highland Press). 19p. 1. Clark family. 2. Clark, Neill Alexander, 1822 or 1823-1864-Family. 3. North Carolina-Genealogy. [G141].

CLARK -- Clark, Chovine R. *Lineage of Chovine Richardson Clark, Manning South Carolina. On Father's Side: Clark, DuPont, Guerry, Graves, Kimmel, Long, Perdriau, Phillips. On Mother's Side: Benbow, Billups, Humphrey, Richardson.* Sumter, SC, Printed by Wilder & Ward. Offset Print, 1969. iii 60p. [A130].

CLARK -- Clark, Edward E. and Daisy. *A Genealogy of the Clarks of Guilford Court House (now Greensboro), N.C.* Mt. Sterling, IL, 1912. 70 leaves. [X189-FW/LI].

CLARK -- Clark, Eva Turner. *Jacob Clark of Abbeville, South Carolina and Some of His Descendants. Notes on Allied Families and Letters of Reverend Jacob Clark, a Family Memorial.* New York, NY, Downs Printing Co., 1926. 121p. "Three hundred copies privately printed." D gives underscored part of title. [L3507: D2474].

CLARK -- Clark, Joliene Byrd. [G141]. See above. BURBAGE. [G106].

CLARK -- Clark, Meribah E. *A Genealogy of the Clarks of Guilford Court House (now Greensboro) North Carolina.* Mount Sterling, IL, Meribah E. Clark, 1968. 72p. [D2484].

CLARK -- Miller, Clara Hunt. *The Clark Family of Orange County, North Carolina.* __, NC, C.H. Miller, 1986. 203p. Limited ed. 200 copies. 1. Clark family. 2. Orange County (N.C.)-Genealogy. [G142].

CLARK -- Wommack, Mildred Clark. *Alston Clark's Descendants of Lancaster District, S. C., Old Letters, Wills, Deeds, Bible and Cemetary Records.* NP, 1970. 224 leaves. [D2511].

CLARKSON -- Clarkson, Francis O. *Thomas Boston Clarkson of South Carolina, His Forebears and His Descendants through His Son,*

William, Including Brief Genealogies of Simons, Heriot, and Marion Families of South Carolina. Charlotte, NC, Clarkson, , 1973, iii, 97 leaves. SC gives: 1 v. (various pagings). D gives underscored part of title. [S505; D2525].

CLAY -- Bryant, Lawrence C. *Historical & Geographical Record of Lee Clay and Related Families of Person County, N.C.* Orangeburg, SC, Bryant, 1972. 70p.
[X192-FW].

CLEGG -- Broughton, W. Harold. *The Cleggs of Old Chatham.* Charlotte, NC, The Association, 1977. x, 470p. [D2549].

CLEVELAND -- Cleveland, James Butler. *A Genealogical Register of the Descendants of Moses Cleveland of Woburn, Mass., An Emigrant in 1635 from England, with a Sketch of the Clevelands of Virginia and the Carolinas.* Albany, NY, Munsell Printer, 1881. 48p. Library of Congress copy replaced by Microfilm. [L3583; VV39].

CLEWELL -- Howell, Gertrude Jenkins. *History of the Clewell, Crabs, Schultz Families in the United States, 1685-1953, Sketch of the Howell - Jenkins Family in North Carolina.* Wilmington, NC, Howell, 1953. 78, 4p. [D2565].

CLINARD -- Gay, Lois Hedgecock. *Generations: The Margaret and Samuel Clinard Clan of North Carolina.* High Point, NC, 1979. 239p. [NG30].

COATE -- Park, Ernest S. *Ancestors and Descendants of Marmaduke Coate of South Carolina and Ohio.* Wolfboro, NH, E.S. Park, 1960. 275p. 2 leaves. [X197-FW].

COATES -- Tucker, D. A. *Coats Kin: From North Carolina to Tennessee to Arkansas.* Houston, TX, D.A. Tucker, 1987. 179p. 1.

Coates family. 2. Southern States-Genealogy. [G146].

COBB -- Maxie, Marie. *Ambrose Cobb of Lincoln County, North Carolina, Ambrose Cobb of Knox County, Kentucky, Vincent Cobb of Jessamine County, Kentucky.* NP, Marie Maxie, 1988. 8 leaves. [DC765].

COCKERHAM -- Cockerham, Dewey Erson. *A Genealogy of the Generations of the Cockerham, Darnell and Tucker Clans, Who Settled in the Foothills of the Blue Ridge Mountains of Northwest North Carolina.* Elkins, NC, 1959. 28 leaves. [L3656].

COCKERHAM -- Kaufman, Nell Shepperd. *John Cockerham and His Descendants: Barnwell District, SC - Amite County, MS: A Progress Report.* Georgetown, TX< Copy-Right, 1987. x, 389p. 1. Cockerham family. 2. Cockerham, Joh, ca. 1735-ca.1844-Family. 3. Mississippi-Genealogy. [G147].

COFFEY -- Coffey, Laurence H. *Thomas Coffey and His Descendants, with a Brief Sketch of the Life of Thomas Coffey, a Pioneer in North Carolina from Virginia, and of Reuben Coffey, a Pioneer in Indiana from North Carolina, and Others.* Chatanooga, TN, N. Sander, 1931. 3, 102p. [L3680; D2623; VV40].

COGBURN -- Raisty, Jewell Cogburn. *The Family of John Cogburn (ca. 1745-1810) of Edgefield District, South Carolina.* NP, Raisty, 1965. vii, 160 leaves. [D2635].

COGGESHALL -- Coggeshall, Chair Pierce. *The Coggeshalls in America: Genealogy of the Descendants of John Coggeshall of Newport with a Brief Notice of Their English Antecedents.* Spartanburg, SC, 1982. 395p. Replaces 1930 ed. [NG31].

COGGESHALL -- Coggeshall, Robert Walton. *Ancestors and Kin.* Spartanburg, SC, Reprint

Co., 1988. xiv, 588p. 1. Coggeshall family. 2. Pauley family. 3. Thomas family. 4. Hansen family. [G148].

COIT -- Coit, John Eliot. *Lineage of the Descendants of John Calkins Coit of Cheraw, South Carolina, 1799-1863.* NP, Coit, 1945. 52p. D gives 50 leaves. [L3708;D2645].

COKER -- Simpson, George Lee. *The Cokers of Carolina; A Social Biography of a Family.* Chapel Hill, NC, Published for the Institute for Research in Social Science by the University of North Carolina Press, 1956. xvi, 327p. [L3719].

COLE -- Sheriff, Pauline Calloway. *Mount Hope. A History of the Cole, Shipman, and Allied Families: Abercrombie, Allen, Anderson, Bailey, Bennett, Bryson, Carson, Channell, Curtis, Hemphill, Hutchins, Keith, Munday, Nixon, Owens, Stephens, and Other Families of Buncombe, N.C., Georgia, Alabama, Mississippi, Arkansas, Texas, Oklahoma, and Elsewhere.* Hollis, OK, P. C. Sheriff, 1982. 256p. [C141].

COLEMAN -- McPherson, Jessie Coleman. *A History of the Coleman - Sloan - Johnson Families.* Columbia, SC, McPherson, 1970. 214p. [D2681].

COLEMAN -- Rosson, Mrs. B. H. *The Descendants of Robert Coleman and Elizabeth Roe, and Some Colemans of Fairfield and Union District, South Carolina.* NP, 1951, 115, 17p. [D2686].

COLLETON -- Easterby, James Harold. *Wadboo Barony, Its Fate as told in Colleton Gamily (sic) Papers, 1773-1793.* Columbia, SC, Univ. of South Carolina Press, 1952. xv, 29p. (South Carolina; Sesquicentennial Series, No. 3). [L3785].

COLLINS -- Collins, Archibald O. *Ole Mann Mose and His Chillun: The Story of Moses Collins of South Carolina, Georgia, Alabama, and Mississippi*. Aransas Pass, TX, Biog. Press. 1974. v, 485p. [X204-FW].

COLLINS -- Dyer, Watson Benjamin. *The Family history of Thompson Collins, 1758-1854 - Celia Self, 1790-1870; from N.C.... to Union County. Part Two: The Family History of William Jackson - Nancy Stanley*. Rome, GA, Author, 1971. B 10 - C 127p., 7 l, 101p. [NG31; X203-FW].

COLLINS -- Field, Sueanne Maxwell. *The Collins Family, Nash County, North Carolina*. Springfield, VA, Field, 1976. ii, 16p. [D2708].

COLLINS -- Sluby, Paul E. [G151]. See above: BISSELL. [G58].

COLLINS -- Tarlton, William S. *Somerset Place and Its Restoration Prepared for the Division of State Parkes, North Carolina Dept. of Conservation and Development*. Raleigh, NC, 1954. 141p. [L3815].

COLTRANE -- Frazier, Robert H. *Descendants of David Coltrane and James Frazier of North Carolina (for seven generations)*. Greensboro, NC, Simpson Print. Co. 1961. 121p. [L3834].

COLTRANE -- Robertson, Minnie Hohn. *The Earth Abideth Forever: A Portrait of the Davis and Coltrane Families of Randolph County, North Carolina*. Welcome, NC, Wooten Print Co., 1984. 557p. 1. Davis family. 2. Coltrane family. 3. Randolph County (N.C.)-Genealogy. [G152].

CONE -- Cone, Sydney M. *The Cones from Bavaria*. Greensboro, NC, 196_. 145p. [X206-FW].

CONNERLY -- Lampton, William A. *Descendants of John Connerly (- 1751) NC and Cullen Conerly (ca.1745-1811) NC to the Present Time.* China Grove, NC, W.A. Lampton, 1986. 880p. [DC811].

CONNOR -- Baer, Mabel Van Dyke. *The Connor Families of North Carolina and Texas and Collateral Families of Murr and Reed (Reid).* NP, 1974. 21 leaves. [D2767].

CONYERS -- Ervin, Samuel J. Jr., *The Conyers Family of Clarendon County, South Carolina.* Morganton, NC, 1973. 12, 14, 9 leaves. [G154; S543].

COOK -- Cook, Rev. Earl L. *... Cook History and Genealogy of Families Originating in North Carolina from 1760-1941... 2nd ed.* Albermarle, NC, The Church Press, 1941. 92p. [L3942].

COOK -- Peoples, David Stuart. [G155]. See above. CALDWELL. [G115].

COOKE -- Cooke, Charlges G. *Many Cooke's and Their Broth; A Genealogical Outline of the Cooke Family of Virginia, North Carolina, Georgia and Alabama.* Alexandria, VA, 1967. 84p. [L3953; VV43].

COOPER -- Bryan, Thomas R. *Cooper Family History, 1730-1982.* Greenville, SC, A Press, Inc., 1982. 192p. [DS149].

COOPER -- Cooper, Homer C. *Cooper, McKenny, Ferrell/ Farrell, Woddell, Gothard, Wilson & Patton Families of Augusta & Rockbridge Counties, Virginia; York & Adams Counties, Pennsylvania; Blount, Knox, & Roane Counties, Tennessee; Pocahontas, Gilmer & Ritchie Counties, West Virginia; Wayne County, Kentucky; Vigo & Sullivan Counties, Indiana; York County, South Carolina.* Athens, GA, 1969. 7 leaves. [L3990; VV43].

COOPER -- Cooper, John Purley. [G156]. See above. BETHEA. [G54].

COOPER -- Reynolds, June Cooper. *Notes on a Cooper Family.* Greenville, SC, J.C. Reynolds, 1986. xiv, 244p. [G156; NG32].

COOPER -- Roberts, Lillian. *Hugh Cooper, 1720-1793 of Fishing Creek, South Carolina and His Descendants.* Fort Worth, TX, Roberts, 1975. xi, 182, 23p. [D2833].

CORCORAN -- Corcoran, Edwin Emmons. *The John Corcoran Family of Charleston, S.C., the Samuel Barnes Emmons Family of Lancaster, S.C.* Asheville, NC, E.E. Corcoran, 1983. 84 leaves, 4 leaves of plates. [DC gives: 1983, 1986. 2 v.] 1. Corcoran family. 2. Emmons family. 3. South Carolina-Genealogy. 4. Corcoran, John, ca. 1790-1819-Family. 5. Emmons, Samuel Barnes, 1800-1881-Family. [G158; DC835].

CORCORAN -- Corcoran, Edwin Emmons. *Addendum update to the John Corcoran Family of Charleston, S.C., the Samuel Barnes Emmon Family of Lancaster, S.C.* Asheville, NC, E.E. Corcoran, 1986. 11 leaves. 1. Corcoran family. 2. Emmons family. 3. South Carolina-Genealogy. 4. Corcoran, John, ca. 1790-1819-Family. 5. Emmons, Samuel Barnes, 1800-1881-Family. [G157].

CORN -- Dorsey, Lois Tichner. *Corn Stalks and Preachers: A Story of the Corn Family* Hendersonville, NC, Genealogy, Ltd., 1981. 406, 22p. [DC842].

COSSART -- Tilley, Mary Ethel. *<u>Cossart or Cozart</u>; A Brief Genealogical Sketch of the Name and Family.* Roudgemount, NC, Tilley, 1944. 75, 5p. D gives underscored part of title. [L4077; D2908].

COSTNER -- Hoffman, Laban Miles. [G160]. See above: BEST. [G54].

COULTER -- Coulter, Victor A. *The Coulter Family of Catawba County, North Carolina.* Oxford, MS, Coulter, 1975. vii, 99p. [X217-NY].

COURTENAY -- Courtenay, Rev. Carlile. *Genealogy of the Courtenay Family of Charleston, S.C. and Distaff Branches.* Columbia, SC, 1932. 2p., 6 numb. leaves. Photostat of Typed Copy. [L4111].

COVINGTON -- Covington, Da Costa Euclid. *Covingtons Remembered: From Gravestones, Wills, Deeds, and Other Records.* Baltimore, MD, Gateway Press, Fayetteville, NC, D.E. Covington, 1991. 544p. 1. Covington family. [G161].

COVINGTON -- McSwain, Eleanor Pratt Covington. <u>My Folk: The First Three Hundred Years, 1670-1970</u>; *A Study of Many First Settlers and Founders of Old Anson and Richmond Counties, North Carolina.* S adds: "Original Research based on first families of America, exp. of Maryland, Virginia, and New England: Covingtons and collateral lines: Dickery, Walls, Leake, Cole, Crawford, Hunter, Everett, Little, Thomas, Morehead, Bennett, Bethune, McKenzie. Steele, Dowd, Phillips, Pratt, Emerson, Belkeley, Blackistone, Gov. James Moore, S. C., De Coursey of Ireland. Albermarle, NC, The Stanley County Historical Society, 1972. 221, 7, 5, 4p. D gives: 221, 4p. [S571; D2944].

COWAN -- NAS. *SAGE - COWAN - STONE - SAUNDERS Families in North Carolina.* Microfilm Reading Room. [L4135].

COWAN -- Fleming, John Kerr. *The Cowans from County Down.* Raleigh, NC, Printed by Derreth Print Co., c1971. xxv, 440p. [S573; D2947].

COX -- Cox, Elza B. *Ambrose N. Cox, Sr., Descendants, 1772-1972.* Lexington, NC, 1973. vii, 626p. [S577].

COX -- Cox, H. E. *Cox Family of Wayne County, N.C. with Historical Notes of the Cox Family in America.* Mount Oilve, NC, H.E. Cox, 1941. 36p. [X219-FW].

COX -- Cox, Rev. Nelson E. *Our Family Genealogy including the Nelson, Johnson, Roach, Smith, Little, Cox, Dawson, Wooton, and Chapman Families.* Southern Pines, NC, The Mary N. Smith Family, 1938. 5, 109, 8p. [X219-SL].

COX -- Jaeckel, Karl T. *The Family of Granville H. Cox, 1822-1888, of Early Ashe County, North Carolina and Atchison County, Missouri.* El Paso, TX, Jaeckel, 1980. 206p. [D2973].

COX -- Wright, Verl F. *As a Tree Grows; A Preliminary History; A Genealogy of the Cox ana Allied Families of Northwestern North Carolina; Known Descendants Who Have Scattered throughout the United States.* 1962. 426 leaves. NG gives underscored part of title. [NG33; X220-FW/NY].

CRAFT -- Collier, Joella Craft. *A Family Called Craft.* Pikeville, KY, Craft Family Reunion Association, Printing by George, 1985. ii, 204p. 1. Craft family. 2. North Carolina-Genealogy. [G163; C155].

CRAIG -- Craig, Eloise. *Descendants of John Craig, Esquire and John Robinson, Senior: Scotch-Irish Immigrants to Lancaster County, South Carolina.* [NGN18-1-92]

CRAIG -- Kirksey, Sadie. *Craig (Family).* Pickens, NC, 1970. 258p. [X221-FW].

CRANSHAW -- Craig, Edna Crenshaw. *Its Waters Returning. - 1st ed.* Danville, VA, URE Press, 1989. 251p. 1. Craig, Edna Crenshaw-Childhood and youth. 2. Craig, Edna Crenshaw-Family. 3. Cranshaw family. 4. Meherrin River Valley (Va. & N.C.)-Biography. 5.

Meherrin River Valley (Va. & N.C.)-Genealogy. [G164].

CRAVEN -- Purvis, Mary Craven. *Craven: Descendants of Peter Craven, Randolph County, North Carolina, USA.* Asheboro, NC, M.C. Purvis, 1985. xxxix, 546p., 1 leaf of plates. [G164].

CRAWFORD -- Anderson, Maude Crawford. *<u>Thomas Crawford</u>; His Ancestors and Descendants, with Sketches of Related Lines.* Spartanburg, SC, Anderson, 1949. 116p. D gives underscored part of title. [L4223; D3032].

CRAWFORD -- Crawford, Charles Travis. *The Crawford Family (North Carolina and Tennessee)... with Interesting Notes of the Origin and History of the "Crawford Clan".* Laurenceburg, TN, Priv. Print, Crawford, 44p. "The Leake Family Genealogy"; 6 p. at end. [L4215].

CREVELING -- Creveling, Louis G. *Creveling Family History and Genealogy.* Charlotte, NC, Herb Eaton Historical Publications, 1988. vi, 369p. 1. Creveling family. [G165].

CROCKETT -- French, Janie Preston Collup. *The Crockett Family and Connecting Lines.* Spartanburg, SC, 1974 (1928), 611p. Reprint of the ed. pub. by King Print Co., Bristol, TN. [S589].

CROOM -- Outlaw, Doris C. *The Crown Family.* Kinston, NC, Jarman's Mimeographing and Letter Service, 1957 (i.e. 1958). v, 332 leaves. [L4295].

CROOM -- Outlaw, Doris C. *The Crown Family. 2nd ed.* Kinston, NC, 1962. 343 leaves. [X228-NY].

CROOM -- Wood, Lillian F. *Daniel Croom of Virginia, His Descendants in North Carolina;*

Data Compiled for the North Carolina Society of the Descendants of the Palatines. New Bern, NC, 1943. 4p, 21 numb. leaves. [L4294; VV47].

CROSLAND -- Ricaud, Lulu Crosland. *The Family of Edward and Ann Snead Crosland, 1740-1957.* Spartanburg, SC, Reprint Co., 1988. xv, 546p., 52p. of plates. Reprint. Originally published in 1958. 1. Crosland family. 2. Crosland, Edward-Family. [G167].

CROWE -- DuPree, Garland Crowe. *People of Purpose: Dr. William Houston of County Antrim, Ireland, and Duplin County, North Carolina; Some of His Descendants, and Some Related Families, Including Crow - Crowe.* Fitzgerald, GA, Walker Printing Co.., <1990-> v. <2 >. 1. Houston family. 2. Crows family. 3. Houston, William, 1715-1795-Family. [G167; DC1864].

CROWE -- Johnson, Catherine Boyd. [G167]. See above: BOYD. [G79].

CURETON -- Cureton, Thomas K. *Lancaster County Curetons and Relatives in the Revolutionary War.* NP, 1956. 25 leaves. [D3165].

CURETON -- Cureton, Thomas Kirk, Jr. *The Curetons of Lancaster County, S. C.* Waxhaw, SC, Cureton, 1949. 67 leaves. [D3166].

CURTIS -- King, Mable LeVert. *Descendants of Michael Curtis, Elisha Felton, John Fennel, Richard King, Jr., Virginia and North Carolina to Lawrence County, Alabama.* Memphis, TN, 1982. pni. [VV49].

CUTHBERT -- Bulloch, J. G. B. *The Cuthberts, Barons of Castle Hill and Their Descendants in South Carolina and Georgia.* Washington, DC, Bulloch, 1906. 100p. L gives: corrections and additions to March,

1928: 6 Typewritten pages inserted at end. [L4434; D3201].

CUTHBERTSON -- Wise, Frank E. *A History of William Cuthbertson and Benjamin Wise, and Adjoining Families: Davis, Wilson, Lonon, Henson, Chandler, Thompson, Turner, and Others.* Nebo, NC, F.E. Wise, 1990. 60, 38p. 1. Cuthbertson family. 2. Wise family. 3. Cuthbertson, William, 1740-1838-Family. 4. Wise, Benjamin, d. 1855-Family. 5. Davis family. 6. Wilson family. 7. North Carolina-Genealogy. [G171].

CUTLER -- Davis, Genevieve L. *Our Cutler Line and Some Allied Families.* Charlotte, NC, Mrs. W.A. Davis. 1961. 20 l. [X235-FW/NY].

D

DAINGERFIELD -- MacRae, Lawrence. *Descendants of John Daingerfield and His Wife, New Kent County, Virginia, 1640, Including Descendants of Elizabeth Meriweather of Essex Co., Va., Apphia Fauntleroy of Richmond Co., Va., Elizabeth Parker of West Moreland Co., Va. and Their Husbands, Also Thomas Deaderick and His Wife of Frederick Co., Va., and Dora Virginia Deaderick and Her Husband, Robert Strange MacRae of Orange County, N. Carolina. Descendants of George Parker and His Wife, Accomac Co., Va., 1650.* Greensboro, NC, 1928. 1p. 15 numb. leaves. [L4465; VV50].

DALRYMPLE -- Russell, Marjorie Douglas. *The Douglas in His Hall.* Jacksonville, FL, M.D. Russell, 1983. vii, 368p. 1. Douglas family. 2. Alabama-Genealogy. 3. Scotland-Genealogy. 4. North Carolina-Genealogy. 5. Harrington family. 5. Dalrymple family. [G173].

DANDRIDGE -- Wolf, Elizabeth Dandridge. *The Bower Dandridge's Ancestors and*

Descendants. Hilton Head, SC, E.D. Wolf, 1988. 140p. 1. Dandridge family. 2. West Virginia-Genealogy. 3. Bowler(W.Va.) [G174].

DANFORTH -- Danforth, Edward Courtney Bullock. *Fifteen Generations of Danforths in England and America.* Columbia, SC, Danforth, 1970. v, 25 leaves. [D3245].

DANIEL -- Castleberry, Amelia S. *Some Daniel and Smith Records, South Carolina.* NP, 1948. 31p. [D3246].

DANIEL -- Gee, Christine South. *John Daniel, Sr., 1724-1819, of Essex County, Virginia and Laurense County, South Carolina.* Columbia, SC, Gee, 196_. iv, 227p. [D3247].

DANIEL -- Gee, Christine South. *John Daniel, Sr., 1724-1819, of Essex County, Virginia and Laurens County, South Carolina; His Virginia Ancestry and Some of His Descendants.* Columbia, SC, McDonald Letter Shop, 1970. iv, 227p. [L4512; VV51].

DANIELEY -- Danieley, Rena Maude Iseley. *An Outline of James Danieley of Alamance, and Boston Gerringer of Guilford and Their Kin.* Burlington, NC, M & W Office Supplies, 1983. 156, A-W, 103, A-Wp. [DC936].

DANTZLER -- Dantzler, D. D. *A Genealogical Record of the Dantzler Family, from 1739 to the Present Time.* Orangeburg, SC, R. Lewis Berry, Printer, 1899. 52p. [L4523; D3254].

DANTZLER -- Dantzler, David H. *The David and Elizabeth Shuler-Dantzler Family.* Orangeburg, SC, Quality Print Inc., 1970. 29p. [X24--FW/LA].

DARGAN -- Revill, Janie. *Timothy Dargan; A Few of His Descendants, Residents of South Carolina.* Sumter, SC, 1962. 26 l. Typed. [L4534].

DAVANT -- Courtenay, Carlile. *Genealogy of the Descendants of the Family of South Carolina.* Columbia, SC, 1p., 6 numb. l. Photostat of Typed Copy. [L4566].

DAVANT -- Hanahan, Hardin Davant. *A Place in History: The Davant Family.* Knoxville, TN, H.D. Hanahan 1972. 224p. 1. Davant family. 2. Georgia-Genealogy. 3. South Carolina-Genealogy. 4. Southern States-Genealogy. X gives author as Elizabeth H. D. Hanahan and publication as: "Columbia, SC, R.L. Bryan".
[G175; X242-FW/NY/PH].

DAVENPORT -- Davenport, Dr. John Scott, *The Davenports of Randolph County, North Carolina. An Interim Report.* Cincinnati, OH, 1971. 11 leaves. [X-GF].

DAVES -- Daves, Major Graham. *A Sketch of the Military Career of Captain John Daves of the North Carolina Continental Line of the Army of Revolution; Together with Some Facts of Local and Family History.* Baltimore, MD, Press of the Friedenwald Co., 1892. 16p. [L4573].,

DAVIDSON -- Davidson, Chalmers Gaston. *Major John Davidson of 'Rural Hill', Mecklenburg Count, N.C.* Charlotte, NC, Lassiter Press, 1943. x, 93p.
[L4584; D3297].

DAVIDSON -- Dixon, Elizabeth Williamson. *The Davidson and Allied Families Originating in North Carolina.* NP, 1956. 2 v. (495 leaves). Supplement: The Davidson Family of North Carolina and Tennessee, 1959 bound separately. Includes a copy of Alexander - Davidson reunion, Swannanoa, N.C., August 26, 1911: addresses by F. S. Sondley and Theo. F. Davidson. [D3298].

DAVIDSON -- Hand, Robert Stephens. *Those Members of the Davison / Davidson Family Who*

Descended from William and Elizabeth Davison of County Armagh, Ireland, and Settled in North Carolina and Tennessee, and Late in Mississippi, Texas, and Elsewhere. Chadds Ford, PA, R.S. Hand, 1990. iv, 206p. 1. Davison family. 2. Davidson family. 3. Davison, William, ca 1684-ca. 1723-Family. 4. Ireland-Genealogy. [G176].

DAVIDSON -- Sondley, F. A. *Samuel Davidson.* Asheville, NC, Theo F. Davidson, 1913, 22, 4p. [D3301].

DAVIS -- NAS. *Genealogical Chart of Susanne Davis.* Asheveille, NC, n.d. pni. [X246-NY].

DAVIS -- NAS. *Davis and Wakefield Families; Some Descendants of Travis Davis (1780) of North Carolina and Franklin Co., Ind.; and Some Descendants of Thomas Wakefield Who Came to Virginia in 1635.* Oakland, CA, 1952. 24p. [X244-FW/MH/NY/SL].

DAVIS -- Battey, George Magruder. *...Copy of a Letter to Mrs. Charles D. (Elizabeth Morgan) Davis...(which) Relates Chiefly to the Origin of Jefferson Davis, Head of the Confederacy, and That Branch of His Numerous Family, which Settled in Cave Spring, Floyd County, Georgia; Also to the Family of Captain William Wilkins and Wife, Ann Elizabeth Terrell of Spartanburg County, South Carolina, and Touches ... on... the Mayos, Shorters, Smiths, and Bankstones of Georgia and Elsewhere.* Washington, DC, 1941. 1p., 9 numb. leaves. [L4623].

DAVIS -- Bunn, Maude D. *Genealogy of the Marion - Davis Families.* Raleigh, NC, Edwards, 1973. 239p. [X245-FW].

DAVIS -- Bugg, William Emmanuel. [G177]. See above: BUGG. [G105].

DAVIS -- Cathey, Frederick A. *Isaac Newton Davis, Oliver Wiley Davis, and Their Descendants.* Gastonia, NC, Cathey & Cathey,

1950. 42p. Bound with: Isaac Newton Davis, Oliver Siley Davis and their descendants. Rev. ed. / by Janett Fayssoux Plank, 1961. [D3309].

DAVIS -- Davis, Carrie L. *Ancestors and Descendants and Allied Lines of Medora Virginia Ray: Union District, South Carolina.* Gaffney, SC, C.L. Davis, 1988. xvi, 313p. 1. Ray family. 2. Davis family. 3. Ray, Medora Virginia, 1839-1899-Family. 4. South Carolina-Genealogy. [G177].

DAVIS -- Davis, Charlie B. *The Ancestors and Descendants of Keziah Wheeler Davis and William Davis III.* High Point, NC, 40p. [DC957].

DAVIS -- Davis, Eleanor M. *Davis: A Quaker Family; Charles Davies, the Immigrant to Pennsylvania about 1725, from there to North Carolina, His Wife, Hannah Matson, and Their Descendants.* Baltimore, MD, Gateway Press, 1985. pni. [VP56].

DAVIS -- Davis, Thomas Frederick. *A Genealogical Record of the Davis, Swann, and Cabell Families of North Carolina and Virginia.* Jacksonville, FL, Davis, 1934. 40p. [D3332].

DAVIS -- Dickinson, Mrs. Ollie. *Notes on the Genealogy of the Davis, Mace-Richey Families of North Carolina, Kentucky and Iowa.* NP, n.d. 6 leaves. [X246-LA].

DAVIS -- Hyatt, Sybil. *Davis Bible Records - Lenoir County, N.C.... Copied from a Bible Belonging to Clifton Noble...* Kinston, NC, 1942. 2 leaves. Typed Carbon Copy. [L4625].

DAVIS -- Lambeth, Mary Weeks. [L4638]. See above: BAILEY: [L757].

DAVIS -- Mentzel, Lawra W. *Davis Families of the Savannah River Valley: Containing a*

Record of the Descendants of Van and Harmon Davis from 1725-1978, Covering the Counties of Newberry, Anderson, Pickens, Oconee Counties (sic) of South Carolina, Habersham, Franklin, Hart, Stephens, Polk, Paulding, Gwinett Counties of Georgia. Salt Lake City, UT, Hobby Press, 1978- . v. [C172].

DAVIS -- Robertson, Irma Matthews. [G178]. See above: ANGLE. [G15].

DAVIS -- Robertson, Minnie Hohn. [G178]. See above: COLTRANE. [G152].

DAVIS -- Sheriff, Pauline Callaway. *Davis Data: John and Mary (Mooney) Davis: Their Ancestors and Descendants as We Know Them, from North Carolina, South Carolina, Georgia, Alabama, Arkansas, Texas, Oklahoma, and Elsewhere.* Hollis, OK, Sheriff, 1988, 351p 1. Davis family. 2. Mooney family. 3. Davis, John, 1803-1871-Family. 4. Davis, Mary Mooney, 1810-1880-Family. 5. Southern States-Genealogy. [G178].

DAVIS -- Wise, Frank E. [G178]. See above: CUTHBERTSON. [G171].

DAVISON -- Hand, Robert Stephens. [G178]. See above: DAVIDSON. [G176].

DAWSON -- Dawson, Charles C. *A Collection of Family Records, with Biographical Sketches, Other Memoranda of Various Families and Individuals Bearing the Name Dawson, or Allied to Families of that Name.* Charleston, SC, Garnier & Co., 1969. viii, 572p. Library of Congress has 1874 edition. [X247-NY/SU].

DEAN -- Wood, Margarette Hall. *The History of John Huson: From North Carolina to Alabama, His Huson, Huston, Houston, Descendants and the Allied Pioneer Families of Clepper, Robinson, Denn, and Gilmore.* Baltimore, MD, Gateway Press, 1990. xxxiii, 335p. 1. Hewson family. 2. Huson, John, b. 1774-Family. 3.

Houston family. 4. Dean family. 5. Gilmore family. 6. Robinson family. 7. Southern States-Genealogy. [G182].

DeCAMP -- DeCamp, Harvey. *The Ancestors and Descendants of Harvey De Camp, 1807-1878.* Morehead, NC, 1968. 86, 67p. [X250-NY].

DEESE -- Starnes, Herman. *Deese Family.* Monroe, NC, Starnes, 1968. 33 l. [D3440].

DE GRAFFENRIED -- Graffenreid, Thomas Pritchett de. *Catalog of the Items in the De Graffenried Family Collection at New Bern, NC.* NP, 1958, 10 l. NG lists under GRAFFENREID. X lists under GRAFFENRIED. [NG47; X381-FW].

DeHART -- DeHart, A. J. *DeHart.* Bryson, NC, DeHart Association, 1935. 38p. [D3453].

DELLINGER -- Dellinger, Paul H. *Cemetary & Death Records.* Lincolnton, NC, Paul H. Dellinger, 1987. 163p. 1. Dellinger family. 2. North Carolina-Genealogy. [G184].

DELLINGER -- Dellinger, Paul H. *Dellinger Genealogy.* Lincolnton, NC, P. H. Dellinger, 1989. 120 leaves. 1. Dellinger family. 2. North Carolina-Genealogy. [G184].

DELLINGER -- Dellinger, Paul H. *John Phillip Dellinger.* Lincolnton, NC, P. H. Dellinger, 1989. 1 v. (various pagings). 1. Dellinger family. 2. Dellinger, John Phillip, ca. 1720 -ca. 1783-Family. 3. North Carolina-Genealogy. [G184].

DELOZIER -- Edwards, Richard Laurence. *Ancestors and Decendants of the Edwards - Mathias, Delozier, and Related Families that Pioneered through Virginia, Carolinas, Tennessee, Kentucky, Illinois, Missouri, Kansas, and Spread to Descendants in Thirty-Seven States and Two Provinces in Canada.* Coffeyville, KS, R.L. Edwards, 1985. xvi,

597p. 1. Edwards family. 2. Mathis family. 3. Delozier family. [G208; C205; VV60].

DENNY -- Denny, Zeb. *Bird Denny.* Roanoke Rapids, NC, Z. Denny, 1982. iii, viii, 141 leaves. 1. Denny family. 2. Denny, Carey Bird, 1846-1921-Family. 3. North Carolina-Genealogy. [G186].

DENNY -- Dixon, Margaret Collins Denny & Elizabeth Chapman Denny Vann. *Denny Genealogy.* New York, NY, Nat'l. Historical Society, 1944. V. 1-3. Partial contents - Book 1: Descendants of Frederick Denny. Walter Denny of Mississippi and his descendants. Dennings of Delaware. Book 2: The Descendants of William Denny of Chester County, Pennsylvania, and allied families of Culbertson, Gaston, McNair, Rodgers, Walker and many others, and the Descendants of George Denny of Lincoln County, North Carolina through his son Alexander. Book 3: The Descendants of David Denny, Sr., of Pennsylvania and the Shenandoah Valley of Virginia and allied families of Brunk, Campbell, Davis, Gaither, Guthrie, Hubbard, Lockhart, Lunsford, Stone, Washington, Weller, and many others. [L4828].

DENNY -- Rankin, S. M. *Denny Families of Buffalo Church, Rown and Guilford Counties, North Carolina.* NP, 1946. 77 l. [D3506].

DE ROSSET -- Meares, Kate De Rosset. *A Group of My Ancestral Dames of the Colonial Period.* Goldsboro, NC, Nash Bros., Book and Commercial Printers, 1901, 17p. "An historical paper read before the N.C. Society of Colonial Dames, by the author, president, March 14, 1901. [L4858; DC1020].

DE ROSSET -- Meares, Catherine De Rosset. *Annals of the De Rosset Family, Hugenot Immigrants to the Province of North Carolina in the Eighteenth Century.* Columbia, SC, R.L. Bryan Co., 1906. 91p. [L4859; S681].

DeROSSET -- Strong, Ludlow Potter. *List of Direct Descendants of the DeRossett Family with Introduction and Brief Notes to Supplement the Annals of the De Rossets.* Compiled 1947-1948. NP, 1949. 48p. (See above De Rossett [L4859; S681]). [L4860].

DERRICK -- Derrick, Charles Alan. *The Derrick Family.* Irmo, SC, C.A. Derrick, 1991. xi, 525p. 1. Derrick family. 2. South Carolina-Genealogy. [G187].

DE SAUSSURE -- Harper, the Hon. William. *Memoirs of the Life, Character, and Public Services of the Late Hon. Henry William De Saussure, Prepared and Readon the 15th February, 1841 at the Circular Church, Charleston, by appointment of the South Carolina Bar Assocation.* Charleston, SC, Printed by W. Riley, 1841. 38p. [L4862].

DEW -- Dew, Sarah Mae. *The Dew Line from England to Virginia and the Carolinas to Alabama, Mississippi, Arkansas, Texas, and Louisiana, with Some Records of Other States.* Magnolia, AK, S.M. Dew, 1988. 13, 514p. 1. Dew family. 2. Great Britain-Genealogy. 3. Southern States-Genealogy. [G188].

DEW -- White, Ernestine Dew. *Genealogy of Some of the Descendants of Thomas Dew, Colonial Virginia Pioneer Immigrant, together with Genealogical Records and biographical Sketches of Families in Virginia, Maryland, North Carolina, South Carolina, West Virginia and Tennessee...* Greenville, SC, White, 1937. 349p. D gives underscored title. [L4891; D3544; VV55].

DE WALT -- McCrary, Clara Johnstone. *The De Walt Family, Connections and Traditions.* Newberry, SC, 1921. 51 leaves. Typed. [L4892].

DEWESSE -- Carter, James M. *Rev. Edmund Alexander Deweese, Caroline Lovingood Deweese,* *and Descendants.* Port Richey, FL, J.M. Carter, 1988. 5 v. 1. Deweese family. 2. Deweese, Edmund Alexander, 1822-1910-Family. 3. Deweese, Caroline Lovingood, 1825-1895-Family. 4. North Carrolina-Genealogy. [G188].

DEWING -- Manly, Charles Gottschalk. *Some Antecedents of Miriam Dewing (1793-1857) Beloved Wife of Adin Manly (1793-1867) of Taunton and Athol, MA.* Charlotte, NC. 1981. pni. [NG37].

DICK -- Hoffman, Muriel M. *History of the Peter and Christina Shutt Dick Family, Frederick Co., Md., Wilkes Co., N.C., Muhlenberg Co., Simpson Co., Ky., Sangamon Co., Cass Co., Ill.* Anchor, Il, 1970. 81p. [X259-FW].

DICKERT -- Dickert, Yancey J. *A History and Genealogy of Peter Dickert of South Carolina.* [NGN16-3-90].

DICKINSON -- Outlaw, Lena Dickinson. *Dickinson Genealogy.* Winston-Salem, NC, Hunter, 1977. 336p. [DC1038].

DICKSON -- Henderson, Jackson G. *Genealogical Data Pertaining to the Descendants of Matthew Dickson.* Charlotte, NC, Henderson, 1954. 37 leaves. [D3591].

DICKSON -- Reynolds, Harriet Dickson. *David Dickson, 1750-1830 of South Carolina and Georgia and Some of His Descendants.* Houston, TX, Reynolds, 1977. iii, 135 leaves. [D3593].

DILLARD -- Dillard, Emmett Urcey. *David L. Dillard: "His Roots and Branches".* Raleigh, NC, U.E. Dillard, 198_. xi, 335 leaves. 1. Dillard family. Dillard, David L., 1815-1878-Family. [G191].

DILLINGHAM -- Haile, Margaret Wallis. *Dillinghams of Big Ivy, Buncombe County, N. C.*

and Related Families. Baltimore, MD, Gateway Press, 1979. xii, 862p. [D3616].

DIXON -- Dixon, Ben F. *The Old Stamping Ground, Some Notes on the quaker Dixons of Chatham County, N. C.* San Diego, CA, 1934. 9 leaves. [NG37].

DOAK -- French, Janie Preston Collup. *The Doak Family*. Spartanburg, SC, The Reprint Co., 1974 (1933). 98p. Reprint of the edition published by Lookout Pub. Co., Chatanooga, TN. [S700].

DOBBIN -- Barekman, June B. *Some Dobbins - Skiles Kin from Pennsylvania to North Carolina at an Early Date. Also with Additional Lines: Coker, Cowan, Dailey, Graham, Hess, Palmer, Barekman*. Chicago, IL, Barekman, 1966. 39 leaves. [L5017; D3650].

DOBBIN -- Barekman, June B. *Some Dobbin - Skiles Kin from Pennsylvania to North Carolina and Tennessee. Additional Lines: Coker, Cowan, Dailey, Graham, Hess, Palmer, Barekman. Ed. 2 Rev and enl.* Chicago, IL, 1968. 44p. X gives: "Library of Congress has 1966 ed." [X265-FW].

DOBSON -- McLean, Albert S. *The Dobson Family of North Carolina*. Asheville, NC, 19__, 4 leaves. [L5019].

DODD -- Henderson, Marion Elizabeth Freeman. *The Dodds I Know*. Charlotte, NC, M.E.F. Henderson, 1986. 4, 27 leaves, 5 leaves of plates. 1. Dodd family. 2. Southern States-Genealogy. [G193].

DODDS -- Colby, Lydia. *The Genealogy and History of the Families of Francis Dodds and Margaret Craig Dodds of Spartanburg, South Carolina*. Geneseo, IL, Colby, 1929. 177p. Bound with 6 leaves of corrections. [D3655].

DODSON -- Williams, Sherril (Mrs. Sherman). *The Dodson (Dotson) Family of North Farnham Parish, Richmond County, Virginia: A History and Genealogy of Their Descendants.* Easley, SC, Southern Historical Press, 1988-1989. 2 v.(xv, 1585, 190p, 145p. of plates). 1. Dodson family. 2. Virginia-Genealogy. DC gives underscored title.
[G194; D1063].

DOGGETT -- Doggett, Anna. *History of the Doggetts of Guilford County, North Carolina.* Greensboro, NC, Piedmont Press, 1969. 78p. [S704: D3672].

DONALDSON -- Edwards, Christine Williams. *The Donaldson Family of Caswell County, North Carolina and Wilson County, Tennessee.* Athens, AL, Mrs. Thomas E. Edwards, 1972. 62 leaves. [D3681].

DOUGHTON -- Doughten, Thomas Edson. *A Monographic Study of Joseph Doughton (...1771-...1832), the Progenitor of the N.C. Branch of the Family.* Toledo, OH, Bryan, OH, Century Pr., 1973. 30p. NG gives underscored title. [NG38; X269-FW].

DOUGLAS -- Russell, Marjorie Douglas. [G198]. See above: DALRYMPLE. [G173].

DOWLING -- NAS. *Biographical Sketches, Darlington, South Carolina Newspaper Material.* Darlington, SC, n.d. See also: BEASLEY Family. [L1281 above] in vertical file at Library of Congress. Ask Reference Librarian. [L5148].

DOWLING -- NAS. *"To the Dowlings Who Served in America's Wars". A Memorial Plaque presented by Maude Dowling Turner at the 1946 Dowling Family Reunion Meeting, Hampton, S.C.* San Antonio, TX, 1946. 20p. [X27-FW/NY].

DOWNS -- Ridings, Beulah Philbeck. *An Index to The Captain Benjamin Newton, Williams (sic)*

Downs, and Other Lineage History by Posey E. Downs. Shelby, NC, Broad River Genealogical Society, 1984. 61p. 1. Downs, Posey E. Captain Benjamin Newton, William Downs, and other lineage-Indexe. 2. Newton family-Indexes. 3. Downs family-Indexes. 4. Proctor family-Indexes. 5. Cleveland County (N.C.)-Genealogy-Indexes. [G199].

DRAKE -- Linn, Jo White. [G199]. See above: ARRINGTON. [G20; DC1093].

DRAKE -- Petitt, Mildred Talbert. *Ancestors and Descendants of James Drake of Devonshire, England and Nash County, North Carolina.* Jerseyville, IL, Petitt, 1963. 60 leaves. [D3749].

DRAKE -- Watson, John Drake. *Descendants of Zachariah Alford Drake Of Marlboro County, SC.* NP, 1981. 1 v. in various pagings. [DS196].

DRAUGHON -- Draugton, Wells Robert. *Descendants of James Draughon of Edgecombe County, North Carolina.* Durham, NC, Draughon, 1974. vi, 333p. [S726; D3757].

DRAYTON -- Taylor, Emily Heyward. *The Draytons of South Carolina and Philadelphia.* Lancaster, PA, Wickersham. 1921. pni. [VP61].

DREW -- Emison, James W. *Drew, Hart, Kerby, Dutton Families of Virginia, North and South Carolina, Georgia, Florida.* NP, 1969. 1 v. (Various foliations). DC gives underscored part of title. [D3761; DC1099; VV57].

DREYER -- Creech, Ruth Ann Matthis. *A New Land, A New Beginning: A History of the Mathis and Dryer Families.* Fayetteville, NC, R.A.M. Creech, 1989. 326p. 1. Mathias family. 2. Dreyer family. 3. Switzerland-Genealogy. 4. Pennsylvania-Gemealogy. [G200].

DRURY -- Kmiecik, Linda Lightholder. *The Early Drury Line of New England: Some Descendants to 1850 of Hugh Drury (c.1617-1689).* Spartanburg, SC, Reprint Co., 1990. 224p. 1. Drury family. 2. Drury, Hugh, ca.1617-1689-Family. DC gives underscored title and 223p. [G201; DC1109].

DUBOSE -- MacDowell, Dorothy Kelly. *Dubose Genealogy: Descendants of Isaac Dubose and Wife, Suzanne Couillandeau, French Hugenot Refugees, Who Settled on the Santee River in South Carolina About 1689.* Aiken, SC, 1972. xvi, 533p. S gives underscored title and publication as: . Columbia, SC, R.L. Bryan Co. [S729; NGS5].

DUCKETT -- King, Marjorie Johnson. *The Ducketts, from Maryland to Texas.* Cary, NC, M.J. King, 142p. 1. Duckett family. [G202].

DUKE -- NAS. *Notebook Concerning Revolutionary Pensioners and Relating Principally to the Duke Family of North Carolina and Virginia.* NP, n.d. 127p. [XA1070-WR; VV58].

DUKE -- Durden, Robert F. *The Dukes of Durham, 1865-1929.* Durham, NC, Duke University Press, 1975. xiv, 295p., 8 leaves of plates. [S736].

DULLES -- Stoney, Samuel Gaillard. *The Dulles Family in South Carolina; A Keepsake Published on th eOccasion of a Commencement Address by the Honorable John Foster Dulles, Secretary of State of the United States, at the University of South Carolina, Monday, the Sixth of June Nineteen Hundred and Fifty-Five.* Columbia, SC, University of South Carolina, 1955. 1955. 29p. D gives underscored part of title. [L5264; D3814].

DUNBAR -- De Huff, Elizabeth W. *Dunbar Family of Barnwell County, South Carolina.*

Rev. ed. Augusta, GA, 1970. 191p. [X278-FW].

DUNN -- Dunn, J. B. (Jewell Beatrice). *Genealogy of the Dunn and Reagan Families of South Carolina, Georgia, and Wisconsin.* Houston, TX, 1948. 4 leaves. [L5323].

DUPRE -- Langley, Emimae. *The Dupre Trail.* Greensboro, NC, Langley, 1965, 1966. 2 v. [D3859].

DUPUY -- Glenn, Willetta Callaway. *The Story of a Hugenot Sword, Being Incidents in the Life of Bartholomew Dupuy, An immigrant to Virginia from France.* Spartanburg, SC, 1926. pni. [NG38].

DUTARTRE -- Garden, Rev. Alexander Graham. *A Brief Account of the Deluded Descendants; Extracted from a Serom (!) Preached by the Author at Charleston, in South Carolina.* New Haven, CT, Printed and sold by James Parker and Company, at the Post Office, 1762. 8p. Library of Congress copy: p. 3-4 wanting. [L5361].

DYER -- Overlander, Rufus M. [G206]. See above: BLUNT. [G63].

E

EADDY -- Eaddy, Elain Y. *The Promised Land. The James Eaddy Family in South Carolina.* Hemingway, SC, Eaddy, 1976. vi, 359p. 8 leaves of plates. X289 lists under EDDY & omits "8 leaves of plates". [X285-NY; X289-FW].

EARLE -- Earle, Julius Richard. *Earle. Short Biographical Sketches and Family History.* Hollands, SC, 1899. 8p. Additions and corrections made in ms throughout the book. [L5400].

EASTER -- Easter, Louise E. *Descendants of Michael Easter of North Carolina.* Bladensbug, MD, Genealogical Recorders, 1961. vii, 179p. [NG39; D3921].

EATON -- Eaton, Hubert A. *The Genealogy of Thomas Spotswood Eaton and Ann (Annie) Burwell. - 1st ed.* Wilmington, NC, Bonapart Press, 1984. ii, 85p. 1. Eaton family. 2. Eaton, Thomas Spotswood, 1820-1900-Family. 3. Eaton, Annie Burwell, 1830-1891-Family. 4. Afro-American Genealogy. [G207].

EATON -- Owen, Thomas McAdory. *Colonel William Eaton, of Granville County, North Carolina.* Charlotte, NC, 1899. 14-190. Detached from Davidson college magazine, Oct. 1899. [L5432].

EBORN -- Cutting, Betty Hicks. *The Eborns of Matchapungo: Hyde and Beaufort Counties, North Carolina and Allied Families.* Greenville, SC, B.H. Cutting, 1987. 949, 56p. NG gives underscored title and 949p. 1. Eborn family. 2. Beaufort County(N.C.)-Genealogy. 3. Hyde County(N.C.)-Genealogy. 4. North Carolina-Genealogy. [G207; NGS5].

ECKEL -- Rubincam, Milton. *The Eckel Family of Maryland, Pennsylvania, Tennessee, North Carolina and Delaware.* Hyattsville, MD., Rubincam, 1955. 70 leaves. [L5499; NG39; D3951; VP65].

EDDENS -- Eddens, Frank Lee. *Geneology (sic) of the Eddens Family from John Elder (1762-1835) to James William Eddens (1821-1867) to 1984. Second edition.* Florence, SC, Eddens, 1984. 94 leaves. [DC1151].

EDMISTON -- Edmiston, Prentess P. *A Branch of the Edmiston Family Tree from Ireland to North Carolina to Pennsylvania to Virginia to Tennessee to Arkansas and to Texas, A. D. 1700-1964.* Harlingen, TX, 1964. 14 leaves. Carbon copy. [L5485; VV59].

EDWARDS -- Dixon, Elizabeth Williamson. *Col. Nathaniel Edwards Family of Brunswick Co., Va., Col. William Eaton Family of Granville, N. C.* NP, 1958. 120 leaves. [D3991; VV60].

EDWARDS -- Edwards, Richard Laurence. [G208]. See above: DE LOZIER. [G184; C205; VV60].

EDWARDS -- Reynolds, Harriet Dickson. *Thomas Edwards, 1785-1853 of North Carolina, Georgia and Alabama and Some of His Descendants ... Collins, Culpepper, Dickson, McCrary, Morris, Morriss ...* NP, 1967. 172 l. [D4007].

EFIRD -- Efird, Oscar Ogburn. *The History and Genealogy of the Efird Family.* Winston-Salem, NC, Efird, 1964, xxiii, 556p. [D4012].

ELAM -- Evans, Regnia E. *The Elam Family.* NP, Mary Adair Chapter, South Carolina DAR G.R.C. Report; Series 2, vol. 3. 1990. 342 leaves. [DC1162].

ELLIOTT -- Elliott, Robert Garrison. *A Tarheel Confederate and His Family. 1st ed.* Daytona Beach, FL, R.G.E. Publications, 1989. xiii, 130p. 1. Elliott family. 2. Elliott, William Harrison, 1841-1914-Family. 3. North Carolina-Genealogy. 4. United States-History-Civil War, 1861-1865-Biography. [G211; NGN16-4-90].

ELLIS -- Andrea, Leonardo. *Ellis Family of South Carolina* Columbia, SC, Andrea, 1949. 35 leaves. [D4062].

ELLIS -- Ellis, Frampton Erroll. *Some Historic Families of South Carolina.* Atlanta, GA, Ellis, 1962. 92 l. [L5618; D4067].

ELLIS -- Ellis, McClintock T. *Records of the Family of Joseph Ellis.* Due West, SC, A.R.P. CO., 1939. 23p. [X295-LA].

ELLIS -- Sheek, Ann Ellis. *History of Twelve Generations of the Ellis Family, 1636-1974.* Clemmons, NC, Sheek, 1974. vii, 193p. [S788].

ELLISON -- Erath, Clara Ellison. *Descendants of John and Robert Ellison of Fairfield County, South Carolina,* Houston, TX, 1972. 131p. [D4080].

ELLISON -- Johnson, Michael P. *Black Masters: A Free Family of Color in the Old South - 1st ed.* New York, NY, Norton, 1984. xvi, 422p. 1. Afro-Americans-South Carolina-Charleston-History-19th century. 2. Afro-Americans-South Carolina-Charleston-Biography. 3. Ellison, William, b. 1790. 4. Ellison family. 5. Charleston(S.C.)-Race relations. 6. Charleston(S.C.)-History-1775-1865. [G213].

ELLSWORTH -- Siebert, Harriett E. *Ellsworth Genealogy... of North Carolina and Virginia.* Alameda, CA, 1955. 105 numb. leaves. [X296-LA; VV61].

ELMORE -- Elmore William E. *"Elmore Papers": Concerning the Early Elmores in Virginia, North Carolina, with Some Information Regarding S. C. and Ky. Early Elmores.* Phoenix, AZ, 1983. 106 leaves. [C210; VV61].

EMMONS -- Corcoran, Edwin Emmons. [G214]. See above: CORCORAN. (Original & Addendum). [G158].

ENGLAND -- Lord, Darice Watson. *England and Allied Families of North Carolina and Georgia.* NP, 1956. 172 leaves. [D4129].

ENSMINGER -- NAS. *The Ensminger Family: Pennsylvania, Maryaland, Virginia (and) South Carolina. Rev.* Washington, PA, Rev. 1961. 1961. 27p. [L5693].

ENSMINGER -- NAS. *The Ensminger Family: Pennsylvania, Maryaland, Virginia (and) South*

Carolina. Rev. Washington, PA, 1965. 28 l. [L5694; VP68; VV61].

ERVIN -- Ervin, Sam J., Jr. *The Ervins of Williamsburg County, South Carolina.* NP, 1972, 1 v. (unpaged). [S805].

ERWIN -- Miller, Annie Elizabeth. *Carolina Pioneers and Their Descendants.* Macon, GA, J.W. Burke, Co., 1927. vii, 143p. [D4159].

ESTEP -- Burgess, Jane Farrell. *The Eastep/Eastep Genealogy. Estep / Eastep / Estepp / Esteb / Eastepp / Eastup.* Rockville, MD, J.F. Burgess, 1988. 105 leaves. 1. Eastep fanily. 2. Maryland-Genealogy. 2. Pennsylvania-Genealogy. 3. North Carolina-Genealogy. [G217].

ETCHISON -- Barekman, June B. *History of Edmund Etchison, Revolutionary Soldier of North Carolina, and His Descendants: Including Atchisons--Virginia, Maryland, Kentucky--and Records of...Kin Throughout America.* Chicago, IL, 1980. 264p. 3 pl. of 1. D gives underscored title. [C215; D4169; VV62].

ETHEREDGE -- Etheredge, Hamlin. *Our Etheredge Family Circles From 1753-1953.* Johnston, SC, 1953. 72p. [NG41].

EVANS -- Evans, Ellen Good. *Evans Family of Virginia and North Carolina, etc.* Joplin, MO, 1931. pni. [VV62].

EVANS -- Harbour, Lizora Powell. [G218]. See above: CHILTON. [G136].

EVERARD -- Haywood, Marshall De Lancey. *Sir Richared Everard, Baronet, Governor of the Colony of North Carolina, 1725-1731, and His Descendants in Virginia.* Washington, DC, 1897. 12p. L gives: "From publications of the Southern historical association". [L5778; VV62].

EVERETT -- Register, Alvaretta K. *Three John Everetts and Jehu Everett, North Carolina, Georgia.* Statesboro, GA, A. K. Register, 1982. 32 leaves. [C217; NG41].

F

FALES -- Fail, Welton Reed. *The Fail - Fales and Related Families: A Tribute to Our Patriot Ancestor, Dixon Fail.* Wolfe City, TX, Henington Pub. Co., Lancaster, TX, 1987. xii, 163p. 1. Fales family. 2. North Carolina-Genealogy. [G221].

FANNING -- Fanning, Lawrence R. *Fannin(g) Family and Their Kin.* Columbia, SC, 1971. 350p. [X310-FW].

FARLOW -- Farlow, Edgar E. *Brief History of the Farlow Family.* Greensboro, NC, 1963. 112p, 2 leaves. [X311-FW].

FARMER -- Bishop, Rachel Parsons Flynn. *Farmer and Field Families of Virginia.* Columbia, SC, 1983. pni. [VV64].

FARMER -- Farmer, Ellery. <u>Descendants of Thomas Farmer Who Came to Virginia in 1616</u>. *A Genealogy; with Sketches of Some of the Families Allied by Marriage to the Farmer Family.* Asheville, NC, 1956. 88p. D & VV give: Henderson, NC. NG, D and VV give underscored part of title. [L5875; NG41; D4255; VV64].

FARRINGTON -- Rochelle, Herschel B. *Farrington and Kirk Family; Ancestors and Descendants of Abraham Farrington (1765-1845) of New Jersey and Ohio and wife Deborah Kirk (1781-1829) of Chester Co., Pennsylvania.* Hillsborough, NC, 1983. 361p. [NG41; VP71].

FARRIOR -- Brown, Leslie H. *Genealogy of the Farrior Family.* Wilmington, NC, Brown, 1948. 345p. [D4278; DC1223].

FARROW -- Farrow, Audry Doris Goolsby. *A Genealogical History of the Farrow, Waters, and Related Families, with Personality Profiles and Brief Skteches of the Times and Experiences of Two Pioneer Virginia, South Carolina, and Mississippi Families.* Ripley, MS, 1973. 104p. DC gives underscored part of title and shows publication as: Fulton, [MS?], Itawamba County Times. [S834; NG41; DC1224; VV64].

FARROW -- Farrow, Mary Cloyd Howe. *A Genealogical History of the Farrow, Nelson and Related Families. With Personality Profiles and Brief Sketches of the Time and Experience of Two Pioneer South Carolina Families.* Greenville, SC, Poinsett Print. & Letter Shop, 1972. 88p. DC gives underscored title. [S833; DC1225].

FAVRE -- Carroll, Alma Yarborough. *Faver and Kindred, 1748-1890: From Virginia to South Carolina, Georgia (Wilkes, Troup, Heard Counties) - 1st ed.* - Roswell, GA, WH Wolfe Associates, 1990. xvi, 383p. 1. Favre family. 2. Southern States-Genealogy. [G224].

FELTON -- Felton, Augustus C. *The Felton Family of North Carolina and Georgia.* Macon, GA, Felton, 1954. 154, 25p. [D4324].

FENNER -- Barrett, Ruth Leslie. *The Fenner Forebears of Samuel Fenner Leslie, 1877-1969: Their Lives, Their Descendants, Their Kin in North Carolina, Virginia, Tennessee, Alabama, Missisisppi, Arkansas, and Texas.* Windom, TX, R.L. Barrett, 1987. 357p. 1. Fenner family. 2. Leslie, Samuel Fenner, 1877-1949. [G225].

FENWICK -- NAS. *The John's Island Stud (South Carolina) 1750-1788.* Richmond, VA, Old Doninion Press, 1931. pni. [VV64].

FERGUSON -- Abbot, Hortense E. *Descendants of the Ferguson Families, Wilkes County, North*

Carolina. Salt Lake Cuty, UT, Paragon Press, 1980. 329p. [DC1240].

FERGUSON -- Ferguson, William Otto. *We Fergusons and Related Families.* Monroe, LA, W. O. Ferguson, 1985. xxix, 418p. 1. Ferguson family. 2. Ferguson, Samuel Maley, b.1778-Family. 3. Southern States-Genealogy. Lineage beginning with Samuel Maley Ferguson, born in 1778 in South Carolina, later moving to Georgia and Mississippi and including descendants in forty other states. [G226; C225].

FESSLER -- Fessler, William T. *Fessler Ancestories: Foreign Origins and Family Summaries and Briefs in Pennsylvania: Also Briefs in California, Illinois, Indiana, Iowa, Kansas, Kentucky, North Carolina, Missouri, Ohio, Virginia: Plus Hundreds of Other Surnames.* Haddonfield, NJ, 1980. [VV65].

FINCHER -- Fincher, Evelyn Davis. *Finchers in the U.S.A., 1683-1900.* Greenville, SC, A Press, 1981. 626p. [DS235].

FINKLEA -- O'Doherty, Mary K. *Pioneers of the Great Pee Dee, Genealogical Notes on Finklea and Related Families: Cain, Coleman, Dewitt, Exum, Finklea, Gibbs, Hyman, Keefe, Kirton.* Myrtle Beach, SC, O'Doherty, 1974. 47p. [S855; D4390].

FINKLEA -- O'Doherty, Mary K. *Finklea, Exum, Purcell, Hyman: Their Roots and Branches.* Columbia, SC, 1984. 190p. [NG42].

FINNEY -- Buchanan, Jane Gray. *Thomas Thompson and Ann Finney of Colonial Pennsylvania and North Carolina: Lawrence, Closs, and John Thompson: Allied Lines of Finney, McAlister, Buchanan, and Hart.* Oak Ridge, TN, J.B. Buchanan, 1987. 402p. 1. Thompson family. 2. Thompson, Thomas, D. ca. 1795-Family. 3. Finney family. 4. McAlister family. DC lists as THOMPSON and gives underscored title. [G229; DC3630].

FISHBURNE -- Fishburne, Henry G. *The Fishburne Family of South Carolina.* St. Petersburg, FL, Genealogy Pub. Service, Sumter, SC, 1989. viii, 350p. 1. Fishburne family. 2. South Carolina-Genealogy. [G230].

FISHER -- Fisher, James L, Arthur W. and Hilbert A. *The Jacob Fisher Family, 1727-1958.* Charlotte, NC, Heritage Printers, 1959. xiv, 385p. [L6091; D4411].

FISHER -- Fisher, P. W. *One Dozen pre-Revolutionary War Families of Eastern North Carolina and Some of Their Descendants.* New Bern, NC, New Bern Historcal Society Foundation, Inc., 1958. 629p. X omits place of publication & pagination. [D4415; X332-SL].

FISHER -- Tate, V. Robins. *Joseph Fisher, 1695-1784 Descendants: Penn., N.C., Ga.* Milwaukee, WI, V.R. Tate, 1987. 149. 1. Fisher family. 2. Fisher, Joseph, 1695-1784-Family. 3. Pennsylvania-Genealogy. 4. North Carolina-Genealogy. 5. Georgia-Genealogy. [G230].

FITCH -- Lewis, Ailene Fitch. *Fitch, Crawford, Davis, McFarland Francis, Holderman and Allied Lines from Pennsylvania, Tennessee, Kentucky, North Carolina, Illinois to Johnson County, Missouri; 1722-1971.* Holden, MO, Lewis, 1971. 42 leaves. [X-NY].

FITCH -- Lewis, Ailene Fitch. *Fitch, Crawford, Davis, Holderman, Francis, McFarland and Allied Lines from Pennsylvania, Tennessee, Kentucky, North Carolina, Illinois to Johnson County, Missouri; 1722-1976.* Holden, MO, Lewis, 1976. 130p. [D4438; VP73].

FLEMING -- Reese, Lee Fleming. *John Fleming: Carolina to California, Some*

Descendants and In-Laws, 1734-1972. San Diego, CA, Printed by Goodway Copy Center, 1972. 1 v. (various pagings). S gives: Contents: Flemings Paternal Descendants and In-Laws. Callarmans: Maternal Descendants and In-Laws. Reese - Taylor Descendants and In-Laws. [S872; D4476].

FLEURY -- Newton, Leroy L. *Genealogical Report, Newton and Flury and Allied Families from Maryland, Virginia, Alabama, South Carolina, Georgia, Southern Arkansas, Red Lands in Indian Territory, Oklahoma, and Other Places.* Altus, OK, L.L. Newton, 1987. 134, a-j pages, 3 leaves of plates. 1. Newton family. 2. Fleury family. 3. Oklahoma-Genealogy. 4. Afro-American-Genealogy. [G233].

FLOWERS -- Johnson, William E. *The Flowers Family of North Carolina.* Winter Park, FL, Johnson, 1964. 77 leaves. [D4509].

FLOYD -- Floyd, Marjorie Dodd. *Descendants of Col. Mathew Floyd, Loyalist of South Carolina and His Son, Abraham Floyd.* Dayton, OH?, M.D. Floyd, 1980. 1 v. (various foliations). [DC1278].

FLOYD -- Floyd, Mildred. *The Floyd Family: Wales to Va., N.C., (S.C.?), Ga., Ala., Miss., & Texas: Evidences of all Families Involved, Threads of Ancestors, Allied Families.* Dallas, TX, Floyd, 1978. iv, 60 l. [C233].

FLOYD -- Floyd, Viola Caston. *Floyd - Ervin Family on Lancaster County, South Carolina.* Summerville, SC, H.J. Floyd, 1963. 127p. X gives 126p. [D4515: X327-FW].

FLOYD -- Ivey, Robert A. *Floyd, Thomas and Allied Families.* Spartanburg, SC,.1972. 94 leaves. [X327-LA].

FOREMAN -- Gage, Mildred Foreman. *Foreman Family Lineage.* Asheville, NC, M.F. Gage, 1986. 107p. 1. Foreman family. [G235].

FORGY -- Wallace, L. F. *Genealogical History of the Forgy, Forgey, and Forgie Families in America*. Greenville, SC, 1957. 330p. [X331-FW].

FORMAN -- Foreman, James A. *Foreman Genealogy*. Jackson, SC, 1958. 45 l. [X331-FW].

FORTENBERRY -- Criminger, Adrianne Fortenberry. *The Fortenberry Family of Southern Mississippi: with Early Records Concerning the Faulkenberry / Fortenberry Families in the South*. Easley, SC, Southern Historical Press, Clarkston, GA, 1984. ix, 456p. 80 pages of plates. [C236].

FOSTER -- Boyd, Margie Milner. *Rigsby Relatives and Related Families: Shephard, Foster, Lawson: Virginia, North Carolina, Georgia, Texas, 1693-1900s: Also Barclay, Bean, Burke...* Port Arthur, TX, M.M. Boyd, 1986. vi, 602p. 1. Rigsby family. 2. Shepard family. 3. Foster family. 4. Southern States-Genealogy. [G236].

FOWLER -- Arthur, Glenn Dora Fowler (Mrs. James Joyce Arthur). *Annals of the Fowler Family with Branches in Virginia, North Carolina, South Carolina, Tennessee, Kentucky, Alabama, Mississippi, California and Texas*. Austin, TX, Arthur, Ben C. Jones & Co., 1901. xvi, 327p. [L6339; D4611; VV69].

FOWLER -- Fowler, Grover Parsons. *The House of Fowler; A History of the Fowler Families of the South, Embracing Descendants of John Fowler of Virginia and Branches in North Carolina, Georgia, Tennessee, Kentucky, Alabama, Texas; Also Records of Allied Families*. Hickory, NC, 1940. 754, 2p. D gives underscored title and note: "Index by Mrs. Frank Cline bound separately." [L6343; D4615; VV69].

FOWLER -- Fowler, Richard Gildart. *A History of the Fowler Family of Southeastern*

North Carolina. Norman, OK, R.G. Fowler, 1985. viii, 109, 136p. Rev. ed. of: History of the Fowlers of Southeastern North Carolina, 1984. 1. Fowler family. 2. North Carolina-Genealogy. [G237].

FOWLER -- Jackson, Miss M. C. Bagley. *A Family Tree of Daniel Fowler, A Colonial Settler in South Carolina.* NP. 18__. Geneal. Table. [L6334].

FOWLER -- Nash, Sara M. *Ancestors and Descendants: Edward and Lucinda (Bell) Nash, John and Ailsey Gray, John and Mary Fowler, George W. and Nancy King, Hugh and Elizabeth (Bridges) Bailey, the Mahaffeys, Solomon and Margaret Hopkins, the Curetons, and Many Others.* Fountain Inn, SC,, 1972. vi, 197p. G gives: "Errata leaf inserted." 1. Nash family. 2. Fowler family. 3. Gray family. S & D list as NASH. S omits author. [S1802a; G237; D9163].

FOWLER -- Stickney, Matthew A. *The Fowler Family, a Genealogical Memoir, Ten Generations, 1590-1882.* Charleston, SC, Garinier & Co., 1883. Reprinted 1969. pni. [X334-NJ/SP].

FOWLER -- Traver, Jerome D. *Fowler Family Facts: Virginia, North Carolina, Tennessee, Illinois, Iowa and Wisconsin.* [NGN18-3-92].

FOX -- Faucette, Shirley. *An Outline of Four Generations of the Family of Henry Fox (1768-1852) and His Wife, Sarah Harrell Fox (1772-1848), of South Carolina and Mississippi.* Hattiesburg, MS, Faucette and McCain. 1971. iv, 267 leaves. [S901; D4629].

FOX -- Fox, Jared Copeland. *The Family History of Virginia Tortat Fox.* Greensboro, NC, Fox. 1968. 26, xviii p. [D4631].

FOX -- McCain, William D. *Eight Generations of the Family of Henry Fox (1768-1852) and His*

Wife Sarah Harrell Fox (1772-1848), of South Carolina, Tennessee, Alabama, and Mississippi. Hattiesburg, MS, McCain, 1975. 4 v. X gives 2 v. [D4637; X4637].

FOX -- Steadman, Joseph E. *Ancestry of the Fox Family of Richard and Lexington Counties, S. C.* NP, n.d. 81, 166p. [X335-FW].

FRANCISCO -- Moon, William Arthur. *Peter Francisco.* Pfafftown, NC, Colonial Publ., 1980. vii, 106p. [DS247].

FRANCK -- Hyatt, Sybil. *Franck, Jones County, North Carolina.* Kinston, NC, 1948. 10 leaves. Typed. [L6391].

FRANKLIN -- Robinson, Elisabeth P. *The Descendants of Johathan Franklin of Burke County, N.C. and Owen County, Ind.* NP, 1977, 112 leaves. [DC1324].

FRASER -- Fraser, Thomas L. *Back When: A Biography of Josceph Bacon Fox and Mary Boulineau Fox of Hinesville, Ga., and Their Children.* Clinton, SC, 1976. v, 179p. [X338-FW].

FREEMAN -- Freeman-Ellis, Mary. *The Way It Was.* Wilson, NC, M. Freeman Ellis, 1986. 76p., 18p. of plates. 1. Freeman family. 2. Afro-America-Genealogy. 3. North Carolina-Genealogy. [G241].

FREEMAN -- Honeycutt, Frances F. *The Ones Who Came Before: A Family History and Memoirs.* Baltimore, MD, Gateway Press, Hendersonville, NC, F.F. Honeycutt, 1986-1989. 2 v, 1. Lyda family. 2. Freeman family. 3. Whitaker family. [G241].

FREEMAN -- Miller, Marianne Freeman. *The Freemans of Surry County, Virginia and Franklin County, North Carolina...* Talladega, FL, Miller, 1988. 154p. [DC1334].

FRIERSON -- Frierson, Lorraine Screven. *Frierson and Allied Families of South Carolina.* Kyle, [SC?], C.H. Young, 1980. 56 leaves. Originally published: 1936. [DC1346].

FRY -- Yoder, G. M. *Fry Family of North Carolina.* Centreville, MD, S.T. Wright, 1970. 4 leaves. [A241].

FULENWIDER -- Bell, Raymond Martin. *The Vollenweider Family in America: Henry Fullenwider--Kentucky, Jacob Fullewider (Fullenwider)--Maryland, Jacob Ful(l)enwider--North Carolina, Ulrich Ful(len)wider--Virginia.* Washington, PA, 1983. pni. [VV71].

FULLER -- Fuller, Theodore A. *Ancestry of Kay and Lynn.* Sylva, NC, Fuller, Fuller, 1978. 1000-9921p. sic. [D4745].

FULLER -- Fuller, Theodore Albert. *Early Southern Fullers.* Sylva, NC, Fuller, 1967. 207p. [D4746].

FULMER -- Folmar, L. W. *Colonial Ancestors of the Fulmers of South Carolina and the Folmars of Alabama.* Pelham, NY, 1972. 94p. Addendum, 1973. 8p. [X345-FW/NY].

FULTON -- Fulton, William Lawrence. *David Fulton of Colonial South Carolina and Some of His Descendants.* Amundsen Pub. Co., 1988. xi, 111p. 1. Fulton family. 2. Fulton, David, d. 1745-Family. 3. Southern States-Genealogy. [G246].

FUNDY -- Irving, Wm. H. *Fundy Family.* Durham, NC, Seaman Print. 1972. 180p. [X489-FW].

FUNCHES -- Kennedy, John T. *The Funchess Family.* Columbia, SC, Kennedy, 1962. 48p. [D4760; X345-NY/SL].

FUNDERBURK -- Funderburk, Guy Bernard. *Funderburk Castles and Conquests.* Pageland,

SC, Funderburk, 1975. iv, 453, 11p. S gives also: 4 leaves of plates. [S940; D4761].

FUNDERBURK -- Funderburk, Guy Bernard. *Funderburk History and Heritage.* Salem College, Salem, WV, Funderburk, 1967. xi, 544p. See just above: Funderburk castles and conquests. [D4762].

FURCHES -- Furches, John Frank. *The Furches Folks.* Clemmons, NC, 1971. 216p. [S943: NG44; X346-FW].

FURCHES -- Furches, John Frank. *A Genealogical Resume of The Furches Folks.* Clemmons, NC, 1974. 23p. 1. Furches family-Addresses, essays, lectures. 2. Furches, John Frank, 1904- Furches folks-Addresses, essays, lectures. [G246].

FURMAN -- Furman, James D. *The Furman Legend.* Greenville, SC, Keys Print. Co., 1978. 85p. [D4770].

FURMAN -- Furman, McDonald. *The South Carolina Furmans as Educators.* Boston, MA, 1897. 2 leaves. [X346-NY].

FURMAN -- Furman, Thomas deS. *The Ancestry of Thomas deSaussure Furman and Harriett Adams Mims.* Edgefield, SC, n.d. Chart. [X347-NY].

FUTCH -- Smith, Evelyn Futch. *North Carolina Palatine - Germans (Futch Family).* Jacksonville, FL, Smith, 1970. 115p. [D4774].

G

GABLE -- Gibson, George. *Ancestry of the Goble Family: From Gabels in Pennsylvania through Maryland to Gobbels in North Carolina.* Columbia, MO, G. and B. Gibson, 1987. 66p. 1. Göbel family. 2. Gable family. [G247].

GAFFNEY -- Gaffney, Michael. *The Journal of Michael Gaffney with an Historical Introduction and Notes by Ronald G. Killion, Bobby G. Moss. 2nd ed., rev. genealogy.* Greenville, SC, A Pres, 1981, 1971. iv, 102p. 1. Gaffney family. 2. Gaffney, Michael, 1775-1854. [G247].

GAGE -- Gage, Clyde Van Tassel. *Gage Family of the South. Existing Genealogical Records Brought Up To Date, Including Many Records of Families Allied by Marriage; Also Includes Historical and Biographical Records of Great Interest.* Worcester, NY, 1962 or 3. 45 l. [L6565].

GAGE -- Gage, Clyde Van Tassel. *The North Carolina Gage Family; A Genealogical, Historical and Bibliographical Record as Developed from Sources Explained Herein.* Worcester, NY, 1963. 111 leaves. D gives underscored part of title. [L6566; D4786].

GAGE -- Gage, Clyde Van Tassel. *The North Carolina Gage Family; A Genealogical, Historical and Biographical Record, with a Comprehensive Study of Members of the North Carolina Group and Other Matters Gage. 2d ed.* Worcester, NY, 1966. 192, 19 leaves. [L6571; A249].

-- *Supplement No. 1 - A Supplementary Record of Changes and Additions to the Text....* Worcester, NY, 1967. [A250].

GAILLARD -- MacDonald, Dorothy K. *Gaillard Genealogy; Descendants of Joachim Gaillard & Esther Paparel.* Columbia, SC, R.L. Bryan, 1974. xxx, 373p. [X350-FW].

GAINES -- Gaines, Thomas R. *Francis Gaines of Albermarle County, Va. and Elbert County, Georgia.* Anderson, SC, Thomas R. Gaines, NP, 1967. viii, 104p. D gives date as 1966. [D4794; X350-NY/SU; VV].

GAITHER -- Dunn, Evelyn W. *A Genealogical and Biographical Review from Wills, Deeds and Bible of the Families of Gaither in Maryland and North Carolina.* NP, 1956. 28p. [D4796].

GAMBLE -- Buck, Robert J. *Trail Blazers of the Thomas Gamble Family...* Asheville, NC, Priv. Print. 1948. [X352-CH].

GAMMON -- Gammon, William J. *Old Gammon Families and Their Descendants.* Montreat, NC, 1965. vii, 176p. [NG45; X352-FW/MH/NY].

GARDNER -- Gardner, Benjamin Hard. *Genealogy of the Gardner Family.* Aiken, SC, 1953. 25 leaves. [L6649].

GARLICK -- Garlick, Norman L. *Garlick Family History and a Journal of a Trip to the Goldfields of California in 1850.* Charleston, SC, N.L. Garlick, n.d. Various pagings. [X354-CH].

GARRETT -- Fisher, Sunie Garrett Talbert Elliott. [G251]. See above: CATLETT. [G128].

GARRISON -- Husband, Cornelia Garrison. *A History of the Descendants of David Garrison, Sr. of Mecklenburg County, N.C.* Charlotte, NC, C.G. Husband, 1973. iv leaves, 140p. 1. Garrison family. 2. Mecklenburg County(N.C.)-Genealogy. [G251; D4877].

GARROU -- Garrou, Hilda Whitener. *Garrou Family of Valdese, N.C.* NP, Garrou, 1967. 61p. [D4880].

GARY -- Updike, Ethel Speer. *Gary Family of England to Virginia to South Carolina.* Phoenix AZ, Updike, 1976. 248p. [D4886; VV73].

GASTON -- Davidson, Chalmers Gaston. *Gaston of Chester. Based Chiefly on the Notes and Records Preserved by Judge Arthur Lee Gaston.*

Davidson, NC, Davidson, 1956. xiii, 146p. D gives underscored title. [L6690; D4890].

GASTON -- Gee, Mary Gaston. *The Ancestry and Descendants of Amzi Williford Gaston II (1841-1911) of Spartanburg County, South Carolina.* Charlottsville, VA, Mrs. Wilson Gee, 1944. x, 48p. D lists under GATSON[?]. [A896; D4903; VV73].

GASTON -- Gee, Mary Gaston. *The Ancestry and Descendants of Amzi Williford Gaston II (1841-1911) of Spartanburg County...* Charlottsville, VA, Gee, 1944, 1974. 2 v. Supplement No. 1, 1944-1974 published by The Amzi Willford Gaston II Family Reunion. [DC1394].

GASTON -- McSweeney, E. F. *Gastons.* Boston, MA, Wright, 1926. 325p. Contents: Judge William Gaston of North Carolina; Governor William Gaston of Mass., Colonel William A. Gaston of Mass. [X356-FW].

GATCH -- Gatch, Frances Anne Amason. *South Carolina Gatches and Their Descendants.* United States, F.A.A. Gatch, 1989, (Columbia, SC, American Print Co.) iv, 341p. [G252]. 1. Gatch family. 2. South Carolina-Genealogy. [G252].

GATES -- Leonard, Carol J. *The Gates Family of Patrick County, VA.* Toast, NC, C.J. Leonard, 1984. i, 208p. [DC1396].

GEDDINGS -- Walker, Lucile Geddings. *The Friendly Swepson Geddings Family of Paxville, South Carolina.* Macon, GA, Walker, 1975. 142p. [D4915].

GEE -- Gee, Maude. *Ancestry and Descendants of Wilson Parham Gee of Lunenberg County, Va., and Union County, South Carolina and His Wife, Drucilla Elizabeth Gilliam Gee, of Union County, South Carolina.* University, VA, 1935. Chart. Geneal. Table. [L6717].

GEE -- Gee, Wilson. *The Gee Family of Union County, South Carolina.* Charlottesville, VA, Privately printed for the Author by Jarman's Incorporated (D gives: Gee), 1935. 29p. [L6714; D4918; VV74].

GEIGER -- Geiger, Percy L. *The Geigers of South Carolina.* NP, L.G. Geiger, 195_. D gives 1945. 191p. [L6724; D4924].

GETTY -- Gettys, Joseph M., Ed. *An American Family Centering in the William Ebenezer and Alice Rosina Gettys Family of York County, South Carolina.* Clinton, SC, J.M. Gettys, 1989. 136p. 1. Getty family. 2. Gettys, William Ebenezer, 1862-1937-Family. 3. Gettys, Alice Rosina, 1876-1957-Family. 4. York County(S.C.)-Biography. 5. York County(S.C.)-Genealogy. [G255].

GIBBES -- Wilson, Robert. *Genealogy of the Gibbes Family of South Carolina.* Charleston, SC, 1899. 1 Genealogical Chart. [X362-FW].

GIBBONS -- Hersperger, Laura Vivian Gibbons. *Memorial to Those Who Lie Buried in Gibbons Cemetary.* NP, Priv. published by L.V.G. Hersperger, 1985. 49p. Clarendon County(S.C.)-Genealogy. 2. Registers of births, etc-South Carolina-Clarendon County. 3. Gibbons famils. 4. Gibbons Family Cemetary (S.C.). 5. Inscriptions-South Carolina-Clarendon County. [G256].

GIBBONS -- Hersperger, Laura Vivian Gibbons. *Michael Gibbons of South Carolina and His Descendants: History and Genealogy of the Gibbons Family and Related Families.* Rockville, MD. H.G. Hersperger, 1988. xviii, 816p. 1. Gibbons family. 2. Gibbons, Michael, d. 1753-Family. 3. South Carolina-Genealogy. DC gives underscored title and Ann Arbor, MI, McNaughton-Gunn. [G256; DC1408].

GIBBS -- Harbour, Lizora Powell. [G257]. See above: CHILTON. [G136].

GIGNILLIAT -- Kenan, Robert Gignilliat. *History of the Gignilliat Family of Switzerland and South Carolina.* Easley, SC, 1977. 286p. [NG46].

GILBERT -- Guffin, R. L. *Gilbert Pioneers and Their Descendants in North Carolina and Georgia.* Tuscaloosa, AL, Guffin, 1974. vi, 168p. [S987].

GILBERT -- Schwartze, Annie James (Andrews). *Gilbert Genealogy, Starting with Abram Gilbert and Elizabeth West Gilbert in Newberry, South Carolina, Following Their Descendants through Georgia, Alabama, and Texas.* NP, 194_. 19p. [L6806].

GILL -- Rowland, Joseph S. *Peter and Robert Gill: Their Ancestors and Descendants.* Tuscaloosa, AL, J.S. Rowland, 1986. iii, 149p. 1. Gill family. 2. Gill, Peter, 1797-1862-Family. 3. Gill, Robert, 1799-1872-Family. 4. North Carolina-Genealogy. [G259].

GILL -- Winn, Mildred Louise. *The Family of Robert Alexander Gill and Jeanette Viola (Prescott) Gill.* Greenville, NC, A.T. Prescott, 1986. iv, 90 leaves, 1 leaf of plates. 1. Gill family. 2. Gill, Robert Alexander, 1859-1931-Family. 3. Florida-Genealogy. [G259].

GILLILAND -- Gilliland, Lyle Willis. *Willis and Gilliland Families of Hanover County, Virginia, Rutherford County, North Carolina, Pendleton County, South Carolina, Brown County, Ohio, Putnam County, Illinois, Douglas County, Oregon.* Eugene OR, Paul A. Grant, 1979. 16 l, 2 leaves. of plates. [C259; VV75].

GILMORE -- Wood, Margarette Hall. [G260]. See above: DEAN. [G182].

GIST -- Gee, Wilson. *The Gist Family of South Carolina and Its Maryland Antecedents.*

Charlottesville, VA, Jarman's Inc. (D gives Gee). 1934. x, 101p. [L6885; D5034; VV75].

GITHENS -- Githens, Sherwood. *The Githens Family in America, 1741-1977.* Based upon earlier work by George Burling Bithens, Durham, NC, Moore Publishing Company, 1978. x, 220 (i.e. 315p.). [D5035].

GLEATON -- Gleaton, Grace N. *Genealogical Record of Joe (Isaac) Gleaton, Our Immigrant Ancestor of London, Eng., and Orangeburg, S.C. with Allied Families.* NP, 1941. Various pagings. [X370-FW].

GLEN -- NAS. *Glenn Family.* North Carolina DAR, G.R.C. ___, NC? 1951. 141 leaves. [DS272].

GLEN -- Bulloch, Joseph Gaston Baillie. *A History of the Glen Family of South Carolina and Georgia.* Washington, DC, 1923. 134p. [NG46].

GLEN -- Bulloch, Joseph Gaston Baillie. *A History of the Glen Family of South Carolina and Georgia. <u>Also, Bayard, Potter Families.</u>* NP, Bulloch, 1923. NG adds underscored part of title and gives: Washington, DC, and 134p. 2, 132, 2p. [L6909; NG46; D5063].

GLENN -- Glenn, Leonidas C. *Genealogies of the John Glenn, John Wilson, Hugh Torrence and Allied Families of Gaston County, North Carolina.* NP, 1953. 201 leaves. [D5065]

GLENN. -- Glenn, Wayne. *The Glenn Family of Lancaster County, Pa. Lincoln County, N.C. White County, TN, Marshall County, TN and Christian County, Mo...* Nixa, MO, W. Glrnn 1985. 13 leaves. [DC1436].

GLENDENING -- Enquist, Anita C. Clendinen. *Thomas Clendinen of Cecil County, Maryland and York County, South Carolina: A Genalogical Record of His Family and Descendants in the*

South, 1774-1985. Columbus, GA, Quill Publications, 1986. vi, 182p. 1. Glendening family. 2. Clendinen, Thomas, 1744-1817-Family. 3. Southern States-Genealogy. [G262].

GLENN -- NAS. *Glenn Family.* NP, North Carolina DAR, G.R.C., 1951. 141 leaves. [DS272].

GLICK -- Glick, Joseph M. Family Historical Committee. *Across the Years; A Story of and a Stream Through the Glick Family in the Shenandoah Vellye (sic) of Virginia.* Charlotte, NC, Delmar Print Co., 1959. 221p. [L6934; VV76].

GOBBEL -- Gobbel, Luther L. *The Genealogical Family of Rowan.* Durham, NC, Gobbel, 1976. xv, 171p., 4 leaves of plates. [X371-FW/LA/NY/PH].

GÖBEL -- Gibson, George. [G262]. See above: GABLE. [G247].

GÖBEL -- Gobbel, Luther L. *The Gobbel Family of Rowan.* Durham, NC, Gobbel, c1976-1985. 2 v. Vol. 2. "An extensive supplement to "The Gobel family of Rowan, written in 1974 and published in 1976, with a combined index to the first book and volume II." 1. Göbel family. 2. United States-Genealogy. [G262].

GOFF -- Bundy, V. Mayo. *Remembering Our Goff - Hodges and Their Kin.* Charlotte, NC, H. Eaton Historical Publications, 1988. xiv, 490p. 1. Goff family. 2. Hodges family. 3. North Carolina-Genealogy. [G263].

GOGGANS -- Eve, Maron Summer. *Our Folks.* Columbia, SC, M.S. Eve, 1987. xxxv, 597p. [DC1444].

GOGGIN -- Eve, Maron Summer. *Our Folks.* Columbia, SC, M.S. Eve, 1987. xxxv, 597p. 1.

Goggin family. 2. Southern States-Genealogy. [G263].

GOODLETT -- Goodlett, Mildred W. *Links in the Genealogical Chain.* Travelers Rest, SC, 1965. 373p. [L6971].

GOODMAN -- McHugh, Matthew Lew. *Some Goodmans and McHughs.* Columbia, SC, Printed by Kohn Print. Co. 1968. 240p. [L6977].

GOODNIGHT -- Berry, Eunice G. *So Proudly They Served. Supplement to Hans Michael Goodnight Clan, 1708-1976.* Drexel, NC, Berry, 1976. 56 leaves. [X375-DP].

GOODNIGHT -- Winecoff, Edgar M. *Descendants of Caleb M. B. Goodnight and the Goodnight (Gutknecht) Allied Families of America: The Goodnight Genealogy.* Winston-Salem, NC, E.M. Winecoff and E.F. Basinger, 1990. 85p. 1. Goodnight family. 2. Goodnight, Caleb Mathias Barnhart, 1837-1916-Family. 3. Gutknecht Family. [G266].

GORDON -- NAS. *Gordon Genealogy. The Great Scottish Historical House. The Descendants of Sir Adam de Gordon and Allied Families of Scotland, England, United States of America, South Carolina, Vermont (and) New York States... 1305-1906.* NP, 1906. 64 leaves. [X376-NY].

GORE -- Prince, B. Otis. *Let's Meet the Gores.* Columbia, SC, B.O. Prince, 1962. 140 leaves. 1. Gore family. [G267].

GORHAM -- Webb, Mrs. Sarah Gorham. *The Gorhams of North Carolina.* Boston, MA, Wright & Potter Printing Co., 1928. 18p. "Reprinted from the New England historical and genealogical register of October, 1928. [L7072].

GOSS -- Heuss, Lois Ione Hotchkiss. *Frederick Goss of Rowan County, North*

Carolina, and His Descendants. Akron, OH, 1968. xii, 616p. NG gives 617p. [L7083; NG47].

GOSSETT -- Jerkins, Grace M. *Chronicles of the Gossett Family.* Gary, IN, G.M. Jerkins, 1985. viii, 263p. "An account of the family, originating in Frances, some of their descendants in the United States, their trek westward from Pennsylvania, Virginia, and North Carolina, several related Gossett families, some other allied families." 1. Gossett family. [G268].

GOTT -- Cook, Rohease Brown. *A Record of the Descendants of John Gott of Maryland, Logan Co., Ky., & White Co., Ill. and of His Son-in-Law, James E. Wrenwick of South Carolina and White County, Ill.* Erie, PA, Cook, 1965. 146, 2p. D gives 145 leaves. [D5169; X378-FW/PH].

GOURDIN -- Gourdin, Peter Gaillard. *The Gourdin Family.* Easley, SC, Southern Historical Press, 1980. 590p. [DS281].

GRACEN -- Dreyer, Gladys Grayson. *Our Gracen (Grayson) Family of South Carolina.* NP, Dreyer, 1958. 127p. [D5184].

GRADY -- Grady, Benjamin. *John Grady (1710-1787) of Dobbs and Duplin, with Some of His Descendants.* Wilson, NC, P.D. Gold Publishing Co., 1030. 93p. D gives underscored part of title. [L7119; D5186].

GRAFFENRIED -- De Graffenried, Thomas P. *The de Graffenried Family Honor Roll (European Branch Only).* NP, 1957. 23 l. [X381-FW/NY]. See above: De GRAFFENRIED [NG47; X381-FW]

GRAFTON -- NAS. *The Grafton Family Connection.* Ontario, Canada, L. Grafton, 1986-1990. 2 v. Contents: Pt. 1. South Carolina and Mississippi - Pt. 2. South

Carolina, U.S.A. - Mississippi, U.S.A., Ontarion, Canada. 1. Grafton family. 2. Canada-Genealogy. [G269].

GRAHAM -- Kell, Katherine Tolle. *David Graham of Chester County, South Carolina and His Descendants, 1772- 1989*. Birmingham, MI, 1990. 610p. [DC1472].

GRAHAM -- Stewart, Frank Graham. *Documentation of a Stewart - Graham Lineage in North Carolina.* Horse Shoe, NC, F.G. Stewart, 1990. xii, 389, 59p. Errate slip inserted. 1. Stewart family. 2. Graham family. 3. North Carolina-Genealogy. [G269].

GRANT -- Coffee, Isabelle Maxwell. *William Grant III of South Carolina.* NP, Coffee, 1975. ii, 13-28 leaves. [S1041].

GRASSE -- Simmons, Agatha Aimar (Mrs. T. Ritchie Simmons). *Charleston, S.C., A Haven for the Children of Admiral de Grasse.* . Charleston, SC, 1940. 16p. [L7175].

GRAVES -- Graves, Aubrey E. *Pioneer Settlers of Blount and DeKolb Counties, Alabama, John Graves , Pioneer and Allied Families of Alabama and North Carolina.* Chatanooga, TN, 1968. 186p. [L7185].

GRAVES -- Graves, Kenneth Vance. <u>*Robert Graves of Anson County, N.C. and Chesterfield County, S.C., Ancestors and Descendants (ca. 1580-1979)*</u>*: A Branch of the Descendants of Capt Thomas Graves, 1608 Immigrant to Jamestown, Va.* Baltimore, MD, Gateway Press, 1980. 408p. DS gives underscored title. [DS282; VV79].

GRAY -- Gray, Hugh C. *The Gray Family.* Charlotte, NC, B.S. Plummer, 1987. 130 l. 1. Gray family. [G270].

GRAY -- Linn, Jo White. <u>*The Gray Family and Allied Lines*</u>*: Bowman, Linsay, Mills, Dick,*

Peebles, Wiley, Shannon, Lamer, McGee. Salisbury, NC, 1976. xvii, 627p. D gives underscored title. [D5238; NG47; X384-NY/PH].

GRAY -- Nash, Sara M. [G270]. See above: FOWLER. [G237; D9163].

GRAY -- Overlander, Rufus M. [G270]. See above: BLUNT. [G63].

GREEN -- Green, C. Sylvester. *Greens from Westmoreland County, Virginia: with Sketches and Index of Interrelated Families, especially Spilman, Hudson, Barham, Owen, Chaplin, Perkins, Short, Reese, and Howell.* Greenville, NC, 1975. vii, 155p. 1. Green family. 2. Westmoreland County (Va.)-Genealogy. 3. United States-Genealogy. [G271; S1053; VV79].

GREEN -- Schwenker, Robert F, Jr. *The Greens of Clear Springs, New Bern, and Breven County: The Genalogical History of a North Carolina Family.* Belle Mead, NJ, R.F. Schwenker, 1989. 1 v. (various pagings). 1 Green family. 2. North Carolina-Genealogy. [G272].

GREER -- Holcomb, Brent. *Greer and Related Families: Sanders, Sims, Glenn, Christmas, Smith, Ferris, and Carver, of the Carolinas and Virginia.* Columbia, SC, B.H. Holcomb, 1987. 109p., 2 leaves of plates. 1. Greer family. 2. Saunders family. 3. Smith family. 4. Southern States-Genealogy. [G273].

GREGG -- Gregg, E. Stuart. *A Crane's Foot (or Pedigree) of Branches of the Gregg, Stuart, Robertson, Dobbs, and Allied Families.* Hilton Head, SC, Gregg, 1975. xix, 681p, 10 leaves of plates. 1. Gregg family. 2. Stuart family. 3. Robertson family. [G273; S1057].

GREGG -- Gregg, E. Stuart. *A Pictorial Pedigree.* Columbia, SC, R.L. Bryan Co., 1977. ix, 175p. 1. Gregg family. 2. Stuart family. 3. Robertson family. [G273].

GREGORIE -- Wilsom, Carrie Price. *Gregorie Family of Midlesex County, Virginia and Charleston, S.C.* NP, 1925. 23 leaves. [D5293; VV80].

GREGORY -- Spears, Josephine Gregory. *Gregory Family Correspondence, 1829-1888 and Josephus Gregory Travel Diary, 1848-1849...* Raleigh, NC, J.G. Spears, Title Pg: " This book was prepared as a companion to Josephus Gregory the Centanarian. [DC1498].

GREENVILLE -- NAS (United States. Circuit Court. (4th Circuit)). *The Charge of Judge Potter to the Jury in the Suit of the Devisees of the Early Granville Against Josiah Collins in the Circuit Court of the United States, December Term, 1803, as Reported in the Raleigh Register, Jan. 20 & 27, 1806.* Raleigh, NC, Printed by J. Gales, 1806. 16p. References: Shaw & Shoemaker 11200. 1. Greenville family-Trials, litigation, etc. 2. Collins, Josiah-Trials, litigation, etc. 3. Ejectment-North Carolina. [G274].

GRIDER -- Barr, James T. [G274]. See above: BARR. [G36].

GRIFFIN -- Griffin, Clarence. *Descendants of Chisholm Griffin.* Spindale, NC, 1931. 163 leaves. D gives: 200 l. [L7317; NG48; D5309].

GRIFFIN -- Griffin, Fred M. *The History and Genealogy of the Thomas Griffin Family.* Monroe, NC, Cory Press, 1949. 92p. [L7319; D5310].

GRIFFIN -- Griffin, Margarette Glenn. *The John Griffin Family of Nash County, North Carolina.* Rocky Mount, NC, Griffin, 1964. 49, 5 leaves. [D5311].

GRIMES -- Grimes, Rufus Nathan. *The Grimes - Llewellyn Families, 1635-1972.* Raleigh, NC, Edwards & Broughton Co., 1972. vii, 61p. [S1065].

GRIST -- Whitehead, Mary Grist. *From Grandmother's Trunk: A Family Portrayal.* Spartanburg, SC, Reprint Co., Publishers, 1989. viii, 434p. 1. Grist, Martha Rebecca Cook, 1845-1888-Family. 2. Grist family. 3. Georgia-Social life and customs-Sources. 4. Georgia-Biography. 5. Georgia-Genealogy. [G276].

GROGAN -- Thoesen, Edythe M. W. *Records of the Grogan Family of North and South Carolina, Georgia and Virginia.* Boulder CO, n.d. 33 leaves. [X391-DP].

GUERARD -- Guerard, George C. *A History and Geneology sic of the Guerard Family of South Carolina from 1679-1896.* NP, 1900, 23 leaves. [D5365].

GUIGNARD -- NAS. *Planters and Business Men; The Guignard Family of South Carolina, 1795-1930.* Columbia, SC, University of South Carolina Press, 1957. xii, 155p. (South Carolinia, no. 6) "A selection from the three thousand Guignard papers." [L7390].

GUION -- Davies, Graham. *In Memoriam: John A. Guion, M.D. New Bern, NC, 1816-1894.* NP, n.d. Unpaged leaflet. [X394-SL].

GULLETT -- Fisher, Joanne M. Gullett. *Ezekiel Gullett and Descendants: North Carolina to Indiana, 1780-1986.* Union City, IN, J.M.G. Fisher, 1986. xii, 265, 11p. [DC1531].

GUNTHER -- Buff, L. H. *Gunters Along the Edisto: Some Descendants of Russel Gunter.* Spartanburg, SC, 1987. 1. Gunther family. 2. Gunter, Rusel, 1777 or 8-1876-Family. 3. South Carolina-Genealogy. [G281].

GURLEY -- NAS. *Notes on William Gurley, One of the First Settlers of Johnston County, N.C., and Some of His Descendants.* Birmingham, AL, 1951. 26 leaves. [L7420].

GUTHRIE -- Guthrie, Laurence R. *American Guthrie and Allied Families; Lineal Representations of the Colonial Guthries of Pennsylvania, Connecticut, Maryland, Delaware, Virginia, North and South Carolina, Some Post-Revolutionary Emigrants and of Some Allied Families.* Chambersburg, PA, Kerr Printing Company, 1933. 6, ix, 743p. [L7445; VV81].

GUTHRIE -- Guthrie, Laurence R. *American Guthrie and Allied Families: Lineal Representations of the Colonial Guthries of Pennsylvania, Connecticut, Maryland, Delaware, Virginia, North and South Carolina, Some Post-Revolutionary Emigrants, and of Some Allied Families.* Baltimore, MD, Gateway Press, 1985. ix, 743p., 21 leaves of plates. 1. Guthrie family. [G282; VV81].

GUTKNECHT -- Winecoff, Edgar M. [G283]. See above: GOODNIGHT. [G266].

GUYTON -- Andrea, Leonardo. *Guyton.* Columbia, SC, Andrea, 1966. 77, 4 leaves. [D5398].

GWIN -- Hornback, Joyce Gwin. *The Gwins of North Carolina and Tennessee.* Pearl, MS, Hornback, 1986. 96p. [DS292].

GWINN -- Hickerson, Thomas Felix. *Happy Vally History and Genealogy.* Chapel Hill, NC, Author, 1941. ix, 244p. "This book deals particularly with the history of the Gwyns, Lenoirs, and any other families connected by ties of kinship, but long identified with the Yadkin Valli - the part from Lenoir to Elkin." [L7453].

H

HABERSHAM -- Bulloch, Joseph Gaston Baillie. *A History and Genealogy of the Habersham Family and the Families of Clay, Stiles, Cumming, King, Elliott, Milledge,*

Maxwell, Adams, Houston, Screvens, Owens, Demere, Footman, Ellis, Newell, Davis, Barrington, Lewis, Warner, Cobb, Flournoy, Pratt, Nephew, Bolton, Bowers, Cuthbert, and Many Other Names. Columbia, SC, R.L. Bryan, Co., 1901. vi, 222p. D gives underscored part of title; NG omits names after Warner. [L7463; NG48; D5401].

HACKNEY -- NAS. *Let the Record Show, the Hackneys: Two Early Prominent Black Families of Chatham and Orange Counties, NC: A History and Genealogy of Charles H. & Antoinette Stone Hackney and Louis Henry and Laura Edwards Hackney. - 1st ed.* San Jose, CA, Gentrace Association, Inc., 1987. xxii, 339p. 1. Hackney family. 2. Hackney, Charles H., 1832-1919 or 20-Family. 3. Hackney, Louis Henry, 1854-1937-Family. 4. Chatham County (N.C.)-Genealogy. 5. Orange County (N.C.)-Genealogy. 6. Afro-American-Genealogy. [G287].

HADDEN -- Hadden, Robert Lee. *The Shamrock and The Fleur De Lys: The Family Histories of the William James Hadden Family and the Whitney Shumate Family.* Greenville, NC, Hadden Pub. Association, 1990. 328p. 1. Hadden family. 2. Hadden, William James, 1892-1954-Family. 3. Shoemaker Family. 4. Shumate, Whitney, 1896-1966-Family. [G287].

HADLEY -- Bradfield, Allen L. *Thomas Lindley and Ruth Hadley: The Wedding of Cindy's Ancestral Lines of Hadley and Lindley, Her Sixth Great Grandmother, Ruth Hadley, and Grandfather Thomas Lindley: A Brief Account of Their Life and Times, Including Analysis of What is Currently Known.* Bridgeport, IL, A.L. Bradfield, 1979. i, 76 leaves. 1. Lindley family. 2. Lindley, Thomas, 1706-1781-Family. 2. Hadley family. 4. Pennsylvania-Genealogy. 5. North Carolina-Genealogy. 6. Indiana-Genealogy. [G288].

HADLEY -- Hadley, Lyle H. *Some Descendants of Jeremiah Hadley, 1741-1786, and Joseph*

Hadle, 1754-ca. 1794, of Chatham County, North Carolina. Edited by Curtis E. Helton, Hadley Genealogical Society of Southern California, Los Angeles, CA, 1974. vi, 231p. (His [sic] a Hadley Genealogy: v. 3). [S1084].

HADLEY -- Healton, Curtis E. *A Hadley Genealogy.* Los Angeles, CA, Hadley Genealogical Society of Soutern California, 1974. 3 v. Contents: v. 1. Ancestry of Simon Hadley, the Immigrant, and Some of His Descendants. - v. 2. Some Descendants of Joshua Hadley, 1743-1815, of Chatham County, North Carolina. - v. 3. Some Descendants of Jeremiah Hadley, 1754-ca. 1794, of Chatham, North Carolina. 1. Hadley family. [G288].

HADLEY -- Perry, Webster. *Genealogical Data Relating to the Earlier Generations of the Hadley Family in America as Compiled from the Records of Spring and Cane Creek Monthly Meeting, N.C...* Richmond, IN, 193_. 54p. Pt. 2 from Stuart and allied lines by F.A. Stuart. [X398-FW].

HAGLER -- Haigler, W. H. *Haiglers of South Carolina: History and Genealogy.* Montogmery, AL, W.H. Haigler, 1975. v, 217p. [S1087].

HAGOOD -- Hagood, Johnson. *<u>Meet Your Grandfather</u>, a Sketchbook of the Hagood - Tobin Family.* Charleston, SC, Hagood, 1946. 165p. D gives underscored part of title. [L7488; D5419].

HAILE -- Green, Dorothy C. *Haile, Ferguson, Chestnut, Owens, Howard, Wills, Tombstone and Records - Virginia, South Carolina, Georgia.* NP, 1958. 28 leaves. [D5420; VV82].

HALCOMB -- Giulvezan, Isabel Stebbins. *Notes on Hiram H. Halcomb (1789-1869) of Caswell County, North Carolina, Robertson County, Tennessee, Logan and Simpson Counties, Kentucky and His 16 Children.* St. Louis, MO, Giulvezan, 1961. 55 leaves. [D5436; X-FW].

HALEY -- NAS. *John Haley Family History.* High Point, NC, High Point Historical Society, 1973. 31p. [X401-FW].

HALL -- Adams, Mary Lizzie Hall. *The Hall Family History.* Statesville, NC, Adams, 1949. 443p. [L7565; D5453].

HALL -- Hall, Marvin F. *History of the Hall-Ayers-Holland Family. Virginia, North Carolina Georgia, Tennessee, Texas.* Scarsdale, NY, Hall, 1976. 100 l. [D5466: VV83].

HALL -- Hartley, Elizabeth J. H. *Descendants of Moses Hall, John Doudna, and Benjamin Hall (Quaker Fams. of Belmont County, Ohio, from Va., and N.C.).* Denver, CO,1958. xxii, 339p. [X401-FP/FW/NY; VV83].

HALL -- Kendall, John S. *The Hall Family of South Carolina, Descended from John Hall of York County, South Carolina. With Notices of the Allied Families of Watson, McDowell, Parks, Davis, Wilson, Venable, Ruffner, Aston, Cocke, Smith, Woodson, and Michaux.* Berekely, CA, 1943. 1p., 14, 24 numb. l. [L7562].

HALL -- Parrish, Verle Hamilton and Efonda S. Doughton. *Who's Who in My Hall Family (of Virginia, North Carolina and Kentucky).* Georgetown, KY, Verle H. Parrish, Farmington, UT, E. S. Daughton, 1982. 128p. [C289; VV83].

HALLAM -- Whitney, Kenneth A. *The Documented Afro-American Family History: Carey Pickens and Mary Hallums, 1765-1910.* Evanston, IL, K.A. Whitney, 1988. xi, 47p., 93 leaves. 1. Pickens family. 2. Hallam family. 3. Pickens, Carey, b. ca. 1835-Family. 4. Hallums, Mary, 1851-1905-Family. 5. Afro-American-Genealogy. 6. South Carolina-Genealogy. [G290].

HALLOWELL -- Hallowell, Barbara G. *Cabin, A Mountain Adventure.* Illustrations by Aline Hansens. Boone, NC, Appalachian Consortium

Press, 1986. 253p. 1. Mountain Life-Appalachian Region, Southern. 2. Appalachian Regions, Southern-Social Life and customs. 3. Hallowell, Barbara, 1924- 4. Hallowell family. [G291].

HAMBRIGHT -- Summers, Bonnie Mauney. *The Colonel Frederick Hambright Family.* Kings Mountain, NC, Summer, 1969, 77, xi p/l?. [D5494].

HAMER -- Hoker, Glora Janie Hamer. *John Hicks Hamer, 1765-1842, His Antecedents, Descendants and Collateral Families, 1744-1949.* Spartanburg, SC, Hooker, 1949. 350p. [D5497].

HAMILTON -- Baskerville, Patrick Hamilton. *The Hamiltons of Burnside, North Carolina, and Their Ancestors and Descendants.* Richmond, VA, W.E. Jones' Sons, Inc., 1916. pni. [VV84].

HAMILTON -- Hendrix, Ge Lee Corley. *A Genealogy of Thomas Hamilton and His Descendants of Ninety-six District, South Carolina.* Greenville, SC, G.L.C. Hendrix, 1980. 30 leaves. [DC1576].

HAMILTON -- McPherson, L. D. *Partial Genealogy of the Families of Hamilton of Ga., S.C., and Reids of N. C.* Chicago, IL, 1933. 6 numb. leaves. [L7642].

HAMILTON -- Parrish, Verle Hamilton. *Hamilton, Mullins, Fleming, and Related Lines. of Ky., W.Va., No. Car., and Tenn.* Stamping Ground, KY, Parrish, 1975. 80p. [S1100].

HAMILTON -- Skelley, Mildred. *History of the Hamilton, Wilfong, Shuford, Warlick, Hoyle, Baker, Bush and Other Families in Indiana and North Carolina.* NP, 1962. 44 leaves. [D5511].

HAMLIN -- Lawson, Percy Bethel. [G292]. See above: BROADNAX. [G90].

HAMMER -- Hammer, Harriette J. *Ancestors and Descendants, 1683-1983, Abraham Hammer of Philadelphia County, Pennsylvania, and Randolphy County, North Carolina. 2nd ed.* NP, 1986. xxiv, 187p. 1. Hammer family, 2. Hammer, Abraham-Family. 3. Philadelphia County, (Pa.)-Biography. 4. Philadelphia County, (Pa.)-Genealogy. 5. Randolph County (N.C.)-Biography. 6. Randolph County (N.C.)-Genealogy. [G292; NGS7].

HAMMER -- Winkler, Ruth Hammer Swearington. *Genealogy of Hammers Relating to North Carolina, 1684-1987.* Summerfield, NC, R.H.S. Winkler, 1987. xiv, 197p. 1. Hammer family. 2. North Carolina-Genealogy. [G292].

HAMMOND -- Tillman, M. N., Comp. *Hammond Family of Edgefield District.* Compiled for the Edgefield County Historical Society. Edgefield, SC, Advertiser, Pr., 1954. 34p. [X406-FW].

HAMPTON -- NAS. *Hampton Family of Virginia, North and South Carolina & Kentucky.* NP, nd. pni. [X406-SL; VV85].

HAMPTON -- Cauthen, Charles Edward. *Family Letters of the Three Wade Hamptons, 1782-1901.* Columbia, SC, U. of S.C. Press, 1953. 181p. [L7668; D5529].

HAMPTON -- Meynard, Virginia Gurley. *The Venturers: The Hampton, Harrison, and Earle Families of Virginia, South Carolina, and Texas.* Easley, SC, Southern Historical Press, 1981. 1114p. D gives underscored title. [NG49; D5533; VV85].

HAMRICK -- Jones, S. C. *The Hamrick Generations.* Raleigh, NC, Edwards & Broughton Printing Co., 1920. 3, 207p. [L7669; D5535].

HAND -- Campbell, Vivian. *Hanner Cousins.* NP, V. Campbell, [Cambridge, [IA] M. A.

Hayden, 1986. 95p. 1. Hand family. 2. North Carolina-Genealogy. [G293].

HANDCOCK -- St. Amand, Jeanette C. . *William Handcock of Virginia and Craven County, North Carolina.* Wilmington, NC, 1960. 20 leaves. [D5547; VV85].

HANES -- Linn, Jo White. *People Named Hanes.* Salisbury, NC, 1980. 281p. [NG51].

HANKS -- Baber, Adin (with a number of Hank descendants). *The Hanks Family of Virginia and Westward; A Genealogical Record from the Early 1600's, Including Charts of Families in Arkansas, the Carolinas Georgia, Illinois, Indiana, Iowa, Kentucky, Missouri, Oklahama, Ohio, Pennsylvania, and Texas.* Kansas, IL, 1965. 1 v. (various pagings). [L7685; VP92; VV85].

HANNA -- NAS. *Some Descendants of James Hanna of South Carolina.* Wolf City, TX, Henington Pub. Co., 1969. 48p. [L7696].

HANNA -- Hanna, Frank A. *The Hanna Family of Enoree River.* Durham, NC, 1969. xi, 113p. [A281].

HANNA -- Montoye, Betty A. (B). *Hanna Family: 1774-1974; Laurens District, S.C. to Carroll County, Indiana.* Knoxville, TN, 1974. 78p. [X409-FW/LA/NY].

HANSEN -- Coggeshall, Robert Walden. [G295]. See above: COGGESHALL. [G148].

HARDAWAY -- Carlisle, Maxine Fallers and Denzil Lark Carlisle. *The Descendnts of John Clack Hardaway and Mary Hardaway Harwell of Virginia, Chambliss and Sarah Carlisle of North Carolina.* San Francisco, CA, Carlisle, Carlisle. 1958. 33 leaves. [L7725; D5582; VV86].

HARDESTY -- Wesley, Irma Hardesty. *Hardesty Family in America.* Charlotte, NC, Wesley, 1981. vii, 223p. [DS311].

HARDY -- Hardee, David L. *The Eastern North Carolina Hardy - Hardee Family in the South and Southwest.* Raleigh, NC, Hardee, 1964. 302p. X gives date as: 1962 [D5610; X413-FW].

HARGETT -- Hargrett, Felix. *The Hargretts of Georgia and Their Origins in Germany and North Carolina. Rev. and corr. ed.* Lynchburg, VA, F. Hargrett, 1986. viii, 139p., 3 leaves of plates. Rev. ed. of The Hargretts of Georgia and Their Ancestors in Germany and North Carolina, 1984. 1. Hargett family. 2. Georgia-Biography. 3. North Carolina-Biography. DC gives place of publication as: Athens, GA. [G298; DC1621].

HARGETT -- Hargrett, Felix. *The Hargretts of Georgia.* Lynchburg, VA, F. Hargrett, 1986. viii, 139p., 3 leaves of plates. Second edition. Previously published as: The Hargretts of Georgia and Their Origins in Germany and North Carolina. 1986. See immediately above. [G298].

HARGETT -- Hyatt, Sybil. *Hargett - Thompson, Onslow County, North Carolina.* Kinston, NC, 1948. 17 l. Typed Carbon. [L7753].

HARGRETT -- Hargrett, Felix. *The Hargretts of Georgia and Their Origins in Germany and North Carolina. rev.* Athens, GA, Georgian Press, 1984. 131p., 4 leaves of plates. 1. Hargrett family. 2. Georgia-Biography. 3. North Carolina-Biography. [G298].

HARGRETT -- Hargrett, Felix. *The Hargretts of Georgia and Their Origins in Germany and North Carolina. rev.* Athens, GA, F. Hargrett, 1986. 139p. [NG50; DC1621].

HARLLEE -- Harlee, William Curry. *Kinfolks, a Genealogical and Biogrphical Record of Thomas and Elizabeth (Stuart) Harlee, Andrew and Agnes (Cade) Fulmore, Benjamin and Mary Curry, Samuel and Amelia (Russell) Kemp, John and Hannah (Walker) Bethea, Sterling Clack and Frances (King) Robertson, Samuel and Sophia Ann (Parker) Dickey, Their Antecedents, Descendants, and Collateral Relatives, with Chapter Concerning State and County Records and the Derivation of Counties of Alabama, Florida, Georgia, Mississippi, North Carolina, Pennsylvania, South Carolina, Tennessee, Texas, and Virginia.* New Orleans, LA, 1934-37. Searcy & Pfaff, Ltd. 4 V. Contents: v. 1. Harllee Section. - v. 2. Fulmore Section. Curry Section. Kemp Section. - v. 3. Bethea Section, Robertson Section, Dickery Section. v. 4. General Indes. [L7764; VP93].

HARPER -- Floyd, Viola Caston. *Descendants of William Harper, Irish Immigrant to Lancaster County, South Carolina.* Lancaster, SC, Floyd, 1965. 583p. [L7783; D5642].

HARPER -- Harper, James E. *Harper, Kennebrew-etc.,* Townville, SC, J.E. Harper, 1982- v. <1 >. 1. Harper family. 2 Killebrew family. [G300].

HARPER -- Reynolds, Troy Harper. *Robert Harper, Revolutionary Soldier of Catholic Presbyterian Church, Shester, South Carolina, 1742-1801.* NP, Reynols, 1980. 31 leaves. [D5645].

HARPER -- Satterfield, Virginia. *Harper Family of Johnston County, North Carolina.* Smithfield, NC, 1977. 31 leaves. [D5646].

HARPER -- Whitaker, C. Bruce. *The Whitaker Family of Buncombe County, North Carolina and Genealogies of the Reed, Harper, and Wright Families. - 1st ed.* Asheville, NC, Ward Pub. Co., xvi, 340, 60, 64, 58p. 1. Whitaker family. 2. Reed family. 3. Harper family. 4. Wright family. [G300].

HARRELL -- Simpson, Virginia Harrell. *Our Harrells of South Carolina.* Chatanooga, TN, V.H. Simpson, n.d. 2 v. Part 2. Descendants of Jacob Harrell. [DC1632].

HARRINGTON -- NAS. *The Harrington Letters.* Chapel Hill, NC, The University, 1914. 62p. (The University of North Carolina. The James Sprunt historical publications, pub. under the direction of the North Carolina historial society... V. 13, no. 2) Letters of the Harrington Family of North Carolina, 1785-1843. "Introductory note" signed: H. M. Wagstaff. [L7790].

HARRINGTON -- Russell, Marjorie Douglas. [G300]. See above: DALRYMPLE. [G173].

HARRIS -- Andrea, Leonardo. *Harris Family of South Carolina.* NP, South Carolina DAR, G.R.C., 1966. 69 leaves. [DC1645].

HARRIS -- Leonard, Calista V. *Harris History: A History of American Descendants of Edward Harris and His Wife Flora Douglas of Scotland, 1650c-1984.* Santa Monica, CA, Computer Assisted Ancestor Tracking Co., 1984-1985, v 1-4. v. 1. without specific title; v. 2. their grandson Samuel Harris (1715-1789) his wife, Martha Laird and their descendants; v. 3. their great grandson, Thomas Harris 1283 (1749-1791) and his wife Mary Baker (1744-1818) of Mecklenburg Co., North Carolina and Greene Co., Georgia; v. 4. Childrene (sic) of Eli Harris 12837. [C300].

HARRIS -- Leonard, Calista V. *Harris History: A History of American Descendants of Edward Harris and His Wife Flora Douglas of Scotland, 1650c-1984.* Santa Monica, CA, Computer Assisted Ancestor Tracking Co., 1984-1987, 6 v. v. 1. without specific title; v. 2. their grandson Samuel Harris (1715-1789) his wife, Martha Laird and their descendants; v. 3. their great grandson, Thomas Harris 1283 (1749-1791) and his wife Mary Baker (1744-1818) of Mecklenburg Co., North Carolina and Greene Co., Georgia; v. 4. Children of Eli Harris 12837; v. 5. Louisiana Children of their great grandson Thomas Harris 1283: Eli Harris, Jr. 128375 and Datus Whitaker Harris 1283770; v. 6. A one-line bibliograpical index, and alphabetical index, of all their known American descendants to 1987 as described in volumes 1-5. [G301].

HARRIS -- Roberson, Erma Harris. *Harris Tree and Branches: Descendants of John Taylor Harris, North Carolina and Tennessee.* Cullman, AL, Printed by Brook Litho c. 19. p. [L7831]

HARRIS -- Roberson, Erma Harris. *Harris Tree and Branches: Descendants of John Taylor Harris, North Carolina and Tennessee.* Cullman, AL, Gregath Pub. Co., c. 1990. 145p. 1. Harris family. 2. Harris, John Taylor, 1775-1868 or 9-Family. 3 North Carolina-Genealogy. 4. Tennessee-Genealogy. [G301]

HARRIS -- Stratton, Mary Harris. *Ancestors and Descendants of Robert Harris, Sr., 1702-1788.* Charlotte, NC, Stratton, 1967, 217p. [L7831; D5692].

HARRIS -- Stratton, Mary Harris. *Ancestors and Descendants of Robert Harris, Sr., 1702-1788.* Charlotte, NC, Stratton, 1967, 1986. 2 v. [DC1646].

HARRIS -- Warren, Jean Pressley. *Leander N. Kirkpatrick, Martha Rachel Smart, & James B. Harris History.* Candler, NC, J.P. Warren, 1984. 39 leaves. 1. Kirkpatrick family. 2. Harris family. 3. North Carolina-Genealogy. [G301].

HARRIS -- Wagstaff, H. M. *The Harris Letters.* Durham, NC, The Seeman Printery,

1916. 91p. The James Sprunt Sprunt historical publications, pub. under the direction of the North Carolina historical society. V. 14, no. 1 "The Harris letters ...represent, for the most past, a collection of the letters of Charles Wilson Harris...to his uncle, Dr. Charles Harris, and his brother, Robert Wilson Harris" - Prefatory note. [L7817].

HARRIS -- Woodruff, Caldwell. *Tucker Harris, M.D. (1747-1821), of Charleston, South Carolina, and His Descendants. Families of Clarkson, Gibson, Finley, Heriot, Mazyck, Simons, and Woodruff. Constituting a Record of the Descendants of the Reverend and Learned Thomas Boston, A.M., (1677-1732), Minister of Ettrick, Scotland.* Linthicum Heights, MD, D. Woodruff, 1946. iv, 282 (i.e. 293) numb. leaves. Forward signed: Caldwell Woodruff. [L7825].

HARRISON -- Harrison, Thomas P., Jr. *The Harrisons of Andersonville, South Carolina.* Austin, TX, 1973. x, 148p. [S1132].

HARRISON -- Harrison, Thomas P., Jr. *The Harrisons of Andersonville, South Carolina. Supplement Only.* Austin, TX, 1975. 47p. [X418-FW].

HARRISON -- Rowe, Ella Harrison. *Rowe and Harrison Families of Eastern North Carolina.* Baltimore, MD, E.H. Rowe, 1988. 83p. 1. Rowe family. 2. Harrison family. 3. North Carolina-Genealogy. DC lists under ROWE. [G302; NGN16-4-90; DC3167].

HARRISON -- Williams, Frank L. *John Garrison of 96 District, South Carolina and Botetourt County, Virginia, between 1771 and 1808.* Hot Springs, AK, 1970. pni. [VV88].

HART -- Beach, Harriett Hart. *The Ancestors and Descendants of Horace and Olive Hart.*

Clovis, CA, H.H. Beach, 1985. 3, 43, 5 leaves. 1. Hart family. 2. Hart, Horace Greeley, 1812-1892. [G302].

HARTNESS -- Hartness, George Bowman. *By Ship, Wagon, and Foot to York County, S. C.* Columbia, SC, Hartness, 1966. 116p. [D5752].

HARVEY -- Shelburne, Robert C. *The Harvey Family*. Asheville, NC, 1963. 4 leaves. [X420-DP/NY].

HATFIELD -- Hatfield, John Bennett. *A Genealogical History of the Hatfield and Sherman Families of Utica, N.Y.* Greensboro, NC, Greensboro Printing Co., 1981. 222p. [DS324].

HATFIELD -- Jones, Virgil. *The Hatfields and the McCoys.* Chapel Hill, NC, University of North Carolina Press, 1948. 293p. [D5975].

HATFIELD -- Waller, Altine L. *Feud: Hatfields, McCoys and Social Change in Appalachia, 1860-1900.* Chapel Hill, NC, University of North Carolina, 1988. 313p. [DC1680].

HATHCOCK -- Haithcock, Richard. *Haithcock Families of Ohio and the Allied Families from North Carolina. Rev. 2nd ed.* Washington Court House, OH, R. L. Haithcock, 1985. viii, 161p. 1, Hathcock family. 2. Ohio-Genealogy. 3. North Carolina Genealogy. [G304; C304].

HATLEY -- Hatley, Coy S. *We Hatleys Are A Hardy Bunch.* Stanfield, NC, C.S. Hatley, 1987. 202p., 2 leaves of plates. 1. Hatley family. 2. North Carolina-Genealogy. [G305].

HAUSER -- Hauser, Kenneth John. *Alsatian-American Family Hauser.* Winston-Salem, NC, Hunter Pub. Co., 1977. 335p. [D5806].

HAVENS -- Woodworth, Esther Deidamia Littleford. *Havens - Austin Genealogy..* Charleston, SC, Woodworth, 1956. 39, 7 leaves. [D5816].

HAWKINS -- Claypool, E. A., Genealogist. *Hawkins Records: South Carolina, North Carolina, Delaware, Kentucky.* NP, 1902. 124p. 9 leaves. [X425-FW].

HAWKINS -- Wulfeck, Dorothy Ford. *Hawkins of Virginia, the Carolinas and Kentucky; Court Records, Queries, Brief Lineages, Genealogical Notes.* Naugatuck, CT, 1962. 86p. D shows 86 leaves and date of 1963. X gives date of 1967. [D5834; X426-SU; VV90].

HAWORTH -- Davis, Charles B. *The Haworth Record. Devoted to Historical Interest of the Family Everywhere.* High Point, NC, Chas. B. Davis, Printers, 1906- . FW has vol 3, no. 12, PH has vol. 1 nos. 1-4, 7, 9, 10; vol. 4 nos 2, 3, 5 (Jan-Nov. 1906 and Oct 1914 - Apr 1915. [X427-FW/PH].

HAY -- Colcock, Charles J. *The Family of Hay: A History of the Progenitors and Some South Carolina Descendants of Col. Ann Hawkes Hay... 500-1908. Reprinted with Later Lines added by Mrs. T. D. Bateman (Erroldine Hay).* New Orleans, LA, Pelican Pub. Co. 1959. xiv, 288p. [X428-FW/NY].

HAY -- Colcock, Charles J. *The Family of Hay: A History of the Progenitors and Some South Carolina Descendants of Col. Ann Hawkes Hay... Third Edition.* Charlotte, NC, J.C. Hay-Steele, 1986. 515p. Originally published in 1908. [DC1692].

HAYDEN -- Linn, Jo White. *A Holmes Family of Fowan and Dividson Counties, North Carolina with Haden, Heilin, Reid, Rex, Linn, Smith, Bernhardt, Snider, Pearson, Graham, White, Sawyer, Foushee, Ballou, Hurley, Morrison, King, Erwin, Pannill, Dillard, Knowles.*

Salisbury, NC, 1988. xvi, 308p. One folded map in pocket. 1. Holmes family. 2. Hayden family. 3. Reed family. 4. North Carolina-Genealogy. DC gives underscored part of title and "Holmes Investment" as publisher. [G327; NGN17-1-91; DC1825].

HAYES -- Hathaway, Bernice F. *Hayes - Maddock - Stubbs and Allied Lines; Many of the Ancestors and Descendants of Bailey Hayes and Mary Stubbs, Married...1802. Early Pennsylvania, Virginia, Maryland, North Carolina, Georgia and Ohio Lines.* Denver, CO, Privatele Publis. 1969. 98p. [X428-DP/FW/MH/NY; VV90].

HAYNE -- Campbell, Julia Anna Francis Courtenay. *The Hayne Family of South Carolina and Some Relatives in These Lines: Martin, Davidge, Barnwell, Courtenay, Beattie, Adams, Hazelhurst, Black, Hasell, Davis, Foster, Houston, McIver, Woodward, Baldwin, Brevard, Trapier, Motte, Shubrick, Perry, Swinton (and) Splatt.* Charlottesville, VA, 1956. 21 leaves. [L8061; VV90].

HAYNES -- Haynes, Ina F. <u>Raleigh Rutherford Hayes</u>. *A History of His Life and Achievements.* Asheville, NC, Haynes [X gives Miller Print], 1954. 99p. D gives underscored title. [D5862; X429-FW].

HAYNES -- Jervey, Theodore D. *The Hayne Family.* In South Carolina historical genealogical magazine. Charleston, SC, 1904. Vol. v, p.(168)-188. Detached copy. [L8072].

HAYNSWORTH -- Haynsworth, Hugh Charles. *Haynsworth - Furman and Allied Families; including Ancestors and Descendants of Sarah Morse Haynsworth.* Sumter, SC, Osteen Publ., Co., 1942. 333p. [L8079; D5869].

HAYWARD -- Heyward, Barnwell Rhett. *Genealogical Chart. Heyward of South*

Carolina. Albany, NY, 1896. Genealogical Table. [L8084].

HAYWARD -- Heyward, James Barnwell. *The Colonial History of the Heyward Family of South Carolina, 1760-1770, Together with an Abbreviated Genealogy, 1770-1870.* Nashville, TN, McQuiddy Printing Company. 1907. 38p. [L8086].

HAZELWOOD -- Watson, Ruth Lancaster Trowell. *Lancaster and Related Families: Williams, Hazlewood, Willirord, West, Gwinn.* Greenville, SC, R.L.T. Watson, 1986. xii, 147p. 1. Lancaster family. 2. Williams family. 3. Hazelwood family. 4. South Carolina-Genealogy. [G308].

HEARN -- NAS. *The Hearne Family in Ohio from N. Car. and Maryland.* Harrison, OH, E. M. Shaver, 1989. 1 v. (various foliations). 1. Hearn family. 2. Ohio-Genealogy. [G308].

HELMS -- Myers, Sarah M. *George and Tilman Helms Pioneers of Anson & Mechlenburg Counties, N.C. History and Genealogy of the Helms Family.* NP, 1981. 1 v. in various pagings. [DS329].

HENKEL -- Van Henkle, et al. *The Ancestors and Descendants of Horace Russell Henkle and Effa Hope (Phelps) Henkle.* Lincoln, NB, Henkle Audio Visuals, 1983. Subtitle: Being the account of one family extending for a dozen generations from the five western European countries through early colonial America in Massachusetts, New York, Pennsylvania, Virginia, and North Carolina to the end of the ninteenth century in these states and West Virginia, Ohio, and Indiana, and then with the last year to the nineteenth century the start of five generations in Colorado. Privately printed. 1. Henkel family. 2. Henkle, Horace Russell, 1870-1949-Family. 3. Phelps family. [G312].

HENLEY -- Bell, Eleanor P. *The Sage of the Family and Descendants of David Vestal Henley and Eleanor Lassiter of Randolph County, North Carolina.* Columbia, SC, Dependable Print, 1986. vii, 1022p., 2 leaves of plates. 1. Henley family. 2. Henley, David Vestal, 1818-1893-Family. [G312].

HENRY -- Van Valin, Minnie D. *Miscellaneous Henry Records.* NC?, 1940. 72 l. [D5979].

HENRY -- Van Valin, Minnie D. *William Henry, Senior, 1715-1819, and Hugh Allison, Senior, 1714-1790 of York County, South Carolina and Some of Their Descendants.* 1933. 155 leaves. [D5980].

HENSON -- Harmon, Terry L. *The Henson Family, 1780-1986: The Genealogy of Charles and Elizabeth Henson and Their Descendants.* Vilas, NC, T.L. Harmon, 1986. 384p., 96p. of plates. 1. Henson family. 2. Henson, Charles, ca. 1780-ca. 1830-Family. [G313].

HERIOT -- Woodruff, Capt. Caldwell. *Family of Heriot of Castlemains, Dirleton, Haddington, Scotland, with Descendants in the United States of Colonel Robert Heriot of Haddington and South Carolina, Revolutionary Soldier; His Brother, William Heriot of Haddington and South Carolina; His Nephew Roger Heriot of Haddington and South Carolina, Their Cousin George Heriot of Haddington and South Carolina in the the Province of Quebec, Canada, of John Heriot, Sheriff Clerk of Haddington, Scotland (brother of above George)....* Baltimore, MD, 1918. 1p, 167 (i.e.168) numb. leaves. Typed. [L8237].

HERIOT -- Woodruff, Caldwell. M.D. *Roger Heriot of South Carolina and His Descendants, with a Record of the Heriots of Ladykirk and Shiels, Berwickshire, Scotland. Also an Account of Maj. Gen'l. the Hon. Fredk. Geo. Heriot, C.B. by J.C.A. Heriot.* Linthicum Heights, MD, 1937. 4p., 87 numb l., xv plates. "A supplement to my account of the Heriots of Scotland and South Carolina". [See HERIOT, L8237 above]. [L8239].

HERIOT -- Woodruff, Caldwell. *Heriots of Scotland and South Carolina... The Ouldfield Family. Genealogical Tables, Letters, Manuscripts, and Documents.* Linthicum Heights, MD, 1939. 2p, iii, 199 numb. leaves "Second Edition". Typed. [L8240].

HERMAN -- Little, Pearl. *Sketch of the Herman Family.* Hickory, NC, 1939. 13 numb. leaves. [L8245].

HERNDON -- Herndon, John Goodwin and Ruth Herndon Shields. *The Herndons of the American Revolution.* Haverford, PA, Priv. Print., 1950-1952. 4 v. (His the Herndon Shields Family of Virginia, v. 2.) (Hers the Descendants of William and Sarah (Poe) Herndon of Caroline County, Va., and Chatham County, North Carolina. Contents: pt. 1. John Herndon (ca.1700-1786) of Charlotte County, Virginia, and his descendants. - pt. 2. Edward Herndon (ca. 1702-1759) of Spotsylvania County, Virginia and his descendants. pt. 3. William Herndon (ca. 1706-1783) of Orange County, Virginia and his descendants. pt. 4. Richard Herndon (prob. b. ca. 1708- d. post 1754) of Caroline County, Virginia and His Known Descendants. [L8250].

HERNDON -- Herndon, John Goodwin. *The Herndon Family of Virginia.* Haverford, PA, Priv. Print. 1947-1952. 2 v. in 5. v. 1 500 copies, v. 2. 100 copies. Continued by Ruth Herndon Shields' "The descendants of William and Sarah (Poe) Herndon of Caroline County, Va., and Chatham County, N.C. Chapel Hill, NC, 1956. 232p. "Continuation of The Herndon Family of Virginia" by Dr. John Goodwin Herndon of Haverford, Pennsylvania.". [L8251].

HERNDON -- Shields, Ruth Herndon. *The Descendants of William and Sarah (Poe)*

Herndon of Caroline County, Va. and Chatham County, N.C. Chapel Hill, NC, Shields, 1956. 232p. [D6008; VV92].

HERNDON -- Wood, Edna Hilliard White. *The Herndon - Hunt and Allied Families.* Raleigh, NC, Bynum Printing Co., 1930. 110p. [D6010].

HERRING -- Herring, Robert A. *The John Herring Family of North Carolina and Mississippi; A Narrative Report by the Author.* NP, 1969. viii, 92 l. [A310].

HERRING -- Sloo, James R. *John Herring of New Hanover County, N. C. and Some of His Descendants, 1705-1941.* Raleigh, NC, Sloo, Sloo, 1941. 81p. X gives 81 leaves. [D6015; X440-SL].

HEWSON -- Wood, Margarette Hall. [G316]. See above: DEAN. [G182].

HEYL -- Rucker, Elizabeth Hoyle. *The Genealogy of Peiter Hyle and His Descendants, 1100-1936, with the Intermarried Families of Arnold, Bess, Byrd, Cansler, Carlock, Carpenter, Costner (Kestner) Davis, Freeman, Friday, Gantt, (Gaunt, Ghent) Green, Hahn, Henkel, Hoffman, Hovis, Huffstetler, Jones, Klein, Lineberger (Leinberger) Mendenhall, McIntosh, Nesbitt, Payne, Patton, Peel, Peeler, Porter, Ramsour, Reinhardt, Rhyne, Reynolds, Robinson, Rudisill, Shuford, Summey, Smith, Thompson, Wells, Warlick, Weidner, and Wilfong.* Shelby, NC, Zolliecoffer Jenks Thompson, 1938. 1539p. D gives underscored part of title. [L8305; D6043].

HIATT -- Hyatt, Sybil. *North Carolina Hiatts and Hyatts.* Kinston, NC, n.d. 11p. [X443-FW].

HICKMAN -- Hilton, Hope A. *Edwin and Elender Webber Chiles Hickman; Some Progenitors and Descendants, Early Pioneers of Virginia, North Carolina, Kentucky, Missouri,* *and Utah.* Salt Lake City, UT, 1967. iv, 167p. [L8315; VV93].

HICKS -- White, Barneta McGhee. *In Search of Kith and Kin: The History of a Southern Black Family.* Baltimore, MD, Gateway Press, 1986. 208p. 1. Magee family. 2. Hicks family. 3. North Carolina-Genealogy. 4. Afro-American-Genealogy. [G317].

HICKS -- Williams, Mary Faison Hicks. *The Hicks Family of North Carolina, U.S.A.* NP, 1942. 51 leaves. [D6064].

HIERS -- Hiers Research Committee. *The Hiers Genealogy.* Columbia, SC, R.L. Bryan Co., 1974. viii, 606p. [D6066].

HIGDON -- NAS. *Descendants of Joseph Hoffman Higdon and Margaret Matilda Berry Higdon.* Asheville, NC, Big Red Q Quickprint, 1983. vxi, 134p. [DS342].

HIGDON -- Smith, Jo Ann. *Leonard Higdon of Anson County, North Carolina and His Descendants.* Raleigh, NC, Business Services Unlimited, 1982. 66p. [DS343].

HIGDON -- Smith, Jo Ann. *The Higdon Family Association.* Raleigh, NC, J.A. Smith, 1986. 53p. [G317].

HIGDON -- Willis, Opal M. *Leonard Higdon of North Carolina, Known Descendants, 1755-1986: Pioneer Families of America.* Provo, UT, Stevenson's Genealogy Center, 1987. x, 490p. 1. Higdon family. 2. Higdon, Leonard, d. 1775-Family. 3. North Carolina-Genealogy. [G317].

HIGHSMITH -- Highsmith, Annette Paris. *<u>Highsmiths in America; Descendants of Daniel Highsmith of Halifax County, North Carolina</u>, with Appendices of Unconnected Highsmith Families.* Provo, UT, Highsmith, 1971. 691p. DC gives 2 v. NG & DC give underscored part of title. [S1202; NG52; DC1775].

HILL -- Hill, George A. *Hill & Hill - Moberly Connections of Fairfield County, South Carolina.* Ponca City, OK, Hill, 1961. 326p. [D6104].

HILL -- Hill, Jobe. *The Jobe Hill Journal, Written about 1904.* Summerville, SC, Hill Family Organization, 1975. 82, 3, 10p., 1 leaf of plates. [S1209].

HILL -- Hill, Stuart H. *Some Allied Eastern North Carolina Families.* NP, 1946-1947. 3 v. [D6109].

HILL -- Hill, Stuart H. *The Hill Family of Bertie, Martin and Halifax Counties, North Carolina. Also Bryan, Whitmel, Blount, Norfleet, Pugh, Hall, Stuart, Weldon, Spruill, Long, Williams, Smith, Jacocks, and Other Allied Families of North Carolina and Virginia.* New York, NY, 1922-36. 4 vols. [X447-NY; VV94].

HILL -- Ivey, Thomas Neal. *Green Hill.* Oxford, NC, Priv. Print. by J. Edward Allen. 1927. 113, 1p. [L8279].

HILL -- McCarthy, Anne L. *The Hill Family of Chowan County, North Carolina.* Edina, MN, McCarthy Publications, 1990. 347p. [DC1786].

HINES -- Hines, Benjamin McFarland. *Hines and Allied Families: Some Descendants of William Hines of Sussex County, Virginia (ca. 1690-1760) and a Record of Their Principal Allied Families, Watson (Virginia, Mississippi) Shackelford, (Virginia, South Carolina, Georgia); Nisbet (North Carolina, Georgia); and Kennon (Virginia).* NP, Dorrance, 1981. vi, 259p., 9 pages of plates. [C322; NG52; VV95].

HINSON -- Whitaker, Mary Hinson. *Our Hinson Heritage in N.C. and S.C.* Monroe, NC, M.H. Whitaker, 1985. 217p. 1. Hinson family. 2.

South Carolina-Genealogy. 3. North Carolina-Genealogy. [G320].

HINTON -- Hinton, Judith Garner. *The Hintons of Nash and Johnson Counties, North Carolina..* Baltimore, MD, Gateway Press, 1990. 281p. 1. Hinton family. 2. North Carolina-Genealogy. [G320].

HINTON -- Hinto, M. H. *Hintons of Earlscote and Chilton Foliot.* Raleigh, NC, 1944. 27p. [X450-FW].

HITCHCOCK -- Hitchcock, Leon Whitney and Gertrude Hitchcock Mounsey. *Genealogical Records of William Hendee Hitchcock and His Descendants.* Durham, NC, 1971. 11 l. [S1214].

HOBBS -- Handley, Helen M. *Some Descendants of William and James Hobbs of North Carolina.* Berkeley, CA, H.M. Handley, 1984. 133, xvii pages. [DC1796].

HOBBS -- Hobbs, R.L. *Hobbs and Related Families.* Winnsboro, SC, Winnsboro Pr., 1976. 396 leaves. [X452-FW].

HOBBS -- Lewis, Ailine F. *The Hobbs: Jacob Henry... Millard F. and Allied Lines from N.C., Va., Ky. 1764-1987.* NP, Missouri, DAR 1987. 105 l. [DC1798].

HOBSON -- Davis, Earl H. *Hobson Descendants of George and Ethel Hobson, Virginia, North Carolina, Ohio, Indiana.* Long Beach, CA, Author, 1957. 323p. [X452-FW/MH].

HOCH -- Hoch, John Hampton. *Hoch - High Family in America; A Record of Some Hoch Immigrants and Their Descendants.* Charleston, SC, Issued by Hoch - High Family Reunion, 1962. iii, 170p. Also: *Supplement* by Fora H. Hoeffner, 1976. 48p. Typed. [X452-PH].

HOFFMAN -- Hoffman, Laban Miles. <u>Our Kin</u>; *Being a History of the Hoffman, Rhyne,*

Costner, Rudisill, Best, Hovis, Hoyle, Wills, Shetley, Jenkins, Holland, Hambright, Gaston, Withers, Cansler, Clemmer, and Lineberger Families. Charlotte, NC, Daniel E. Rhyne, Laban L. Jenkins, L.M. Hoffman, 1915 584p. D gives underscored part of title and 586p. [L8492; D6196].

HOFFMAN -- Hoffman, Max Ellis. *The Hoffmans of North Carolina; A Genealogical Presentation of the Original Hoffmans Who Settled in North Carolina.* In this the author gives a brief historical review of the European origin; the conditions which caused them to leave their native country; their migrations through Pennsylvania and Virginia to North Carolina and the Genealogical Development of their descendants to the present day.. Asheville, NC, Hoffman, 1938. 192p. [L8495; D6197].

HOGE -- Tyler, James Hoge. *A Genealogy. The Family of Hoge.* Greensboro, NC, James Fulton Hoge, 1927. 141p. D & NG give underscored part of title. X gives: Jos. J. Stone, Printers. [D6201; NG53; X454-PH].

HOGG -- Hitt, Susie Juanita. *Newton Thomas Hogg.* Newberry, SC, Sun Printing Co., 1970. 61p. [D6202].

HOGG -- Tyler, James Hoge. *The Family of Hoge.* Greensboro, NC, James Fulton Hoge, J.J. Stone & Co., Printers. 1927. 3, 141p. [L8500].

HODGES -- Bundy, V. Mayo. [G322]. See above: GOFF. [G263].

HOFFMAN -- Hoffman, Laban Miles. [G322]. See above: BEST. [G54].

HOFFMAN -- Hoffmann, Una McLeod. *Friedrich Hoffmann Family, 1845-1987.* __, SC, U.M. Hoffmann, 1987. xiv, 93 leaves. LC copy unbound phtocopy of typescript. 1. Hoffman family, 2. Hoffmann, Friedrich, 1845-1918-Family. [G322].

HOLBROOK -- NAS. *Joseph Halbrook(s) Born 9 April, 1781, N.C. Died 27 May, 1863, Mo. Son of John Holebrooke.* Birmingham, AL, W.B. Halbrooks, 1975. 49p., 2 leaves of plates. [S1226]

HOLLAND -- Holand, Irma Ragan. *The Hollands from Virginia to North Carolina.* NP, 197_. 144p. [D6224; VV95].

HOLLAND -- Holland, Mary Detus Deen. *Holland Genealogy.* NP, Holland, 1966. 64 leaves. v. 1: Deen, Miles, Kemp, Hall;. v. 3: A genealogy of the descendants of Jacob Carter of South Carolina; v. 4: A genealogy of the descendants of John Miles. [D6226].

HOLLEMAN -- Whitehurst, Anna Holleman. [G326]. See above: CHRISTOPHER. [G138].

HOLLER -- Atay, Joanne Holler, et al. *The Holler Family of Catawba and Iredell Counties, North Carolina.* NP, The Authors, 1990. xii, 115p. [DC1815].

HOLLOWELL -- Hollowell, Lucy Elliott. *The Hollowells.* Woodland, NC, Hollowell, 1969. 88 leaves. [D6245].

HOLMAN -- Holman, Olive B. *German-Swiss and Scotch-Irish Settlements in Souther Carolina. Brownlee - Holman and Collaterals.* Anderson, SC, 1937. 84 l. Typed. Includes Padgett, Caldwell, Acker, Brown, Hubbard, Waddell, Wannamaker, and Rumph Families. [L8552].

HOLMES -- Holmes, James G. *Holmes Family, Charles Town, South Carolina.* Charleston, SC, 1882. Broadside. [X458-MH].

HOLMES -- Linn, Jo White. [G327]. See above: HAYDEN. [G306; NGN17-1-91; DC1825].

HOLT -- Tatum, V. Holt (from notes provided by Madie Holt Black & others). *The Holt Family in Europe and American, 1248-1971; A*

Brief Account of the Genealogy, History, and Armory in England and Germany in Europe: Also in the State of Massachusetts, Connecticut, Virginia, North Carolina, Tennessee, Mississippi and Utah in America. Cincinnati, OH, 1971. 16p. [S1236; VV96].

HOO -- Ross, Robbie Lee Gillis. *Your Inheritance.* Matthews, NC, Delmar Print Co., 1972-1978. 2 v. [D6279].

HOOKER -- Maes, Virginia I. *The Descendants of Samuel Hooker of the Carolinas, Tennessee, Indiana and Illinois.* Rushville, IL, 1942. 8p, 12 numb. leaves. X gives just 8p. Reproduced from typed copy. [L8600; X462-OH].

HOOPER -- Alderman, Edward A. *Address on the Life of William Hooper, "The Prophet of American Independence." Guilford Battle Ground, July 4, 1894.* Chapel Hill, NC, University Press. 1894. 73p. Publ by the Guilford Battle Ground Company. [L8086].

HOPKINS -- Bruhn, Reva Hopkins. *Hopkins Forever: James Hopkins, Revolutionary Soldier, Virginia, North Carolina, Kentucky, Tennessee, Illinois, and Missouri.* Visalia, CA, R. H. Bruhn, 1984. ii, 74p. 110 pages of plates. [C332; VV96].

HOPKINS -- Hopkins, Laura Jervey. <u>*Lower Richland Planters*</u>*: Hopkins, Adams, Weston and Related Families of South Carolina.* Hopkins, SC, Hopkins, 1976. xi, 530p. D gives underscored part of title. [D6308; X464-FW/LA/NY].

HOPKINS -- Kincaid, Helen H. *Hopkins Hoax.* Williamston, NC, Kellogg Research, 1973. 288p. Concerns the Mark Hopkins Estate, 1813-1878. [X464-FW].

HOPPER -- Sturgill, Lorene Moxley. *Hoppers, Moxley, Toliver and Related Families.* Winston-Salem, NC, Hunter Pub. Co., 1985. 1.

Hopper family. 2. Hoppes family. 3. Moxley family. 4. Tolliver family. 5. North Carolina-Genealogy. [G330].

HOPPES -- Sturgill, Lorene Moxley. See above: HOPPER. [G330].

HORN -- Gillespie, Rollin Wilson. *The Descendants of Jesse Horn of Rutherford County, North Carolina.* McLean, VA, Gillespie, 1975. 86 leaves. [D6325].

HORNE -- Hyatt, Sybil. *Bible Record in Possession of Miss Della Hyatt, Tarboro, N.C.* Kinston, NC, 1943. 1 leaf. Typed. [L8649].

HORTON -- Barlowe, Texie Horton. *The Hortons of Western North Carolina.* Lenoir, NC, Barlowe, 1934. 77p. [D6341].

HORTON -- Evans, Reta M. *Descendant of David Horton of North Carolina.* Blacksburg, VA, Southern Print Co., 1987. 1. Horton family. 2. Horton, David, 1724-1784-Family. 3. North Carolina-Genealogy. [G331].

HORTON -- Outen, Lon D. *Hortons on Lynches River and Red Oak Woods Plantation.* Kershaw, SC, L.D. Outen, 1989. xvi, 284p. 1. Horton family. 2. South Carolina-Genealogy. [G331].

HOUSE -- Loeb, Helen House. *Source Records of the House, Houze, Howse, Jenkins and Clift Families of Maryland, Virginia, and North Carolina.* NP, Louisiana DAR, 1980. ??v. DAR library has v. 1. early members of the House family. [Dd6380; VV97].

HOUSTON -- DuPree, Garland Crowe. [G332]. See above: BOYD. [G79; DC1864].

HOUSTON -- DuPree, Garland Crowe. *People of Purpose: Dr. William Houston... Duplin County, North Carolina.* Fitzgerald, GA, Dupree, 1988, 1990. 2 v. DAR library holdings: v. 2. [DC1864].

HOUSTON -- Wood, Margarette Hall. [G333]. See above: DEAN. [G182].

HOWARD -- Padgett, Dora Adele. *The Howard Family of Ocracoke Island, N.C.* Washington, DC, 1955. 41 leaves. X gives 41 pages and date of 1954. [NG54; X471-FW].

HOWARD -- Padgett, Dora Adele. *William Howard, Last Colonial Owner of Ocracoke Island, North Carolina, His Family and Descendants.* Washington, DC, Padgett, 1974. NG gives underscored title & Padgett, WA[?], 117p. [S1264; NG54].

HOWE -- Whitley, Olga Mary Rolater. *Colonel Joseph Howe, York County, South Carolina: His Descendants and His Brothers.* Commerce, TX, 1960. 97 leaves. [L8760].

HOWE -- Whitley, Olga Rolater. *The Howe Line, Pennsylvania, South Carolina, Kentucky; With Connections, Dunlap, McKenzie, Patrick, and Biggers.* Commerce, TX, 1967. lix, 316 leaves. [L8763; VP110].

HOWELL -- Clark, Benjamin Clarence. *Barnabus and Martha Howell of Darlington County, South Carolina and some Descendants.* Santa Ana, CA, 1985. 22 leaves. [NG54].

HOWELL -- Clark, Betty Lane. *Joseph Howell Revolutionary Soldier of Old Barnwell District, SC.* NP, 1971. 163 l. [D6421].

HOWELL -- Tayloe, Margaret Howell. *Howell: One Southern U.S. Family: Joseph Howell of Concord, N.C., His Descendants and Some Related Families.* Tappahannock,VA, Margaret Howell Tayloe, 1986. i, 159 leaves. Spine Title: Howell - Stonemets - Kyler families. 1. Howell family. 2. Steinmetz family. 3. Koehler family. [G334].

HOWELL -- Tayloe, Margaret Howell. *Howell: One Southern U.S. Family: Joseph Howell of*

Concord, N.C... Revised edition. Tappahanock, VA, 1989. 139p. Revises Genealogy of the southern line of the family of Howell / Clark. [DC1875].

HOYLE -- Rucker, Elizabeth Hoyle. [L8801]. See above: HEYL. [L8305; D6043].

HUBBARD -- Wilson, Evelyn Hubbard. *Hubbard Family of Marlborough County, S.C.: Ancestors and Descendants of Laughlin Bouie Hubbard and Mary Adams Hubbard.* Winston-Salem, NC, F.M. Hubbard, 1988. 107p. [DC1882].

HUMBLE -- Smith, Ione R. Card. *David (H)umble (1775-) of Montgomery County, North Carolina, Salisbury District & Two of His Sons: Randle (H)umble (1821-1878) of North Carolina, Clay County, Indiana, and Marion County, Iowa, Benager (H)umble (1823-1894) of North Carolina, Owen County, Indiana & Marian & Pottawattamie Counties, Iowa & Their Descendants.* Elkhorn, NB, I.R.C. Smith 1988. iii, 96 leaves. [G337].

HUGER -- Brown, Thomas L. *Descendants of John Huger of South Carolina, Son of the Emigrant, Daniel Huger.* Charleston, WV, 1911. 3p. VV omits author. [L8850; VV98].

HUGER -- Juger, Mary Esther. *The Recollection of a Happy Childhood.* Pendelton, SC, Research and Publication Committee, Foundation for Historic Restoration in Pendleton Area, 1976. 85p. [D6488].

HUGER -- Wells, T. Tileston. *The Hugers of South Carolina.* New York, NY, Priv. Print. 1931. Includes an account of Francis Kinloch Huger's Participation in an Attempt to Liberate Lafayette from the Austrian Prison of Olmütz. [L8851]. (Version in French) [L8852]).

HUGHES -- Hughes, David D. *Hughes and Allied Families.* Charleston, SC, Garnier & Co., 1968. 239p. [X475-NY].

HUGHES -- Hughes, Lydia Annie and Richard Hughes Sullivan. *Hughes Family of Kentucky and Virginia.* Columbia, SC, 1920. 48p. Previously Published in 1902. [L8858; X475-FW; VV98].

HUGUENIN -- Davis, Harry Alexander. *Some Hugenot Families of South Carolina and Georgia; Supplement number 2: David Huguenin, Gideon Mallet, Francois Gabriel Ravot.* Washington, DC, 1937. 1p, 85 numb. leaves. Mimeographed. [L8867].

HUMPHREY -- Abee, Blanche Humphrey. *Colonists of Carolina in the Lineage of Hon. W. D. Humphrey. Also Thomas Family.* Richmond, VA, William Byrd Press, Inc., 1938. 259p. NG lists as HUMPHRIES. D & VV give underscored title. D notes: Index by Catherin Brumbaugh, bound separately." [NG55; D6517; VV99].

HUMPHREY -- Holcomb, Brent. *Ancestors and Descendants of Charles Humphries (d. 1837) of Union District, South Carolina, 1677-1874: Including Records from Virginia, North Carolina, South Carolina, Mississippi, and Other States.* Columbia, SC, 1985. 228p. NG lists as HUMPHRIES. [NG55; VV99].

HUMPHREY -- Humphries, J(ohn) D(avid). *Descendants of Charles Humphries of Virginia, Nathaniel Pope of Virginia, Reuben Brock I of Ireland and Aaron Parker of Virginia.* Atlanta, GA, 1938. 63p. L gives: "This booklet intended as a supplement to 'Georgia Descendants of Nathaniel Pope of Virginia, John Humphries of South Carolina, and Allen Gay of North Carolina' published by John D. Humphries, July, 1934". [L8906; NG55; VV99].

HUMPHRIES -- Humphries, John David. *Descendants of Charles Humphries of Virginia, Nathaniel Pope of Virginia, Reuben Brock of Ireland and Aaron Parker of Virginia.* Altanta, GA, 1938. 63p. [NG55].

HUNT -- Banister, Eme O. *Hunt Fishing.* Anderson, SC, 1967. 2 v. [D6535].

HUNT -- Banister, Eme O. *Hunt Hunting; Several Hunt Family Lineages.* Anderson, SC, Priv. Print., 1966/ 1 vol. in 2 (various pagings). Additions and Corrections, 1967. 54 leaves. [X479-FW/NY].

HUNT -- Kellam, Ida Brooks. *Hunt Family Records.* Wilmington, NC, Kellam, 1959. 42 leaves. [D6543].

HUNT -- Wyman, T. B. *Genealogy of the Name and Family of Hunt.* Charleston, SC, Garnier, 1969. xv, 414p. [D6551].

HUNTER -- NAS. *Address of Joseph M. Morehead on the Life and Times of James Hunter, 'General' of the Regulators; of Professor J.M. Weatherly on the Presentation of David Clarks's Portrait of John Penn; and of Hon. Charles M. Stedman on the Dedication of the Schenck Museum, Guilford Battle Ground, July 3, 1987 [sic].* Greensboro, NC, Guilford Battle Ground Co., 1897. 66p. [D6553].

HUNTER -- Barekman, June B. *Hunters of Early Rowan Co., North Carolina; from Records in the McCubbins Files and Court Records, Salisbury, N.C.* Chicago, IL, Barekman, 1971. 21 leaves. D gives underscored part of title and date of 1972. [S1288; D6555].

HUNTER -- Briggs, Willis G. *Hunters of Wake County, N. C.* Raleigh, NC, 1940. 16p. [X480-FW].

HUNTER -- Hollingsworth, Leon Stephens. *A History of the Origin and Development of Our Family in America and a Genealogy of the Descendants of John Hunter, II..* Greenville, SC, Hunter History Publishing Commitee, 1952. 176p. Cover Title: Hunters Then and Now. [L8952].

HUNTER -- Hunter, Walter M. *The Hunters of Bedford County, Virginia; Notes and Documents on the Family of James Hunter, Regulator Leader of N.C. Including Forebears in Pennsylvania, Virginia, North Carolina, Louisiana and Texas.* Cottonport, LA, Polyanthos, 1973. 296p. X gives: "..Medford County, Virginia"[?]. [NG55: X480-FW/LA/NY; VV101].

HUNTER -- Hunter, William May. *The Hunter Family.* Charlotte, NC, Observer Printing House. 1920. 144p. [D6563].

HUNTINGTON -- Hogan, William Johnston. *Huntington Silversmiths, 1763-1885.* Durham, NC, Sir Walter Press, 1977. 136p. [D6567].

HUNTLEY -- Huntley, Virgil W. *Thomas Huntley, Sr. of Anson County, North Carolina: His Descendants in the Carolinas and Elsewhere.* Mystic, CT, V.W. Huntley, 1988. 1. Huntley family. 2. Huntley, Thomas, ca. 1745-1802-Family. 3. North Carolina-Genealogy. [G338].

HURT -- Blevins, Ray E. *Hurts from South Carolina to Wayne County, Kentucky.* Johnson City, TN, Overmountain Press, 1989. 216p. 1. Hurt family. 2. South Carolina-Genealogy. 3. Kentucky-Genealogy. [G339].

HUTCHINS -- Bugg, William Emmanuel. [G339]. See above: BUGG. [G105].

HUTCHINS -- Townsend, Rita Hineman. *Hutchins - Hutchens, Descendants of Strangeman Hutchins, Born 1707, of the James River in Virginia and Surry (Yadkin) County, North Carolina.* Baltimore, MD, Gateway Press, 1979. 908p. [NG56; VV101].

HUTCHINSON -- Hutchinson, Frederick McAlpine. *The Hutchinson Family of Laurens County, South Carolina and Descendants.*

Houston, TX, Anson Jones Press, 1947. 263p. [D6609].

HYER -- NAS. *Progeny Record of John Henry Hyer, Charleston, South Carolina.* NP, n.d. Unpaged. [X484-FW].

I

INABNIT -- Lefvendahl, Georgie Inabinet Adams. *The Inabnit Family of South Carolina; Some of the Inabnit, Inabnet, Inabinet and Inabinett Families of Colletion, Charleston and Lower Orangeburgh Districts and Counties.* Orangeburg, SC, Culler, Lefvendahl, 1970. 3 v. pni. A does not indicate numb. of vols. DAR library has v. 3 only. D gives underscored part of title. [A342; D6646].

INNES -- Martin, Elizabeth Innis. *Innis - Lane Genealogy: Charles Lane Innis, Sr., the Only Direct Male Descendant and Progeny of William Porterfield Innis and Jessie May Lane.* Tryon, NC, E.I. Martin, 1988. 226p. 1. Innes family. 2. Lane family. 3. Innis, Charles Lane, 1905-1966-Family. 4. Innis, William Porterfield, 1894-1932-Family. [G341].

IRVING -- Irving, Wm. H. [X489-FW]. See above: FUNDY. [X489-FW].

IRWIN -- Ervin, Sam(uel) J., Jr. *Ervins of Williamsburg County, South Carolina.* NP, 1972. 1 v. (unpaged). 1. Irwin family. [G342].

IRWIN -- Ervin, Sam(uel) J. *Ervins of South Carolina.* Morgantown, NC, S.H. Ervin, 1980. 1 v. (various foliations). Rev. and enl. ed. of: Ervins of Williamsburg County, South Carolina. 1972. 1. Irwin family. 2. South Carolina-Genealogy. [G342].

ISBELL -- Kruemcke, M. R. *Isbell Family of Virginia, North Carolina, South Carolina,*

Georgia, and Texas. NP, 1986. 50 leaves. [DC1960].

ISLER -- Hyatt, Sybil. *Descendants of Christian Isler.* Southern Pines, NC, 1915. 1 leaf. Reprinted from The Free Press. [X490-NY].

ISLER -- Hyatt, Sybil. *Isler (Family).* Kinston, NC, 1943. 1p, 7 numb. leaves. Typed. "(Records) collected by Sybil Hyatt, Kinston, N.C., in 1914, and given to the North Carolina Society of the Descendants of the Palatines. Compiled October 1, 1943. [L9136].

IVEY -- Ivey, George Franks. *The Ivey Family in the United States.* Hickory, NC, Southern Pub. Co., 1941. 5, 113p. [L9139; D6691].

J

JACKSON -- Haemmel, W. G. *Jackson and Related Families: 300 Years in America, a Genealogical and Biographical Compilation.* Waynesville, NC, 1972. 172p. [X492-FW].

JACOBS -- Jacobs, Thornwell. *My People.* Clinton, SC, 1954. 79p. [X493-FW].

JACOBS -- Symmonds, Dorothy. *A History and Genealogy of the Pritchett, Rimmer, Jacobs, Hamilton, Eldridge, Etheridge, Smith, Brown, and Davidson Families from North Carolina, Tennessee, Illinois, Missouri, and Kansas in the Early 1800s to 1900s.* Bellaire, TX, D. Symonds, c1985-<c1989 >. v. <1-2 >. Vol. 2 has title: A history of the genealogy of the families of Howland, Brown, Follett, Van Dyke, Lamb, Spaulding, and Davidson with related lines of Tret, Botsford, Parker, Burwell, Clark, Andrews, Symmonds, Burnaman, Ashbaugh, and Smith from Holland, England, Scotland, and France to Massachusetts,

Connecticut, New York, New Jersey, Ohio, Iowa, Indiana, Nebraska, Kansas, and Texas from "The Mayflower" pilgrims in 1620 to the 1980s. 1. Pritchard family. 2. Rimmer family. 3. Jacobs family. DC lists as: PRITCHETT. [G345; DC2965].

JACOCKS -- Jacocks, William Picard. *Descendants of Thomas Jacocks.* Chapel Hill, NC, Jacocks, 1957. 89 l. [L9177; D6725].

JARNIGAN -- Powers, Lee Leeper. *Captain Thomas Jarnigan, 1746-1802.* Lake Lure, NC, Powers, 1978. x, 102p. [DS388].

JARRETT -- Speegle, Charles Martin. *The Spiegel Family and Their Kin: Including the Jarrets, Lentzs, Epplers, Cobbs, Massengils, Thomases, Coopers, McGees, Alexanders, McCoys, and Millers: and Records of the Zion Evangelical Lutheran Church of Catawba County, North Carolina: A Story of Migrants to the West.* Fayetteville, NC, Historic Records Pub. Co. of Fayetteville, 1986- v. <1 >. 1. Spiegel family. 2. Jarrett family. 3. Lentz family. 4. Zion Evangelical Lutheran Church (Hickory, N.C.)-Registers. DC lists under SPIEGEL & gives underscored title. [G346; DC3427].

JEFFCOAT -- Jeffcoat, Mrs. Wilson (Vera Rell Spires). *Seed of Jacob Jeffcoat Family, History and Genealogy. - 1st ed.* West Columbia, SC, Wentworth, Print. 1975. xi, 269, 18 leaves of plates. [S1337].

JEFFERIES -- Jefferies, James L. *The Jefferies Pioneers and Their Descendants of Union and Cherokee Cos., S.C.* NP, 1941-43. Typescript. pni. [D6757].

JENKINS -- Keith, Frances Peale, ED . *The Stephen Jenkins, Senior Family, 1775-1988: 203 Years of Jenkins Heritage.* __, NC, The Stephen Jenkins, Senior Executive Committee, 1988- . v.<1 >. 1. Jenkins family.

2. Jenkins, Stephen, 1810-1899-Family. [G347].

JENKINS -- Bowen, Nettie Jenkins. *The Jenkins Family of Virginia and North Carolina and three Allied Families: Yarboro, Crask, and Cook.* Raleigh, NC, M. Bowen Moore, 1966. 152p. [L9254; VV104].

JENKINS -- Jenkins, James. *Experience, Labours, and Gospel Sufferings of Rev. James Jenkins, of the South Carolina Conference.* [NGN-18-4-92].

JENKINS -- Rhyne, Martha McJunkin. *McJunkin- A Family of Memories.* Greenville, SC, M.M. Rhyne, 1989. viii, 188p. 1. Jenkins family. 2. South Carolina-Genealogy. [G347].

JERNIGAN -- Powers, Lee Leeper. *Captain Thomas Jarnagin, 1746-1802: The Story of One of Tennesssee's Early Pioneers and His Wife Mary Witt Jarnagin, 1753-1829. Enl. and corr. ed.* Lake Lure, NC, Powers, 1978. x, 209p. 1. Jarnagin, Thomas, 1746-1802-Family. 2. Jaragin, Mary Witt, 1752-1829-Family. 3. Hamblen County (Tenn.)-Biography. 4. Pioneers-Tennessee-Hamblem County-Biography. 5. Jernigan family. 6. Witt family. [G349].

JERNIGAN -- Powers, Lee Leeper. *Captain Thomas Jarnagin, 1746-1802: The Story of One of Tennesssee's Early Pioneers and His Wife Mary Witt Jarnagin, 1753-1829. Enl. and corr. ed.* Lake Lure, NC, Powers, 1985. x, 326p. 1. Jarnagin, Thomas, 1746-1802-Family. 2. Jaragin, Mary Witt, 1752-1829-Family. 3. Hamblen County (Tenn.)-Biography. 4. Pioneers-Tennessee-Hamblem County-Biography. 5. Jernigan family. 6. Witt family. [G349].

JERNIGAN -- Worley, Lillian J. *Jernigan Reunion; A Gathering of Some Descendants of Thomas Jernigan, Immigrant 1635 to Nansemond*

County, Virginia... Clinton, NC, 1971. xxiv or xxv, 229p. D gives underscored title. [D6787; X499-NY; VV105].

JEWETT -- Moore, Joanne Cullom. *Some History and Genealogy ofthe Jouett Family.* Frenchman's Bayou, AK, J.C. Moore, 1988. 33 leaves. 1. Jewett family. 2. Virginia-Genealogy. 3. North Carolina-Genealogy. 4. Tennessee-Genealogy. [G350].

JOHNSON -- NAS. *History of the Johnson Family.* Dunn, NC, Upchurch Printing Co., 1939. 78p. [D6817].

JOHNSON -- Davis, Annie Dent. *Abraham Johnson and Descendants.* Greensboro, NC, Fitchfotolith Service, 1939. 1p, 64 numb. leaves. [L9346].

JOHNSON -- Johnson, C. B. *Brief History of the Descendants of Samuel Johnson, Founder of the Cape-Fear River Johnsons.* Champagne, IL, Times job. pr., n.d. 29p. [X504-FW].

JOHNSON -- Johnson, Falba Love. *Johnson - McCall and Related Families.* Columbia, SC, R.L. Bryan, 1979. xiv, 328p. [DC2003].

JOHNSON -- Powers, Mary Rebecca Watson (Mrs. James Alderman Powers. *Johnsons of Argyll... Our Clan of Johnsons (Argyll, Scotland and America).* Kingston, NC, Powers, 1940. 126p. D gives underscored part of title. [L9350; D6852].

JOHNSON -- Reynolds, Katherine. *Some Descendants of Gideon Johnson, Sr. of Virginia and North Carolina.* NP. 1966. 3 v. [D6854; VV105].

JOHNSON -- Weight, Verl F. *Captain Samuel Johnson of Wilkes County, North Carolina: Ancestry and Descendants.* Carmichael, CA, V.F. Weight, 1988- . v. <1- >. Contents: v. 1. Descendants of Robert and

Celia Bourne Johnson. 1. Johnson family. 2. Johnson, Samuel, 1757-1834-Family. 3. North Carolina-Genealogy. [G353; NGN16-6-90].

JOHNSTON -- NAS. *The Spur and the Phoenix: The Newsletter of Clan Johnston in America.* Hemingway, SC, 1977- . _v. Quarterly, See DAR shelflist for library holdings. [DC2017].

JOHNSTONE -- Johnstone, James D. *The Johnstone Papers.* Georgetown, SC, Johnstone, 1975. 1 v. (various foliations). [D6879].

JOLLEY -- Duncan, Constance J. *Through Tinted Lenses, A True Historical Narrative of the Willis Alexander Jolley Family in Rutherford, N.C.* Spruce Pine, NC, 1959. 124p. [X505-FW].

JONES -- Cunningham, Caroline. *Jones Records.* Raleigh, NC, Cunningham, 1964. 137p. L omits pagination. [L9443; D6896].

JONES -- Ewing, Evelyn Jones. *Joseph Jones of Gates County, North Carolina: Ancestors and Descendants, 1635-1985.* Emporia, VA?, 1985. pni. [VV106].

JONES -- Hooker, Ruth N. *Jones of Albermarle in Carolina.* Memphis, TN, 1948. 24 leaves. [X506-MH].

JONES -- Hosier, Scott Foye. *The History of Jacob Jones of Franklin Co., N.C., and His Descendants.* [NGN18-3-92].

JONES -- Jones, Colonel Cadwallader. *A Genealogical History.* Columbia, SC, A. I. Robertson (Ye Bryan Printing Co.) 1900. vii, 73p. [L9403; D6907].

JONES -- Jones, Hazel Parker. <u>The History of the Samuel Jones Family</u>, *Kershaw County, S.C., 1756-1960 Including Allied Families.* Kershaw, SC, Jones, 1961. 180p. D gives underscored part of title: [L9437; D6913].

JONES -- Jones, Mary Eloise. *History of Jeremiah Jones of Orangeburg District, South Carolina.* Columbia, SC, R.L. Bryan, 1967. xv, 283p. [D6921; X508-FW].

JONES -- Jones, Walter B. *John Burgwin Carolinian * * * John Jones Virginian, etc.* Montgomery, AL, 1913. pni. [VV107].

JONES -- Jones, Wilburn L. *William and Robert Jones and Alvin Wooten Families of North Carolina, 1804-1989.* NP, 1990. 146 leaves. [DC2029].

JONES -- Hoffmann, Una McLeod. *Abel Samuel Jones Family, 1215-1990.* Lexington, SC, U.M. Hoffmann, 1990. iv, 183, 24p. of plates. 1. Jones family. 2. Jones, Abel Samuel, 1818-1879-Family. 3. McLeod family. 4. South Carolina-Genealogy. [G353].

JORDAN -- Purvis, Frankie Jordan. *Jordan Tracks and Trails.* Albany, GA, F. J. Purvis, 1988. 141p. 1. Jordan family. 2. Alabama-Genealogy. 3. South Carolina-Genealogy. [G355].

JORDAN -- Zoellner, L. R. *Jordan Family of Virginia and North Carolina.* Los Angeles, CA, 1945. 29p. [X509-LA; VV107].

JOYNER -- Joyner, Ulysses P. *Joyner of Southampton. Thomas Joyner of Isle of Wight County, VA, and His Descendants in Eastern VA and NC.* Orange, VA, 1975. 233p. [NG58].

JULIAN -- Hine, Frances J. *Julian Family.* Winston-Salem, NC, Julien de Roquetaillade, 1974. vi, 92p. [X511-FW].

K

KAY -- Kay, William D. *The Descendants of John Kay, 1777-1855, Abbeville County, South*

Carolina. Ann Arbor, MI, McNaughton and Gunn, 1984. 136p. 1. Kay family. 2. Kay, John, 1777-1855-Family. [G360].

KEITH -- Henderson, Marion Elizabeth Freeman. *Of Keith & Kin.* Charlotte, NC, M.E.F. Henderson, 1987. vi, 162p., 2 leaves of plates. 1. Keith family. 2. Scotland-Genealogy. 3. Great Britain-Genealogy. [G361].

KELLER -- Keller, Andrew King. *The Ancestors and Descendants of Andrew King Keller and Marie Trapper.* Surfside Beach, SC, 1987. v, 149p. 1. Keller family. 2. Trapper family. 3. Keller, Andrew King, 1922- -Family. 4. Trapper, Ann Marie, 1922- -Family. [G361; NG59].

KELLER -- Keller, Andrew King. *Descendants of the Kellers of Leemersheim, Kuhardt and Neupfotz, Rhineland-Pfolz, Germany.* Surfude (sic) Beach, SC, 1987. 2v. [NG59].

KELLY -- Van Staaveren, Elizabeth Kelly. *David Kelly, 1763-1838 and William Warren Kelly, 1807-1882 of Darlington County, South Carolina and Bradford County, Florida.* Alexandria, VA, E.K. Van Staaveren, 1990. xi, 295p. [DC2070].

KELSEY -- Kelsey, Mavis Parrott. *Samuel Kelso / Kelsey, 1720-1796: Scotch-Irish Immigrant and Revolutionary Patriot of Chester County, SC. Also Mills, Gill, Pagan, Wylie, Morrow, Jones, Sealy, Jaggers, Reeves, Mauldin, Moore, Stevenson, McAlexander Fam.* Houston, TX, 1984. 683p. [NG59].

KENNEDY -- Brown, Leslie. *Kennedy Sketches.* Warsaw, NC, 1943. 12p. [X519-MH/NY].

KENNEDY -- Kennedy, Gayle Marie. *My Kennedy Ancestors of Fairfield County, South Carolina.* Spartanburg, SC, Kennedy, 1969. 77 leaves. [D7072].

KENNEDY -- Kennedy, John T. *The Kennedy Family; A Brief Record of the Kennedy Family of Lenoir and Wayne Counties, North Carolina.* Columbia, SC, 1963. v, 97p. [L9611; D7075].

KEPPEL -- NAS. *Some Early Keppel Families: Keppel's of Pennsylvania, Maryland, North Carolina. Various Spellings: Keppel, Keppele, Kepple, Kappel, Koeppel, Koppel, Copple, Coppel, etc.* Hollis, NY, 1952. Unpaged. [L9636; VP122].

KERN -- Garrard, Mary Margaret Kern. *The Kern Family of Rowan County, North Carolina; Nicholas County, Kentucky; Boone, Clinton, Lawrence, Monroe Counties, Indiana; Hancock County, Illinois; Lee County, Iowa.* NP, 1968. 53p. [L9643; D7094].

KERR -- Kerr, Alexa McColl. *The Family of George Bigger Kerr, 1919-1981.* Bennettsville, SC, A.M. Kerr, 1985. vii, 120 leaves, 6p. of plates. 1. Kerr family. 2. Kerr, George Bigger, 1919-1981-Family. [G366].

KERSHNER -- Kerschner, George C. *History of the Kershner Family of Windsor, Twp., Berks Co., Pennsylvania.* Charlotte, NC, Kershner Family Association, 1983. iv, 146p. [DC2088].

KERSHNER -- Kershner, W. E. Ed. *Kershner Kinfolk.* Charlotte, NC, Kershner Family Association, 1982- . __ v. See DAR shelflist for library holdings. [DC2089].

KEY -- Padgett, Irene Frances Key. *Key Is My Name.* Shelby, NC, Padget, 1980. 157p. [D7127].

KILLEBREW -- Harper, James E. [G368]. See above: HARPER. [G300].

KILLIAN -- NAS. *The History of the Killian Family in North Carolina.* Newton, NC, 1940. 20 leaves. [X524-MH/NY].

KILLIAN -- Killian, George W. *The Killian Family and Particularly the Ancestors and Descendants of Andreas Killiam, 1702-1785. Arrived in America 23 September, 1732.* Rochester, NY, 1 v. (unpaged). Contents: The History of the Killiam Family in North Carolina by J.Y. Killian, Killian in Europe by C.H. Killian. Account of Talk at the unveiling of the Andreas Killian Memorial on 19 October, 1952, by C.H. Killian. Colonial Killians and their families, by C.H. Killian. An essay about Phillip Killian, a grandson of Andreas through John, by C.H. Killian. Andreas Killian and some of his descendants in Georgia, by T.C. Killian. Killians and the Mormon Church from 1942 minutes by G.W. Killian. Wills and Miscellaneous. Cletus Killin's comments after reading the History of the Killiam Family in North Carolina by C.H. Killian. [L9695].

KILLIAN -- Killian, J. Yates. *The History of the Killian Family in North Carolina.* NP, 1955. 27p. X omits author, gives Newton, NC, and 26p. [D7149; X524-FW].

KINCAID -- Kincaid, Clyde Edward. *Kincaid: The Family of John Kincaid Sr. (1710-1811) and Kincaids of the Carolinas and Virginia with Expanded Research in Burke and Cladwell Counties, North Carolina.* Asheville, NC, 1983. pni. [VV110].

KINDLEY -- Black, Fleta K. *Supplement to the William Kindley Genealogy.* __, NC, F.K. Black, 1986. xi, 396p. Supplement to: The William Kindley family genealogy. Bessie Jewel Mayes Wimberly. 1. Kindley family. 2, Kindley, William, 1792-1858-Family. [G369].

KING -- NAS. *History of William King, Jr., His Foregathers, Descendants.* Darlington, SC, The New and Press, 1961. 148p. [D7182].

KING -- Blankenship, Gayle King. *Families of Warren, Franklin & Granville Counties, North*

Carolina & Virginia Ancestry: King, Tharrington, Shearin, & Timberlake. Poquoson, VA, G.K. Blankenship, 1989. v, 203p. 1. King family. 2. Timberlake family. 3. Torrington family. 4. Shearin family. 5. Timberlake family(sic). 6. Virginia-Genealogy. 7. North Carolina-Genealogy. DC gives underscored title. [G369; DC2104].

KING -- King, Henry Lee. *A King Genealogy: Some Descendants of Michael King of Nansemond County, Virginnia, 1667-1987.* Cary, NC, H.L. King, 1988 2 v. in 1. 1. King family. 2. King, Michael, d. 1700-Family. 3. Southern States-Genealogy. [G370].

KING -- King, William A. *"Grandfather" Robert King, 1750(56) - 1826.* Anderson, SC, J.M. King, 1937. 3 leaves. [X526-NY].

KING -- Newman, Chapman H. *A Brief History of George King (1760-1820) of Lower Chesterfield County, S.C. and His Descendants.* McBee, SC, 1955. 48 leaves. [DC2106].

KING -- Turner, Louise King. *Descendants of William Albert King and Elizabeth Helen Harris King.* Durham, NC, Turner, 1986. 35 leaves. [DC2107].

KING -- Wilson, Reba S. *Lees and Kings of Virginia and North Carolina, 1636-1976.* Ridgely, TN, Wilson and Glover Pub. Co., 1975. 185p. NG gives: "also by Betty S. Glover". D lists under LEE. X indicates 2 leaves of plates. [NG62; D7572; X527-FW/SL; VV110].

KINNICK -- Waggener, Nettie Edna. *The Kinnick Family. A Genealogical History of the Kinnick Family of America; Descendants of John Kinnick and Ann Kinnick of Davie County, North Carolina.* Franklin, IN, 1953. xix, 355p. [L9781].

KINSEY -- Hyatt, Sybil. *Kinsey, Jones County, North Carolina.* Kinston, NC, 1948. Typed. 8 leaves. [L9785].

KINSLER -- Beckham, William Kinsler. *The Kinslers of South Carolina.* Columbia, SC, 1964. 90p. [L9786; NG60; D7209].

KIRKLAND -- Green, Mrs. Robert L, et al. *Kirkland Source Book of Records.* Greenwood, SC, 1977-<1988 > v. <1-2 >. [G371].

KIRKLAND -- Anderson, Jean Bradley. *The Kirklands of Ayr Mount.* Chapel Hill, NC, University of North Carolina Press, 1990. 1. Kirkland family. 2. Ayr Mount (N.C.) 3. Dwellings-North Carolina-Orange County. 4. Plantations-North Carolina-Orange County. 5. Orange County (N.C.)-Biography. 6. Orange county (N.C.)-Genealogy. 7. Plantation Owners-North Carolina-Orange County-Biography. [G371].

KIRKPATRICK -- Kirkpatrick, Martin Glen. *John and Priscilla Kirkpatrick of Prince William County, Va., and Their Descendants; Records.* Skyland, NC, 1959. pni. [VV111].

KIRKPATRICK -- Kirkpatrick, Melvin E. *A Kirkpatrick Genealogy, Being an Account of the Descendants of the Family of James Kirkpatrick of South Carolina, ca. 1715-1786.* Bloomington, MN, M.E. Kirkpatrick, 1985. 17, 231, 42p., 20p. of plates. NG gives underscored titled and 231p. 1. Kirkpatrick family. 2. Kirkpatrick, James, ca. 1715-1786-Family. [G371: NG60].

KIRKPATRICK -- Stone, Mrs. L. H. *The Family of John Kirkpatrick, Revolutionary Soldier of Charlotte, North Carolina, and Related Families.* NP, 1944. 65 leaves. [D7233].

KIRKPATRICK -- Warren, Jean Pressley. [G372]. See above: HARRIS. [G301].

KITTRELL -- Alexander, Mrs. U. B. *Our Family Mosaic; (the Kitrells, the Earls, the Joneses, Gills, Ellingtons, Rowlands, Mitchells, Fullers, Youngs, and Others.* Kittrell, NC, 1959. 40p. [L9831].

KLEIN -- Cline, Archey Campbell. *Descendants of Michael Klein.* Charlotte, NC, Crabtree Press, 1973. 270p. [NG60; X532-FW/NY/PH].

KLOTZ -- Kluttz, Ralph Dean. *The Descendants of Johann Jacob Klotz in America, 1690-1990: Kluttz, Klutts, Kluts, Clutts, Clutz.* Salisbury, NC, R.D. Kluttz, 1990. xxv, 546, 64p. 1. Klotz family. 2. Klotz, Johann Jacob, b. 1690-Family. [G373].

KNIPPERS -- Knippers, Prentiss A. *Descendants of Thomas Theopolus Knippers and Margaret Deseria Lambert of Holland, South Carolina and Allied Families.* Tylertown, MS, Knippers, 1983. 338p. [DS413].

KNOTT -- Amato, Irene E. *William and Eleanor Nutt of Virginia and Carolina: Their Descendants and Allied Families.* Carson City, NV, 1977. pni. [VV111].

KNOTT -- Knotts, Robert Homer. *Knotts Family Records.* Salisbury, NC, R.H. Knotts, 2 v. (535p). (Michael Thorn & Sarah Knotts; v. 8, section 1-2). 1. Knott family. [G374].

KNOX -- Goodman, Hattie S. *The Knox Family; A Genealogical and Biographical Sketch of the Descendants of John Knox of Rowan County, North Carolina, and Other Knoxes.* Richmond, VA, Whittset & Shepperson, 1905. 2, 266p. [L9899; VV111].

KOONTZ -- Koontz, Douglas J. *The Koontz and Leonard Families in Davidson County, North Carolina.* Winston-Salem, NC, Koontz, 1976. 49 leaves. [D7315].

KORNER -- Körner, Jules Gilmer. *Joseph of Kernersville, Being the Story of the Families Körner - Kerner, Kastner, Spach, Gardner, Pike, and Weisner and Their Descendants in the Town of Kernersville, North Carolina.* Durham, NC, Seeman Printery, 1958. xxii, 215p. D gives underscored part of title. [L9915; D7318].

KRESS -- NAS. *The Descendents[sic] of Johann Nicholaus Heinrich Kress (Cress).* Indian Trail, NC, B.J. Cruse, Jr., 1987. xxiii, 559p. 1. Kress family. [G378].

KUNKEL -- Kunkle, James m, and Doris M. *History of the Kunkle Name.* Fort Mills, SC, J.M. Kunkle, 1975. 115 leaves. [S1494].

KYLE -- Kellough, Gene Ross. *The Ancestry of Gene Ross: Including the Ross Line and Associated Lines of Bennett, Grimes, Llewellyn, Knighton, Turnbull, and Kyle. Including Wills, Letters, and Contents of Kyle Estate Sale, Plus "Samplings" the Account of Growing Up in Texas.* Sececa, SC, G.R. Kellough, 1986. xvi, 137, 152p., 5p. of plates. 1. Ross family. 2. Turnbull family. 3. Kyle family. 4. Kellough, Gene Ross-Childhood and youth. 5. Kerens(Tex.)-Biography. 6. Kerens(Tex.)-Social life and customs. [G381].

L

LACKEY -- Lackey, Mrs. Jay and Mrs. H.G. Duncan. *A History of the Lackey Family.* Wilkesboro, NC, 1962. 59p. [L9956].

LaFEVER -- LaFever, Ira C. *LaFever.* Columbus, NC, LaFever, 1964. 100p. [D7365].

LAFITTE -- Davis, Harry Alexander. *Some Hugenot Families of South Carolina and*

Georgia, Peter Lafitte, Andre Verdier, Samuel Montague, Henri Francois Bourguin, Peter Papot, Benjamin Godin. Washington, DC, 1926. 1p., 59 numb leaves. [L9974].

LAFITTE -- Davis, Harry Alexander. *Some Hugenot Families of South Carolina and Georgia, Peter Lafitte, Andre Verdier, Samuel Montague, Henri Francois Bourguin, Peter Papot, Benjamin Godin.* Washington, DC, 1927. 1p., 78 numb leaves. [L9975].

LAMBERT -- Doggett, Mary Norton and Sophie S. Martin. *The Lambert / Lambeth Family of North Carolina.* Greensboro, NC, Lambeth Family Convention. 1974, x, 945p. [S1506; NG61; D7389; X547-FW/SP].

LANCASTER -- Watson, Ruth Lancaster Trowell. [G385]. See above: HAZELWOOD. [G308].

LANDER -- Sherrill, William L. *A Brief History of Rev. Samuel Lander, Senior, and His Wife, Eliza Ann (Miller) Lander... Their Two Sons William and Samuel Lander and Their Grandson Samuel A. Weber.* Greensboro, NC, The Advocate Press, 1918. 63, 1p. [L10036].

LANE -- Martin, Elizabeth Innis. [G386]. See above: INNES. [G341].

LANE -- Haywood, Marshall DeLancy. *Joel Lane, Pioneer and Patriot. A Biographical Sketch Including Notes About the Lane Family and the Colonial and Revolutionary History of Wake County, North Carolina.* Raleigh, NC, Alfred Bynum & Christophers, 1900. 30p. [L10053].

LANE -- Haywood, Marshall DeLancy. *Joel Lane, Pioneer and Patriot. A Biographical Sketch Including Notes About the Lane Family and the Colonial and Revolutionary History of Wake County, North Carolina.* Raleigh, NC, Alfred Williams & Co., 2d ed. Rev. 1925. 30p. [L10057].

LANE -- Haywood, Marshall DeLancy. *Joel Lane, Pioneer and Patriot.* Raleigh, NC, Alfred Williams & Co., 1925, c1900. 30p. [D7420].

LANE -- Simon, Marilyn Lane. *The Ancestry and Known Descendants of Joseph Lane, 1770-1850 of Marion County, South Carolina, and Simpson County, Mississippi.* NP, 1986. iii leaves, 470p. 1. Lane family. 2. Lane, Joseph, 1770-1850-Family. [G386].

LANEY -- Funderburk, Guy B. *Laney: Lineage and Legacy.* Monroe, NC, Carey Press, 1974. 303p. [S1515].

LANGSTON -- Langston, Carroll Spencer. *Descendants of Solomon Langston of Laurents County, South Carolina, Through His Son, Bennett. Rev. and Partly Brought Up to Date.* Williamsville, IL, 1969. 57 leaves. 1. Langston family (Solomon Langston, 1732-1825). [G387; A383].

LANIER -- Sawyer, Mamie Chambers. *The Lanier Family of France, England, Virginia, and Duplin County, N.C.; A Genealogy of Stephen Lanier (1760-about 1838) or Duplin County, N. C., His Ancestors and Descendants.* Elizabeth City, NC, 1972. 108p. D gives underscored title.
[S1522; D7442; VV113].

LANIER -- Sawyer, Mamie Chambers. *Rabbi Moses ha-Kohen of Tordesillas and His Book 'Ezer ha-emunah' - A Chapter in the History of the Judeo-Christian Lanier (1760-about 1838) of Duplin County, N.C. His Ancestors and Descendants.* Elizabeth City, NC, 1972. iii, 108 leaves. [S1523].

LANPHERE -- Lanphere, Edward E. *Genealogy and History: Lanphear, Lamphier, Lanphere and Related Families in America.* Chapel Hill, NC, 1967. 87 leaves. [X551-FW/NY].

LANPHERE -- Lanphere, Edward Everett. *Lanphere and Related Families Genealogy.* Chapel Hill, NC, Lanphere, 1970. xi, 175p. [A gives: 1967 ed. published under title: Genealogy and History: Lanphear, Lamphier, Lanphere and Related Families. See just above]. [S1525; A385; D7448].

-- *The Bates Family in America, and Corrections and Additions to the Lanphere and Related Families, 1970 Revised edition.* Chapel Hill, NC, 1972. ii, 41 leaves. [S1525].

LAPP -- Cast, Marion Lopp. *Lopp - Lapp Genealogy: North Carolina - Rowan - Davidson Counties... Tennessee, Missouri...* Belton, MO, Cast, 1988. 99 leaves. [DC2178].

LARRIMORE -- Lawrimore, Eugene S. N. *William Andrew Lawrimore and His Descendants.* Georgetown, SC, E.S.N. Lawrimore, 1986. 38 leaves. 1. Larrimore family. 2. Lawrimore, William Andrew, 1804-1886-Family. 3.South Carolina-Genealogy. [G388].

LAWRENCE -- NAS. *History of the Lawrence Family in England, Virginia, and North Carolina, with Historical Sketches and Genealogical Outlines of the Lawrence Family in Connecticut, Maryland, Massachusetts, New Jersey, New York, and South Carolina. Also Including Genealogical Records of Other Families Coverging with the Lawrence of Virginia-North Carolina: Vaughan with Lawrence 1805, Rea with Lawrence 1836, Jordan with Darden 1825, Darden with Pruden 1844, Pruden with Lawrence 1870, Moorman with Lawrence 1901.* Bristol, VA/CT? 1964. 1 v. Various Pagings. [L10177; VV113].

LAWRENCE -- NAS. *History of the Lawrence Family in England, Virginia, and North Carolina, with Historical Sketches and Genealogical Outlines of the Lawrence Family in Connecticut, Maryland, Massachusetts, New*

Jersey, New York, and South Carolina. Also Including Genealogical Records of Other Families Coverging with the Lawrence of Virginia-North Carolina: Vaughan with Lawrence 1805, Rea with Lawrence 1836, Jordan with Darden 1825, Darden with Pruden 1844, Pruden with Lawrence 1870, Moorman with Lawrence 1901. Bristol, VA/CT? 1964-65. 2 v. Vol. 2 has title: The related families of Jameson family [sic] of Virginia and Norfleet family [sic] of Virginia and North Carolina. [A386].

LAWSON -- Bulkley, Caroline Kemper. *Lawson of Virginia, North Carolina and Georgia.* NP, 1932. 111 leaves. [D7499; VP114].

LAWSON -- Willis, B. L.. *Sketches and Genealogy of the Bailey - Craddock - Lawson Families of Virginia and North Carolina.* Alexandria, VA, 1974. 218p. [VV114; X557-FW].

LAWTON -- Breese, Clyde. *How Grand A Flame: A Chronicle of a Plantation Family, 1813-1847.* Chapel Hill, NC, Algonquin Books of Chapel Hill, 1991. pni. 1. Charleston (S.C.)-Biography. 2. Lawton family. 3. Plantation life-South Carolina-Charleston-History. 4. Charleston (S.C.)-History. [G391].

LAWTON -- Inabinette, E. L. *The Lawton Family of Robertville, S.C.* Columbia, SC, South Caroliniana Library, 1963. 12, iv p. [DC2196].

LEA -- Dixon, Elizabeth W. *The Lea Family of Virginia, North Carolina and Mississippi.* NP, 1958. 360 l. D adds: "See also: Williamson - Bethel and allied families of North Carolina, 1956. See also: The Williamson family of Isle of Wight County, Virginia, Southampton County, Virginia, Norhampton County, North Carolina, Caswell County, North Carolina, 1958." [D7513; VV114].

LEA -- McPherson, Jessie Coleman. *A History of the Lea - Lattimore - Hadden - Pagaud Families.* Columbia, SC, McPherson, 1978. x, 162p. [D7516].

LEA -- Rose, Ben L. *Report of Research on the Lea Family in Virginia & North Carolina Before 1800.* Richmond, VA, B.L. Rose, 1984. 157p. [DC2199].

LEAGUE -- Willia, Betty. *The League Family of Virginia and South Carolina.* Amarillo, TX, 1976. A-B, 114p. [D7523; VV114].

LEE -- NAS. *Some of the Descendants of Capt. Thomas Lee of Hawkins Co., Tenn and John Lee, Esq. of Johnston Co., North Carolina.* NP, 1972-1975. 1 v. in various foliations. [DS427].

LEE -- Couling, Mary P. *The Lee Girls.* Winston-Salem, NC, J.F. Blair. 1987. 242p., 16p. of plates. 1. Lee family. 2. Lee, Robert E. (Robert Edward), 1807-1870-Family. 3. Virginia-Biography. [G393].

LEE -- Dudley, Geraldine Martin. *Family of (Asa B. Lee) of Johnston County, North Carolina, a Descendant of John Lee, Esquire.* Princeton, NC, Dudley, 1986. 181p. [DC2210].

LEE -- King, Henry Lee. *The Henry Lee Society Present "Henry Lee of Bertie Co., N.C. and Henry Lee of Gates Co., N.C., 18th Century."* Carey, NC, H.L. King, 1986. 81p. 1. Lee family. 2. Lee, Henry, of Bertie Co., N.C.-Family. 3. Henry Lee of Gates Co., N.C.-Family. 4. North Carolina-Genealogy. DC gives underscored title and publisher as: "The Henry Lee Society." [G394; DC2212].

LEE -- Lee, Agnes. *Growing Up in the 1850's: The Journal of Agnes Lee.* Chapel Hill, NC, Pub. by Robert E. Lee Memorial Association by the University of North Carolina Press, 1984. xx, 151p. 1. Lee, Robert E. (Robert Edward), 1807-1870-Family. 2. United States-Social life and customs-19th century. 3. Lee, Agnes, 1841-1873-Diaries. 4. Children-United States-Diaries. 5. Lee family. [G394].

LEE -- Lee, Dosson Lavell. *The Family Register of Peyton Lee, 1801-1873, of New Hanover County, North Carolina, and Hancock County, Mississippi. Rev. ed.* Leetown, MS, 1986. 56, 32p. 1. Lee family. 2. Lee, Peyton, 1801-1873-Family. [G394].

LEE -- Lee, Janice Gartman. *Reb's Roots.* West Columbia, SC, J.G. Lee, 1986. viii, 206p., 6p. of plates. [G394].

LEE -- Lee, Joseph Britton. *The Lee and White Families of Bertie, Chowan, Hertford, and Perquimans Counties, North Carolina, 1660-1983.* Washington, DC, 1983. 147p. [NG62].

LEE -- Lee, William A. *Genealogy: Lee; South Carolina Branches. This Pedigree and Deeds Were Abstracted by Us.* NP, 189_, Genealogical Chart. [X559-NY].

LEE -- Read, Thomas C. <u>*The Descendants of Thomas Lee of Charleston, S.C*</u>*. 1710-1769.* Columbia, SC, R.L. Bryan Co., 1964. xxv, 465p. D gives underscored title. [L10286; NG62; D7566].

LEE -- Rose, Ben Lacey. *Report of Research on the Lea Family in Virginia & North Carolina Before 1800.* Richmond, VA, 1984. 157p. [NG62; VV116].

LEE -- Rose, Ben Lacey. *The Lea Ancestry of Margaret Lea, Wife of Gen Sam Houston.* Richmond, VA, B.L. Rose, 1987. 15p. "Addendum #2 to Report of research on the Lea family in Virginia & North Carolina before 1800 by Ben L. Rose. 1. Lee family. 2.

Houston, Margaret Lea, 1819-1867-Family. [G394].

LEE -- Royall, Luby F. *The Lees of Johnston County, North Carolina.* Smithfield, NC, Royall, 1978. 256p. [D7567].

LEE -- Sirmon, Marilyn Lane. *The Ancestors and Known Descendants of Solomon Lee, 1758/60-1818 of New Hanover County, North Carolina. - 3rd ed.* Hattiesburg, MS, M.L. Sirmon, 1988. iii, 520p. 1. Lee family. 2. Lee, Solomon, ca. 1758-1818-Family. 3. Southern States-Genealogy. [G394].

LEE -- Wilson, Reba S(hropshire). [D7572; X560-DP/LA/NY/SL; VV116]. See above: KING. [NG62; D7572; X527-FW/SL; VV110]

LEEPER -- Andrea, Leonardo. *Leeper and Looper Families of South Carolina.* NP, 1949. 24 leaves. [D7577].

LEFVENDAHL -- Lefvendahl, Georgie I. Adams. *Lefvendahl, Smoak and Related Family Records.* Orangeburg, SC, Lefvendahl, 1966. 74 l. [L10321; D7589].

LEGARE -- Fludd, Eliza C. K. *Biographical Sketches of the Huguenot Solomon Legaré, and of His Family, Extending Down to the Fourth Generation of His Descendants Also Reminiscences of the Revolutionary Struggle with Great Britain, Including Incidents and Scenes Which Occurred in Charleston, of John's Island, and in the Surrounding Country of South Carolina During the War.* Charleston, SC, Edward Perry & Co., 1886. 142p. D gives underscored part of title. [L10323; D7590].

LENTZ -- Lentz, John Paul. *Lenta Heritage: Records and Descendants of the Four Lentz Brothers Who Settled in Rowan County, North Carolina Between 1778 and 1782.* Bulington

[sic], NC, J.P. Lentz, 1986. 1 v. (various paginations). [DC2227].

LENTZ -- Speegle, Charles Martin. [G397]. See above: JARRETT. [G346].

LEONARD -- Koster, Fanny L. *Annals of the Leonard Family.* Charleston, SC, Garnier & Co., 1911. Reprinted 1969. pni. [X565-NJ].

LESLIE -- Murphy, Marion Emerson. *Early Leslies in York County, South Carolina: Their Migration to Tennessee, Missouri, and Arkansas, Their Ancestry and Descendants - 1st ed.* San Diego, CA, 1972. xvi, 210p. "Sequel to Tennessee Murphys - Murpheys and Allied Families. Vol. 1.". [S1560].

LESLIE -- Murphy, Marion Emerson. *Early Leslies in York County, South Carolina: Their Migration to Tennessee, Missouri, and Arkansas, Their Ancestry and Descendants - 3rd ed.* San Diego, CA, 1976. xvi, 210p., 1 leaf of plates. [X567-NY].

LEWIS -- Lewis, Harrison. *Our Lineage.* Chapel Hill, NC, Lewis, 1981. 34p. [D7661].

LEWIS -- Lewis, P. Loyd. *James Lewis and Ann Elizabeth Stewart Lewis of North Carolina and Missouri. Their Ancestry and Descendants.* Ferguson, MO1934. 5, 23p. [L10463].

LEWIS -- Mock, Ella M. L. *Some Surry County Lewises and Their Kin, 1791-1976.* Elkin, NC, Blackwell print., 1976. 104p. [X569-FW].

LEWIS -- Stevenson, Mary Lewis. *William Lewis of Horry County, South Carolina.* Columbia, SC, Charlotte Stevenson, Printed by R.L. Bryon Co., 1960. viii, 181p. D gives 81p? [L10470; D7677].

LEWTER -- West, Belle Lewter. *Luter - Lewter Family of England, Virginia, North*

Carolina, and States South and West. Durham, NC, West, 1974. 157p. NG lists as LUTER. [S1571; NG65; VV118].

LIDE -- Green, Fletcher M. *The Lides Go South...and West.* Columbia, SC, University of South Carolina Press, 1952. vi, 51p. [D7685].

LINDEMAN -- Boswell, Imogene May. *The Ancestors and Descendants of Henry D. Lendermon: Randolph County, North Carolina, Greenville County, South Carolina, Maury County, Tennessee, Carroll County, Tennessee, Marshall County, Mississippi.* Wolfe City, TX, Henington Pub. Co., 1988. 337p. 1. Lindeman family. 2. Lendermon, Henry D., 1788-1845-Family. 3. Southern States-Genealogy. [G402].

LINDER -- Linder, Billy R. *Edward L. Linder of Georgia, South Carolina, and Mississippi, 1801 to after 1866.* Vienna, VA, Linder, 1975. 9p. FW shows: Bound with Ferguson Chart by C. W. Ferguson. [D7715; X573-FW].

LINDER -- Linder, Billy R. *John Lewis Linder of South Carolina, Georgia, and Mississippi, 1765-1843.* Vienna, VA, 1975. 13pages. [X573-FW].

LINDER -- Linder, Myrtle Kinard. *Jacob Somon [sic] Linder of Colleton County, South Carolina.* Arlington, VA? Kinard, et al. 1988. v, 346p. Southern Linders v. 2. [DC2264].

LINDLEY -- Bradfield, Allen L. [G402]. See above: HADLEY. [G288].

LINDSAY -- Brien, Lindsay B. M. *Clan Lindsay; Lindsay Families of Virginia, North Carolina, South Carolina.* NP, n.d. pni. [VV118].

LINDSAY -- Elizabeth Dick. *Diary of Elizabeth Dick Lindsay, Feb. 1, 1837 - May 3, 1861.* Salisbury, NC, 1975. [NG63].

LINEBERRY -- Lineberry, Winfield S. *Lineberry Family.* Locust Grove, NC, 1918. 22p. [X574-FW].

LIPSCOMB -- NAS. *Genealogy of Calesta Carroll Lipscomb Fitzhugh. - 1st ed.* San Jose, CA, Gentrace Associates, Inc. 1985. 2 v. 1. Lipscomb family. 2. Sherrill family. 3. Fitzhugh, Calesta Carroll Lipscomb, 1943- Family. 4. Afro-American Genealogy. 5. South Carolina-Genealogy. [G404].

LITTLE -- Covington, O. McRae. *The Littles of Carlisle.* Wadesboro, NC, Covington, 1970. 188p. [D7752].

LITTLE -- Little, Lawrence L. *Geneology sic of the Little Family of Georgia and North Carolina.* Portales, NM, Cora Stewart Little Family Association, 1971. iii, 210p. [D7756].

LITTLE -- Little, Lawrence L. *Genealogy of the Little - Odom Family of Georgia and North Carolina.* Chicago, IL, or Creve Coeur, MO, Adams, Pr., Ed. 2, 1974. 191p. [X576-FW/LA].

LITTLEFORD -- Woodsworth-Barnes, Esther Littleford. The Littleford Family of Downers Grove Township, DuPage County, Illinois: *The Ancestors and Descendants of George Wellington Littleford, 1825-1910, Born Buckinghamshire, England and His Wife, Ann Jones. 1830-1891, Born Monmouthshire, Wales.* Clemson, SC, E.L. Woodworth-Barnes, 1990. 121 leaves. 1. Littleford family. 2. Littlefore, George Wellington, 1825-1910-Family. 3 Jones family. 4. Littleford, Ann Jones, 1830-11891-Family. DC gives underscored title and 121p. [G404; DC2274].

LITTLEJOHN -- McKowan, Iris Littlejohn. *Littlejohn Genealogy; Oliver Littlejohn*

Descendants. Gaffney, SC, Gaffney Ledger, 1953. 1109p. [L10600].

LIVINGSTON -- Ericson, Jack T. *The Robert R. Livingston Papers, 1658-1888: A Guide to the Microfilm Edition.* Sanford, NC, Microfilming Corp. of America, 1980. ix, 53p. 1. Livingston family-Archive-Microfilm catalogs. 2. Livingston, Robert R., 1746-1813-Manuscripts-Microfilm catalogs. 3. Manuscripts, American-NewYork(State)-Microfilm catalogs. 4. New York Historical Society-Microfilm catalogs. [G405].

LIVINGSTON -- Livingston, Lucius Wilmot. *Historical and Geneological sic Record of John Livingston, the First, of Orangeburg County, South Carolina.* Orangeburg, SC, Printed by Walter D. Berry, 1940. 91p. [D7775].

LLHUYD -- Fair, Mildred Caroline Lide. *Llhuyd, Loyd, Lloyd, Lide, from Wales to Pennsylvania, through Virginia to South Carolina with Extensive Records for Evan James Lide.* Orangeburg, SC, Fair, 1971. 94p. X lists as LLOYD. D gives underscored part of title. [D7779; X578-FW/NY].

LOFTUS -- Bernstein, Dorothy Loftis. *Loftis and the Descendants of Lemuel Loftis of South Carolina.* __, TX, J.L. Loftis, Jr., 1987. 87p. 1. Loftus family. 2. Loftis, Lemuel, ca.1774-1838-Family. 3. South Carolina-Genealogy. [G406].

LOGAN -- Barry, Byrdella Logan. *Timothy Logan of North Carolina and Kentucky.* NP, 1953. 37 leaves. [D7806].

LOGAN -- Conley, Katherine Logan. *The Genealogy of Major Francis Logan.* Rutherford, NC, Printed by Associated Services, [illegible] [illegible] leaves. D gives: Cover Title: Major Francis Logan and his wife, Hannah Trimble. [S1599; D7807].

LOGAN -- Logan, George William. *A Record of the Logan Family of Charleston, South Carolina.* Cincinnati, OH, Morrill, 1923. 70p. [L10661; D7811; VV119].

LOGAN -- Logan, Lide A. *The Logans of Old Ninety Six and Their Descendants. Revised Edition.* Columbus, NC? 1986. 316, 76p. [DC2283].

LOGAN -- Logan, Wilson. *Historical Record of the Logans and Daniels of South Carolina.* Charleston, SC, 1905. 21p. [X580-FW].

LOGAN -- McConnell, Richard Bland. *Logan Cousins: A Chart Index of Some of the Descendants of Colonel George Logan of Charles Town, South Carolina and His Wife, Frances.* NP, McConnell, 1966. 99, xxxvii, 14 leaves. Edition limited to 80 copies. 1. Logan family. [G407].

LOGUE -- Buchanan, Jane Gray. <u>*John Logue of North Carolina*</u>*: History and Hypothesis: Logue and Related Families of Delaware, Maryland, Pennsylvania, Virginia, and Tennessee.* Oak Ridge, TN, Buchanan, 1980. iv, 47 leaves. D gives underscored title. [D7814; VV119].

LONG -- NAS. *A Long Journey: A Genealogical look at the Family of Benjamin Thomas (B.T.) and Nancy Long of Johnson County, North...* NP, Smithfield Bryan Chapter, North Carolina DAR, G.R.C., 1985. 90 leaves. [DC2290].

LONG -- Evans, Eytive (Long). *A Documented History of the Long Family: Switzerland to South Carolina, 1758 - 1956, Including Allied Families; A Documentery Record of the Long (Lang) Family of Newberry, Edgefield, and Saluda Counties, South Carolina.* Atlanta, GA, 1956. xii, 316p. [L10698; NG64; D7821].

LONG -- Frost, Earle W. *A Genealogical Brouchure of the Long and Doub Families of*

North Carolina and Their Midwestern Descendants. Kansas City, MO, Frost, 1975. ix, 19p. [D7822].

LONG -- Fulk, John D. *Tobias Long, 1781-1856, Surry County, N. C. and Greene County, Ind.* NP, 1929. 55p, 4 l. Related Families: Ferguson, Graves, Fulk. [X581-FW].

LONG -- Long, Jasper S. *Long Family Records; and a Genealogy of the Descendants of Henry and Catherina Kern Long, born 1718, Heidelberg, Germany and the Holcomb Family and Descendants of the Widow Rachel Reinhardt.* Yadkinville, NC, Long, 1965. 270p. D gives underscored part of title. X gives publication data as: Winston-Salem, NC, Clay Print. [D7825; X581-FW/NY].

LOTT -- Lott, Dewel C. *"Lott" of Cousins.* Hartselle, AL, 1975. 284p. Descendants of George Lott, ca. 1750-1812 of Fairfield Co., S. C. [X583-FW].

LOVE -- NAS. *The Love Family Historical and Genealogical Quarterly. V. 1 - Sept. 1953 -* Camden, SC, Love Family Historical and Genealogical Association. Published by R. A. Love. [L10768].

LOVE -- Andrea, Leonardo. *Love Families of South Carolina.* NP, 1949. 44 l. [D7863].

LOVE -- Love, Robert A. *General Thomas Love of Western North Carolina and Western Tennessee and His Brothers Robert and James, 2nd ed. with additions and corrections.* St. Petersburg, FL, Love, 1955. 43, 2 leaves. D gives underscored title; no notice of edition. [L10760; D7868].

LOVELACE -- Miller, Anne V. *A Lineage in the Vestal Family and the Lovelace Family of Yadkin County, N.C., 1793-1985.* Sterling, VA, Old Mill Printers, 1985. iv, 51 leaves, 8 leaves of plates. 1. Vestal family. 2.

Lovelace family. 3. Yadkin County (N.C.)-Genealogy. DC gives publisher as: Miller. [G410; DC3773].

LOVELL -- Rhodes, May Lovell and T. D. *A Biographical Genealogy of the Lovell Family in England and America.* Asheville, NC, Biltmore Press, 1924. 6p, 15, 221, 3p. [A412].

LOWE -- McDuffie, Eva Loe. *The Lowe - Loe - Low Family in Virginia, North Carolina, Mississippi, Tennessee, Kentucky, and Missouri.* NP, 1955. 109 leaves. [D7888; VV120].

LOWE -- West, Carrie M. *John Lowe of North Carolina and Indiana, 1800-1868; His Ancestry, Descendants, and Some of the Allied Families, 1729-1977.* No Imprint. 177p . [X584-KH].

LOWNDES -- Chase, George B. *Lowndes of South Carolina.* Boston, MA, A. Williams & Co., 1876. 81p. [L10799; D7894].

LUCAS -- Lucas, Pauline. *Tell It Again: The Story of a Family.* Charlotte, NC, Herb Eaton Historical Publications, 1987. vii, 640p. 1. Lucas family. 2. North Carolina-Genealogy. [G411].

LUMPKIN -- Lumpkin, Martha Neville. *Minor, Scales, Cottrell, and Gray Families of Virginia, North Carolina, and Mississippi.* Clarksville, B.G. Lumpkin, TN, 1974. vii, 139p. [S1626; VV120].

LUTER -- West, Belle Lewter. *The Luter-Lewter Family of England, Virginia, North Carolina, and States South and West.* Durham, NC, West, 1974. 157p. [D7939].

LUTHER -- Hagan, Janice. <u>North Carolina Luthers; Three Generations</u> *being Michael, George, Jacob, Christian, Luther and Barbara Luther Auman, Their Children and*

Grandchildren. 2nd revision. Athens, GA, J. Hagan, 1988. 22p. 1. Luther family. 2. Luther, Michael, 1751-1834-Family. 3. North Carolina-Genealogy. DC gives underscored part of title. [G413; DC2315].

LUTZ -- Lutes, Margaret D. *The Lutz Family of Central North Carolina.* Boise, ID, Lutes, 1969. 32, 65 leaves. [L10854; D7942].

LYDA -- Honeycutt, Frances F. [G413]. See above: FREEMAN. [G241].

LYNCH -- Deans, Frances Lynch. *The Lynches from Ireland to Eastern North Carolina: In the Counties of Craven, Johnston, Bobbs, Wayne.* Goldsboro, NC, F.L. Deans, 1989. xiv, 577p. DC gives underscored title and 576p. 1. Lynch family. 2. Ireland-Genealogy. 3. North Carolina-Genealogy. [G414; DC2323].

LYONS -- Linn, Jo White. *The Ancestry of Nathalie Fontaine Lyons: Also: Lyons, Nunes, Miranda, Luria, Cohen, Hart, Clayland, Maffit, Beach.* Salisbury, NC, Linn, 1981. xi, 260p. DS gives underscored title. [NG65; DS446].

M

MACKLENDON -- McClendon, S. E. *Macklendon Family to America, 1696; McClendon, 1700, McLendon, 1725, of North Carolina.* NP, 1949. 17 leaves. [D7996].

MacLEAN -- Sinclair, Brevard D. *An Historical Account of the MacLeans of Duart Castle, and the Genealogy of the Children and Grand-children of Rev. John Campbell Sinclair...* Columbus, OH, 1879. 37p. Contains also sketches of the Davidson and Brevard Families of Mecklenburg, N.C. [X-PH].

MacMASTER -- McMaster, Fitz Hugh. *MacMaster - McMaster Family.* Columbia, SC, Stet Co., 1926. 142p. [D8001].

MACMILLAN -- Stubbs, Sallie McMillan. *MacMillan Genealogy.* Lumberton, NC, Freeman Printing Co., 1956. 79p. [D8003].

MacNEIL -- NAS. *The MacNeil Memorial, Red Springs, North Carolina... Unveiled May 23, 1928. Clan MacNeil Association of America.* Brooklyn, NY, Flatbush Prtg. Co., 1928. 20p. [X613-LI/NY].

MacQUEEN -- MacElyea, Mrs. Annabella Bunting (MacCallum). *A Biography of Col. James MacQueen and His Descendants.* Charlotte, NC, 1916. 261p. [NG67].

MacQUEEN -- MacElyea, Annabella Bunting. *The MacQueens of Queensdale.* Charlotte, NC, Observer Printing House, 1916. 261p. See also below: McQUEEN: [X614-FW/LI/NY]. [D8010].

MACRA -- Macra, Mrs. John. *A Genealogical Account of the Macras, Transcribed by Farquhar Macra.* Camden, SC, 1879. 36p. [X615-LI].

MacRAE -- MacRae, Lawrence. *Descendants of Duncan & Ann (Cameron) MacRae of Scotland and North Carolina.* Greensboro, NC, 1927. 1p., 23 numb. leaves. [L11278].

MacRAE -- MacRae, Lawrence. *Descendants of Duncan & Ann (Cameron) MacRae of Scotland and North Carolina.* Greensboro, NC, MacRae, 1929. 62p. [D8014].

MAGILL -- Jones, Hazel Parker. *Descendants of James Boyd Magill, 1787-1880, Emigrant from Ireland to Chester County, S.C. in 1823; A Biographical and Historical Genealogy, Including Allied Families.* Kershaw, SC, 1963. 195p. [L11296].

MALONE -- Malone, Randolph A. *Malone and Allied Families, Including Records From*

Virginia, North and South Carolina, and Georgia. Ann Arbor, MI, McNaugton and Gunn, Thomasville, GA, Malone, 1986. viii, 389p. [G420; NGS8; DC2348].

MALPAS -- Brinson, Seavy Wooten. *The James Malpas Family; A History of the Descendants of James Malpas of the Moore's Creek Community in New Hanover, now Pendar County near Currie, N.C., with the Line of Lineage of Cholmondeley Malpas of England as taken from Burke's Peerage as found further along in this expose covering the period from William La Belward, Lord of the Moity of the Barony of Malpas Including Calmundelai. With as Complete a History as possible from 1760-1964.* Wilmington, NC, Brinson, 1966. 216p. D gives underscored part as title. [L11347; D8056].

MALPUS -- Malphurs, Muriel Ward. *Genealogy of the Early Malpus of Virginia, North Carolina, South Carolina, Georgia, Florida, and Alabama: Including Malpas, Malpass, Malphurs, and All Similar Names. ; With Allied Families.* National City, CA, 1987. 940p. DC gives underscored part of title and xxxii, 728, 72p. [NGS8; DC2350].

MANGUM -- Palmer, John T. *The Mangums of Virginia, North Carolina, South Carolina, Georgia, Alabama & Mississippi.* Santa Rosa, CA, J. T. Palmer, 1988. viii. 74p. 1. Mangum family. 2. Southern States-Genealogy. [G421].

MANLEY -- Manly, Charles Gottschalk. *A Genealogy and History of Adin Manly (1793-1867) and Howard Manly (1791-1852): Together with Some Descendants and Some Related Families: Almost 200 Years of Manlys.* Charlotte, NC, 1988, x, 180p. NGS lists as MANLY and gives 180p. [G421: NGS8].

MANLY -- Manly, Louise. *The Manly Family; An Account of the Descendants of Captail Basil Manly of the Revolution and Related Families.*

Greenville, SC, Manly, Keys Printing Co., 1930. xv, 351p. Contents: Captain Basil Manly and his four children; Governor Charles Manly; Rev. Basil Manly; Judge Mathias Evans Manly, Mrs. Louisa Manly. - Syng, Murray, and Rudolph Lines and Descendants of Rev. Basil Manly, Sr. D gives underscored part as title. [L11357; D8069].

MARBRET -- Hammond, Joan Marbret. *The Marbret Heritage.* Summerville, SC, Printing Associates of Summerville, 1980-1990. 2 v. [DC2358].

MARION -- Atkinson, Ola Marion. *Marion Family.* Siloam, NC, Atkinson, 1964. 90 leaves. [D8095].

MARION -- Bunn, Maude Davis. *The Genealogy of Marion - Davis Families.* Raleigh, NC, Edwards & Broughton, 1973. 239p. [S1710; D8096].

MARLOWE -- Marlowe, James I. *The Marlows of the Waccamaw River Region.* [Mill Creek, Brunswick County, NC, J.I. Marlowe, 1988. 64, 39 leaves. 1. Marlow family. 2. Virginia-Genealogy. 3. South Carolina-Genealogy. 4. North Carolina-Genealogy. [G424].

MARSH -- Price, Walter R. *The Marsh Family of Eastern North Carolina.* NP, 1959. 124 leaves. [D8121].

MARSH -- Marsh, U. Bowdoin. *John Marsh of Craven and Kershaw Counties, South Carolina and His Descendants and Research Notes on Marsh.* Tallahasee, FL, U.B. Marsh, 1987. ix, 243p. 1. Marsh family. 2. Marsh, John, d. 1803 or 4-Family.
[G425].

MARSHALL -- Turner, Alienne Wiggins. *John Marshall, Sr.; A Genealogy and History of Some of the Descendants of John Marshall, Sr of Brunswick County, Va., 1732-1956.*

Henderson, NC, Turner, 1956. 36p. [D8138; X624-FW/NY].

MARTIN -- Fagg, Jenny Martin. *A Family History of Thomas Martin, Sr. a North Carolinian American Revolutionary Soldier - 1st ed.* Fort Worth, TX, Arrow/Curtis Print. Co., 1976. x, 385p. 1. Martin Family. [G426; X627-FW/NY].

MARTIN -- Gee, Christine Smith. *Some of the Descendants of Daniel Martin (1745-1829) of Laurens County, South Carolina, and the Allied Families of Hudgens, McNeese, Rodgers, and Saxon.* Greenwood, SC, printed privately by Key Print. Co., Greenville, SC, 1963. v, 97p. [L11500].

MARTIN -- Lewis, Eulalie M. *A History of the William Henry Martin Family.* Raleigh, NC, 1973. 40p. [X627-NY].

MARTIN -- Martin, Arthur Morrison. *The Flemington Martins.* Columbia, SC, State Printing Co., 1970. vii, 114p. [A439].

MARTIN -- Woodson, Hortense. *The Martins of Martin's Mill in South Carolina.* NP, Woodson, 1980. 104p. [D8171].

MASHBURN -- Simpson, Edna Grant. *The Mashburn Family of North Carolina and Georgia.* Knoxville, TN, Simpson, 1975. 425 leaves. [DC2380].

MASSEY -- Smith, Carmae Massey. *Descendants of Arthur Massey, Cheraws District, South Carolina, 1769.* Owensboro, KY, Cook-McDowell Publications, Inc., 1980. 193p. [C444; D8200].

MASSENGILL -- Butler, Florence Roberta Walker. *The Massengills of Johnston County, N. C.* Hamlet, NC, R.W. Butler, c1984-c1986. 2 v. 1. Massengill family. 2. North Carolina-Genealogy. [G428].

MATHIAS -- Creech, Ruth Ann Matthis. [G429]. See above: DREYER. [G200].

MATHIS -- Mathis, Robert Butler. *The Thomas Charles Mathis Family.* Advertiser Press, Edgefield, SC, 1969. 151p. NG gives title as: "The Charles Thomas Mathis Family". D gives date of 1968.
[S1739; NG69; D8227].

MATTHEWS -- Robertson, Irma Matthews. [G430]. See above: ANGLE. [G15].

MAXWELL -- Cannon, A. Charles. *The Maxwells of Greenville.* Greenville, SC, A.C. Cannon, 1989. 325p. 1. Maxwell family. 2. South Carolina-Genealogy. [G431].

MAY -- Mays, Rayford Glynn. *Mays and Pullen Pioneers: Tideland Virginia to Tennessee and North Alabama: Across Four Centuries.* Franklin, NC, 1983. pni. [VV126].

MAY -- Mays, Samuel E. *Genealogical Notes on the Family of Mays, and Reminiscences of the War Between the States, From the Notes Written Around the Campfires by Samuel Elias Mays, Born in South Carolina, Nov. 12th, 1834; Died at Plant City, Fl., Nov 27th, 1906; and Some References to the Earle Family.* Plant City, FL, Printed by Plant City Enterprises, 1927. 324p. [L11641].

MAY -- Renard, Laura Foster. *The May, Lang, Joyner, Williams Families of North Carolina (Pitt County Area).* Durham, NC, L.F. Renard, 1974. 197, 1p., 8 leaves of plates.
[S1750].

MAY -- Woodson, Hortense. *Charles May and His Descendants.* Edgefield, SC, May Family Association, 1956. 287p. [D2821].

McADAMS -- McAdams, Edward Pope. *A McAdams Family History.* Charlotte, NC, E.P. McAdams, 1990. 317p. [DC2419].

McADOO -- Lemons, Nova A. *John McAdoo of Virginia, North Carolina, Tennessee, and Kentucky.* Dallas, Lemons, 1991. iv, 52p. [DC2424].

McALISTER -- McAlister, Frank Dicken. *Notes on the Family of Alexander McAlister of Pendelton, South Carolina.* Conway, AR, 1979. 46 leaves. [NG65].

McALLISTER -- Buchanan, Jane Gray. [G432]. See above: FINNEY. [G229].

McALLISTER -- McAllister, Rev. D. S. *Genealogical Record of the Descendants of Col. Alexander McAllister, of Cumberland County, N.C.; Also of Mary and Isabella McAllister.* Richmond, VA, Whittet & Shepperson, 1900. 244p. D gives underscored title. [L10908; D8300; VV126].

McALPIN -- Hazelton, Trica Willey. *Some Descendants of Alexander McAlpin, Sr., of Abbeville District, SC, and Wilkes Co., GA, and Alexander McAlpin, Jr., of Green Co., TN and Henry McAlpin of Greene County., TN, and Daniel McAlpin of Johnson Co., IN.* Las Cruces, NM, 1987. 11p. [NG65].

McALPINE -- Russell, Doris McAlpin . *McAlpin(e) Genealogies, 1730-1990: Alexander McAlpin of South Carolina and Georgia and His Descendants, Plus Other McAlpin(e) Families of North America.* Baltimore, MD, Gateway Press, 1990. xi, 735p. 1. McAlpin family. 2. McAlpin, Alexander, d. 1790-Family. [G433].

McANDREWS -- Skeen, A. T. *Clan McAndrew.* Winston-Salem, NC, A.T. Skeen, Jr., 1988. xii, 312p. 1. McAndrews family. [G433].

McBRAYER -- Whitaker, Hattie Katerine Reed. *McBrayer.* Southern Pines, SC, Whitaker, McBrayer, 1926. 151p. [D8312].

McBRYDE -- Patterson, A. M. *History of John and Mary Wilkerson McBryde and Their Descendants.* Raleigh, NC, 1963. pni. [NG65].

McBRYDE -- Patterson, A[lex]. M. *History of John and Mary Wilkerson McBryde and Their Descendants.* Raleigh, NC, 1967. iv, 153p. D gives bracketed name of author and title as: "The clan McBryde." [NG65; D8316].

McCAA -- McCaa, John. *Dr. John McCaa of Camden, South Carolina, 1793-1859, His Descendants.* Anniston, AL, McCaa, 1975. 267p. [D8317; X594-FW/NY].

McCAIN -- McCain, W. D. *Seven Generations of the Family of Alexander Hamilton McCain (1786-1838) and His Wife Naomi Neely McCain (1880-1874) of N.C., S.C., Ga., Ala., and Miss.* Hattiesberg, MS, 1973. vii, 448p. [X594-FW].

McCALL -- Whitfield, Marguerite L. *McCall and McLaurin Families of Ballachulish in Scotland County, North Carolina.* Southern Pines, NC, 1978. pni. [NG65].

McCAY -- Couch, Sara Crenshaw. *The Martin Stanley McCay and Martha P. Collins McCay Family Genealogy.* Greenville, SC, S.C. Couch, 1988. 441p. [DC2441].

McCLAREN -- Greenway, Carol Forrest. *Alexander McClaren with excursis sic on Related Families of Va., N.C., S.C., and Tenn.* 1977. 306 leaves. [D8345; VV127].

McCLELLAN -- McClelland, Clifton A. *Silas and Penelope (Anderson) McClelland and Some of Their Descendants..* Baltimore, MD, Gateway Press, Whiteville, NC, C.A. McClelland, 1987. xiii, 327p., 1 leaf of plates. 1. McClellan family. 2. McClelland, Silas, Ca. 1790-1875-Family. [G434].

McCONNELL -- McConnell, Joes P. *The McConnell Families of Davidson's Creek Settlement, Iredell County, North Carolina 1748-1982.* Mooresville, NC, J.P. McConnell, 1983. 179p. [DC2452].

McCORMICK -- McCormick, Andrew Phillip. *Scotch-Irish in Ireland and America, as Shown in Sketches of the Pioneer Scotch-Irish Families McCormick, Stevenson, McKenzie, and Bell in North Carolina, Kentucky, Missouri and Texas.* New Orleans, LA, 1897. 1 v. various pagings. [L10983].

McCOWN -- Clement, Louise McCown. *The McCown Familiy of the Peedee Section of South Carolina.* Columbia, SC, R.L. Bryan Co., 1966. xi, 246p. [L10990; D8392].

McCRACKEN -- McCracken, Franklin Y. *McCrackens of Haywood County, N. C.* Waynesville, N. C. Atlas, Pr., 1965. 29p. [X599-FW].

McCRAY -- McCray, Percie. *The James McCray Family of Erie County, Pennsyulvania.* Hendersonville, NC, 1982. 122p. [NG66].

McCULLOUGH -- Harmon, Lillian B. *Descendants of John McCulloch (McCully) Born about 1777 in the Vicinity of Asheville, N. C.* NP, 1976. 39 leaves. Typed. [X600-GF].

McCULLOUGH -- Lowery, Edna Hazel McCullough. *Descendants of McCullough: Includes Genealogy of the Family of Mary McCulloch, 1722-1792, of Orange County, N.C.* NP, 1986. pni. [NG66].

McCURDY -- Zook, B. Jesse. *McCurdys: Long Canes, South Carolina to Upshur County, Texas.* Camden, IN, 1985. 85p. [NGS8].

McDANIEL -- McDaniel, Steven L. *The McDaniel Pedigree.* San Francisco, CA, S.L. McDaniel, 1985-<1987 >. v. <1-3 >. 1.

McDaniel family. 2. North Carolina-Genealogy. [G437].

McDONALD -- McDonald, J. Milton. *McDonalds & Perritts of Marion County, S.C.* [NGN18-1-92].

McDONALD -- McDuffie, Eva (Loe). *John and Flora McDonald McDuffie of the Isle of Skye, Scotland and North Carolina, Mississippi, and Louisana.* Oak Ridge(?), LA, 1957. 91 leaves. [NG66].

McDOUGALL -- McDougall, Dennis C. *Descendants in America of Robert McDougal, 1720-1816 and Collateral Families.* Parris Island, SC, 1939. Unpaged. [X602-FW].

McDOW -- Corcoran, Edwin Emmons. *The John Cunningham McDow, Sr. Family of Lancaster South Carolina.* Asheville, NC, Corcoran, 1980. 46 leaves. Suppl. to McDow Family in America/Ida McDow Rodman. [See just below]. [D8436].

McDOW -- Rodman, Ida McDow. *The McDow Family in America.* NP, 1954. 109 leaves. [D8437].

McDOWELL -- Avery, Judge A. C. ... *Historical Homes of North Carolina - Quaker Meadows.* Raleigh, NC, E.M. Uzzell & Co., Printers, 1994. (The North Carolina Booklet; Great Events in North Carolina history, Vol IV, no. 3, July, 1904). Contains biographical notices of the McDowell family, owners of Pleasant Gardens and Quaker Meadows in Burke Co., N. C. [L11054].

McDOWELL -- Crook, John A. *McDowell and Related Families: A Genealogy.* Reidsville, NC, Crook, 1975. xi, 116p., 16 leaves of plates. [X603-FW/LA/NY].

McDOWELL -- Perdue, Lemuel Ford. *A Brief History of Ephraim and Joseph McDowell of Virginia and North Carolina.* Houston, TX,

Southwestern Press, 1912. 32p. [D8446; VV128].

McDUFFIE -- McDuffie, Eva Lee. *John and Flora McDonald McDuffie of the Isle of Skye, Scotland, and a Record of Their Descendants , Who Settled in North Carolina, Mississippi, and Louisiana.* Oak Ridge, LA, 195_. 91 leaves. [L11057].

McELWEE -- McElwee, Pinckney G. *Genealogy of Mary McElwee Enloe, Wife of Benjamin Enloe and Daughter of William McElwee of Clarks Fork of Bullocks Creed of York County, South Carolina.* Washington, DC, Elwee[sic], 1964. 52p. [D8454].

McELWEE -- McElwee, Pinckney Glasgow. *Geneology sic of William McElwee, II of Clarks Fork of Bullocks Creed of York County, South Carolina.* Washington, DC, McElwee, 1959. 227 leaves. [L11062; D8455].
-- *Supplement,* i.e. *Chapter 7; Genealogy of Mary McElwee Enloe.* Washington, DC, 1964. a-j, 52p. [L11062].

McELWEE -- McElwee, Pinckney Glasgow. *Geneology sic of William McElwee, II, of Clarks Fork of Bullocks Creek of York County, South Carolina.*

McFADDEN -- Skinner, William Thomas. *A McFadden Chronology, 1710-1900.* Richburg, SC, 1983. 64p. [NG66].

McFADDIN -- NAS. *The McFaddin Dedication, Sardinia, South Carolina...* Clinton, SC, Jacobs and Company, 1937. 98p. [L11063].

McFADDIN -- Blanding, A. L. *McFaddin, 1730-1930.* Clinton, SC, 1931. 99p. [X603-LI].

McFADIN -- McFadin, Maude A. *The John Stephen McFadin Family of North Carolina, Kentucky, Indiana, and Kansas.* North Newton, KS, Mennonite Press, 1971. 111p. Includes memoirs of George E. McFadin. [NG66; D8462; X603-FW/LA/NY/SP].

McFARLAND -- Campbell, Kathryn Hutcherson. *The McFarland Clan of North Carolina, Kentucky, Missouri.* Dallas, Campbell, 1974. vii, 188 leaves. [D8464].

McGIRT -- Love, Louise W. *The Descendants of Archibald McGirt, III, and John McGirt.* Wilmington, NC, Love, 1969. 103p. [D8479].

McGOWAN -- NAS. *Proceedings of the Reunion of the McGowan Family, Held at Liberty Springs Church (Presbyterian)...* August 3, 1915. 51p. [L11090].

McGREW -- McGrew, Clinton Jackson. *Genealogy of Alexander McGrew of Amelia Township, South Carolina.* Spring Hill, FL, C.J. McGrew, Jr., 1989. 370p. 1. McGrew family. 2. McGrew, Alexander, 1768-1828-Family. 3. Amelia (S.C.)-Genealogy. 4. South Carolina-Genealogy. [G440; DC2484].

McGRIFF -- Hill, Joseph Edward. *Colonel Patrick McGriff of Chester County, South Carolina, and Montgomery County, Georgia, <u>His Children and Grandchildren</u>.* Leesburg, FL, Hill, 1973. 66 leaves. S shows 60 leaves. X adds underscored part to title. [S1666; NG67; D8487; X605-FW].

McGUINN -- McGuinn, Margaret C. S. *The Descendants of Michael McGuinn.* Spartanburg, SC,.1954. 107 leaves. [X605-NY].

McINTYRE -- McIntrye, Lucy E. *The McIntyres of Montgomery County, North Carolina, <u>1835-1965.</u>* Red Oak, NC, McIntrye, 1965. 1 v. unpagedd. D gives 71p; omits underscored part of title. L [L11130; D8505].

McINTYRE -- McLean, Angus Wilton. *Lumber River Scots and Their Descendants: the McLeans, the Purcells, the McIntyres, the*

Torreys, the Gilchrists. Richmond, VA, W. Byrd Press, 1986, 1942. xxx, 839p., 1 leaf of plates. 1. McLean family. 2. Purcell family. 3. McIntyre family. 4. North Carolina-Genealogy. [G441].

McIVER -- Kelly, Kenneth Low. *McIver Family of North Carolina.* rev. of Genealogy of the McIver Family of North Carolina by Helen H. McIver, 1922. Washington, DC, McIver Art and Publications, Inc., 1964. 382p. D omits underscored note. [L11134; NG67; D8506].

McIVER -- McIver, Helen H. *Genealogy of the McIver Family of North Carolina.* NP, 1922. 168p. [D8507].

McIVER -- McIver, Helen H. *Genealogy of the McIver Family of North Carolina.* Richmond, VA, Whitter & Shepperson, 1943. L omits pagination. D gives 53p. [L11133; D8508; VV128].

McIVER -- McMaster, Louise M. *Roderick McIver and His Family.* Charleston, SC, Legerton, 1952. 45 leaves. [X606-NY].

McKAY -- Couch, Sarah Crenshaw. *The Martin Stanley McCay and Martha P. Collins McCay Family Genealogy.* Clemson, SC, S.C. Couch, 1988. 22, 441p., 1 leaf of plates. 1. McKay family. 2. McCay, Martin Stanley, 1806-1876-Family. [G441].

McKAY -- McKoy, Henry Bacon. *The McKoy Family of North Carolina Including Ancrum, Berry, Halling, Hasell, and Usher.* Greenville, SC, 1955. 198p. D lists under McKoy and gives title as: "The McKoy Family in North Carolina." [L11147; NG67; D8538].

McKELDEN -- Frink, James L. *Something about the McKeldens and the McIntoshes and Other Ancestors.* Greensboro, NC, Office Service Co., 1972. 138p. [D8523].

McKINSEY -- Barry, Ruby M. *The McKinsey's (sic) (McKensey, McKensie, McKinsey) Family; Descendants of George W. McKinsey and His Wife Sarah (Thomas) McKinsey of Newberry, S. C. and Warren County, Ohio and the Migration of Their Children into Indiana.* Indianapolis, IN, R. M. Barry, 1969. 216p.
[X609-FW/NY].

McKISSICK -- Graydon, Nell S, et al. *The McKissicks of South Carolina. The Stories of a Piedmont Family and Related Lives.* Columbia, SC, 1965. xv, 485p.
[L11185].

McLARTY -- McLarty, Adelaide. *The McLarty Family of Kintyre, Scotland and Mecklenburg County, North Carolina and Their Descendants.* Lexington, NC, 1974. 962p. NG gives underscored part of title.
[S1673; NG67; X610-FW].

McLEAN -- McLean, Angus Wilton. [G443]. See above: McINTYRE. [G441].

McLEAN -- McLean, Angus Wilton. *Lumber River Scots and Their Descendants.* Lumberton, NC, McLean, 1942, xxvii, 839p. [Earlier edition of work just above]. [D8541].

McLEMORE -- Lee, Margaret McLemore. *McLemore - Johnson Family of Johnston County, North Carolina.* NP, 1976. 107 leaves. [D8544].

McLEMORE -- McLemore, James L. *The Early History of the McLemore Family of Virginia and the Carolinas.* Suffolk, VA, J.L. McLemore, 1988. 2, 117p., 12p. of plates. 1. McLemore family. 2. Virginia-Genealogy. 3. North Carolina-Genealogy. 4. South Carolina-Genealogy. [G443].

McLENDON -- NAS. *The McLendons of Anson County, (1695-1957).* Wadesboro, NC, 1958. 112p. [L11211].

McLENDON -- Redfearn, Rosalind McLendon. *The McLendons of Anson County.* Wadesboro, NC, 1958. 112p. [D8546].

McLEOD -- Hoffman, Una McLeod. [G444]. See above: JONES. [G353].

McLEOD -- MacLeod, James B. *The Descendants of Alexander McLeod.* United States, Published by Scot Press for the Clan MacLeod Society USA, 1985. 34p. (Migration project publication series; no. 5.) 1. McLeod family. 2. McLeod, Alexander, ca. 1730-1815-Family. 3. North Carolina-Genealogy. 4. Scotland-Genealogy. 5. Great Britain-Genealogy. [G444].

McMASTER -- McMaster, Fitz Hugh. *The History of MacMaster - McMaster Family.* Columbia, SC, 1926. 142p. [L11223; NG67].

McMURRAY -- White, James Westley. *History of the McMurray Family in Guilford County, North Carolina.* NP, 1951. 24 l. [D8557].

McNAIR -- Humphries, Lillie Marvin (Mrs. John D. *Descendants of Daniel McNair of Georgia, Jacob Miller of South Carolina, James Nisbet of Georgia, and Robert Jones of South Carolina.* Atlanta, GA, Humphries, 1935. 65p. [L11244; D8564].

McNEILL -- Reynolds, Harriet Dickson. *James and Jane McNeill of North Carolina, Georgia, and Alabama.* NP, 1963, 48 l. [D8572].

McNEILL -- Rose, Ben Lacy. *Thomas McNeill of Caswell County, North Carolina; His Forebears & Descendants.* Richmond, VA, B.L. Rose, 1984. 154p. [NG70; DC2510].

McNIEL -- Hayes, Johnson J. Genealogy of the McNiel Clan *Descendants of Rev. George McNeil, b. in Scotland.* Wilkesboro, NC, Hayes, 1934. 113p. X gives "McNeil" throughout. [D8578; X613-FW].

McPHAIL -- Simmons, Fannie Vann. *Daniel Alexander McPherson and His Descendants.* Raleigh, NC, Print. by Litho Industries, 1968. x, 148p. [L11259].

McQUEEN -- McEleyea, Mrs. R. T. *The McQueens of Queensdale: A Biography of Colonel James McQueen and His Descendants, 1765-1908 with an Introduction by Hon. A. W. MacLean, and the Proceedings of the First Clan McQueen Meeting at Maxton, N.C., June 3 - 5, 1913.* Charlotte, NC, Observer Printing House, 1916. 6, 261p. D gives underscored title and Wilmington, NC, 1916. 261p. [L11272; D8010].

McQUEEN -- McEleyea, Mrs. R. T. *The McQueens of Queensdale: A Biography of Colonel James McQueen and His Descendants, 1765-1908.* Wilmington, NC, 1908. 91p. See also above MacQueen [D8010; X614-FW/LI/NY].

McSWAIN -- McSwain, Eleanor (Davis). *Some Descendants of David McSwain (B/Isle of Skye-d. N.C); The Families of Hamrick, Washburn, McGowan, McWilliams, Ware, Wells, Randle.* Macon, GA, Nat. Print., 1974. viii, 234p. D gives underscored title. [S1684; NG68; D8594; X615-FW].

McWILLIE -- Johnson, Robert D. *Genealogy of the McWillie and Cunningham Families.* Columbia, SC, R.L. Bryan Co., 1938. iv, 219p. [D8603].

MEADOWS -- Arrington, Clarence H. [G447]. See above: ARRINGTON. [G20].

MEANS -- McBryde, Sara C. *Genealogy of the Means Family Fairfield County, South Carolina.* NP, 1935. 12, 5, 6 leaves. [D8632].

MEHERRIN -- Mayfield, George R. III. *The Living Dream; A Story of Upper-South Carolina Pioneers.* Columbia, SC, R.L. Bryan Co., 1971. 239p. [A449].

MERCER -- Mercer, Joseph C. *Descendants of Noah Mercer and Wife, Sarah, Born in Jones County, N.C. about 1773, Died in 1823 in Jones County, Gray, Georgia.* Gray, GA, 1964, c1967. iii, 58p. [L11745].

MERRILL -- Merrill, William Ernest. *Captain Benjamin Merrill and the Merrill Family of North Carolina.* Penrose, NC, Merrill, 1935. 90p. [L11774; D8693].

MERRITT -- Merritt, Edward. *The Merritts of Sampson and Duplin Counties, North Carolina.* NP, 1968. ix, 136 leaves. [D8701].

MERRITT -- Turner, Lynne Slater. *The Merritt Families of North Carolina...* NP, n.d, __v. DAR library holdings: v. 2(1700-1850). [DC2545].

MICK -- Romine, R. R. *The Mick Family of West Virginia: A Genealogy and History.* Raleigh, NC, R.R. Romine, 1989. 74 l. 1. Mick family. 2. West Virginia-Genealogy. [G454].

MIDDLETON -- Middleton, Alicia Hopton. *Life in Carolina and New England During the Nineteenth Century as Illustrated by Reminiscences and Letters of the Middleton Family of Charleston, South Carolina, and of the De Wolf Family of Briston, Rhode Island.* Bristol, RI, Priv. Print. 1929. xii p. 2 leaves, 233p. 500 copies. Contents. - A family record by Alicia H. Middleton. - Record by Nathaniel Middleton. - Reminiscences by Nathaniel Middleton. Record of the Marston family from the reminiscences of Annie E. Marston De Wolf. [L11849].

MILES -- Miles, Ralph J. *A Genealogy of the Miles Family Mainly of the Carolinas and Georgia.* Birmingham, AL, Miles, 1984. 173p. [DC2559].

MILHOUS -- Milhous, Evelyn Perry (Mrs. A.P. Ferguson). *History of the Milhous Family in*

South Carolina. Miami, FL, Printed by cooperation of the Miami Herald, 1944. 12 leaves. [L11863].

MILLER -- DeHuff, Elizabeth W. *Miller Family of North and South Carolina.* Augusta, GA, 1967. 81p. [XA1074].

MILLER -- Hunt, June Perkins. *John Miller of Marion County, South Carolina.* NP, 1976. 160 leaves. [D8773].

MILLER -- Miller, Danny. *The Miller Family of Ashe County, North Carolina.* Winston-Salem, NC, Hunter Pub. Co., 1979. 422p. [D8781].

MILLER -- Miller, Geraldine Trexler. *Wendel Miller and His Descendants.* United States: G.T. Miller, 1985. xvi, 608p. 1. Miller family. 2. Miller, Wendel, 1728/9-1805-Family. 3. North Carolina-Genealogy. [G455].

MILLER -- Miller, Ruth Suitor. *Some Descendants of Daniel Miller (d. 1816) of Adams Pennsylvania and Mahoning Co., Ohio.* Asheville, NC, Ward Pub. Co., 1986. xii, 88p. 1. Miller family. 2. Miller, Daniel, d. 1816-Family. 3. Ohio-Genealogy. [G455; DC2569].

MILLER -- Niemann, Rubinetta Miller. *Our Heritage.* Burlington, NC, Niemann, 1981. 253p. [DS493].

MILLER -- Overlander, Rufus M. [G456]. See above: BLUNT. [G63].

MILLER -- Whitaker, Harriet Katherine Reed. *Genealogy of the Miller Family.* Southern Pines, NC, Dixie Printing Co., 1926. 20p. [D8812].

MILLER -- White, Margaret Miller. *The Hugenot Millers: A Family History.* Fulton, MS, Itawamba County Times, 1986. 435p. 1.

Miller family. 2. Mournier family. 3. South Carolina-Genealogy. [G456].

MILLING -- Fletcher, Azile Milling. *The Milling Family of South Carolina, 1771-1976.* NP, 1976. 174p. [D8815].

MILLS -- Mills, Laurens Tenney. *A South Carolina Family: Mills - Smith and Related Lines.* Addenda by Lilla M. Hawes and Sarah M. Norton. NP, 1960. 158p. NG omits underlined part of title. [L11933; NG71].

MILLS -- Potter, Hazel Alexander. *Mills - Mitchell and Allied Families, 1720-1987.* NP, H.A. Potter, 1987. 339p. 1. Mills family. 2. Mitchell family. 3. South Carolina-Genealogy. 4. Georgia-Genealogy. [G456].

MINOR -- Lumpkin, Martha Neville. *Minor, Scales, Cottrell, and Gray Families of Virginia, North Carolina, and Mississippi.* Clarksville, TN, 1974. 133p. NG lists with Lumpkin. [NG65].

MITCHELL -- Allen, Estill Franklin. *Cousins: Handbook and Family History of Mitchell, Allen, Gilleland, and Related Families from Virginia into Georgia, North Carolina, Kentucky, Tennessee, Missouri, Mississippi, Illinois, Iowa, Arkansas, Louisiana, Oklahoma, New Jersey, Texas, California, Florida, and Idaho, mid 1700's to 1980.* Brownwood, TX, Howard Payne University, 1981. xxiv, 347p. [C477; VV132].

MITCHELL -- Mitchell, B. S. *Mitchell - Pearman Families.* Honea Path, SC, 1967. 1 v. (various pagings). [L11990].

MITCHELL -- Mitchell, Lily E. *American Branch of the Mitchell Family of Scotland and Its Major Allied Families.* Cary, NC, 1960. 175p. [X657-FW].

MITCHELL -- Potter, Hazel Alexander. [G458]. See above: MILLS. [G456].

MITCHENER -- Mitchiner, William A. *The Mitchener and Mitchiner Families of North Carolina and Other States and Related Families of Turner, Stevens, Nance, and Powell.* Baltimore, MD, Gateway Press, 1989. 1, Mitchener Family. 2. Mitchner, Samuel, 1768-1836-Family. 3. Turner family. 4. Stevens family. 5. North Carolina-Genealogy. [G458].

MOAD -- Horlacher, Gary T. [G459]. See above: CHAMBERS. [G131].

MOAK -- Moak, Lennox Lee. *The Moak and Related Families of South Carolina and Mississippi, 1740-1960; with Notes as to Members of the Family in Tennessee and Illinois and Also Notes as to Other Moak Families in New York, Pennsylvania, Maryland, and Virginia.* Fort Washington, PA, 1960. 310 leaves. [L11996; VP157; VV132].

MOISE -- Moïse, Harold. *The Moïse Family of South Carolina and an Account of the Life and Descendants of Abraham and Sarah Moïse, Who Settled in Charleston, South Carolina, in the Year 1791 A.D.* Columbia, SC, Moïse, Printed by R.L. Bryan Co., 1961. xvi, 304p. [L12011; D8873].

MONK -- Bowman, Charles H, Jr.. *The Monk Family.* Southern Pines, NC, 1969. 40 leaves. 1. Monk family. X gives 75 leaves. [G460; A461; X660-NY].

MONROE -- Patterson, Alex M. *The Monroes of the Upper Cape Fear Valley.* Miami, FL, McAskill Pub. Co., 1976. 145p. [X660-LA].

MONTGOMERY -- Bryan, Catherine Cameron Wilkerson. *Montgomery's of South Carolina, Mississippi, and Other Southern States.* West Point, MS, Bryan, 1959. 75 l. [D8898].

MONTGOMERY -- Williams, Robert T. *John Sumner Williams and Helen Katherine Montgomery, Their Ancestors and Descendants, 1461-1987.* Cary, NC, R.T. Williams, C.P. Williams, 1987. 87 leaves. 1. Williams family. 2. Montgomery family. 3. Williams, John Sumner, 1862-1943-Family. [G462].

MONTS -- Wright, William Howard. *Our Monts Family: A History of the John Casper Monts Family of South Carolina.* Ann Arbor, MI, Wright, 1990. vii, 1089p. [DC2602].

MOOD -- Stubbs, Thomas McAlpin. *Family Album, An Account of the Moods of Charleston, South Carolina, and Connected Families.* Atlanta, GA, Stubbs, 1943. 2, ix, 246p. D lists under MOODS. [L12082; D8907].

MOODY -- Moody, Helen Belden. *Richard Moody, 1810-1892: His Ancestors, Family and Descendants.* Dillon, SC, H.B. Moody, 1990. vi, 225p. 1. Moody family. 2. Moody, Richard, 1810-1892-Family. 3. South Carolina-Genealogy. [G462].

MOONEY -- Sheriff, Pauline Calloway. [G463]. See above: DAVIS. [G178].

MOORE -- Austin, Nancy Jane Moore. *The Moore Family of Anson and Union Counties, North Carolina, 1750-1986 [i,e,1988].* Peachland, NC, Charlotte, NC, M.L.M. Yandle, 1988. viii, 362p. 1. Moore family. 2. North Carolina-Genealogy. [G463; DC2607].

MOORE -- Cope, Robert. *The Moore Family of North Carolina dates - 1742.* NP, 1954. 58 leaves. [D8922].

MOORE -- Guess, Dorothy Moore. *Genealogy of the Moore Family of Londonerry, New Hampshire and Peterborough, New Hampshire.* Columbia, SC, R. L. Bryan Co., 1976. 285p. [D8925].

MOORE -- More, Grace Van Dyke, Ed. *Chronicles of the Moore Family. Published upon the occasion of the Sixty-Fifth Anniversary of the Organization of the John More Association.* Greensboro, NC, 1955. xvi, 424p. [L12133].

MOORE -- Moor, Steven Richard. *The Moore Huffman Family: with Subsequent Related Materials of the History of the Moore (More), Williard (Viellard), Huffman (Hoffman), and Lail (Lagle) Branches and Their Arrival and Settlement in the Areas of Pennsylania, Maryland, Virginia, and North Carolina.* Jamestown, NC, 1978. pni. [VV133].

MOORE -- Revill, Janie. *Abstract of Moore Records of South Carolina, 1694-1865.* Columbia, SC, The State Co., 1931. 46p. [L12121; D8945].

MOORE -- Van Valin, Minnie D. *John Moore, Senior, Revolutionary War Patriot of Anson / Tryone i.e. Tryon / Lincoln / Gaston County, North Carolina.* NP, 1968. 104 l. [D8950].

MORAGNE -- Moragne, Mary E. *The Neglected Thread.* Columbia, SC, University of South Carolina Press, 1951. 256p. [D8955].

MOORHEAD -- Moorhead, Paul A. *The John Moorhead Family of South Carolina; A Short History and Genealogy (1st ed.)* Largo, FL, 1973. 33 leaves. [S1788a].

MOREHEAD -- Edmunds, Mary Lewis Rucker. *Governor Morehead's Blandwood and the Family Who Lived There.* Greensboro, NC, 1976. 52p. 1. Greensboro, N,C. Blandwood, 2. Morehead, John Motley, 1796-1866. 3. Morehead family. 4. Governors-North Carolina-Biography. [G465; X666-FW].

MOREHEAD -- Morehead, John Motley, III. *The Morehead Family of North Carolina and*

Virginia. New York, NY, Morehead, 1921. 57 leaves. [D8961; VV133].

MOREHEAD -- Morehead, John Motley, III. *The Morehead Family of North Carolina and Virginia.* New York, NY, Morehead, Edition of 50 copies printed by De Vinne Press, 1921. x pages, 2 leaves, 147p. [L12147].

MORRIS -- Morris, Whitmore. *A Morris Family of Mecklenberg County, North Carolina.* San Antonio, TX, 1956. 128p. [L12206].

MORRISETTE -- Shannonhouse, Edna Morrisette. *The Morrisettes of North Carolina and Other Southern States.* Elizabeth City, NC, Shannonhouse, 1972. iv, 186p. X gives: M.S. Raper as publisher. [D9012; X669-FW/NY].

MORRISON -- Lore, Adelaide. *The Morrison Family of the Rocky River Settlement of North Carolina.* NP, Eugenia Lore, 1950. 543p. [L12216; D9014].

MORRISON -- Morrison, Barclay. *Dust to Dust.* Hilton Head, SC, B. Morrison, 1988. 266p. 1. Morrison, Barcley, 1912- -Family. 2. Morrison family. 3. United States-Biography. 4. World War, 1939-1945-Personal Narratives, American. 5. Engineers-United States-Biography. [G468].

MORROW -- Morrow, J. T. *Morrow Family of South Carolina, Mississippi, Alabama, and Texas; Ancestors and Descendants of Jane Peden and Samuel Morrow...* Chicago, IL, 1934. 44 leaves. [X669-FW].

MORSE -- Ballinger, Dwight Gail. *White - Morse Family History, 1790-1985.* Cincinnati, OH, Mr. & Mrs. D.G. Ballinger, 1987. iv, 54 leaves. 1. White family. 2. Morse family. 3. North Carolina-Genealogy. [G468].

MORSE -- Haynsworth, Hugh Charles. *Ancestry and Descendants of Sarah Morse Haynsworth a South Carolina Supplement to the Histories of Morse (Moss) Tomlinson, Welles, Curtis, and Shelton Families of Connecticut.* Sumter, SC, Priv. Printed by Osteen Pub. Co., 1939. 52p. [L12232].

MORTON -- McKenney, Ruby Griffin. *Genealogical Records of John Morton and His Descendants of Pennsylvania, Virginia, North Carolina, Georgia, & Florida.* NP, 1961. 26 leaves. [D9043; VP160; VV135].

MORTON -- Morgan, Donna Morton. *The Lookout Mountain Mortons and Their Descendants: Plus Ancestors and Relatives from York Co., Pennsylvania, Mecklenburg Co., North Carolina, Blount Co., Tennessee, and Walker Co., Georgia.* Baltimore, Gateway Press, New Orleans, LA, D.M. Morgan, 1989. viii, 256p. 1. Morton family. 2. Georgia-Genealogy. [G468].

MOSELEY -- Moseley, Thomas Byrd. *A Moseley Genealogy: England, Holland, Virginia, The Carolinas, Georgia, Alabama, Mississippi, Louisiana, Texas, to the West Coast.* Baltimore, Gateway Press, 1985. xv, 3287p., 2 leaves of plates. C & VV list under MOSLEY. [C489; DC2655: VV135].

MOSLEY -- Mosley, Modie Young. *The Search for West Mosley / Moseley and His Descendants.* Clyde, TX, M.Y. Mosley, 1989. xiv, 519p. 1. Mosley family. 2. West, 1751-1821-Family. 3. North Carolina-Genealogy. [G469].

MOSS -- Moss, T. C. *The David Moss Family; Warren and Granville Co., N.C. Green, Adair, Mercer, Boyle, Barren, Hart and Warren County, Ky. Williamson and Maury Co., Tenn. Mississippi.* Memphis, TN, Print by C. Johnson and Assocs., 1968. 79p. [L12274].

MOUNIER -- White, Margaret Miller. [G470]. See above: MILLER. [G456].

MOXLEY -- Sturgill, Lorene Moxley. [G471]. See above: HOPPER. [G330].

MULLIKEN -- Mullican, N. Spencer. *Mullikins and Mullicans of North Carolina; A History of Lewis Mulliken and His Descendants, Covering the Period Since His Arrival in Rowan County, North Carolina in 1781 from the Western Shore of Maryland.* Winston-Salem, NC, Mullican, 1950. 218p. D lists under MULLIKIN. [L12341; D9099].

MULLINAX -- Mullinax, Otto B. *Some Mullinax Roots, South Carolina to Texas.* Austin, TX, O.B. Mullinax, 1982. xv, 242p. [NG73; DC2671].

MULLINS -- Sturgill, Wanda Hutchinson. *Ths John Mullins and Nancy Gentry Family Tree.* Mathews, NC, W.H. Sturgill, 1983. 37p. [DC2672].

MULLIS -- Mullies, William Arthur. *A History of the English Speaking Mullis Family.* Kansas City, MO? W.A. Mullies, 1984- v. <1 >. Contents: v. 1. C 874 A.D. to 1774

A.D. 1. Mullis family. 2. Virginia-Biography. 3. North Carolina-Biography. 4. England-Biography. [G472].

MURPHREE -- Linder, Billy Royce. *Daniel Murphree of Bertie, Orange, and Chatham Counties, North Carolina.* Vienna, VA, 1973. 8 leaves. [D9122; X677-FW].

MURRAY -- Murray, Alton J. *Kindred Murrays: A Story of the Murrays Who Imigrated from the Cape Fear in North Carolina to the Province of Georgia in 1769 and Their Kindred.* St. Mary's, GA, Murray, 1981. xv, 104p., 2 leaves of plates. [C495; DS511].

MUSGRAVE -- Shartle, Stanley Musgrave. *A History of the Quaker Branch of the Musgrave Family of the North of Ireland, Pennsylvania,*

North Carolina, Illinois, and Elsewhere, with Selected Papers Relating to the Ancient and Landed Musgraves of England. Indianapolis, IN, 1961. 200p. NG gives underscored title: [L12376; NG73; VP162].

MYERS -- Martin, Sophie Stephens. *Ancestors and Descendants of William R. Myers.* Chapel Hill, NC, S.S. Martin, 1984. 91, 38p. 1. Myers family. 2. Myers, William Rayford-Family. [G475].

N

NACHAMSON -- NAS. *"Always Good to Each Other"; The Story of the Nachamsons as told by Jennie B. and the Nine Children.* Durham, NC, 1968. vii, 172p. [S1800].

NANCE -- Mitchiner, William A. [G476]. See above: MITCHENER. [G458].

NANCE -- Nance, Davidson. *The History and Genealogy of the Nances; but More Particularly of the Descendants of Dr. John and Jane Nance of Mecklenburg County, Virginia.* Marshallville, NC, Nance, 1930. 149p. D gives undersored part of title. [D9155; X681-FW].

NASH -- Nash, James Henry. *The Georgia Descendants of Edward Nash of Greenville County, South Carolina and Some Related Families.* Somerville, TN, 1973. 111p. NG gives underscored part of title. [S1802b; NG73].

NASH -- Nash, Sara M. [G476]. See above: FOWLER. [G237; S1802a; D9163].

NASH -- Nash, Shepard. K. *Nash.* Sumter, SC, Nash, 1954. 36p. [D9164

NATION -- Nations, Loye E. *Descendants of Mattison Nations and Myrtle Della Sands.*

Columbia, SC, 1969. 173p. 1. Nations family. [G477].

NEAL -- Reynolds, Katherine. *Some Descendants of Younger Neal of Chatham County, North Carolina; with Notes on the Neal Family.* NP, 1965. 175 leaves. [D9182].

NEATHERY -- Neathery, John Marshall. *A Partial History of the Neathery Family, of Mecklenburg, Virginia.* Rolesville, NC, J.M. Marshall, 1979. 39 leaves. [DC2699].

NEELY -- Neely, Juanita Henderson. *Neely Family History, 1730-1939.* Rock Hill, SC, Neely, 1959. 55p. [D9189].

NELSON -- Cox, William E. and Mrs. Olivia Cox McCormoc, et al. *Our Family Genealogy, Including the Nelson, Johnson, Roach, Smith, Little, Cox, Dawson, Wooten, and Chapman Families, each Related to the Others by Descent or Marriage, or Both.* Southern Pines, NC, The Mary Nelson Smith Family, 1938. 5, 109, 8p. [L12460].

NELSON -- Cox, William E. *Our Family Genealogy.* Raleigh, NC, Mary Nelson Smith Family, 1967. 279p. [D9210].

NELSON -- Nelson, Wm. D. *Reflections of Five Generations, 1760-1967.* Reynolds, NC, 1967. 161p. [X685-FW].

NESBIT -- Nisbet, Newton Alexander. *Nisbet Narrations (1st ed).* Charlotte, NC, Printed by Crayton Print Co., 1961. 439p. [L12474].

NEUENSCHWANDGER -- Lanphere, Edward Everett. *The Neuenschwandger (Nighswander, Niswanger) Line Genealogy.* Chapel Hill, NC, Lanphere, 1970. 134 leaves. X gives 114p, 19 leaves, and Rev. ed. [D9223; X686-FW].

NEWBURY -- Collar, Grant Harold. *Newbury Family and In-Laws: Ten Generations, John*

Newberry I + Joanna Swain, Married 1786 in North Carolina. Little Rock, AK, G.H. Coller,Jr., 1989. 413p. 1. Newbury family. 2. Newberry, John, b. ca. 1754-Family. 3. Southern States-Genealogy. [G480].

NEWKIRK -- Newkirk, Elizabeth. *Newkirk Family in North Carolina.* NP, 1958. 266 leaves. [D9245].

NEWLIN -- Newlin, Algie I. *The Newlin Family, Ancestors and Descendants of John and Mary Pyle Newlin.* Greensboro, NC, 1965. x, 578p. D gives underscored title. [L12525; NG74; D9251].

NEWTON -- Newton, Leroy L. *Genealogical Report: Newton and Flury and Allied Families: from Maryland, Virginia, Alabama, South Carolina, Georgia, Southern Arkansas, Red Lands in Indiana Territory, Oklahoma, and Other Places.* Altus, OK, L. L. Newton, 1987. 134, a-j pages, 3 leaves of plates. 1. Newton family. 2. Fleury family. 3. Oklahoma-Genealogy. 4. Afro-American-Genealogy. [G480].

NEWTON -- Riddings, Beulah Philbeck. [G480]. See above: DOWNS. [G199].

NGUYEN -- Nguyen, Trieu Dan. *A Vietnamese Family Chronicle: Twelve Generations on the Banks of the Hat River.* Jefferson, NC, McFarland, 1991. pni. 1. Nguyen family. 2. Kim Bài (Vietnam)-Genealogy. [G481].

NICHOLSON -- NAS. *Genealogy of Nicholson and Allied Families.* Edgefield, SC, Edgefield County Historical Society, 1944. 68p. [D9274; X689-FW].

NICHOLSON -- Nicholson, Kenneth J. *John & Mary Williams Nicholson: North Carolina Pioneers to Indiana and Iowa. - 1st ed.* Falls Church, VA, P.N. Briggs, Falls Church, VA, 198_-1989. 7 v. Vols. [2]-7 have subtitle:

North Carolina pioneers to Indiana and Iows, with known descendants. Vol. [6] by K.J. Nicholson adn Geanell Brooks Carman. Vol [1] Rev. 1989. Contents: [1] Introduction - [2] A chapter on their son Andrew Nichsqson (sic), and his wife, Sarah Ann Lamb, and known descendants - [3] A chapter on their son Joseph Nicholson, and his wife, Sarah Murray, and known descendants - [4] A chapter on their son Williams Nicholson, and his wife, Ruth Bond, and known descendants - [5] A chapter on their daughter Sarah Nicholson, and husband Thomas Murray II, and known descendants - [6] A chapter on their son James Taylor Nicholson, and his wife, Sarah Veal, and known descendants - [7] A chapter on their daughter Jane Nicholson, and her two husbands, Thomas F. Madison and John Larkin Stahl and known descendants. 1. Nicholson family. 2. Nicholson, John, 1784-1868-Family. 3. Nicholson, Mary Williams, 1782-1852-Family. 4. North Carolina-Genealogy. 5. Iowa-Genealogy. 6. Indiana-Genealogy. [G482; NGN17-1-91].

NORRIS -- Morrison, Leonard A. *Lineage and Biographies of the Norris Family from 1640 - 1892. With References to the Norrises of England...* Boston, MA, Damrell & Upham, 1892. Charleston, SC, Garnier & Co. 1968. 207p. [X693-PH].

NORRIS -- Young, Pauline. *"Norris Family" of Abbeville, South Carolina (Old Ninety-Six District).* Abbeville, SC, 1948. 9, 8p. Typed. [X693-FW].

NORTON -- Norton, Sarah Mills. *Generations Back: Norton & Related Lines.* Wallhala, SC, 1977. 336p. [NG75; D9332].

NORWOOD -- Norwood, Margaret Dial. *Capt. John Norwood and Mary Warren Norwood.* Goldsboro, NC, Hillburn Printing Corp., 1979. 217p. [D9338].

NORWOOD -- Nowrood, William Howard. *'General' John Norwood.* Dallas, TX, Trumpet Press, 1964. 424p. Typescript addends: Norwood families of South Carolina by Mable Van Dyke Baer, 1973, bound separately. [D9339].

NYE -- Nye, L. Bert. *A Genealogy of American Nyes of German Origin.* Wilkesboro, NC, 1984. 2 v. [DC2756].

O

OAKES -- Oaks, William Bryant. *Descendants of Isaac Oakes/Oaks, Born in North Carolina in 1777, Died in Tennessee in 1870.* Renton, WA, W.B. Oaks, Jr., 1985. 1. Oakes family. 2. Oakes, Isaac, 1777-1870-Family. [G488].

O'BANNON -- De Huff, Elizabeth Willis. *The Family of Thomas O'Bannon of Fauquier County, Virginia, and Barnewell County, South Carolina.* August, GA, 1969. 60p. [S1832; VV140].

O'CONNER -- Cox, Lula Price O'Conner, (Mrs. William Edward) *The O'Conner - Conner - Simmons Families.* Southern Pines, NC, W. E. Cox, Jr., 1941. vi, 81p. [L12696; D9376].

O'HEGERTY -- Hagerty, John C. *History of the Nobel O'Hegerty Family; Ancient Lords of Magherabeg and Clainsullagh... Donegal... Ireland.* Charleston, SC, Hagerty, 1959. Various pagings. [X699-FW].

O'HIGGINS -- Lord, Robert A. *Contribution Toward a Bibliography of the O'Higgins Family in America.* Durham, NC, 1932. p.107-138. "Reprinted from the Hispanic American historical review. vol. XIII, No. 1 February, 1932. [L124764].

OLIPHANT -- NAS. *The Oliphant Family. Descendants of William and Betsy Gordy*

Oliphant. Wilmette, IL, Oliphant Family History, 1975. pni. [NG75].

OLIPHANT -- NAS. *Descendants of William Oliphant of North Carolina. Also Collateral Families: Weatherlee, Colee, Hale, Vaughn, Slough, Morgan, Burch, Martindale Families. Rev. ed. addenda and corr. with Index.* Mt. Prospect, IL, Oliphant Family History, 1976. ?vol. [X701-FW].

OLIPHANT -- NAS. *Descendants of William Oliphant of North Carolina. Also Martindale, Burch, Morgan, Hale, Vaughn, Slough, Colee, Mitchell, King Families. Rev.* Wilmette, IL, Oliphant Family History, 1977. pni. [NG75].

OLIPHANT -- Stein, Nancy Hawlick. *Descendants of Wm. Oliphant of North Carolina.* Wilmette, IL, Oliphant Family History, 1974. 248, 29p. [D9420].

OLIVE -- NAS. *James Olive Family, Wake County, N.C.* Fort Worth, TX, Olive Family Association, 1965. iv, 281p. [L12777; D9421].

OLIVER -- Oliver, Hugh R. *Sketches of the Olivers: A Family History, 1726-1966. - 1st ed.* Pinehurst, NC, H.R. Oliver, 1987. xii, 571p. 1. Oliver family. [G491; DC2769].

OLIVER -- Lefvendahl, Georgie I. Adams. *Oliver - Sistrunk Families.* Orangeburg, SC, Lefvendahl, 1964. 73 l. [L12789; D9424].

ORMOND -- Ormond, Ben F. *Ormand History and Decendants [sic] of James Ormand, Sr., 1669-1976: Some History of the Orman's, Ormand's, and Ormonds, [sic] also Descendants of James Ormand, Sr., and Related Families, Dixon, Huffstetler, Goforth, Price, Thornburg.* Greenville, SC, A Press, 1983. 200p. 1. Ormond family. 2. Ormand, James, 1669-1766-Family. [G495].

OUDERKIRK -- Ouderkirk, Henry John. *The Ouderkerk Family Genealogy from 1660.* Charlotte, NC, 1982. 1 v. [NG76].

OUDERKIRK -- Ouderkirk, Henry John. *The Ouderkerk Family Genealogy from 1660.* Charlotte, NC, Delmar Publishers 1982-<1990- >. v. <1-2 >. Vol. 2 edited by H. John Ouderkirk and Raymond D. Ouderkirk. Contents: v. 1. From 1660 - v. 2. Families Ouderkerk, Ouderkirk, Oderkirk, and Odekirk. 1, Ouderkerk family. [G497].

OUTLAW -- Outlaw, Albert Timothy. *Outlaw Genealogy, and An Account of the First Grady - Outlaw Reunion.* Wilson, NC, P.D. Gold Pub. Co., 1930. 71p. D gives underscored title. [L12885; NG76; D9475].

OUZTS -- Woodson, Hortense. *Peter Ouzts I and His Descendants.* Edgefield, SC, Edgefield Advertiser, 1949. 345p. [D9477].

OWEN -- Bagley, Miss M. C. *A Family Tree of John Owen, a Colonial Settler in North Carolina.* Jackson, NC, 18__. Geneal. Table. [L12896].

OWNBY -- Morgan, Boyce M. *The Ownby - Ownbey Families of Rutherford and Buncombe Counties, North Carolina, and Eastern Tennessee.* El Paso, TX, B.M. Morgan, 1988 [1989]. 63, 233p. Some copies may be imperfect: p176 blank. 1. Ownby family. 2. North Carolina-Genealogy. 3. Tennessee-Genealogy. [G498].

OZMENT -- Reynolds, Fanny O. *Record of the Descendants of Richard Ozment (1800-1866) and His Wife Rebecca (Polly) Eddings (1801-1843)...* Greensville, NC, 1957 58 l. [X71 -].

P

PADGETT -- Padgett, Bob. *Paper Mansions.* Asheville, NC, Bright Mountain Books, 1986.

242p., 1p. of plates. Illustrated by Dianne Cable. 1. Black Mountain Region (N.C.)-Biography. 2. Padgett family. 3. Padgett, Bob, 1925- 4. Black Mountain Region (N.C.)-Social life and customs. [G499].

PAGE -- Page, Jesse M. *The Page Family of North Carolina, 1685-1850: A Compilation of Primary Records.* Raleigh, NC, 1987. vii, 849p. NGS gives underscorted title and 749p. [G499; NGS9].

PAINE -- Bivins, Caroline Pasteur Holmes. *Pedigree Chart of Dolley Payne, b. May 20, 1768 at New Garden, N.C., d. July 12, 1849 at Washington, D.C. m. first John Todd, Jr., Jan 7, 1790 and second, James Madison, Jr., Sept. 15, 1794.* Greensboro, NC, 1970. 4 leaves. 1. Madison, Dolley, 1768-1849. 2. Paine family. [G500].

PALLEN -- Lambeth, Mary Weeks. See above: BAILEY. [L757]

PALMER -- Palmer, John T. *The Palmers and Parmers of North Carolina, Alabama, and Mississippi: With Related Lines of Gates,Hays, Layton, May, Mangum, Ponder, Ross, Rouse, Drury, and other Early Simpson County, Mississippi Families.* Santa Rosa, CA, J.T. Palmer, 1988. ix, 332p. 1. Palmer family. 2. Gates family. 3. Hayes family. 4. Mississippi-Genealogy. [G501].

PARIS -- Paris, Maurice Hudson Thatcher. *Threlkeld - Paris Genealogy, Including Twenty-Fofour Allied Families.* Georgetown, SC, Lawrimore Corp., 1989. viii, 132p. 1. Threlkeld family. 2. Paris family. 3. Price family. 4. Shaw family.. [G502].

PARK -- Creech, William Douglas. *A Parks Family Album Featuring Berry Amaziah Parks and His Wife, Mary Eliza Smith and Their Descendants.* Charlotte, NC, W.D. Creech, 1988. 1 v. 1. Park family. 2. Parks, Berry

Amaziah, 1848-1911. 3. North Carolina-Genealogy. [G502].

PARK -- Miller, Helen Hill. *Colonel Parke of Virginia: The Greatest Hector in the Town: A Biography*. Chapel Hill, NC, Algonquin Books of Chapel Hill, 1989. xx, 232p. 1. Parke, Daniel, 1664 or 5-1710. 2. Politicians-Virginia-Biography. 3. Virginia-History-Colonial period, ca. 1600-1775. 4. Park family. 5. Spanish Succession, War of 1701-1714-Campaigns. 6. Colonial Administrators-Great Britain-Biography. [G502].

PARK -- Park, Evelyn Potter. *Allen Park, 1745-1805 of Rowan County, North Carolina and Madison County, Kentucky; Including Some of His Descendants and Allied Families*. Chandler, OK, W. R. Park, 1970. x, 300p. [A517].

PARKER -- NAS. *Nathaniel Parker (2), 1651-1737, Reading Massachusetts and His Descendants, Showing Their Ancestry in America from Thomas Parker (1), 1609-1683, Puritan Emigrant from England to Massachusetts in 1635; A Biographical and Historical Genealogy*. Kershaw, SC, 1966, xvi, 146p. [L13076].

PARKER -- Bagley, Miss M. C. *A Family Tree of John Parker, a Colonial Settler in North Carolina. Drawn from data furnished by B.F. Bullard of Savannah, GA.* Jackson, NC, 1906. Geneal. Tab. [L13054].

PARKER -- Kirkpatrick, Eunice Temple. *The Parker Family of Johnston County, North Carolina, and Related Families*. Durham, NC, Kirkpatrick, 1980. iii, 127p. [D9583].

PARKER -- Kirkpatrick, Eunice Temple. *The Parker and Temple Families*. Durham, NC, E.T. Kirkpatrick, 1984. 89 leaves. [DC2820].

PARKER -- Parker, Ellen. *Record of the Parker Family of the Parish of St. James Goose*

Creek and of Charleston, South Carolina. Charleston, SC, 1930. 2p. 8 numb. leaves. [L13066].

PARKER -- Parker, Frances Elizabeth. *The Family of Parker: A Catalog of Members of the Parker Family of Hertford County, North Carolina and Their Descendants.* Rosemead, CA, 1971. 198 leaves. 1. Parker family. NG gives underscored title. [G503: NG77].

PARKER -- Peyton, Helen E. Hart. *Some Early Pioneers of Western Kentucky: Their Ancestors and Descendants - 2nd ed.* Charleston, SC, H.E.H. Peyton, 1990. xiv, 786p. 1. Parker family. 2. Hart family. 3. Sisk family. [G503].

PARKER -- Zoellner, Leslie R. *Parker Family of North Carolina.* Los Angeles, CA, 1946. 40 leaves. [X717-LA].

PARROTT -- NAS. *The Parrott Family.* NP, North Carolina DAR. 1954. 20 leaves. [D9620].

PARSONS -- Bishop, Rachel Parsons Flynn. *The Parsons Family of Natural Bridge Virginia.* Columbia, SC, W. Smith Associates, 1987. 80 leaves, 24 leaves of plates. DC gives: "80 [99] leaves." 1. Parson family. 2. Natural Bridge (Va.)-Genealogy. [G504; DC2831].

PARTRIDGE -- Strangward, Ethel Partridge. *Nathaniel Partridge of Charles Town, South Carolina and His Descendants: Three Centuries of an Anglo-American Family.* Sylvester, GA, E. P. Strangward, 1985. xviii, 149p., 20p. of plates. 1. Partridge family. 2. Partridge, Nathaniel, 1687-1722-Family. 3. South Carolina-Genealogy. [G505].

PATE -- Pate, Julia Claire. *Pate - Adams - Newton and Allied Families Principally in Richmond, Scotland, and Robeson Counties in North Carolina and Marlboro County, South*

Carolina. Red Springs, NC, Pate, 1958. 153 leaves. [L13129; D9643].

PATTERSON -- NAS. *Papers Relating to John Patterson of Mecklenburg County, North Carolina.* NP, North Carolina DAR, G.R.C., 1944. 24 leaves. [D9655].

PATTERSON -- Patterson, Alex M. *Highland Scots Pattersons of North Carolina and Related Families.* Raleigh, NC, 1979. 519p. [NG78].

PATTERSON -- Shields, Ruth Herndon. *Some Orange County, North Carolina Families, Includes a History of the Patterson Family.* Chapel Hill, NC, Shields, 1967. 19, 3 leaves. D gives underscored title. [D9664; DC2838].

PATTON -- Patton, Helen. *A Remembrance: Mamie Dickey Slagle Patton, April 4, 1888-March 29, 1935.* Franklin, NC, H. Patton, 1984. 109p. 4 folded leaves of plates. 1. Patton, Mamie Dickey Slagle, 1888-1915-Family. 2. Patton family. 3. North Carolina-Biography. [G506].

PAULEY -- Coggeshall, Robert Walden. [G506]. See above: COGGESHALL. [G148].

PEACE -- Peace, Richard Raymond. *The Descendants of of Silas Peace, 1775-1968.* Greensboro, NC, Arnold Copy Centers, 1978. 318p. [D9698].

PEACH -- Peach, John Harding. *The Peach Tree Handbook.* Baltimore, MD, Gateway Press, <1988- >. Contents: v. 2 Southern Maryland Branch. 1. Peach family. 2. Maryland-Genealogy. 3. South Carolina-Genealogy. [G507].

PEDEN -- Peden, Jessie. *The Pedens of America; An Outline of the Ancestry and Descendants of John Peden and Margaret McDill Peden: Scotland, Ireland, America.* Greenville, SC, Hiott Press, 1961. 654p. [L13231; D9731; X726-SP].

PEEBLES -- Whitley, Edythe R. *Peebles Family of Virginia, North Carolina, Kentucky, Illinois, Missouri, etc.* Seattle, WA, n.d. 50p. [X726-SP; VV144].

PEELER -- Peeler, John W. *A Record and History of the Peeler Family.* Charlotte, NC, J.W. Peeler, 1935, xvi, 248p. 1. Peeler family. [G509; D9736].

PENCE -- Pence, Maxine E. *The Pence Family of Georgia, North & South Carolina: From Their Beginnings They Moved to almost All Parts of the U. S.* Cheney, WA, Pence Publications, 1985-1986. xxxiv, 412p. [G510: DC2856].

PENDERGASS -- Pendergraft, Allen. *Descendants of Job Pendergrass (1754-1831).* Sedona, AZ, Pendergraft, 1974. 40p. [D9769].

PENDERGASS -- Pendergraft, Allen. *Pendergass of Virginia and the Carolinas, 1669-1919.* Sedona, AZ, 1977. 67p. VV lists as PENDERGAST and gives author as Pendergast. [NG78; VV144].

PENDERGRASS -- Pendergrast, Robert Allison. *Family History, John Pendergrass of Butte County, North Carolina and Lancaster County, South Carolina.* Atlanta, GA, R. A. Pendergrast, 1980. iii, 291p. [C535].

PENDLETON -- Hilldrup, Robert Leroy. *The Life and Times of Edmund Pendleton.* Chapel Hill, NC, University of north Carolina Press, 1939. 363p. [D9771].

PENLAND -- Browder, Blanch Penland. *The Penland Family of North Carolina.* NP, 1959. 41 leaves. [D9780].

PENLAND -- Browder, Blanch Penland. *The Penland Family of North Carolina. Rev. and enl. edition of the Penland Family of North Carolina, 1959 and Lists of Descendants and Short Sketches of George Penland, 1778-1877,* *and Harvey Penland Monroe, 1812-1889. 1958.* NP, Browder, 1975. viii, 182 leaves. DC gives 226p. [S1931; DC2858].

PEOPLES -- Peoples, David Stuart. [G510]. See above: CALDWELL. [G115].

PEOPLES -- Reynolds, Katherine. *Some Descendants of Hugh Peoples of Chatham County, North Carolina.* NP, 1965. 62 l. [D9798].

PERISHO -- Gmelich, Berniece Perisho. *The Perisho Parisho Family.* West Union, SC? B.P. Gmelich, 1979- . __ v.. [DC2868].

PERKINS -- Scott, William Walter. *'Gentleman' John Perkins.* Lenoir, NC, Lenoir News-Topic, 1920. 84 4 columns. [D9814].

PERKINSON -- Robinson, Quay H. *Perkinson Kin: Warren County, North Carolina, Granville County, North Carolina, Vance County, North Carolina, Mecklenburg County, Virginia.* Macon, NC, Q.H. Robinson, 1982. 1. Perkinson family. 2. North Carolina-Genealogy. 3. Virginia-Genealogy. [G512].

PERRY -- Winborne, Benjamin B. *The Perry Family of Hartford County, North Carolina.* Raleigh, NC, Edwards & Broughton Printing Co., 1909. 64p. D gives underscored part as title. [L13382; D9828].

PERRYMAN -- Bruhn, Reva Hopkins. *"Lest We Forget, the Perriman Story," 1707-1987: Maryland, North Carolina, Tennessee, and Missouri.* Visalia, CA, R.H. Bruhn, 1987. 79 leaves, 52 leaves of plates. 1. Perryman family. 2. Southern States-Genealogy. [G513].

PETREA -- Jorgensen, Ada Petrea. *Genealogy of Petrea and Hunter Families From Rowan and and Cabarrus Counties, North Carolina.* Silver Spring, MD, 1980. 65 leaves. D gives underscored title. [NG79; D9849].

PETREA -- Jorgensen, Ada Petrea. *The Petrea Family of Cabarrus County, North Carolina.* Silver Spring, MD, 1980. 68 leaves. [NG79; D9850].

PETTAWAY -- NAS. *Micajah Pettaway, Edgecome County, North Carolina.* NP, 1982. 24, 16 l. [DS548].

PETTIGREW -- Lemon, Sarah McCulloh, Ed. *The Pettigrew Papers.* Raleigh, NC, State Dept. of Archives and History, 1971-<1988 > v. <1-2 >. Selected papers of the Pettigrew family in he Southern Historical Collection, Library of the University of North Carolina at Chapel Hill and the North Carolina State Dept. of Archives and History. Vo. <2 > puslished by: North Carolina Dept. of Cultural Resources, Division of Archives and History. Contents: v. 1. 1685-1818 - v. 2. 1819-1843. 1. North Carolina-History-Sources. 2. Pettigrew family. [G515].

PETTUS -- Pettus, Mary Elizabeth. *Pettus History and Genealogy* Charlotte, NC, J&J Sales Co., 1965. 277p. [D9857].

PETTY -- Hodges, Alice Amis. *Ancestors and Descendants of Dr. John Wright Petty of Madison Co., Ala.* Pendleton, SC, Hodges, 1978, 38, 46p. [D9860].

PEYTON -- Ross, Helen Pate. *Pait, Payte, Pate: Virginia, North Carolina, Tennessee, Georgia.* Sturtevant, WI, H. P. Ross, 1986. 53p. 1. Peyton family. [G515].

PHELPS -- Phelps, Daniel LeRoy. *Phelps Veterans of the Revolutionary War.* Camden, SC, D.L. Phelps, 1990. 19 leaves. [DC2891].

PHELPS -- Van Henkle, Charles, et al. [G516]. See above: HENKEL. [G312].

PHIFER -- Phifer, Charles H. *Genealogy and History of the Phifer Family* Charlotte, NC,

George E. Wilson, 1910. 53p. L adds: Written in 1883, but not previously published. "The Phifer Family of North Carolina, a genealogical abstract compiled by Rovert S. Phifer... Jackson, MS, 1922." 75 numbered leaves consisting of manuscript notes, mounted newspaper clippings, and mounted photographs inserted in front of book." [L13547; D9883].

PHILLIPS -- Bayless, Mary Phillips. *Ancestry of Gadsden Phillips, 1860-1945 and Aurelia (Teasdale) Phillips, 1867-1919 of Charleston, South Carolina and Savannah, Georgia - 1st ed.* - Ashville, NC, Ward Pub. Co., 1985. xix, 158p. 1. Phillips family. 2. Tisdale family. 3. South Carolina-Genealogy. [G516].

PHILLIPS -- Friel, Shirley Phillips. *The Phillips family, Our History, Our Heritage.* Angola, IN, S.P. Friel, 1988. 1. Phillips family. 2. North Carolina-Genealogy. [G516].

PHILLIPS -- Paschal, Emma Phillips. *The John Phillips Family: Eleven Generations Originating in Moore County, North Carolina.* Charlotte, NC, H. Eaton Historical Publishers; Merceline, MO, Walsworth Pub. Co., 1982. 519p. 1. Phillips family. 2. Phillips, John, d.ca. 1799-Family. 3. North Carolina-Genealogy. DC gives pulication data as: Carthage, NC, E.P Phillips. [G516; DC2895].

PHILLIPS -- Phillips, John. *Descendants of Philomen Phillips of North Carolina and Indiana.* Cabin John, MD, J. Phillips, 1986. 57 leaves. 1. Phillips family. 2. Phillips, Philoman, b. ca. 1790-Family. [G517].

PHILLIPS -- Phillips, John. *Descendants of Thomas H. Phillips of North Carolina, Indiana, and Missouri.* Cabin John, MD, J. Phillips, 1986. 1 v (various pagings). 1. Phillips family. 2. Phillips, Thomas H.-Family. [G517].

PHILLIPS -- Walker, Alice America Beaufort. *Phillips Family of South Carolina.* NP, 1959. 26 leaves. [D9912].

PHILPOTT -- Philpot, Charles Hughes. *Alexander Martin Philpott.* Durham, NC, Philpott, 1967. 19 leaves. Bound with: English and American Backgrounds of a Philpott family Line of Virginia and Maryland, 1970. 30 leaves. [D9913].

PHILPOTTS -- Philpott, Jane. *Philpotts in Patrick and Henry Counties, Virginia (1772-1843).* Durham, NC, 1966. pni. [VV146].

PHIPPS -- Mullins, John C. *The Phipps Family of N.C. and Va.: Being the History of Some of the Descendants of Joseph Phipps Senior of Guilford Co., N.C.* Clintwood, VA, 1982. pni. [VV146].

PICKENS -- Pickens, Monroe. *Cousin Monroe's History of the Pickens Family.* Easley, SC, Day, 1951. 279p. [L13585; D9926].

PICKENS -- Whitney, Kenneth A. [G518]. See above: HALLAM. [G290].

PIERPONT -- Ambler, Charles H. *Francis H. Pierpont, Union War Governor of Virginia and Father of West Virginia.* Chapel Hill, NC, University of North Carolina Press, 1937, xiii, 483p. [L13612a].

PINCKNEY -- Powell, Mary Pinckney. *Over Home: The Heritage of Pinckneys of Pinckney Colony, Bluffton, South Carolina.* Beaufort, SC, 1982. 374p. [NGS9].

PINDER -- Johnston, Francis Claiborne. [G519]. See above: ELLIOTT. [G212].

PINNIX -- NAS. *Pinnix Family genealogy.* North Carolina DAR, 1959. 51 l. [D9964].

PINSON -- Andreas, Leonardo. *Pinson and Allied Families of South Carolina.* NP, 1949. 26 leaves. [D9965].

PLAXCO -- Mendenhall, Samuel Brookes and William Boyce White, Jr. *Plaxco - Robinson; Being an Account of Tow of the Ancient Presbyterian Families of Upper South Carolina (particularly situtated in York and Chester Counties) - 1st ed.* Rock Hill, SC, 1958. xviii, 160p/ "Limited to three hundred copies". [L13675].

PLOWDEN -- Plowden, Jessie Samuel. *History of the Descendants of Edward Plowden I in America.* Greenville, SC, 1937. 82p. [S1970].

PLUNKETT -- Ivy, Emma P. *The Thousand Plunketts; A Paritally Documented Record of the Families of Charles Plunkett of Newberry County, S. C. and Related Families.* Athens, GA, J.S. Ivy, 1969-74. 2 v. FW gives: 528p. [X744-DP/FW/IG/NY/SL/SP].

PLYLER -- Starnes, Herman. *The Plyler Genealogy, 1688-1965.* Monroe, NC, Starnes, 1966. xi, 196p. [L13695; D10011].

POLHILL -- DuPriest, Rosa Polehill. *That Your Days May Be Long.* Greenville, SC, DuPriest, 1977. 92p. [DS558].

POLK -- Angellotti, Mrs. Frank M. *The Polks of North Carolina and Tennessee.* Easley, SC, Published for the James K. Polk Memorial Association, by the Southern Historical Press. 1984. viii, 105p. "Reprinted from the New England historical and genealogical register, volume 77...volume 78". 1. Polk family. 2. North Carolina-Genealogy. 3. Tennessee-Genealogy. NGS gives only title, author, and 105p. [G524; NG80].

POLK -- McGuire, Mrs. Fannie. *Polk or Pollock - Weddington Families and Their Relations with the Shelby and McClarty Families in N.C.* NP, F. McGuire, 1921-1922. 214p. [DC2918].

POLK -- Rogers, Wilmot Polk. *Ezekiel Polk and His Descendants.* San Francisco, CA, 1939. 114, 32 numb. leaves. "Some of this material was included in a series of articles "The Polks of North Carolin and Tennessee", which appeared in the New England historical and genealogical register beginning with the issue of April, 1923 and concluding in the issue of July, 1924" - Foreword. "Vindication of the revolutionary character and services of the late Colonel Ezekiel Polk of Mecklenburg, N.C..." Also includes the Alexander, Campbell, McNeal, and Rogers families. [L13714].

POND -- Pond, Rachel Adams Cloud and Clifton Ray Pond. *John Pond of North Carolina; His Ancestry from the Pioneer, Samuel Pond, and His Descendants including Dailey, Stitt, and Frazee Lines.* New York, NY, 1965. 283p. "Revised edition of the Pond, Dailey, Stitt, and Frazee lines to be found in the Pond - Adams families, produced by the compilers in 1959. [L13737].

PONDER -- Ewald, A. L. *Ponder Family of Maryland and Delaware and of Hezekiah Ponder of N. C.* NP, 1967. 20p. [X746-FW].

PONDER -- Ewald, Annie Laurie. *Family of Hezekiah Ponder of Buncombe County, N.C., S.C., Georgia and Texas.* NP, n.d. 16p. [NG80].

POOL -- Lamb, Bessie Pool. *A Genealogical History of the Poole, Langston, Mason Families and Kindred Lines of Upper South Carolina.* Enoree, SC, 9, 1, 251p. [L13743].

POOLE -- Owens, Tench Pool. *Tench Carson Pool: His Ancestors and Descendants.*

Clinton, SC, T.P. Owens, 1986. 47p. 1. Poole family. 2. Pool, Tench Carson, 1848-1911. [G525].

POND -- Pond, Rachel Adams Cloud. *John Pond of North Carolina.* New York, Pond, Pond, 1965. 283p. [D10038].

PONDER -- Ewald, Annie Laurie. *Ponder Family of Maryland and Delaware and of Hezekiah Ponder of N.C.* NP, 1967. 20 leaves. [NG80].

PONDER -- Ewald, Annie Laurie. *Family of Hezekiah Ponder of Buncombe County, N.C., S.C., Georgia and Texas.* NP, 1968. 16p. NG omits date. [NG80; X746-FW].

POOLE -- Poole, William Lee. *Early North Carolina Pool Clan of Bladen, Anson, Rowan, & Davidson Counties: Eleven Generations of Edward Pool and His Descendants from the Early 1700's to the Present 1983.* Macon, GA, W. L. Poole, 1983. vi, 220p. [C551].

POPE -- Humphries, John D. *Georgia Descendants of Nathaniel Pope of Virginia, John Humphries of South Carolina and Allen Gay of North Carolina.* Atlanta, GA, Humphries, 1934. 40p. [L13761; D10050; VV148].

PORTER -- Porter, Bertha N. W. *Porter Genealogy; William Porter, 1786-1862 and Wife Lucy Cook, Married ca. 1816. Natives of North Carolina. Pioneer Settlers of Stewart County, Ga.* Newburn, GA, 1971. 47p. [X749-FW/NY].

POSTON -- Landers, Erma K. Poston. *A Poston Family of South Carolina; Its Immigrant Ancestor and Some of His Descendants, A Family Genealogy.* Atlanta, GA, Landers, 1965. 100p. NG & D give underscored title. [NG80; D10077; X-DP/FW/NY/PH].

POTEET -- Buchanan, Paul C. *Poteet / Petite Families of Colonial Maryland, Virginia, and*

North Carolina. Springfield, VA, Buchanan, 1990. 38p. [DC2929].

POULTON -- Carroll, Sarah Potter. *South Carolina's English Lady: Mrs. Thomas Nuckolls Dawkins (1820-1906) of Union County and Her Poulton Kin.* Greenville, SC, Press Printing Co., 1989. 142p. 1. Poulton family. 2. Dawkins, Thomas Nuckolls, Mrs., 1820-1906-Family. 3. Union County (S.C.)-Biography. 4. Union County (S.C.)-Genealogy. [G527].

POWE -- Godfrey, William. *The Line of Descent of Thomas Powe, 1931. Revised 1936 by J.R.T. (sic).* Cheraw, SC, 1936. Geneal. Table. [L13816].

POWELL -- Lucas, Silas Emmett. *The Powell Families of Virginia and the South: Being an Encyclopedia of the Eight (8) Major Powell Families of Virginia and the South In General.* Easley, SC, 1977, 1969. 637p. NG & D give underscored title and date as 1977. D adds: "See also: Powell family of Norfolk and Elizabeth City / Lucas, 1961. [NG80: D10096; VV149].

POWELL -- Lucas, Silas Emmett. *The Powell Families of Virginia and the South.* Vidalia, GA, Lucas, 1969. 584p. [D10098].

POWER -- McNees, Lucien L. *Descendants of Alexander Power of Laurens County, South Carolina.* Lexington, MS, McNees, 1967. 195p. [X752-FW].

POWER -- McNees, Lucien L. *Descendants of Alexander Power of Laurens County, South Carolina. 2nd edition.* Lexington, MS, McNees, 1988. 176, 13p. [DC2933].

PRATHER -- Prather, John William. *Documentation for Lineage of John William Prather, Jr.* Spartanburg, SC, 1979. 82p. [NG80].

PRATHER -- Prather, John William. *Praters in Wiltshire, 1480-1670.* Hendersonville, NC, J.W. Prather, 1987- . v.<1 > 1. Prather family. 2. Wiltshire (England)-Genealogy. 3. Great Britain-Genealogy. DC lists as: PRATER. [G529; DC2936].

PRATT -- Lofquist, Margaret U. *The Pratt Family of North Carolina and Alabama; Includes Sketches of Allied Families, Beavers, Vernon, and Hampton.* NP, 1966. 58 leaves. D gives underscored part of title. X gives 43, 15 leaves. [D10127; X753-FW].

PRATT -- Shook, Marion A. H. *Carolina Roundup, Kay - Clink - Scales - Pratt and Related Families.* Dallas, TX, 1965. 117p. [X753-FW].

PRESCOTT -- Ellis, Leila Mae Prescott. *The Family of Owen Melvin and Mary Elvina (Wildes) Prescott.* Greenville, NC, A. T. Prescott, 1985. iii, 22 l., 1 leaf of plates. [G530].

PRESCOTT -- Johns, Manda Lee Prescott. *The Family of Henry Oliver and Mary Alice (Wainwright) Prescott.* Greenville, NC, A. T. Prescott, 1986. iv, 42 leaves. 1. Prescott family. 2. Prescott, Henry Oliver, 1873-1942-Family. 3. Georgia-Genealogy. [G530].

PRESCOTT -- Moore, Ruby Inez Harris. *The Family of Benjamin Simon and Annie Clara (Gibson) Prescott.* Greenville, NC, A. T. Prescott, 1986. iv, 95 leaves. 1. Prescott family. 2. Prescott, Benjamin Simon, 1875-1951-Family. 3. Georgia-Genealogy. [G530].

PRESCOTT -- Moyer, Mabel Padgett. *Henry Prescott of Appling, Pierce, and Charlton Counties, Georgia: Son of John Prescott of Appling County, Georgia.* Greenville, NC, A.T. Prescott, "Printed Privately", 1989. iii, 36 leaves. 1. Prescott family, 2. Prescott, Henry, 1839-1903-Family. 3. Georgia-Genealogy. [G530].

PRESCOTT -- Prescott, Adell Taylor. *The Ancestors and Known Descendants of Banjamin Prescott of North Carolina and Sumter District, South Carolina: Born ca.1752, Died Prior to 1830 - Rev.* Greenville, NC, A.T. Prescott, 1988, 1980. v, 124 leaves. 1. Prescott family. 2. Prescott, Banjamin, b. ca. 1752-Family. 3. North Carolina-Genealogy. 4. South Carolina-Genealogy. [G530].

PRESCOTT -- Prescott, Adell Taylor. *The Ancestors of the Appling County, Georgia Prescotts.* Greenville, NC, Printed Privately. 1985, vi, 46, 10 leaves. 1. Prescott family. [G530].

PRESCOTT -- Prescott, Adell Taylor. *Moses and Susanna (Warren) Prescott and Their Descendants.* Greenville, NC, 1985. 1 v. (various foliations). 1. Prescott family. 2. Prescott, Moses, ca. 1787-1862-Family. 3. Florida-Genealogy. [G530].

PRESCOTT -- Prescott, Adell Taylor. *Three Early American Prescotts: Progenitors of Thousands.* Greenville, NC, A.T. Prescott, 1985. vi, 16 leaves. 1. Prescott family. [G530].

PRESCOTT -- Prescott, William. *The Prescott Memorial: or a Genealogical memoir of the Prescott Family in America.* Asheville, NC, Ward, 1983. 653p. [DC2944].

PRESCOTT -- Prescott, Winnie Holland. *The Family of John Allen and Cassie Oregon "Aug" (Ammons).* Edited by Adell Taylor Prescott. Greenville, NC, A.T. Prescott, 1989, iii, 19 leaves. 1. Prescott family. 2. Prescott, John Allen, 1868-1915-Family. [G530].

PRESCOTT -- Prescott, Winnie Holland. *The Family of Joseph Lee and Civility (Aldridge) Prescott.* Edited by Adell Taylor Prescott. Greenville, NC, A.T. Prescott, 1989, iii, 7p.

1. Prescott family. 2. Prescott, Joseph Lee, 1880-1950-Family. 3. Prescott, Civility-Family. 4. Southern States-Genealogy. [G530].

PRESGRAVES -- Presgraves, James Cawood. *Presgraves Genealogy, 1086-1976.* Potomac, MD. 1980. pni. [NG80].

PRESGRAVES -- Presgraves, James Cawood. *Presgraves in North America.* Fripp Island, SC, 1981. 150p. [NG80].

PRESGRAVES -- Presgraves, James Cawood. *The Presgraves Heritage.* Beaufort, SC, J.C. Presgraves, 1986. iv, 123, 2 leaves of plates. 1. Presgraves family. 2. England-Genealogy. [G530].

PREY -- Jorgensen, Ada Petrea. *The Descendants of John Dale Prey and Margaret Wilson Gibson. also Buckland, Goodwin, Stoops Families.* Hendersonville, NC, 1985. 76p. [NG81].

PRICE -- Lee, Janice Gartman. *The George Jacob Price Family History.* West Columbia, SC, J.G. Lee, 1986. vii, 360p. 1. Price family. 2. Price, George Jacob-Family. 3. South Carolina-Genealogy. DC gives: 359p. [G531; DC2951].

PRICE -- Mask, Margaret Hall. *The Price Families on Richardson Creek, Union/Anson Co., N.C.* Wilmington, DE, M.H. Mask, 1985. x, 289. 1. Price family. 2. North Carolina-Genealogy. [G531; DC2952].

PRICE -- Paris, Maurice Hudson Thatcher. [G531]. See above: PARIS. [G502].

PRICE -- Price, Jim. *A Visit to North Carolina.* Arlington, VA, Price, 1974. 10p. [S2007].

PRICE -- Sheppard, Jennifer M. *My North Carolina Ancestors of Beaufort, Bladen,*

Columbus, Martin & Washington Counties, NC and Isle of Wight County, VA. Williamston, NC, Modlin's Ancestral Treesearch, 1990- v.<1- >. 1. Sheppard family, 2. Sheppard, Jennifer M., 1944- -Family. 3. Price family. 4. North Carolina-Genealogy. [G531; NGN18-5-92].

PRIEST -- Linville, Thomas Merriam. *Descendants of Dwight Solomon Priest of Massachusetts and John Henry Linville of North Carolina.* Schenectady, NY, 1978. 97p. [NG81].

PRINCE -- Prince, Vivian Christine. *Prince: Descendants of William Prince, 1788-1869 of Union County and Pickens County, South Carolina.* NP, 1985. 98, 25 l. [DC2962].

PRITCHARD -- Symmonds, Dorothy. [G532]. See above: JACOBS. [G345; DC2965].

PRITCHETT -- Symonds, Dorothy. [DC2965]. See above: JACOBS. [G345; DC2965].

PROCTOR -- Riddings, Beaulah Philbeck. [G532]. See above: DOWNS. [G199].

PRUITT -- Prewitt, Richard A. *Prewitt - Pruitt Records of [name of state].* R. A. Prewitt, <1981-1988 > <5 > v. Contents: [1] Georgia- [2] South Carolina- [3] Tennessee- [4] Texas- [5] Virginia. 1. Pruitt family. 2. Southern States-Genealogy. [G533].

PUCKETT -- Gee, Christine South. *The Roots and Some of the Branches of the Puckett Family Tree.* Greenwood, SC, 1958. vi, 136p. [L13975].

PUCKETT -- Gee, Christine South. *The Roots and Some of the Branches of the Puckett Family Tree.* Columbia, SC, State Commercial Printing Co., 1958. 68 l. [DS567].

PULLEN -- Smith, Hester Moore & Edward S. *William Pullen (1757-1845) An Account of his*

Life in Virginia, Georgia, South Carolina and Alabama. Baltimore, MD, Logical Prod., 1971. 15p., A1-A24. [NG81: X760-FW].

PURCELL -- McLean, Angus Wilton. [G536]. See above: McLEAN. [G443].

PUTNAM -- Mehringer, Corrine P. *Colonial Putnam Families of the Province of South Carolina.* NP, Mehringer, 1950. 1 vol. looseleaf. [X761-OS/SL].

PUTNAM -- Putnam, Thomas Russell. *Putnam Genealogical Chart from 16th Century until 20th Century, Tracing the Descendants of the Early Virginia, Kentucky, Carolina Putnams, Who are Descended from Thomas Putnam, Who Landed in Virginia 1647 from England...* NP, 1938. Genealogical Table. [L14008].

PUTNAM -- Putnam, Thomas Russell. *Putnam Genealogy (Recording the Descendants of Thomas Putnam, the Immigrant to Virginia 1647) - Also an Enumeration of the Living Descendants of the "Virginia-Carolina-Kentucky" Putnams; Also Brief Genealogies of the Harper, Grover, and McGlasson Families.* Okmulgee, OK, 1938. 107p. [L14009; VV151].

PYATTE -- Pyatte, Marhta A. *The Pyatte Family of Western North Carolina.* Banner Elk, NC, Lees-McRae College, Puddingstone Press, 1977. 114p. [D10238].

PYLANT -- Griffin, John M. *The Pilands of Diamond Grove: A Family History Spanning Eight Generations.* Roanoke Rapids, NC, Michael Press, 1988. 72p. 1. Plyant family. 2. Virginia-Genealogy. 3. North Carolina-Genealogy. [G537].

QR

QUATTLEBAUM -- Quattlebaum, Paul. *Quattlebaum a Palatine Family in South Carolina.* Conway, SC, 1950. 240p. Reprinted by South Carolina Historical and Genealogical Magazine, vol. 48, no. 1, Jan. 1947. D gives underscored as title. [L14030; D10248].

QUERY -- Alexander, Eugene. *The Query History.* Gastonia, NC, Hugh A. Query, 1934. 21, 50p. [D10250].

RACKLEY -- Potter, Eloise F. *Rackley, A Southern Colonial Family: The Descendants of Edward Rackley of Virginia: with Appendixes Treating Other Rackley Family Groups Living in the United States Prior to 1900.* Zebulon, NC, Potter Pub. Services, 1984. pni. [VV152].

RADCLIFFE -- NAS. *American Radcliffes: Carolina, Kentucky, Pennsylvania Branch.* NP, 1963. 2 Genealogical Tables. [L14053].

RADCLIFFE -- Ratcliff, Clarence E. *John Ratcliffe Genealogy, Chatham County, N. C. Descendants.* Spring Arbor, MI, 1963. 41 l. [L14052].

RADCLIFFE -- Radcliffe, Edward J. *The Radcliffes of Carolina; A Genealogical Record.* NP, 1923. 6 leaves. [X765-NY/PH].

RADCLIFFE -- Radcliffe, Edward J. *The Radcliffes of Carolina; A Genealogical Record.* NP, n.d. 4p. [X765-PH].

RADCLIFFE -- Radcliffe, Edward J. *The Radcliffes of Carolina; A Genealogical Record.* NP, n.d. 10. [X765-PH].

RADCLIFFE -- Radcliffe, Edward J. *The Radcliffes of Carolina; A Genealogical Record.* NP, 1939. 16p. [X765-PH].

RADER -- Cannon, Cecile Rhodes. *Henry Rader and His Descendants.* Lenoir, NC, C.R. Cannon, 1987. xiii, 131p. 1. Rader family. 2. Rader, Henry, d. 1779-Family. 3. North Carolina-Genealogy. [G539].

RAGAN -- Ragan, Elizabeth H. *The Lineage of the Amos Ragan Family. Also Sowers Family.* Greensboro, NC, Family of Herbert T. Ragan, Quaker Collection of Guilford College, 1976. xiv, 264p. D, DC & X give underscored title. [NG82; D10264; DC2992; X766-NY].

RAGLAND -- Ragland, Charles J. *The Raglands.* Winston-Salem, NC, Ragland, 1978. 278p. [D10266].

RAGLAND -- Ragland, Charles James. *The Raglands.* Winston-Salem, NC, Ragland, 1978, 1987, 2 v. [DC2939].

RAGSDALE -- Wester, June Hart. *Elijah Ragsdale, Born Virginia, November 1, 1778 to South Carolina. Died Georgia, May 1, 1858: His Antecedents and Known Descendants. The Ragsdale Family in England and America by Mrs. Blake Ragsdale Van Leer.* Canton, GA, Wester, 1975. 269p. NG & D give underscored title. [G540; S2034; NG81; D10268; VV152].

RAIFORD -- Raiford, William Russell. *History of the Raiford Family.* Spartanburg, SC, Reprint, 1989. xiii, 191p. [DC2995].

RAMAGE -- Ramage, Mary. *Revolutionary Patriots, John Ramage and Joseph Ramage of Laurens District, South Carolina.* NP, 1987, 53 leaves. [DC3003].

RAMAGE -- NAS. *South Carolina Revolutionary Patriot, Capt. Joseph Ramage.* Verona, NC?, 1988. 28p. [DC3004].

RAMPY -- Rampy, Gordon A. *Palatine Roots: A Study of the German Origins of the Rampy Family with a Narrative Describing the Emigration of Johan Nicholas Rempi to South Carolina with a Large Group of Palatines in 1764.* Warrenton, VA, G.A. Rampy, 1988. 56, 38p. 1. Rampy family. 2. Rempi, Johan Nicholas, 1729-ca. 1801-Family. 3. Palatine

Americans-South Carolina-Genealogy. [G542].

RAMSEY -- Clark, Atenas Ramsey. *Ramseys and Related Families: Stroud, Stubblefield, Macon...* Charlotte, NC, Clark, 1986. various paginations. [DC3007].

RAMSEY -- Ramsey, James Thomas. *The Ramseys of Edgefield: Samuel and Ealanor[sic] Ramsey of Edgefield County, South Carolina and Their Descendants.* 1971. 246 leaves. NG gives underscored part of title. S gives: Published in 1962 under title: Genealogy of the Ramsey family in the southern United States, 1740-1962. [S2036; NG81].

RAND -- Esker, Katie-Prince Ward. *Rand Family of Virginia-North Carolina-Alabama.* NP, 1947. 46 leaves. [D10280].

RANEY -- Brandon, Rosa R. *Raney Days. Rayney Family.* Wilson, NC, 1974. 122p. [NG82].

RANEY -- Waldenmaier, Inez. *One Branch of the Raney Family.* Tulsa, OK, I.R. Waldenmaier, 1985- . 3 v. Contents: part 2 Traveling westward from New Jersey to North Carolina, through Tennessee and Indpendence County, Arkansas. [DC3009].

RANKIN -- Rankin, S. M. *The Rankin and Wharton Families and Their Genealogy.* Greensboro, NC, Rankin (Jos. J. Stone & Co.), 1931. viii, 295p. [L14104; D10301].

RAOUL -- Mills, Mary R. *Family of Raoul; A Memoir.* Asheville, NC, Miller, 1943. xi, 224p. [L14112; X769-FW].

RATLIFFE -- Craig, Marjorie. *Family Records of Henrietta Alberta Ratliffe and Jasper Newton Craig.* Reidsville, NC, 1955. 2 vols. in 1. [X770-NY].

RAVENEL -- Ravenel, Henry Edmund. *Ravenel Records. A History and Genealogy of the Hugenot Family Ravenel, of South Carolina; with Some Incidental Account of the Parish of St. John Berkeley, which was Their Principal Location.* Atlanta, GA, Franklin Printing Co., 1898. v, 279p. [L14127].

RAVENEL -- Ravenel, Rose P. *Charleston Recollections and Receipts: Rose P. Ravenel's Cook Book.* Columbia, SC, University of South Carolina Press, 1989, 1983. 91p. 1. Cookery, American-Southern style. 2. Cookery-South Carolina. 3. Revenel family. 4. Charleston, (South Carolina)-Social life and customs. [G544].

RAY -- Davis, Carrie L. [G544]. See above: DAVIS. [G177].

RAYLE -- Jones, Jean E. *The Rayle Family of Chester County... Guilford... East Tennessee.* Thousand Oaks, CA, Jones, 1980. 203p. [DC3020].

REA -- Rea, Hugh Calvin. *Rea Family Data.* Charlotte, NC, Rea, 1952. 28 l. [D10336].

READ -- Knight, Rosa Talbot. *Genealogy of the Reid Family of North Carolina and Georgia.* NP, 1924. 2p., 57 numb. l. With her genealogy of the Talbot and Wingate Families. [L14166].

REAVIS -- Hall, Marie Reavis. *The Reavis Family, in American Since 1700, Being the Descendants of Edward Reavis, Immigrant from England, Who Settled on the James River in the Colony of Virginia...* Yadkinville, NC, Hall, 1971. 576p. D gives underscored title. S gives: On Spine: Reavis Family History Based on material contained in w v. ms in the North Carolina State Library, Raleigh. [S2056; D10353].

RECTOR -- King, Larry. *Rector Records: Ancestors and Descendants of John Jacob Rector* *and Elisabeth Fischbach 1714 Immigrants... Germanna, Virginia.* Hendersonville, NC, King, 1986. vi, 474p. [DC3030].

REED -- Linn, Jo White. [G546]. See above: HAYDEN. [G306].

REED -- Whitaker, C. Bruce. [G546]. See above: HARPER. [G300].

REED -- Whitaker, Harriet Katherine Reed. *Reed Genealogy.* Southern Pines, NC, Dixie Printing Co., 1926. 24p. [D10389].

REEP -- Reep, Jacob Eli. *Reep Family History, North Carolina.* Huntsville, AL, J.E. Rep, 1978. x, 226p. [D10394].

REESE -- Reyes, Jeaness Reese. *Jane Harris of Rocky River; She Linked the Carolinas.* Oakland, CA, 1964. 273p. [L14223].

REEVES -- NAS. *Ancestral Sketches. (A Chronicle of the Pioneer East Tennessee Families: Reeves, Miller, De Vault, and Range of Washington County; Robeson of Sullivan and McMinn Counties; Easley, Hamilton, Acuff, and Vincent, of Sullivan County; and Certain of Their Antecedents in New Jersey, Pennsylvania, Maryland, Virginia, and North Carolina).* Lynchburg, VA, J.P. Bell Co., 1951. ix, 113p. [L14226; VV155].

REID -- Reid, Louis E., Jr. *David Reid of Mecklenburg County, N.C., and His Descendants.* Bethesda, MD, 1982. 104p. [NG82].

RENTZ -- Sherwin, Ann C. *The Renz Family: Featuring Jakob Ulrich Renz and Maria Barbara Schneider of Weil im Schönbuch and Pfrondorf, and Including the Schwarz Family of Münster and Neckar. Illustrations by Cynthia A. Sherwin.* Raleigh, NC, A.C. Sherwin, 1988. 106p. Errata slip inserted. 1. Rentz family. 2. Renz, Jakob Ulrich, 1811-1864-Family. 3. Schwartz family. 4. German-Genealogy. [G549].

REYNOLDS -- Reynolds, John Fewell. *Genealogical Sketches of Reynolds, Fewells, Walls and Kindred Families..* Winston-Salem, NC, Press of the Commercial Printers, 1923. 56p. D gives: 56p, 63 l. [L14278; D10445].

REYNOLDS -- Reynolds, Mary Kennedy. *Descendants of Benjamin Reynolds and Richard Reynolds of South Carolina.* Selma, AL,M.K. Reynolds: A.R. Day, 1986. 1 v. (various pagings). 1. Reynolds family. 2. Reynolds, Benjamin, b. 1710-Family. 3. Reynolds, Richard, 1672-1758-Family. 4. South Carolina-Genealogy. [G551].

REYNOLDS -- Reynolds, William Wayne. *Reynolds and McGuire Ancestors: An Account for Some of the Ancestors of a Virginia Family.* Raleigh, NC, 1978. pni. [VV156].

RHODES -- Ladson, J. E. *Rhodes Story: Rhodes of Virginia, North Carolina, South Carolina, and Georgia.* Moultrie, GA, 1955. 12p. [X782-FW; VV156].

RHODES -- Rhodes, Raymond C. [G552]. See above: BEERS. [G45].

RHODES -- Rhodes, Troas Etta. *Some of the Early Settler of Pennsylvania, Virginia, Missouri, North Carolina, Indiana, Ohio, Illinois.* Palm Desert, CA, Artisan Printing Co., 1977. iii, 236, iv p.. [D10465; VV156].

RICE -- Moore, Elizabeth. *Rice, Hasell, Hawks, and Carruthers Families of North Carolina.* Bladensburg, MD, Moore, [X gives Genealogical Recorders], 1966. 144p. [D10472; X783-NY].

RICE -- Mosher, Merrill Hill. *John Rice, Sr. of Louisa County, Virginia & Caswell County, North Carolina.* Coos Bay, OR, M.H. Mosher, 1984. 16 leaves. [DC3065].

RICH -- Hogan, Julia R. *William Rich (Richee) Sr., The Record of Some Rich Families in Maryland, Pennsylvania, North Carolina, Tennessee, Indiana and Utah. 2d. ed.* Houston, TX, Rich Family Assoc. 1968. --_ vol. LA has vol. 3. [X783-LA/SU].

RICH -- Thomas, Everett Eri. *Eri Rich Family Tree; Ancestors and Descendants to and from Chester County, Pa; Guilford and Randolph Counties, NC; Wayne County, IN; Hamilton County, IN; Grant County, Indiana.* Indianapolis, IN, 1963. 63 l. L adds: Prefaced with an account of the Rich family in England. [L14332; NG83].

RICHARDSON -- Burgess, James M., M.D. *Chronicles of St. Mark's Parish, Santee Circuit, and Williansburg Township, South Carolina, 1731-1885.* Columbia, SC, C. A. Calvo, Jr., Printer, 1888. 108p.

-- *Index.* NP, 19__, 1p., 6 numb. leaves. Typed copy. [L14343].

RICHARDSON -- Richardson, Thomas F. *Richardson - Hartley - Arender and Related Families; A List of the Known Descendants of Elijah Richardson of Tennessee and Frank Hartley of South Carolina, Both of Whom Moved to Mississippi about 1815.* NP, 1969. 399p. [L14361].

RICHBOURG -- Ervin, Sam J, Jr. *The Richbourg Family of South Carolina.* NP, 1971 or 72. 27 leaves. 1. Richbourg family. [G554; S2087].

RIDDLE -- Duncan, Alice Y. *Our Riddle Family; Stephen Riddle and His Descendants, North Carolina, Indiana and Iowa.* Manhattan, KS, 1971. 14p. Typed. [X787-FW].

RIDGE -- Whitehurst, Anna Holleman. [G555]. See above: CHRISTOPHER. [G138].

RIDGELY -- Olds, Dan W. *William Henry Riegely (1786-1859) His Ancestors and Descendants.* Spartanburg, SC, 1969. 184p. [NG83].

RIDLEY -- Lewis, Henry W. *Southhampton Ridleys and Their Kin.* Chapel Hill, NC, Lewis, 1961. 125 leaves. X gives 125p. [D10531; X788-FW].

RIGBY -- Boyd, Margie Milner. [G556]. See above: FOSTER. [G236].

RIMMER -- Symmonds, Dorothy. [G557]. See above: JACOBS. [G345].

ROACH -- Perry, Max. *The Descendants of the Roach Family of York County, South Carolina: Including Allied Families and Genealogical Briefs of Drennan, Springs, Workman, Hanna, Harris, Thomasson, McConnell, Sturgis, Reid, Edwards, Dodds, Polk, Latham.* Midland, TX, M. Perry, 1983. 126 leaves. 1. Roach family. 2. Southern States-Genealogy. D gives underscored title and date of 1984. [G559; DC3095].

ROBARDS -- Farrior, Bessie Robards. *A History of the Robards Family.* Oxford, NC, 1959. 1 v. [L14447]

ROBBINS -- Robins, Sydney S. *Letters on Robins Family History.* Ashboro, NC, Durham Print. 407p. [X793-FW].

ROBBINS -- Lehman, S. F. *Robbins of Randolph (Co., N.C.).* Winston-Salem, NC, 1972. 68p. [X793-FW].

ROBERDEAU -- Buchannan, Roberdeau. *Genealogy of the Roberdeau Family: Including a Biography of General Daniel Roberdeau, of the Revolutionary Army, and the Continental Congress, and Signed of the Articles of Confederation.* Columbia, SC, R.L. Bryan, Co.,

1979. 280p., 2 leaves of plates (1 folded). Reprint: Originally published: Washington, J.L. Pearson, printer, 1876. 1. Roberdeau family. G & D indicate: Roberdeau family genealogy: 1876-1979 / comp. by Irene McPherson McNulty, 1979 located at p.197-280). D & NG give underscored title. [G560; NG84; D10577].

ROBERTS -- Clark, Mary Frances Roberts. *Roberts Homesteads.* Lexington, SC, M.F.R. Clark, 1988. vii, 228p. 1. Roberts family. 2. South Carolina-Genealogy. [G560].

ROBERTS -- Craine, Lloyd Bascombe. *The First of the Roberts and Crane Families, Who Settled in Western North Carolina and Some of Their Descendants.* St. Paul, MN, 1955. 148p. [L14474].

ROBERTS -- Hayworth, Marianne Browne. *Lt. John Roberts, Revolutionary War: His Descendants and Antecedents. John Mushro Roberts and Mary Eliza Jones, Their Ten Children... and Continuing Lines of Descent.* High Point, NC, Hayworth, 1960. 32 leaves. [D10581; X794-NY].

ROBERTS -- McLeod, Warren Hollingsworth. *Descendants of William Roberts Who Migrated from England, Settled in Sumter District, SC...* NP, 1989. 238 leaves. Originally typed: 1933. [DC3102].

ROBERTSON -- Gregg, E. Stuart. [G561]. See above: GREGG. [G273]. - 2 Entrys.

ROBERTSON -- Robertson, Julian Hart. *The Family of William and Elizabeth Bolling Robertson of Richmond, Virginia, 1585-1981.* Salisbury, NC, Salisbury Printing Co., 1982. viii, 273p. [DS608; VV].

ROBINSON -- Wood, Margarette Hall. [G562]. See above: DEAN. [G182].

RODDENBERRY -- Thurston, George Lee, III. *The Roddenberry / Roddenbery Family Book: Rottenberry, Roddenberry, Roddenbury, Rodenberry, Descendants and Ancestors of George Rottenberry / Roddenberry, Revolutionary War Veteran of South Carolina and Georgia.* Cairo,, GA, Julian B. Roddenbery, 1979. 357p. [C591; NG84; D10662].

RODGERS -- Harrington, Sarah Rodgers. *The Families of Jacob Franklin Rodgers and David Henry Hanna of Williamsburg County, S.C.* Atlanta, GA, Harrington, 1977. 43 l. [D10668].

ROGERS -- Banister, Eme O'dell. *Rogers Family of the Piedmont Section of South Carolina and Allied Families.* Anderson SC, 1965. Unpaged. NG gives underscored part of title. [NG84; X800-FW].

ROGERS -- Banister, Eme O'dell. *The Family of Rogers of the Piedmont Section, South Carolina.* Anderson, SC, Banister, 1966. 1 v. (various foliations). [D10676].

ROGERS -- Banister, Eme O'dell. *The Rogers Line.* NP, 1966. Unpaged. [X800-NY].

ROGERS -- Comer, James Vann . *Rogers, Our Common Bond.* Sanford, NC, J.V. Comer, 1987. iii, 491p. 1. Rogers family. 2. North Carolina-Genealogy. [G563].

ROGERS -- Rogers, F. M. *Rogers Family of the Pee Dee, South Carolina.* Florence, SC, Rogers, 1958. 128, 10p. [D10696].

ROLLINS -- Mayfield, Eddie Stokes. *Ancestors and Descendants of Joel Woodward Rawlinson I.* Rock Hill, SC, A.S. Mayfield, 1985- 1 v. (various pagings). 1. Rollins family. 2. Rawlinson, Joel Woodward, 1822-1888-Family. [G565].

ROOP -- Roop, Phyllis Gale. *Family Portraits.* Fries, VA, P.G. Roop, 1988. x,

367p., 1 leaf of plates. Cover subtitle: The Roops, the Stuarts, and their kin. Limited ed. 300 copies. 1. Roop family. 2. Stuart family. 3. North Carolina-Genealogy. 4. Virginia-Genealogy. [G567].

ROPER -- Walton, June Roper. *Known Ancestry of Samuel Clyde Roper and Tyre Lee Roper.* Ozark, MO, Yates Pub, Co.; Four Oaks, N.C., J.R. Walton, 1986. iv, 80p. 1. Roper family. 2. Georgia-Genealogy. [G568; DC3146].

ROSE -- Rose, Ben Lacy. *Alexander Rose of Person County, North Carolina and His Descendants.* Richmond, VA, 1979. 268p. NG gives underscored title. [NG85; D10745].

ROSE -- Rose, Christine. *Ancestors and Descendants of Frederick Rose of Sussex County, Virginia, Orange County, North Carolina, and Hardin County, Tennessee.* San Jose, CA, Rose Family Bulletin, 1980. 77p. [DS618; VV160].

ROSS -- Crouse. Camille Izar. *The Descendants of William Alfred Ross and Mary Ann Redding of Macon, Georgia.* Charlotte, NC, Crouse, 1983. 86, 63 leaves. [DC3154].

ROSS -- Kellough, Gene Ross. [G569]. See above: KYLE. [G381].

ROSS -- Ross, Robbie Lee Gillis. *Your Inheritance. Ross, Toke, Hoo, Harwell, Wilson Families.* Matthews, NC, 1972. xiii, 343p. S gives underscored title. [S2123; NG85].

ROSS -- Ross, Vaden Elizabeth Easley. *James Ross of Alamance and His Kin.* Clayton, NC, Ross, 1978. 78p. [DS624].

ROSS -- Ross, Vaden Elizabeth Easley. *James Ross of Alamance.* Clayton, NC, Ross, 1978. 78p. [D10761].

ROSS -- Whitsett, Dr. William Thornton. *A History of the Ross Family. Extracts from the Historical Address at the Annual Reunion of the Ross Family at Pleasant Garden, N. C., on August 9th, 1928.* Greensboro, NC, 1928. 1p. From Greensboro Patriot, N.C., August 9, 1928. [L14701].

ROUNTREE -- Ware, Charles Crossfield. *Rountree Chronicles, 1827-1840; Documentary Primer of a Tar Heel Faith.* Wilson, NC, North Carolina Christian Missionary Convention, 1947. 64p. [L14736 & L14738a].

ROUTH -- Routh, Lawrence W. *The Rouths of Randolph County, North Carolina: With Supplementary Information on Connected Families.* NP, 1980. 310p. DC underscored title & no date. [NGS10; DC3162].

ROWE -- Godley, R. O. *Roe / Rowe: The Desendents [sic] of William Roe's (d.1721 Va.) Sone, John.* Washington, NC, R.O. Godley, 1987. 1 v. (various pagings). 1. Rowe family. 2. Roe, William, d. 1721-Family. [G572].

ROWE -- Ella Harrison. [G572]. See above: HARRISON. [G302; NGN16-4-90; DC3167].

RUBENKING -- Rubenking, Gordon. *A Family Reunion; Being a Narrative and Factual Genealogy of the Families, Rubenking, Beverman, Broehl, Hamman.* Tryon, NC, 1983. 402p. [NG85].

RUMPH -- Salley, Alexander S. *Genealogy of the Rumph Family of South Carolina.* Birmingham, AL, Leslie Pr. and Pub. Co., 1903. 10p. [L14806; X812-NY].

RUNYON -- Runyon, Robert and Amos. *Runyon Genealogy; A Genealogy of the Runyon Families Who Settled Early in Kentucky, North Carolina, Virginia and West Virginia.* Brownsville, TX, 1955. 194p. [L14811; VV162].

RUSH -- Broadwater, Mary Jane (Rush). *David Rush and His Descendants.* Bradley, SC, 1953. 238p. [L14821; NG86].

RUSH -- Zoellner, L. F. *Rush Family of North Carolina.* NP, 1946. 15 leaves. [X813-LA].

RUSSELL -- Mchugh, Matthew Lee. *Celena (Lena) Jane Russell Smith.* Columbia, SC, Mchugh, Mchugh, 1974. iv, 511p. [D10863].

RUTHERFORD -- Picras, Sadie Rutherford. *Rutherfords in North Carolina, South Carolina, Alabama, and Georgia.* NP, 1960. 83 l. [D10877].

RUTLAND -- Camp, Helen Moore, et al. *Forging Our Families: Rutland, Askew, Bonner, and Chappell Connection.* Charlotte, NC, Camp, et al., 1988. 155p. [DC3188].

RUTLEDGE -- Bodie, Idella. *A Hunt for Life's Extras: The Story of Archibald Rutledge. - 1st softcover ed.* - Orangeburg, SC, Sanlapper Pub., 1987, 1980. 176p. Summary: A biography of South Carolina's first poet laureate. 1. Rutledge, Archibald Hamilton, 1883-1973-Biography. 2. Poets, American-20th century-Biography-Juvenile literature. [G577].

RYLE -- Ryle, Herbert E. and Elbert Stephens Ryle. *Sone of the Descendants of John Ryle of Anson County, North Carolina and the Ryle Family of Boone County, Kentucky.* Stevensville, MD, 1961. 107 l. [L14885].

RYLE -- Ryle, Herbert E. *The Stephens / Ryle Book: the History and Descendants of Benjamin Stephens, Sr., of Orange County, Virginia and Campbell County, Ky.and John Ryle, Sr., of Anson County, North Carolina Who Died in 1777 and Whose Children Settled in Boone County, Kentucky.* Upper Marlboro, MD, H. E. Ryle, 1987. 454p. 1. Stevens family. 2. Ryle family. 3. Ryle, John, ca.1735-1777-Family.

4. Stephens, Benjamin, 1754-1839-Family. [G578].

S

SAGE -- NAS. [L14915]. See above: COWAN. [L4135].

St. ARMAND -- St. Armand, Jeannette Cox. *Our Family Genealogy, Including the Nelson, Johnson, Roach Families. 2nd ed.* Wilmington, NC, 1967. 279p. [NG91].

SANDERS -- Revill, Janie. *Sanders - Saunders Records of South Carolina, Colonial.* NP, 1939. 74 leaves. [D10933].

SANDERS -- Sanders, Charles Richard. *A History of the Family of Dr. William Josiah and Fannie Adams Sanders of Rutherford County, Tennessee.* Durham, NC, C.R. Sanders, 1982. 77 leaves. [DC3201].

SAUNDERS -- NAS. [L15029]; See above: COWAN. [L4135].

SAUNDERS -- Sanders, Robert W. *Sanders Family History.* Greenville, SC, 1920. 40p. X gives 44p. and lists under SAUNDERS. [L14915; X821-FW/LI].

SARGENT -- Harpole, Agnes S. *Major Sargents and Their Minors; from James Sargent, ca. 1765-ca. 1845, North Carolina through Tennessee, Mississippi, and West.* West Point, MS, 1961. 47 l. [X823-FW/MH/NY/PH].

SATCHER -- Early, Charles L. *Satche of Sussex, England, Pennsylvaia, and South Carolina; Lines of Willis, Wesley, Satcher, 1845-1921.* NP, 1956. 4 leaves. Typed. [X823-PH].

SATTERFIELD -- Satterfield, Frances C. G. *From Whence We Came.* Raleigh, NC, Addressing Duplicating Service, 1973. 114p. [X823-OH].

SAUNDERS -- Holcomb, Brent. [G583]. See above: GREER. [G273].

SAWYER -- Riner, Charles Robert. *The Sawyer Genealogy.* Port Wentworth, GA, C. R. Riner, 1985. 19, 5 leaves, 2 leaves of plates. "The direct line of descent... beginning in October, 1784 with John Sawyer of Old Ninety-six District, South Carolina and ending in December 1985 with descendants of Bennie Lee Sawyer of Worth County, Georgia, and including one family descended through John Warren Sawyer of Mitchell County, Georgia." [G585].

SCANLON -- Scanlon, David Holcomb. *Genealogy of the O'Scanlon, (Scanlon, Scanlon) Family.* Durham, NC, 1938. 23p On Cover: "I am Fond of Ireland". [L15065].

SCHAUB -- Russell, Annie Mary Vest. *The Schaubs and Vests of North Carolina and Washington, D.C.* NP, Russell, 1966. 46, 56, 23 leaves. [L15076; D11016].

SCHENCK -- Schench, David. *Historical Sketch of the Schenck and Bevens Families.* Greensboro, NC, Thomas, 1884. 45p. [X829-FW].

SCHOLL -- Glover, Elizabeth (Bettye) K. & E. Bryan Keisler. *Shull: John W. & Margaret Moak, Descendants.* Gilbert, SC, 1971. 40p. [S2195].

SCHULER -- Shuler, Rebecca Ann Dantzler. *Brightly Shines Her Lamp: The Diary of Rebecca Ann Dantzler Shuler: The Last Years at Cedar Lane - 1st ed.* Roswell, GA, W.H. Wolfe Associates; Bowman, SC, S. Shuler, 1987. xii, 322p. 1. Shuler, Rebecca Ann Dantzler, 1844-1918-Diaries. 2. Schuler family. 3. Cedar Lane Plantation (S.C.). 4. Plantation life-South Carolina-History. 5. South Carolina-Biography. 6. South Carolina-Genealogy. [G591].

SCHWARTZ -- Sherwin, Ann C. [G592]. See above: RENTZ. [G549].

SCOFIELD -- Scofield, Harriet and Henry B. Whipple. <u>*A Scofield Survey*</u>*: Daniel Scofield (d. ca. 1669) and Richard Scofield (1613-1670) and Their Descendants, for about Six Generations, Rufus Scofield (1774-1854) and His Descendants.* High Point, NC, Whipple, 1972. 133 leaves. D gives underscored title. NG omits Scofield dates and the part of title begining with: "for about...". [S2214; NG87; D11078].

SCOTT -- Freel, Margaret Walker. *Unto the Hills.* Andrews, NC, Freel, 1976. 224p. [D11090].

SCOTT -- Scott, Carol S. *William Scott, 1792/3-1800 [i.e. 1732/3-1800] of Cabarrus County, North Carolina and Some of His Descendants with Allied Lines (Cline, Goodnight, Winecoff, Goodman, Suther): A Social History.* Rock Hill, SC, S.D. Scott, 1987. vii, 138p., 1 leaf of plates. 1. Scott family. 2. Scott, William, 1732 or 3-1800-Family. 3. Cabarrus County (N.C.)-Genealogy. 4. North Carolina-Genealogy. [G594; NGN16-4-90].

SCOTT -- Scott, Keith S. M. *Scott, 1118-1923, Being a Collection of Scott Pedigrees Containing All Known Male Descendants from Buccleuch, Linton, Harden, Balweary, etc..* Charleston, SC, Garnier, 1969. 312p. [X837-DP/SU].

SCOTT -- Turner, Herbert S. *The Scott Family of Hawfields.* Haw River, NC, Ralph H. Scott, 160p. [D11102].

SCOTT -- Wiese, O'Levia Neil Wilson. *William Scott of Fairfield ccounty [sic], South Carolina and His Descendants.* Waco, TX, O'L. N.W. Wiese, 1987. 1 v. 1. Scott family. 2. Scott, William, ca. 1760-1805-Family. [G594].

SEARS -- Smith, W. Wayne. *Sears Family of Rowan County, North Carolina, Nicholas County, Kentucky, Indiana, and Missouri.* Moscow, ID, Author, n.d. 18p. [X-FW].

SEAWRIGHT -- Reeves, Nell Seawright. *The Saga of the Seawrights.* Greenwood, SC, 1987. 338p. [NG88; DC3249].

SEGRAVES -- Day, Savannah S. *The Reverend William Segraves and His Descendants.* Blacksburg, VA, Manuscript Memories, 1989. pni, 1. Segraves family. 2. Segraves, William, b. ca. 1817-Family. 3. Seagraves, William, c. ca. 1817-Biography. 4. North Carolina-Genealogy. [G596].

SEILERS -- Slagle, Lucy, et al. *The Family of Alber Siler, 1829-1904 and Joanna Chipman Siler, 1832-1884.* Franklin, NC, Ideal Pub., 1987. 36p. 1, Seiler family. 2. Siler, Albert, 1829-1904-Family. 3. North Carolina-Genealogy. [G597].

SELBY -- Selby, Forest T. *The House of Selby.* Charlotte, NC, 1962. 1, 44p. [L115258].

SELLERS -- Marlowe, James I. *Records Pertaining to the Sellers Family of Brunswick County, N.C.* Manassas, VA, J.I. Marlowe, 1986. 96 leaves. 1. Sellers family. 2. North Carolina-Genealogy. DC omits place of publication and publisher. [G597; DC3261].

SELLERS -- Watters, Clark H. *Some Descendants of William Sellers, Who was in Tarboro, North Carolina in 1750.* Tarboro, NC, 1974. 44p. [X842-NY].

SETZER -- Lyon, Josephine E. Wood. *From Tom's Creek to Sherrill's Ford: The Wood, Sherril and Related Families.* High Point, NC, E.S. Wood. 1985. xiii, 230p. 1. Woods family. 2. Sherrill family. 3. Setzer family. 4. North Carolina-Genealogy. [G598].

SETZLER -- Hampton, Luther W. *Setzlers of the Dutch Fork, South Carolina.* Columbia, SC, L.W. Hampton, 1984. 141p. 1. Setzler family. 2. South Carolina-Genealogy. [G598].

SEVIER -- Armstrong, Zella. *The Sevier Family.* Spartanburg, SC,. The Reprint Co., 1974 (c1926). 81, 325p. (Her notable southern families, v. 4) Reprint of the ed. published by Lookout Publishing Co., Chatanooga. [S2238].

SHANDS -- Shands, Wayland Arthur. *Shands Family History.* Greenwood, SC, Bagpipe Press, 1986- v.<1 > 1. Shands family. DAR library holdings: part 1. [G601; DC3272].

SHANKS -- Littlejohn, Rachael S. *Shanks: South Carolina to Texas.* Lubbock, TX, R.S. Littlejohn. 1974. 56 leaves. [DC3273].

SHANNON -- Shannon, William Gilmore. *Shannon Family and Connections.* Columbia, SC, Shannons, 1973. 163p. [D11223].

SHARP -- Macaulay, Neill W. *The Sharps of the Carolinas and Georgia.* Columbia, SC, Macaulay, 1972. 58p. [DC3279].

SHAW -- Blake, Tyther B. S. *Shaw Brothers: Rev. Murdock Wesley Shaw, Sr., Roderick (Lodd) Shaw of Chesterfield Co., S.C. and Their Descendants.* Kershaw, SC, 1976. XV, 215p. [X847-FW].

SHAW -- McCain, W. D. *Eight Generations of the Family of John Shaw (178-1858) and His Wife, Nancy Worthy Shaw (1788-1846) of N.C., S.C., and Miss.* Hattiesburg, MS, 1974, xi, 463p. [X847-FW].

SHAW -- Paris, Maurice Hudson Thatcher. [G602]. See above: PARIS. [G502].

SHEARER -- Shearer, Edna S. *The Shearers of Glenluce Parish, Wigtownshire, Scotland and*

Allied Families, 1730-1990. Chapel Hill, NC, Shearer, 1990. 181p. [DC3284].

SHEARER -- Sherer, Iva Larou. *Carolina Shearer - Sherers and Others.* Boone, NC, Miinor Pub Co., 1978. 460p. [D11251].

SHEARIN -- Peters, Norman R. [G603]. See above: KING. [G369].

SHEEK -- Sheek, Ann Ellis. *The History of the Sheek Family, 1753-1973.* Clemmons, NC, 1973. 78p. [S2255].

SHELBURNE -- Shelburne, Robert C. *The Shelburne Family.* Asheville, NC, 1964. 4 leaves. [X848-LI/NY].

SHELOR -- Shelor, Sue (Jefferson). *Pioneers and Their Coats of Arms of Floyd County. Shelor, Howard, Jefferson Families.* Winston-Salem, NC, Hunter Publishing Co., 1961. 213p. DS gives underscored title and "First section reprinted from 1938 edition." [NG89; DS648].

SHELTON -- Barrett, Joseph Milton. *Shelton: The Descendants of William Shelton and Nancy Deatherage of Surry County, North Carolina, 1805-1984.* St. Peters, MO, J.M. Barrett, 1984. iii, 526p. 1. Shelton family. 2. Shelton, William, 1805-1873-Family. 3. Surry County (N.C.)-Genealogy. [G604].

SHEPARD -- Boyd, Margie Milner. [G604]. See above: FOSTER. [G236].

SHEPPARD -- Sheppard, Jennifer M. [G605]. See above: PRICE. [G531; NGN18-5-92].

SHERRILL -- NAS. [G605]. See above: LIPSCOMB. [G404].

SHERRILL -- Clark, Wanda Lee. *The Sherril Saga: History of William Sherrill (Sherwill), the Conestoga Fur Trader, 16? to 1725, and His Son, Adam Sherrill, the North Carolina*

Pioneer, 1699-1772, Together with the Genealogical Records of jacob Sherrill, the Seventh Son of Adam Sherrill, the North Carolina Pioneer, and of Jocob's Wife, Hulda(h) Wilson. McAlister, OK, W.L. Clark, 1987. 1 v. (various pagings). 1. Sherrill family. [G605].

SHERRILL -- Lyon, Josephine E. Wood. [G605]. See above: SETZER. [G598].

SHIRLEY -- Arnett, Ethel Stephens. *From England to North Carolina: Two Special Gifts.* New Bern, NC, Tryon, Palace Restoration, 1964. 93p. 1st ed. D omits underscored part of title and reference to edition. [L15561; D11336].

SHIRLEY -- King, Harry Tracy. *John Shirley and His Descendants of Virginia and South Carolina.* Snyder, TX, Feather Print, [VV gives Roby, TX; omits published], 1972. 292p. [X854-FW; VV168].

SHOEMAKER -- Hadden, Robert Lee. [G607]. See above: HADDEN. [G287].

SHOOTER -- Kyles, Carolyn Shooter. *The Shooter Family of Marion County, S. C., 1760-1973.* Charlotte, NC, Kyles, 1974. 60p. [S2279].

SHORE -- Shore, Leo Jane, et al. *Ancestors and Descendants of Frederick Shore, Switzerland, 1570 - Surry County, North Carolina 1750...* Hillsboro, NC, Multi Business, 1983. 814p. [DC3315].

SHOTT -- Shott, Gloria Rich. *The Shott Family.* Clemson, SC, Rich, 1985. 52p. [DC3318].

SHRUM -- Schrum, Vernon J. *The Histor of the Schrum - Shrum Family.* Raleigh, NC, 1968. 83 leaves. [L15593].

SHUFORD -- Shuford, Julius H. *A Historical Sketch of the Shuford Family.* Hickory, NC, A.L. Crouse & Son, 1901. 156p. [D11377; X856-FW].

SHULL -- Glover, Elizabeth K. *Shull: John W. and Martha Mosk, Descendants.* Gilbert, SC, 1971. 34p. [X856-FW].

SIBERT -- Beeson, J. Luther. *The Sibert Family of South Carolina and Alabama.* Mobile, AL, Press of Acme Printing Company, 1928. 17p. [L15621].

SIBERT -- Sibert, Vasco B. *The Sibert Family of South Carolina, Alabama, Tennessee.* NP, 1967. 116 leaves. [D11391].

SIDES -- Sides, Roxie. *Early American Families: Sides, Spach, Nading, Rominger, Longworth, Fortz, Rothrock, Shoat, Vogler.* Winston-Salem, NC, Sides, 1963. xii, 140p. D gives underscored part of title. [D11397; X857-FW].

SILER -- NAS. *Siler Family Reunion Held in Macon County, N.C. 1901. Addition, 1926.* Franklin, NC, Franklin, Pr., 1926. 30p. [X858-FW].

SILER -- Porter, Leona Bryson. *The Family of Weimar Silar, 1755-1831.* Franklin, NC, The Committee appointed at the 100th meeting. 1951. 178, 9p. [D11407].

SILLIMAN -- Silliman, Robert B. *The Silliman Family, Pennsylvania and South Carolina Lines.* Dumaguete City, Phillipines, Silliman University Press, 1966. xiii, 206p. [L15644].

SILLS -- Bryant, Laurence C. *Historical and Genealogical Record of Fanny Sills, and Related Families of Nash County, N.C.* Orangeburg, SC, State College, 1968. v, 84p. [L15645; X858-FW].

SILLS -- Sills, Louise J. *Sills Family and Related Lines.* Orangeburg, SC, Orangeburg Historical and Genealogical Society, 1969. 68p. [X859-NY].

SILLS -- Sills, Louise, J. *Sketch of the Sills Family.* Orangeburg, SC, L.C. Bryant, 1969. 32p. [X859-NY].

SILVER -- Harris, John Silver. *Silver, Our Pioneer Ancestors.* Boca Raton, FL, J.S. Harris, 1987. 81 leaves. 1. Silver family. 2. North Carolina-Genealogy. [G610].

SIMMONS -- Simmons, Samuel William. *Descendants of John Simmons of North Carolina, 1760.* Atlanta, GA, 1979. 133p. NGS gives 132p. [C638; NGS10].

SIMMONS -- Williams, Minnie Simmons. *A Colloquial History of a Black South Carolina Family Named Simons.* Washington, DC, M.S. Williams, 1990. iii, 200, 80p. 1. Simmons family. 2. South Carolina-Genealogy. [G611].

SIMONS -- Simons, Robert Bentham. *Thomas Grange Simons III.* Charleston, SC?, 1954. ix, 211p. [D11432].

SIMPSON -- Perry, Mex. *The Descendants of Simpson - Roach Families of South Carolina.* Midland, TX, Perry, 1973. 252, vi p. [D11437].

SIMS -- Sharp, E. M. *A History of the Sims Family: Descendants and Antecedents of Nathan Sims of Coronaca Community in Greenwood County, South Carolina.* Memphis, TN, Greenwood County Historical Society, 1971. 97 leaves. [DC3348].

SIMS -- Sims, Henry Upson. *The Genealogy of the Sims Family of Virginia, the Carolinas and the Gulf States.* Kansas City, MO, 1940. pni. [VV169].

SINCLAIR -- Sinclair, Brevard D. *An Historical Account of Duart Castle with the Genealogies of the Children and Grandchildren of Rev. John Campbell Sinclair, Together with an Obit of the Latter.* Columbus, OH, Columbus Steam Printing Works, 1879. 33p. A short sketch of the Davidson and Brevard families of Mecklenburg, North Carolina. P. 35." [L15685].

SINEATH -- Baver, William R. *The Sineath Family and Affiliated Family Lineages.* Columbia, SC, Bryan Co., 1971. 379p. [X861-FW/LA].

SINGLETON -- Patty, C. R. S. *Some of the Georgia Singletons and Their Cousins Who Are Descendants of Dr. J. J. Singleton and His Wife, Mary Ann Terrell.* Chapel Hill, NC, 1956. 60p. [X861-FW].

SINGLETON -- Singleton, Virginia E. G. *Singletons of South Carolina.* Columbia, SC, 1914. 53p. [X861-FW].

SINYARD -- Blalock, Delton D. *France to America: Sinyard and Related Families in Alabama, Georgia, South Carolina and Pennsylvania. -- 1st ed. --* Hanceville, AL, D. Blalock, 1984. 107p., 26 pages. of plates. [C639].

SISK -- Peyton, Helen E. Hart. [G612]. See above: HART. [G302].

SISK -- Sisk, Luther L. *The Sisk Family: Virginia--North Carolina--South Carolina--Kentucky--Alabama--Tennessee--Georgia--Missouri--Texas.* Escondido, CA, 1980. 1 v. various foliations. [C640; VV170].

SITTON -- Sitton, Enid W. *Sitton and Gibson Genealogy; Descendants of Three Revolutionary War Soldiers: Joseph Sitton, North Carolina; Guyon Gibson, South Carolina, Thomas Kennedy, Virginia.* Houston, TX, 1967. ix, 433p. [X862-DP/FW/NY/SP; VV170].

SKENE -- Skeen, A.T. *Clan Skeen.* Winston-Salem, NC, A.T. Skeen, 1987. ix, 324p. 1. Skene family. 2. Soctland-Genealogy. [G613].

SKIDMORE -- Skidmore, Warren and William F. *Skidmore; Rickmansworth, England-Delaware-North Carolina and West, 1555 to 1983.* Akron, OH, W. F. Skidmore, 1983. vi, 623p. [C641; NG90].

SLADE -- Slade, Leonard L., Jr. *Samuel Slade of Cheraw District, South Carolina and His Descendants.* Baltimore, MD, Gateway Press, 1975. 193p. 1 folded leaf of plates. [S2311].

SLAPPEY -- Hargrett, Felix. *The Slappeys of South Carolina and Georgia: A Sketch with a Glance at the Allied Family Hatfield.* Athens, GA, Georgian, 1984. [DC3559].

SLAPPEY -- Hargrett, Felix. *The Slappeys of South Carolina and Georgia: A Sketch with a Glance at the Allied Family Hatfield.* Lynchburg, VA, 1984. pni. [VV170].

SLAUGHTER -- Longmire, Norma L. *Jacob Slaughter of Granville County, North Carolina.* Raleigh, NC, Longmire, 1971. 88p. [D11493].

SMARR -- Shannon, William G. *The Smarr Family.* Columbia, SC, Shannons, 1971. 179p. [D11514].

SMATHERS -- Patton, Sadie Smathers. *Smathers from Yadkin Valley to Pigeon River* Hendersonville, NC, Patton, 1954. 56p. [D11515].

SMILIE -- Reynolds, Harriet Dickson. *The Smilies of North Carolina, Georgia and Alabama.* NP. 1963. 19 leaves. [D11522].

SMITH -- Bennett, H. L. *Genealogy of John Henry Smith and Rachel Smith.* Greensboro, NC, 1963. Various paging. [X870-FW].

SMITH -- Cheek, Linda G. *Ancestors and Descendantsof Smiths*. Easley, SC, L.G. Cheek, 1987. 308p. 1. Smith family. [G616].

SMITH -- Draughon, Elanor Daphine Smith. *Descendants of Elijah Smith of Duplin County, North Carolina*. Durham, NC, 1971. vii, 416p. [S2323].

SMITH -- Hodges, Alice Amis. *Ancestors and Descendants of Jessie Smith of . Charleston District S.C. and Lowndes County, Miss.* Pendleton, SC, Hodges, 1978. 32p. in various pagings. [D11542].

SMITH -- Holcomb, Brent. [G616]. See above: GREER. [G273].

SMITH -- Klemcke, Ethel Uhl. *Robert Mays Smith from South Carolina to Texas (the long way)*. Wolfe City, TX, Hennington, 1988. viii, 295p. [DC3376].

SMITH -- LaFever, Ira C. *Smith, 1763-1971*. Columbus, NC, LaFever, 1971. 46p. [D11551].

SMITH -- Poyas, Mrs. Elizabeth Anne. *The Olden Times of Carolina*. Charleston, SC, Courtenary & Co., 1855. iv, 202p. Contains the genealogy of the Thomas Smith Family. [L15785].

SMITH -- Pierce, Sara Amarette Perry. *Genealogy of the Descendants of Huffman, Miller, Pierce, and Smith Families*. Shallotte, NC, S.A.P. Smith, 1986. 1 v. (various foliations). [DC3383

SMITH -- Smith, Evelyn A. F. H. *Charn Cuimhne (Cairn of Memories) to Our Scots of North Carolina*. Jacksonville, FL, Smith, E. A.F.H. Smith, 1969. 309p. Ancestors and Descendants of Archibald Y. Smith. [X871-FW/LA/SL].

SMITH -- Smith, J. Fletcher. *Genealogy of the Smith Family of Rockingham County, N.C.* Cedar Grove, GA, Smith, 1903. 119 leaves. [D11599].

SMITH -- Smith, Pearl O. *Peter Smith: Some of His Virgina, North Carolina, and Kentucky Descendants.* Washington, DC, 1976. 71, 13, 13 l, 12 leaves of plates. [C648; VV172].

SMITH -- Smith, Wolbur Bell. *Smith Family, 1750-1990, Rowan County, N.C., Tipton County, Tn.* Dallas, TX, Baylor University, 1990. 186p. [DC3392].

SMITHWICK -- Bennett, William D. *Smithwick Family in North Carolina: A First One Hundred & Fifty Years.* Raleigh, NC, W.D. Bennett, 1985. ix, 159p. 1. Smithwick family. 2. North Carolina-Genealogy. [G619].

SNEAD -- Butler, Florence Roberta Walker. *The Sneads of Johnston County, N.C., and Related Families.* __, NC, R.W. Butler, 1988. xiii, 328 leaves. 1. Snead family. 2. North Carolina-Genealogy. [G619].

SNEARY -- Sneary, Eugene C. *The Sneary Family in America.* Taylors, SC, The Sneary Family Association, 1975. vii, 142p. [D11636; X874-FW/GF/NY/PH].

SNELL -- Long, Hallock Porter. *Snell Family - Palatines, Virginia, N.C., etc.* Washington, DC, 1934. 2 v. [NG91].

SNELLGROVE -- Snellgrove, Harold Sinclair. *The Snellgroves of Mississippi; Their South Carolina Forebears, and rertain [sic] Pioneer Snellgroves of Georgia and Alabama and Their Descendants.* State College, MS, Mississippi State University, 1968. iv, 44 l. [A622].

SNIPES -- Fisher, James W. *The Ancestors and Descendants of Elbert Monroe Snipes in England, Virginia, North Carolina, South*

Carolina. NP, Snipes Family Association, et al. 1984. 163p. 1. Snipes family. [G620; VV172].

SNIPES -- Fisher, James W. *The Snipes Family of South Carolina and Connections with the Early Virginia, Barbados, and England.* New Orleans, LA, 1989. 478p. 1. Snipes family. 2.South Carolina-Genealogy. [G620].

SONDLEY -- Sondley, F. A. *My Ancestry.* Asheville, NC, 1930. 289p. [D11668].

SOUTH -- Gee, Christine South. *Genealogical Notes on the South Family from New Jersey, Pennsylvania, Maryland, Virginia, South Carolina, Kentucky, and Texas.* Greenville, SC, 1963. v, 163p. [L15974; VV172].

SOWER -- Owen, Ruth Sowers. *A Thousand Doors; The History of Phillip Sauer (Sowers) and His 14 Children.* Lexington, NC, 1971. 157p. [S2355].

SPACH -- Foltz, Henry Wesley. *The Descendants of Adam Spach.* Winston-Salem, NC, Wachovia Historical Society, 1924. xxvi, 202p. [D11690].

SPAIGHT -- Wheeler, John H. *Sketch of the Life of Richard Dobbs Smith of North Carolina (with Genealogy).* Baltimore, MD, W. K. Boyle, 1880. 29p. [X878-FW/LI].

SPALDING -- Mitchell, Louis D. *A Story of the Descendants of Benjamin Spauldingm 1773-1862.* Greensboro, NC, Deal Printing Co., 1989. 121p. 1. Spalding family. 2. Spaulding, Benjamin, 1773-1862-Family. 3. North Carolina-Genealogy. 4. Afro-Americans-Genealogy. [G624].

SPARGER -- Creasy, W.M. *Genealogy of the Sparger and Allied Families.* Wilmington, NC, Creasy, 1936. 126 leaves. [D11700].

SPENCER -- Rigby, Henry W. *early Spencers of Virginia.* Charlotte, NC, Rigby, 1986. 391p. [DC3422].

SPENCER -- Spencer, William F. *Spencer and Allied Families in North Carolina and Virginia...* Roxboro, NC, Taylor, 1984. 62p. [DC3423].

SPICER -- Spicer, Bernard Frederick. *Spicers of Wilkes County, North Carolina and Their Related Families.* Richmond, VA, B.F. Spicer, 1978. iv, 109 leaves. [DC3426].

SPIEGEL -- Speegle, Charles Martin. [G626; DC3427]. See above: JARRETT. [G346; DC3427].

SPRATT -- Spratt, Thomas Dryden. *Thomas Dryden Spratt's Recollections of His Family.* NP, 11963. 64, 5, 27 leaves. Includes History of the old Indian Fort at Fort Mill, S.C. by Zack Spratt. [D11758].

SPRING -- Perry, Max. *Descendants of John Springs (Springsteen) and Sophia Gassaway of Mecklenburg County, North Carolina: Including Genealogical Briefs of the Springsteen and Storm Families.* Midland, TX, M. Perry, 1988. 281p. 1. Spring family. 2. Springs, John, 1717-1790-Family. 3. Springsteen family. 4. Storm family. DC gives underscored part of title & lists under SPRINGS. [G627; DC3434].

SPRINGER -- Springer, M. C. *A Genealogical Table and History of the Springer Family in Europe and North Carolina.* Amesbury, MA, Guild & Cameron, 1917, xvii, 134p. [D11765].

SPRINGS -- Springs, Katherine Wooten. *The Squires of Springfield* Charlotte, NC, William Loftin, 1965. viii, 350p. [D11767].

SPRINGSTEEN -- Perry, Max. [G627]. See above: SPRING. [G627].

SPRUILL -- Lambeth , Mary Weekes. [L16091]. See above: BAILEY. [L757].

STACKHOUSE -- Stackhouse, William R. *The Stackhouse Family.* Marion, SC, Stackhouse, 1935. 241p. [D11779].

STANALAND -- Stanaland, Schuyler D. *Meet the Stanalands.* Baltimore, MD, Gateway Press, Shallotte, NC, S.d. Stanaland, 1986. 425p., 2p. of plates. 1. Stanaland family. [G628].

STANDISH -- Read, Harry Humphrey. *Myles Standish; Notes, Comments, and Genealogy.* Charleston, SC, Thomas Carpenter Read, 1961. 21p. [L16124].

STANFIELD -- Hieronymous, Goldie Smith. *Descendants of Sampson Stanfield, Who Went from Anson County, North Carolina into Knox County, Kentucky, in the Early 1800's, was Son of John Stanfield and Wife Mary.* Falls Church, VA, Hieronymous, 1978, 158p. Rev. ed. published as Descendants of Sampson Stanfield, who went from Anson County, North Carolina into Knox County, Kentucky in the early 1800's. Rev. ed. 1981. [C661].

STANLEY -- Flaherty, Elnora S. *Whither Thou Goest; A Story of the Stanley Family in Virginia, North Carolina, Kansas, and Oklahoma.* Irving, TX, 1973. 66, 5 leaves. [X886-FW/KH/NY; VV174].

STANLEY -- Stanley, Haywood A. *Sands Stanley of the Pee Dee Valley....* Marion, SC, Stanley, 1978. viii, 183p. [DC3451].

STANLEY -- Stanley, Haywood A. *Sands Stanley of the Pee Dee Valley....* Marion, SC, Stanley, 1978, 1979. viii, 183p. [D11814].

STARK -- Abbott, Jane H. *James Stark, Jr. with Wife "Cathron" of Virginia. "Died in the*

Carolina." *Genealogical Notes and Records.* NP, 1929. 71 l. [A634; VV174].

STARK -- Abbott, Jane H. *Thomas Stark of Virginia, to South Carolina, South Carolina to Tennessee and Returned to South Carolina. Genealogical Notes and Records.* NP, 1929. pni. [VV174].

STARNES -- NAS. *Starnes Family of North Carolina.* NP, North Carolina DAR, G.R.C., 1970. 33 leaves. [D11842].

STARNES -- Starnes, W. Oscar. *Descendants of Hilliard Judge Starnes and Julia Ellen Irby.* Monroe, NC, S.E. Starnes, 1964. 34 leaves. [D11843].

STATON -- Staton, John Samuel. *Staton Family* Charlotte, NC, Staton, 1960. xix, 406p. [D11853].

STATON -- Staton, John Samuel. *Staton History: Every Staton We Could Find From 750 to 1982 AD. Revised edition* . Charlotte, NC, Delmar, 1982. 951p. Originally published: 1960. [DC3460].

STEADMAN -- Steadman, Joseph Earle. [G630; DC3463]. See above: BARTON. [G38; DC3463].

STEELE -- Renn, Lydia S. *The Reverend Robert Luckey Steele: Gleanings, Biographical, Filil (sic), Ancestral.* Wake Forest, NC, Renn, 1976. 186p. [DC3464].

STEELMAN -- Steelman, Harold M. *Descendants of Mathias and Ruth Steelman of Surry County, N. C.* Kinston, NC, Steelman, 197_. 157p. [X890-IG/OS/PH].

STEELMAN -- Thurston, Ruby S. *The Steelman Relatives.* Winston-Salem, NC, Family Projects and Printers, 1981. iv, 207p. [DC3465].

STERRETT -- Shearer, Edna Starrett. *The Stewart Sterrett Family Tree.* Chapel Hill, NC, Shearer, 1979, ii, 185p. [D11918].

STEPHENSON -- Stephenson, Thomas Benton. *Stephensons of Nicholas County.* Charleston, SC, Coulter, n.d. 18 leaves. [DC3473].

STEVENS -- NAS. *Stevens Family (North Carolina) and Allied Families.* Des Moines, IA, n.d. 16p. Typed. [X895-FW].

STEVENS -- NAS. *The Legacy of Wilson and Adeline Stephens: A Celebration of the Past, a Vision of the Future: First National Stephens Family Reunion, July 4-6, 1987, at the Augusta Landmark Hotel, August, Georgia and in Aiken and Barnwell Counties, South Carolina.* New York, NY, Stephens Family Reunion, 1987. 84p. 1. Stevens family. 2. Stephens, Wilson, 1838-1914-Family. 3. South Carolina-Genealogy. [G634].

STEVENS -- Mitchener, William A. [G634]. See above: MITCHENER. [G458].

STEVENS -- Ryle, Herbert E. [G634]. See above: RYLE. [G578].

STEVENSON -- Stevenson, Charles Perry. *The Stevenson Family Record Charles Perry Stevenson [sic].* Starr, SC, C.P. Stevenson, 1981. 71 leaves. [DC3479].

STEVENSON -- Stevenson, Charlotte. *The Stevenson Reference Book.* Columbia, SC, R.L. Bryan Co., 1973. 193p. [S2398].

STEVENSON -- Stevenson, Samuel H. *A History and Genealogical Record of the Stevenson Family from 1748-1926.* Cheraw, SC, 1926. 238p. 2d. ed. Brought up to date from book published ca. 1898. [X895-FW].

STEWART -- Kelly, Jeanette H. *My Stewart and Other Kin of Iredell County, N.C.* York,

SC. J.H. Kelly, xiv, 863p. [DC3481].

STEWART -- Lee, Henry. *History of the Stewart or Stuart Family.* Charleston, SC, Garnier & Co., 1970. 125p. X gives: Reprint of 1920 ed. [D11956; X897-FW].

STEWART -- Stewart, Frank Graham. [G635]. See above: GRAHAM. [G269].

STEWART -- Stone, Martha Jane. *The Genealogy and History of the Stewart Family of Halifax County, Virginia, Caswell and Person Counties, North Carolina, Trigg County, Kentucky.* Lexington, KY, 1986. 141p. [NG94].

STIKELEATHER -- Kelly, Jeanett H. [G635]. See above: ALLEN. [G9].

STILL -- Irons, Ava Ray. *The Stills in South Carolina, Georgia, Texas, and Oklahoma.* Camarillo, CA, Irons, 1984. 185p. [C668; DC3490].

STILLEY -- Perry, Mae Carlyle (Bonner). *The Stilley Families of North Carolina.* NP, 1972. 100, 60 leaves. [D11978].

STILLEY -- Perry, Mae (Bonner). *Stilley Facts and Other Families of Eastern North Carolina.* NP, 1973. 60 leaves. [NG93].

STOKES -- Stokes, John L. *The Book of Stokes, 1201-1915.* Yorkville, SC, Enquirer Print, 1915. 28p. rev. ed. [X900-FW/NY].

STONE -- NAS. [L16406]. See above: COWAN [L4135].

STONE -- Charles H. *The Stones of Surry* Charlotte, NC, The Observer Printing House, 1955. 499p. [D12023].

STORM -- Perry, Max. [G637]. See above: SPRING. [G627].

STOUT -- Richardson, David A. *History and Genealogy of Peter Stout of Pennsylvania and North Carolina.* Logan, UT, 1931. 10, 6 leaves. [X902-LA].

STOWE -- Hoke, Rachel Hanna. *The Stowe Family: Descendants of William and Mary Stowe, From Virginia to North Carolina, 1718-1976.* Myrtle Beach, SC, 1977. x, 227p. [D12057; VV177].

STRACHEY -- Sanders, Charles Richard. *The Strachey Family, 1588-1932; Their Writings and Literary Associations.* Durham, NC, Duke University Press, 1953. x, 337p. [L16454].

STRADLEY -- Walton, June Roper. *Some American Descendants of John Stradley.* Four Oaks, NC, J.R. Walton, 1986. iv, 194p. [DC3510].

STRAIN -- Parker, James C. *The Strain Family: A Genealogy of the Descendants of Andrew Strain, Sr., of North Carolina.* Toccoa, GA, Commercial Print. Co., 1985. xiv, 400p. 1. Strain family. 2. Strain, Andrew, d.1826-Family. 3. North Carolina-Genealogy. DC omits underlined part of title. [G639; DC3511].

STRANGE -- Strange, Hubert E. *Strang(e) Genealogy, Scotland, North Carolina, Annapolis, Maryland.* NP, 1972. 24p. [X905-FW].

STRONG -- Strong, Dale G. *The Descendants of John Strong, 1770-1837 and Martha Watson, 1772-1851 of Drumhome Parish, Co., of Donegal, Ireland.* Cassatt, SC, Mr. & Mrs. Dale G. Strong, 1983. 98 l. [DS694].

STROTHER -- Eubank, Hazel Bentley. *Strother and Allied Families.* Easley, SC, Southern

Historical Press, 1982. xix, 305p. 1. Strother family. 2. Georgia-Genealogy. [G641; DS6695].

STROUD -- Perry, Octavie Jordan. *A Sage of Strouds & Strodes.* High Point, NC, Perry, 1966. 159p. [D12099].

STROUP -- Priest, Lyman W. *Johannes and Elisabeth (Löliger) Strub, Basel-Land, Switzerland, Rowan, Surry, Stokes, Forsyth Counties, North Carolina, Bartholomew County, Indiana, Edwards County, Illinois, 1719-1844: A Three Generation Study: Related Families Included: Alberty, Aldridge, Billetter, Boehlo / Belo, Bonn, Brietz, Butner, Chitty, Geiger, George, Greter, Hamilton, Hanke, Hauser, Henning, Hinkston, Holland, Kenyon, Loesch, Mücke / Mickey, Pfaff, Pfohl, Rights, Ruede, Seiler, Sims, Spach, Stoltz, Stolz , Transou, Vickery, Wesner.* Charlottesville, VA, L.W. Priest, 1988. iii, 125p. 1. Stroup family. 2. Strub, Johannes, 1719-1789-Family. 3. Moravians-North Carolina-Genealogy. 4. North Carolina-Genealogy. [G641].

STUART -- Gregg, E. Stuart. [G643]. See above: GREGG. [G273]. - 2 Entrys.

STUART -- Kelly, Jeannette H. [G643]. See above: ALLEN. [G9].

STUART -- Peoples, David Stuart. [G643]. See above: CALDWELL. [G115].

STUART -- Roop, Phyllis Gale. [G643]. See above. ROOP. [G567].

STUART -- Stone, Martha Jane. *The Genealogy and History of the Stewart Family of Halifax County, Virginia, Caswell and Person Counties North Carolina, Trigg County, Kentucky.* Lexington, KY, 1986. 141p. [NG94].

STUART -- Stone, Martha Jane. *The Genealogy and History of the Stewart Family of Halifax*

County, Virginia, Caswell and Person Counties North Carolina, Trigg County, Kentucky. Lexington, KY, M. J. Stone, 1986-<1987 >. v. <1-2 >. [G643].

STUBBS -- Andrea, Leonardo and Joseph E. Hill. *Abstracts of Division of Estates of Stubbs and Allied Families of Marlboro County, South Carolina.* Columbia, SC, 1964. 323 l. [NG94: D12114].

STUBBS -- Boswell, Jimmie John Stubbs. *John Stubbs, 1718-1788 of Williamsburg, South Carolina and His Descendants.* Bryan, TX, J.R. Boswell, Sr., 1990. vii, 244p. 1. Stubbs family. 2. Stubbs, John, 1718-1788-Family. 3. Virginia-Genealogy. 4. South Carolina-Genealogy. 5. Texas-Genealogy. [G643].

STURMAN -- NAS. *Thomas Sturman and Ann: Col. William Hardwick and Elizabeth Sturman; Jeffrey Johnson and Margaret of Virginia, and Their Descendants in North Carolina and Knox County, Tennessee.* NP, 1974. 98 l., 99-110p. [X2424].

SUGG -- Sugg, Eugene. *Sketches of the Sugg Family (of Orange County, North Carolina).* NP, 1940. 11 numb. leaves. [L16610].

SUITER -- Miller, Ruth Suiter. *Some Suitor Families of Canada and the United States of America - 1st ed.* Asheville, NC, Ward Pubb. Co., 1987. xxiii, 150p. 1. Suitor families. 2. Canada-Genealogy. DC gives: "xviii, 149p." [G644; DC3544].

SUITS -- Suits, George Drexel. *Suits and Allied Families of North Carolina and Illinois.* Hillsboro, IL, G.D. Suits, 1989. 1 v. (various paginations). [DC3545].

SULLIVAN -- Simpson, Edna Grant. *The Sullivan Family of Virginia, North Carolina, and Georgia.* Knoxville, TN, Simpson, 1975. ca 450 leaves. [DC3546].

SULLIVAN -- Sullivan, Hazel and Milton. *The Sullivan Family: William Dunklin Sullivan Line.* Enka, NC, Mrs. Milton A. Sullivan, 1961. 40p., 2 leaves of plates. D gives underscored part of title. [S2426; D12149].

SUMMERS -- Hammers, Marian G. *John and Richard Sumner and Their Descendants.* Utica, KY, McDowell Publications, 1986. 154p. 1. Summers family. 2. Sumner, John, ca.1765-ca.1837-Family. 3. North Carolina-Genealogy. [G645].

SUTHERLAND -- NAS. *Clan Sutherland Association. Annual Bulletin ... (of the) 7th - Annual Gathering(s), 1939 -* Rosehill, NC, 1939- Issues from 1939-1940 reproduced from typed copy. [L16632].

SUTHERLAND -- Sutherland, Henry C. *Sutherland Records Found in Georgia, Illinois, Indiana, Kentucky, Maryland, North Carolina, South Carolina and Virginia.* Crown Point, IN, 1968. 245p. [L16635; VV179].

SUTHERLAND -- Sutherlin, E. T. *A Short Genealogy of the Sutherland Family in America.* Kenansville, NC, Clan Southerland Association, 1941. 24p. [D12171].

SUTTENFIELD -- North, Mae Belle Barrow. *History of the Suttenfield and Taylor Families of Virginia and North Carolina.* Summerfield, NC, 1973. 11. 39 leaves. [D12173; VV179].

SYMONS -- Lambeth, Mary Weeks. See above: BAILEY. [L757].

SWAN -- Shank, Henry M. *Genealogy of Thomas Swan of Rowan County, North Carolina.* Denver, CO, 1968. 1 Genealogical Table. [X917-FW].

T

TANNER -- Hussey, Marguerite Carleton. *The Family of Rev. John Tanner - Baptist Preacher; Virginia - North Carolina - Kentucky - Missouri.* Berkeley, CA, 1972. 52 leaves. [S2446; VV181].

TATE -- Plyler, Mattie Adams. *Samuel Pinkney Tate Family Records.* Lancaster, SC, Plyler, 1960. 89 leaves. [D12269].

TATTNALL -- Smith, D.E. Huges. *An Account of the Tattnall and Fenwick Families in South Carolina.* Charleston, SC, 1913. 19p. [L16790].

TATUM -- Ballard, B. Vincent. *Tatum Narrative, 1735-1983: The Tatham Family of South-west Virginia and Western North Carolina.* Cary, NC, B.V. Ballard, 1987. ix, 86p. 1. Tatum family. [G651].

TATUM -- Linder, Billy Royce. *Christopher Tatum of Orangesbusg [sic] District, South Carolina and Perry, Greene, and Jasper Counties in Mississippi.* Vienna, VA, Linder, 1975. 19 leaves. [DC3589].

TAYLER -- NAS. *A History of William Taylor and Sarah Jones and Their Descendants.* Raleigh, NC, Tayler Family Committee, Litho Industries, 1972. 423p. [D12291; X927-FW].

TAYLOR -- Hyatt, Sybil. *Taylor Record, Lenoir County, N. C.* Kinston, NC, 1916. 2 Typed leaves. [L16816].

TAYLOR -- Smith, Cora Taylor Younger. *The Reverend Daniel Taylor, Senior of Virginia.* Florence, SC, Smith, 1981. 277, 11p. [D12298].

TAYLOR -- Taylor, L. Rhea. *Pioneer Moses Taylor and Elizabeth Prevatte Taylor, sr. of*

Kentucky and North Carolina. 1968 Revision. Bowling Green, KY, L. R. Taylor, 1968. 145 leaves. [X927-FW/NY].

TAYLOR -- Taylor, Walter Carroll. *Taylor Kinfolks - 3rd ed.* West Columbia, SC, A. Rawlinson, 1988. 165 leaves. 1. Taylor family. 2. South Carolina-Genealogy. [G653].

TEAGUE -- NAS. *The Teague Family Magazine.* Winston-Salem, NC, Teague Family Memorial Association, 1968- ?? v. DAR library holdings: Vol 1, no. 1, 1968 - Vol. 4. no. 4, 1972. NY holdings: vol. 1-4. July 1968 - Apr 1972. X indicates Quarterly; "No more pub." [A652; D12318; X928-NY].

TEMPLE -- Kirkpatrick, Eunice Temple. *The Temple Family of Wake County, North Carolina and Related Families.* Durham, NC, Kirkpatrick, 1978. 79 leaves. [D12327].

TEMPLETON -- Templeton, L. B. *Templeton Family History.* Union, SC, Templeton, 1953. 155p. [D12332].

TENNENT -- Tennent, Mary A. *Light in Darkness.* Greensboro, NC, Greensboro Printing Co., 1971. 822p. [D12336].

TERRELL -- NAS. *Terrell Trails.* Douglasville, GA, Terrell Society of America, 1985. _ v. Quarterly. See DAR Library Shelflist for Holdings. [DC3608].

TERRELL -- Battey, George Magruder. *Terrell Notes (on the English Terrells Who Settled in Virgina, the Carolinas and Georgia).* Washington, DC 1943. [VV182].

TERRELL -- Terrell, Lynch Moore. *Lynch Moore Terrell Genealogy.* Charlotte, NC, Terrell Society, 1988- v. <1- >. "Comments on Lawrence Fontaine LeStourgeon" - V. 1, 3rd prelim. p. 1. Terrell family. 2.

Terrell, Lynch Moore, 1834-1924-Family. [G655].

TERRELL -- Terrell, William Henry Harrison. *The Terrell Family.* Charlotte, NC, Terrell Society of America, 1989. 1 v. (various pagings). [G656].

TERRY -- Moon, Maude Terry and Gifford Clark Terry. *Genealogy of the James Terry 1701 Branch of the Virginia-North Carolina Terry Family Tree. With Special Emphasis on the Descendants of William H. and Hemima Norwood Terry, 19th Cent. Residents of Chatham County, N. C.* Sandwich, IL, 1964. pni. [VV183].

THAMES -- Kaskin, Frances Thames. *Thames Family History.* Hampton, SC, F.T. Kaskin, 1986. 44p., vi leaves of plates. 1. Thames family. [G656].

THOMAN -- Thoman, Austin Jacob. *The Thoman Family History, Volume II.* Hilton Head Island, SC, 1980. pni. [NG96].

THOMAN -- Thoman, Austin Jacob. *The History of Hans Jacob Thoman, Switzerland and the U.S., 1684-1974.* McLean Va. 1974. 84p. [NG96].

THOMAN -- Thoman, Austin Jacob. *Ancestors and Relatives of Susanna Bauman Thoman.* Hilton Head Island, SC, 1980. 42 l. [NG96].

THOMAS -- NAS. *Thomas Family of Maryland and South Carolina.* NP, n.d. 14 leaves. [X934-LA].

THOMAS -- Coggeshall, Robert Walden. [G658]. See above: COGGESHALL. [G148].

THOMAS -- Wingert, Grace Harper. *Our Kinsmen, A Record of the Ancestry and Descendants of Griffith Thomas, a Pioneer Resident of Orange County, North Carolina.* Springfield, OH, 1938. 135p. [L16963].

THOMPSON -- Beckman, L. A. *Alexander Thompson of Fairfield District, South Carolina.* Ellisville, MS, Beckman, 1950. 56p. [D12400].

THOMPSON -- Buchanan, Jane Gray. [G659; DC3630]. See above: FINNEY. [G229;DC3630].

THOMPSON -- Hendrix, Ge Lee Corley. *The Matthew Thompson Lineage Documentation and Their Relation to Allied Families.* Greenville, SC, Hendrix, 1980. 27 leaves. [DC3635].

THOMSON -- Buck, Robert J. *Trail Blazers of the Thomson Gamble Family; with a Genealogical Record of Some of Their Descendants.* Asheville, NC, 1948. 99p. [X937-CH/FW].

THORN -- Clark, William Alexander Graham. *Ancestors of Dr. Samuel Thorne (1767-1838) of Halifax County, N. C.* Washington, DC, Geneal Table. [L17027].

THORN -- Clark, William Alexander Graham. *Decendants of Dr. Samuel Thorne (1767-1838) of Halifax County, N. C.* Washington, DC, A Chart... [L17028].

THRELKELD -- Paris, Maurice Hudson Thatcher. [G661]. See above: PARIS. [G502].

THURMAN -- Humphries, John D. *Descendants of John Thurman of Virginia, William Graves of Virginia and James Jones of South Carolina.* Atlanta, GA, Humphries, 1938. 81p. [D12468; VV185].

TILLETT -- Allison, Charles Walker. *Reverend John Tillett Family History* Charlotte, NC, Allison, Observer Print. House, 1955. 194, 64, 171p. X gives: "Includes Allison, Wyche. [D12495; X941-SU].

TILLINGHAST -- NAS. *Pardon's Progeny; A Publication of the Tellinghast Family in*

America. Asheville, NC, Tillinghast, 1974- . __v. DAR library holdings: Vol. 1, nos. 1-4. D gives underscored title. [D12497; DC3649].

TIMBERLAKE -- Blankenship, Gayle King. [G662]. See above: KING. [G369].

TIMBERLAKE -- Foster, Clarice Jones. *Look Where The Sun Is: Timberlake Reflections*. Columbia, SC?, Bryan, 1985. 196p. [DC3650].

TINGEN -- Franklin, Leallah. *Garrett Tingen Descendants: Early Settler of Person County, North Carolina*. Baltimore, MD, Gateway Press, 1989. vi, 406p. 1. Tingen family. 2. Tingen, Garrett Robert, ca. 1789-ca. 1847-Family. 3. North Carolina-Genealogy. [G663; DC3654].

TISDALE -- Bayless, Mary Phillips. [G663]. See above: PHILLIPS. [G516].

TISON -- McCormick, Sarah Gray. *Forebears and Descendants of Reuben Henry Tison and Rebekah Mary Jane McKenzie and Facts and Traditions Gleaned throughout the Years...* Dillon, SC, Herald Office Supply. 1966. 74 leaves, 33 leaves of plates. [S2515].

TOLLIVER -- Sturgill, Lorene Moxley. [G664]. See above: HOPPER. [G330].

TOMS -- Toms, Maude. *Descendants of Francis Toms of the Colonial Friends of Eastern North Carolina, 1650-1947*. NP, M. Toms,.. 1947. 11, 8p. [X945-FW].

TORREY -- McLean, Angus Wilton. [G665]. See above: McLEAN. [G443].

TORRINGTON -- Blankenship, Gayle King. [G665]. See above: KING. [G369].

TOUCHTONE -- Sandel, Mary Eleanor and Elias Wesley Sandel. *The Touchtones of Maryland, Virginia, North & South Carolina, Georgia,*

Mississsippi, and Louisiana. NP, 1972. 36 leaves. VV lists as TOCHUTONE. [G666; S2530; VV187].

TOWER -- Read, Thomas Carpenter. *The Tower and Converse Families, Ancestors of Rosa Georgiana (Tower) Read.* Charleston, SC, 1962. 12p. [NG97].

TOWNLEY -- Quattlebaum, Christine Pollard. *The Townley Family History.* Columbia, SC, Quattlebaum, 1969. 22 leaves. [D12586].

TOWNSEND -- Reynolds, Harriet Dickson. *Samuel Townsend, 1751-1849, Revolutionary Soldier of South Carolina, Georgia and Alabama.* NP, 1977. 102 l. [D12594].

TOWNSEND -- Townsend, Malcolm. *The Townsends.* Charleston, SC, Garnier, 1969. Unpaged. [X948-NY].

TRAPPER -- Keller, Andrew King. [G667]. See above: KELLER. [G361].

TREZEVANT -- Trezevant, Thomas Timothée. *The Trezevant Family in the United States, from the Date of the Arrival of Daniel Trezevant, Hugenot, at Charles Town, South Carolina, in 1685, to the Present Date.* Columbia, SC, Printed by the State Company, 1914. 122p. [L17300].

TRIPLETT -- Abbott, Hortense E. *Descendants of the Triplett Families of Virginia, North & South Carolina.* Hemet, CA, 1982. pni. [VV187].

TROGDON -- Trogdon, Willard F. *Trogdon Family History.* Gastonia, NC, Loftin & Co., printers, 1926. 117p. [X952-FW/LA/LI/NY].

TRUESDALE -- Truesdale, Karl. *Descendants of John Truesdale of Cumberland Co., Pennsylvania.* NP, 1952. 79, 100, 70 leaves. Bound with Trusdells of Kentucky, Descendants of John Truesdel of South Carolina and James Truesdale of Rochester, New York. [DC3698].

TRUESDELL -- Truesdale, Karl. *Descendants of John Truesdale of Orange County, North Carolina.* Ithaca, NY, J.B. Truesdale, 1960. 216p. [L17347].

TRUESDALE -- Truesdale, Karl. *Truesdell Genealogy.* Negative. Microfilm 4511. [L17348].

TUCKER -- Fred L. *Tucker, A Genealogy, 1784-1982: The Family and Descendants of Hiram Tucker and Catherine Hendry Tucker of North Carolina and Alabama -- 1st ed.* Decatur, GA, F. L. Tucker. 1982. ix, 174 pages. [C705].

TUCKER -- Tucker, Reuel Walter. *Memoirs and History of the Peyton Tucker Family; Ancestors and Descendants of England, Wales, Vermont, Massachusetts, Maryland, Virginia, the Carolinas, Georgia, Tennessee, Kentucky, Illinois, Missouri, Arkansas, Louisiana, Texas, Oklahoma, and California; and Genealogy.* Baltimore, MD, Gateway Press, 1975. xxvii, 256 p. 2 fold. leaves of plates. [S2558; VV187].

TUCKER -- Woodruff, Caldwell. *The Tucker Family of Bermuda and South Carolina (from Notes by George Haig Tucker).* Linthicum Heights, MD, 1941. 2p., 34 numb leaves. [L17369].

TURNAGE -- Turnage, Richard Wentworth. *The Turnage Family.* Hartsville, SC, R.W. Turnage, 1964. 14 leaves. [DC3704].

TURNBULL -- Kellough, Gene Ross . [G675]. See above: KYLE. [G381].

TURNER -- Fitts, Ruth Turner. *Turner, Georgia - South Carolina.* NP, 1982. 162 l. [DS715].

TURNER -- Mitchener, William A. [G676]. See above: MITCHENER. [G458].

TUTTLE -- Whitman, Joyce Bruner. *Andrew Hull Tuttle, 1775-1845: His Ancestry and Descendants.* Baltimore, MD, Gateway Press, Lenoir, NC, J.B. Whitman, 1985. xi, 517p. 1. Tuttle family. 2. Tuttle, Andrew Hull, 1775-1845-Family. 3. North Carolina-Genealogy. [G677].

TYNER -- Townsend, Peggy Tyner. *Tyner Family, 1704-1971 and Bruce Relations in Roberson Co., N. C.* NP, 1972. 30 leaves. [S2572].

TYSON -- Hyatt, Sybil. *Tyson and Sugg - Beaufort County, N.C. Records.* Kinston, NC, 1941. 12 numb. leaves. Typwritten. [L17467].

TYSOR -- Broughton, W. Harold. *The Tysors of Old Chatham.* Durham, NC, Seeman Printery, 1971. [X gives 1972]. 300p. [D12758; X958-FW/NY/PH].

U

UPCHURCH -- West, Belle Lewter. *Upchurch Family of England, Virginia and North Carolina.* Durham, NC, West, 1972. 126p. [S2579; NG98; D12758; VV189].

V

VAIL -- Vail, Wm. Penn, M.D. *Genealogy of Some of the Vail Family Descended from Thomas Vail at Salem, Massachusetts, 1640, Together with Some Collateral Lines.* Charleston, SC, Presses of Walker, Evans & Cogswell Company, 1937. 6, 359, 14p. [L17534].

VALENTINE -- Valentine, John Jackson. *John Valentine of Newberry District, South Carolina.* Memphis, TN, Valentine, 1957. 134 l. X gives 6, 134p. [NG98; D12807;X963-FW].

VANCE -- Dixon, Elizabeth Williamson. *The Vance Family of Virginia, Pennsylvania, North Carolina, Tennessee; the Brank Family of North Carolina and Kentucky.* NP, 1958. 315 l. [D12825; VP233; VV189].

VANCE -- McCaine, W. D. *Eight Generations of the Family of William Vance (1786-1844) and His Wife, Mary G. McAnulty Vance (1784-1863) of S.C., Alabama, and Mississippi.* Hattiesburg, MS, 1974. xii, 673p. [X965-FW].

VANCE -- Smith, Vance Voss, Ed. *The Vance Family of Piedmont, North Carolina, Vans, De Vaux, DeVallibus...* Winston-Salem, NC, Hunter Publishing, 1981. 396p. [DC3751].

VANDERBILT -- MacDowell, Dorothy Kelly. *Commodore Vanderbilt and His Family: a Biographical Account of the Descendants of Cornelius and Sophia Johnson Vanderbilt.* Hendersonville, NC, D.K. McDowell, 1989, ix 235p. 1. Vanderbilt family. 2. Vanderbilt, Cornelius, 1794-1877-Family. [G685].

VANDEVEER -- Baer, Mabel Van Dyke. *The Vandeveers of North Carolina, Kentucky, and Indiana.* Richmond, VA, Whittet & Shepperson, 1960. xi, 180p. [A680; NG98; D12860].

VANDIVER -- Atkinson, J. Russell. *Decendants (sic) of Edward Calloway Vandiver and Margaret Amelia Welch.* Columbia, SC, Atkinson, 1972. 115 l. [DS727].

VAN ZANDT -- Dean, Ralph H. *Our Dutch Ancestors: Van der Grift, Van Zandt, Van Horn, and the Lee (Lea) Family of North Carolina and Virginia.* Woodland, CA, n.d. iv, 89p. [X972-FW; VV190].

VAUGHAN -- Winborne, Benj. B. *The Vaughan Family of Hertford County, N. C.* Raleigh, NC, Edwards & Broughton Printing Co., 1909. 104p. Contains also the De Berry, Jenkins, and Dew Families. [L17684].

VEEDER -- Veeder, Edwin Henry. *The Vedder Family in America, 1657-1973.* Amherst, NY, Vedder, 1974. 258p. 1. Veeder family. [G688].

VEEDER -- Veeder, Edwin Henry. *The Vedder Family in America, 1657-1985.* Clemson, SC, E.H. Vedder, 1987. 568p., 4 pages of plates. Updated edition of The Vedder Family in America, 1657-1973, 1974. Veeder family. [G688].

VEREEN -- Andrea, Leonardo. *The Vereens of Horry.* NP, Vereen Family Association (Raleigh, N.C.: Joseph J. Vereen), 1957. 20p. [D12961].

VESTAL -- Miller, Anne V. [G689; DC3773]. See above: LOVELACE. [G410; DC3773].

VREELAND -- Vreeland, Louis Beach. *Annals of the Vreeland Family* Charlotte, NC, Vreeland, 1950. 78 leaves. [L17775].

VREELAND -- Vreeland, Louis Beach. *Annals of the Vreeland Family* Charlotte, NC, Vreeland, 1956. 119p. [D12996].

VUNCANNON -- Vuncannon, Samuel H. *The Vuncannon - Voncannons of Randolph County, North Carolina: A Study of Their Past History.* Clearwater, FL, S.H. Vuncannon, 198_. vi, 618p. 1. Vuncannon family. 2. Randolph County (N.C.)-Genealogy. [G693].

W

WADE -- NAS. *The Wades; The History of a Family, Dealing with the Kith and Kin of*

Zachary and Mary Hatton, Their Descendants and Related Lines, Male and Female, in Maryland, Virginia, Tennessee, South Carolina, North Carolina, and Other States. Cairo, IL, 1963. pni. [VV191].

WADE -- Elliott, Margaret Axson. *My Aunt Louisa and Woodrow Wilson.* Chapel Hill, NC, The University of North Carolina Press, 1944. vii, 302p. An account of the author's life spent in the homes of her aunt and brother-in-law. [L17792].

WADE -- Wade, Ophelia R. *Wade - Waid - Waide; A Research Book primarily of Census,Cemetary, and Courthouse Records for the States of Ala., Ark., Ga., Ind., Ky., Mass., Mo., N.C., Okla., S.C., Tenn., Texas and Va.* Bragg City, MO, Author, 1975. 260p. [X981-FW/MH].

WAGGONER -- Vaughan, Lewis Elmo. *Woggoner - Yount Odyssey; from Germany to North Carolina and Points West.* Baltimore, MD, 1982. 50p. [NG99; DC3786].

WAGNER -- Leonard, Frances Wagner, Ed, et al. *"Old" Jacob Wagner of Davidson (Old Rowan) County and Some of His Descendants - Limited ed.* - Lexington, NC, F.W. Leonard, 1984. xx, 429p. 1. Wagner family. 2. Wagner, Jacob, 1717-1789-Family. 3. Rowan County (N.C.)-Genealogy. 4. Davidson County (N.C.)-Genealogy. 5. North Carolina-Genealogy. [G693].

WAGNER -- Thoman, Austin J. *The William Washington Wagner Family History.* Hilton Head, SC, 1980. pni. [NG99].

WAGNER -- Wagner, William F. *Letters of William F. Wagner, Confederate Soldier.* Wendell, NC, Broadfoot's Bookmark, 1983. vi, 103p., 2 leaves of plates. 1. Wagner, William F., 1831-1864-Correspondence. 2. United States-History-Civil War, 1861-1865-Personal narratives,Confederate. 3. Wagner family-Correspondence. 4. North Carolina-History-Civil War, 1861-1865-Personal narratives. 5. Soldiers-North Carolina-Catawba County-Correspondence-Correspondence. 6. Catawba County (N.C.)-Biography. [G694].

WAINNER -- Jeter, Merle (Wainner) and George D. Wainner. *The Family History of Wainner, Overton, McMurray (McMurry) and Interconnecting Lines.* Columbia, SC, 1972. 232p. NG gives underscored part of title. [NG99; X983-FW/NY].

WAKEFIELD -- Pugh, Hazel, et al. *The Family of Henry Wakefield, North Carolina, 1805-1950.* NP, 1950, 78p. [L17830].

WALCOTT -- King, Mrs. James A. *The Walcott Family in America, 1628-1840.* NP, Rachel Caldwell Chapter, North Carolina DAR, G.R.C., 1986. 29 LEAVES. [DC3792].

WALKER -- Bell, Annie W. Burns. *Ward Family History (Which Originated in North Carolina).* Frankfurt, KY, 1931 138 leaves. Various pagings. Typed from official records and local publications. [X985-NY].

WALKER -- Griffin, Clarence. *Revolutionary Service of Co. John Walker and Family and Memoirs of Hon. Felix Walker.* Forest City, NC, The Forest City Courier, 1930. 23, 1p. [L17857].

WALKER -- Jackson, Bill (William H.) *The Descendants of Moses Walker of Orange County, North Carolina.* Carlsbad, NM, B. Jacksln, 1990. 69 leaves. 1. Walker family. 2. Walker, Moses, ca. 1735-1806-Family. 3. Southermn State-Genealogy. [G696].

WALKER -- Walker, Alice A. [G696]. See above: BAKER. [G31].

WALKER -- Walker, Legare. *The Walker Family, Originally of the Wycomico River Section of Northumberland (subsequently Westmoreland) County, Virginia, Stemming from William Walker, 1622/23-1657, and Through One of His Descendants, Josephy Rabley Walker, 1768-1816, Who Immigrated from Mecklenburg County in that State to South Carolina, circa 1806, and Settled in Edgefield County Near the Town of That Name; also a Correction of Certain Errors in a Chart of the Adams Family, with which Walkers are Connected by Marriage.* Summerville, SC, 1945. pni. [VV192].

WALL -- Thomas, Anne Wall. *The Walls of Walltown; The Known Descendants of James Wall of Anson County, North Carolina.* Carrboro, NC, Thomas, 1969. 180p. D gives underscored part of title. [A689; D13072].

WALLER -- NAS. *Edgecombe County, N.C., Records - Waller...* NP, 1942. 3 numb. leaves. Typed. [L17897].

WALLER -- Waller, John Edmund. *800 Years of History of the Waller Family.* Asheville, NC, J.E. Waller, 1984. 197, 8 leaves, p. 198-199. 1. Waller family. 2. Virginia-Genealogy. [G697].

WALLS -- Brumfield, MarciA Conrad. *John P. Walls, 1834/N.C.--1898/Ohio.* Maysville, KY, Brumfield, 1990. 28p. [DC3805].

WALSER -- Walser, Richard. *Five Walsers.* Raleigh, NC, Wolf's Head Press, 1976. 99p. [D13090; X989-FW/LA/OH/PH/SP].

WALTHAL -- Walthall, Malcolm Elmore. *The Walthall Family; A Genealogical History of the Descendants of William Walthall of Virginia.* Charlotte, NC, 1963. pni. [VV192].

WANNAMAKER -- Wannamaker, J. Skottowe. *The Wannamaker, Salley, Mackay, and Bellinger*

Families. Charleston, SC, Walker, Evans, and Cogswell, Co., 1937. 485p. [D13107].

WARD -- NAS. *Newspaper Notices and Family Records of Ward, Jones, Hill, Moore*. NP, North Carolina DAR, 1960. 132 l. [D13124].

WARD -- Bell, Annie W.B. *Ward Family History of the Records of the Eastern Cherokee Indian Tribe, Copied at the National Archives in Washington, D.C. to Honor the Famous Cherokee Woman, Nancy Ward of Tennessee*. Washington, DC, 1988. 86 leaves. FW gives date as 1961. [X992-FW/NY].

WARD -- McGhee, Lucy K. *Ward Family History of Virginia, Showing Their Links with the States of North Carolina, Tennessee and Kentucky Branches of Wards*. Washington, DC, 1957. 29a, 81, A-I l. [X992-FW/NY; VV193].

WARD -- Mosback, Lucille W. *History of Alfred and Elizabeth Robinson Ward, Their Antecedents and Descendants*. Wallace, NC, Wallace Enterprises, 1971. 588p. Rev. and Suppl. to ed. 1 by H. W. Taylor, 1945. [X992-FW].

WARE -- Fisher, Sunie Garrett Talbert Elliott. [G700]. See above: CATLETT. [G128].

WARING -- Waring, P. N. *A Short History of the Warings*. Tyrone, PA, Printed by the Herald, 1898. 60p. Geneal. Tables Inserted. Descendants of Richard of Boston, Mass., 1664, Benjamin of Charleston, S.C., 1691, and the Warings of Herefordshire, Eng. [L17995].

WARLICK -- Warlick, Alfred Caldwell. *A Genealogy of the Warlick Family from Palatinate, Germany*. Gastonia, NC, Warlick, 1960. 93, 13 leaves. [D13148].

WARREN -- Warren, Edward French. *We Live Forever; A Genealogical Study of Thirteen*

Generations Over a Four Hundred Year Period, 1570-1980. Hilton Head Island, SC, 1987. vi, 104p. NG gives title as: "We Live Forever, Warren and Wilson Families, 1570-1980, and 104p. 1. Warren family. 2. Wilson family. [G701; NG100].

WARREN -- Warren, George Corbett. *Warren Kith and Kin: A Genealogy.* Sumter, SC, G.C. Warren, 1986. v, 137p. 1. Warren family. [G701].

WARREN -- Warren, Holland D. *Warrens and Related Families of North Carolina and Virginia.* Lynchburg, VA, H.D. Warren, 1990. 442p. 1. Warren family. 2. North Carolina-Genealogy. 3. Virginia-Genealogy. [G701].

WATERS -- Waters, James McCoy. *From Where the Waters Flow: A Biographical Account of the Waters Family of South Carolina, Florida, and Alabama.* Robertsdale, AL, J.M. Waters, 1985. 62p. 1. Waters family. 2. Southern States-Genealogy. [G702].

WATKINS -- Watkins, Francis N. *A Catalog of the Descendants of Thomas Watkins of Chickahomony, Va. ; Who Was the Common Ancestor of Many of the Families of the Name in Prince Edward, Charlotte, and Chesterfield Counties, Va.* Henderson, NC, Atlas Print, 1899. 50p. [D has NP, 1955. 41 leaves. Typescript of 1899 edition.] [D13211; X999-FW].

WATKINS -- Watkins, William B. *The Watkins Family of North Carolina.* Jackson, TN, McCowat-Mercer, 1925. 85p. [D13213].

WATKINS -- Watkins, Walter Barker Critz. *Family Portrait: 1840-1890: Virginia-Carolina Puritans, Drawn from Their Letters.* Laurel, VA?, W.B.C. Watkins, 1957. 187p. [DC3845].

WATSON -- Watson, Harry L. *Elihu Watson and Permelia Wright Niswanger Watson and Descendants.* Greenwood, SC, Index-Journal Co., 1933. 54p. [D13222].

WATSON -- Watson, Sparkie. *Isham and Mary's Children.* __, SC, S. Watson, 1986. 259p. 1. Watson family. 2. Watson, Isham, 1788-1864-Family. [G703].

WAYLAND -- Wayland, John Walter, Jr. *Wayland Family Genealogy. Bauserman, Blankenbaker, and Dresler Families.* Charleston, SC, 1980. 137 leaves. [NG101].

WEATHERSBEE -- DeHuff, Elizabeth W. *The Weathersbee Family of Halifax and Martin Counties, North Carolina and Barnwell County, South Carolina.* August, GA, 196_. 63p. FW has 50p. dated 1965. [X1002-FW/NY].

WEAVER -- Weaver, Pearl M. *The Tribe of Jacob; The Descendants of the Reverend Jacob Weaver of Reems Creek, North Carolina, 1786-1868 and Elizabeth Siler Weaver.* Weaverville, NC, 1962. viii, 141p. [L18195].

WEAVER -- Weaver, Robert B. *William Weaver, Jr.* Jefferson, NC, Carolina Printing & Supply, 1981. ix, 171p. [DS743].

WEBB -- Hollifield, Hazel Webb. *The Webb Family: Descendants of Isaac & Mary (Polly) Blanton Webb - 1st ed.* Spruce Pine, NC, H.W. Hollifield, 1989. 158p. 1. Webb family, 2. Webb, Isaac-Family. 3. Webb, Mary Blanton-Family. 4. North Carolina-Genealogy. [G705].

WEBB -- Webb, David G. *Webb Family of Bearwallow Ridge.* Columbia, SC, R.L. Bryan, 1983. vi, 435p. [DC3863].

WEBB -- Webb, William James. *Our Webb Kin of Dixie.* Oxford, NC, Webb, 1940. 205p. [D13266].

WEBSTER -- Scarborough, Quincy J. *North Carolina Decorated Stoneware: The Webster School of Folk Potters.* Fayetteville, NC, Scarborough Press, 1986. 93p. 1. Webster family. 2. Gurdon Robins & Co. 3. Stoneware-North Carolina. 4. Decoration and ornament-North Carolina-Themes, motives. [G705].

WEEKS -- Lambeth, Mary Weeks. [L18244]. See above: BAILEY: [L757].

WELBORN -- Wilburn, Hiram Coleman. *Welborn-Wilburn, History - Genealogy; The Families in Virginia, North Carolina, South Carolina.* Waynesville, NC, 1953. 104p. [L18270].

WELLMAN -- Lane, Herbert V. *A Genealogical Record of Some Descendants of Bennett Wellman of Maryland, Virginia, West Virginia, Kentucky and North Carolina.* Bradenton, FL, 1978. 349p. [D13323; VV197].

WELLMAN -- Lane, Herbert V. *A Genealogical Record of Some Descendants of Bennett Wellman of Maryland, Virginia, West Virginia, Kentucky and North Carolina 1754-1978.* NP, 1978. 349p. [D13323].

WELLMAN -- Lane, Herbert V. *A Genealogical Record of Some Descendants of Bennett Wellman of Maryland, Virginia, West Virginia, Kentucky and North Carolina 1754-1978.* Bradenton, FL, H. V. Lane, [1978]-<1983 >. V. <1-3 >. Contents: v. 1. 1754-1978, v. 2. 1754-1980, v 3. 1754-1983. Vol. 2-<3 > called "Supplementary Edition", Have Imprint: Decorah, Iowa, Anundsen Publising. Co. [C742].

WELLS -- Wells, James W. *Descendants of Jacob Wells of Duplin County, North Carolina.* Benton, AK, Wells, 1973. 830p. [D13339].

WELLONS -- Bundy, V. Mayo, Ed. *Charles Wellons of Johnston County, North Carolina,*

His Ancestors and Descendants. Charlotte, NC, Herb Eaton, 1984. 399p. [DC3876].

WESLEY -- NAS. *Memoirs of the Wesley Family. 2d. ed. 1848 Rev., Corr. and Considerably Enlarged.* Taylor, SC, Van Hooser Publications, 1976. 659p. [X1012-LA].

WESSON -- Lawsion, Percy Bethel. [G710]. See above: BRAODNAX. [G90].

WEST -- Boyle, Blodwen (West). *Isaac West's Family of N.C., S.C., and Dickson County, Tenn, 1745-1850.* Cayucos, CA, 1974. 34p. NG gives underscored part of title. X gives 34 leaves and omits place of publication. [NG101; X1014-FW].

WEST -- Hopper, George Henry. *A Study of the West - Hopper and Allied Families.* Durham, NC, West, 1973. 105 leaves. [D13370].

WEST -- Moll, Verna Doane. *Miles West, Born 1796, His Children and Grandchildren: with Appendixes Regarding the Allied Families of Doyle Bowden and Benjamin Williams of North Carolina and Indiana.* Sonoma, CA, 1987. xiv, 234p. 1. West family. 2. West, Miles, 1796-1841-Family. [G710; NGS11].

WEST -- Murff, Vaughn W. *Some Descendants of Henry West, Born in 1785 in N. C.* Floydada, TX, 1961. 72p. [X1013-IG].

WEST -- West, Broadus B. *Genealogy of Isaac West of Greenville County, South Carolina.* Spartanburg, SC, West, 1929. 53p. [D13379].

WEST -- West, Fred. *The Wests of the Cape Fear Valley.* Whitsett, NC, F. West, 1983. (Utica, KY: McDowell Publications) 217p. 1. West family. 2. North Carolina-Genealogy. [G710].

WEST -- West, Fred. *The Wests of the Cape Fear Valley.* Carbondale, IL, F. West, 1987.

341p. "Second edition"-Pref. 1. West family. 2. North Carolina-Genealogy. [G710].

WEST -- West. George Henry. *A Study of the West - Hopper Families.* Durham, NC, 1973. 105 l. Cover Title: West Genealogy, Hopper Genealogy. [S2687].

WHALEY -- Barton, W. Baynard and Fannie May Dolley Barton. *A Limited Genealogy Study of the Descendants of Maj. Gen. Edward Whalley (the Regicide) Featuring Private Thomas Whaley, Lieut. Archibald Whaley of 1776 Era Descendants, Edward Charles Whaley, Joseph Whaley of Edisto, Island, S.C. and Descendants of Nathaniel Whaley in Delaware, Virginia, and Maryland with Appropriate Ancestral Review, Discussion and History 1067-1956.* Stonega, VA, 1956 [i.e. 1967]. 143 leaves, 34 plates. Cover title: Whaleys, 1066; 1660-1967. "This second edition is limited. 22 copies completed". VV gives date of 1956 (probably 1st edition) pni. [G711; VV198].

WHETSTONE -- Routt, Joanne Whetstone. *The Whetstone Family; Switzerland, South Carolina, Alabama.* Harvest, Al, 1972. 151p. [S2690].

WHIDDON -- Alexander, Virginia Wood. *Whitten and Allied Families - 2nd ed.* Columbia, TN, V.W. Alexander, Clenson, SC, W.C.Whitten, Jr. 1984. 668p. 1. Whitten family. 2. Witten family. 3. Whiddon family. 4. South Carolina-Genealogy. 5. Southern States-Genealogy. DC lists as: WHITTEN. [G712; DC3931].

WHIPPLE -- Whipple, Henry Burdette. *A Partial List of the Descendants of Matthew Whipple, the Elder, of Bocking, Essex County, England.* High Point, NC, Whipple, 1965. 2 v. D gives underscored title and shows: 2 v. (v, 197, III, 184 leaves). [A703; NG102; D13441].

WHITAKER -- Honneycutt, Frances F. [G713]. See above: FREEMAN. [G241].

WHITAKER -- Whitaker, C. Bruce. [G713]. See above: HARPER. [G300].

WHITAKER -- Whitaker, Harriet Katherine Reed. *Genealogy of the Whitaker Family, 1431-1926.* Southern Pines, NC, Dixie Printing Co., 1926. 24p. [D13449; X1017-FW].

WHITE -- Ballinger, Dwight Gail. [G713]. See above: MORSE. [G468].

WHITE -- Linn, Jo White. [G714]. See above: ARRINGTON. [G20].

WHITE -- Strawn, Anne White. *The Ancestors and Descendants of John White and Sarah Elizabeth Green with Allied Lines.* Salisbury, NC, Salisbury, Printing, 1984. 472p. [NG102; DC3917].

WHITE -- White, Bonner Dale. *The White Family.* Chester, SC, 1968. 115p. [D13479].

WHITE -- White, Gail. *Emigrants from the Emerald Isle and Related Families: White, Hoke, Dorsey, Hendrick, and Fizwaters / Fitzwaters.* Inman, SC, 1977. 138p. D gives underscored part of title. [NG102; D13486].

WHITE -- White, Iona Ann Gomel. *Descendants of David White, North Carolina and Joseph & Sarah King White...* NP, William White Chapter, Missouri DAR, G.R.C., 1983. 260 leaves. [DC3916].

WHITEHEAD -- Dimond, E. Grey. *The Reverend William W. Whitehead, Mississippi Pioneer: His Antecedents and Descendants: Including Some Notes Concerning the Whiteheads of the Isle of Wight and Southampton, Virginia, Edgecombe, Halifax, Nash, and Wake, North Carolina, Wayne, Indiana, Territory, La Porte, Indian, Points West, and Those Massaced (sic) in the Nat Turner Slave Uprising of 1831.* St. Louis, MO, 1985. pni. [VV200].

WILBURN -- Wilburn, Hiram C. *The Wellborn - Wilburn History and Genealogy.* Waynesville, NC, Wilburn, 1953. 104p. [D13567].

WHITMER -- Owens, Robert James. *The Whitmires of Whitmire, SC and Kin: History & Genealogy of the Descendants of George Frederick Whitmire with a Genealogy of Many of the Maternal Lines.* Canon City, CO, R.J. Owens, 1989. 2 v. (v, 429p.) 1. Whitmire family. 2. Whitmire, George Frederick, 1742-1829-Family. 3. South Carolina-Genealogy. 4 Missouri-Genealogy. [G715].

WHITMER -- Owens, Robert James. *The Whitmires of Whitmire, SC and Kin.* Canon City, CO, R.J. Owens, 1989. 2 v. (v, 429p.) 1. Whitmire family. 2. Whitmire (S.C.)-Genealogy. 3. South Carolina-Genealogy. 4. Whitmire, George Frederick, 1742-1829-Family. [G713].

WHITMER -- Pruett, Haskell. *The Families of the Sons of Christopher Columbus Whitmire, Sr., 1774-1842, NC and SC.* Stillwater, OK, H. Pruett, 1986. 344p. 1. Whitmer family. 2. Whitmire, Christopher Columbus, 1774-1842-Family. 3. North Carolina-Genealogy. 4. South Carolina-Genealogy. [G715].

WHITESIDE -- Whiteside, Don. *Whiteside(s) Listed in North Carolina Census for Selected Counties, 1787-1880 and Other Papers on the Whiteside Family.* Edminton, Canada, 1965(-1970). 1 v. (various pagings). On spine: Whitesides listed in N.C., S.C., & Tenn. census for selected counties. [S2700].

WHITESELL -- Whitsell, William Thornton, PH.D. *A Brief History of Alamance County, North Carolina, with Sketches of the Whitesell Family and the Huffman Family.* Burlington, NC, A.D. Pate & Co., Printers, 1926. 32p. On Cover: Whitsett Historical Monographs, no. 4. [L18547].

WHITTEN -- Alexander, Virginia Wood. [G716; DC3931]. See above: WHIDDON. [G712; DC3931].

WICKER -- Wicker, Richard F. *The Wicker / Whicker Family: Devonshire, Virginia, North Carolina.* Baltimore, MD, Gateway Press, Virginia Beach, VA, R.F. Wicker, 1989. xi, 322p. 1. Wicker family. 2. England-Genealogy. 3. Virginia-Genealogy. 4 North Carolina-Genealogy. [G716; NGN17-6-91; DC3938].

WIDENHOUSE -- Albright, William T. *History of the Widenhouse, Furr, Dry, Stallings, Teeter, and Tucker Families.* Greensboro, NC, 1950. 145p. Also: Supplement to the history of the Furr family (Greensboro, NC, 1956), 63p. [X1024-NY].

WIGGS -- Elvey, Gerald, et al. *The Wigg Family.* Chichester, Susses, England: Phillimore, 1989. 220p. "Introduction" - 1 leaf inserted. 1. Wiggs family. 2. Great Britain-Genealogy. 3. South Carolina-Genealogy. [G717].

WILCOX -- Payne, E. S. *Our Wilcoxon Family from North Carolina to Kentucky to Indiana and Westward.* New Albany, IN, 1970. 452p. [X1026-FW].

WILCOX -- Albertson, Martha S. *A Willcox Family History, 1689-1977: Including Willcox, Wilcox and Allied Families of Pennsylvania, North Carolina, South Carolina, Georgia, Alabama, and Missouri.* Tucker, GA, M. S. Albertson, 1981. ca 550p. "Compiled to again update, enlarge upon and correct the author's previous volumes published in 1972 and 1977." - Preface. [C753].

WILFONG -- Wilfong, Neal D. *The Descendants of Major and Mrs. George Wilfong of North Carolina.* Cleveland, NC, N.D. Wilfong, 1985. ii, 43p. 1. Wilfong family. 2. Wilfong,

George, 1740-1818-Family. 3. North Carolina-Genealogy. [G718].

WILKINS -- Barnhill, Celeste Jane Terrell. *The 16 Children of Capt. William Wilkins and Wife, Ann Elizabeth Terrell of Virginia and South Carolina.* Washington, DC, 1943. 1 leaf. Copied by George Magruder Beatty. [L18696].

WILKINS -- Johnson, Evalyn Park Selby (Mrs. Palmer W.). *The Family of Wilkins.* Marion, SC, 1937. 3, 88p. [L186].

WILLCOX -- McIver, Helen H. *Willcox Family of Pennsylvania, North Carolina, South Carolina, Georgia.* NP, 1930. 119 leaves. [D13627; VP245].

WILLETT -- Willett, Albert James. *The Willett Families of North America: Being a Comprehensive Guide Encompassing Willett, Willett, Willette...[sic].* Easley, SC, Southern Historical , 1985. 2 v. [DC3955].

WILLIAMS -- Ames, Joseph. S. *The Williams Family of Society Hall[sic].* X gives: "Society Hill." Columbia, SC, Pee Dee Historical Association, X gives State Co., 1910. 20p. [D13632; X1030-FW].

WILLIAMS -- Banister, Eme V. O. *Daniel, Paul and Jeremiah Williams, Their Ancestors and Descendants.* Anderson, SC, Banister, 1968. Unpaged. [X1032-FW3].

WILLIAMS -- Perry, John Ben. *The Williams Family of Kershaw County, S.C. and Yalobusha and Grenada Counties, Mississippi.* Grenada, MS, Perry, 1954. 31 leaves. [D13660].

WILLIAMS -- Rosser, John C. *Caharie to Cape Fear: The Descendants of John Williams and Katharine Galbreth of Sampson and Cumberland*

Counties in North Carolina, 1740-1990. Godwin, NC, J.C. Rosser, 1990. 3 v. (xxiv, 1924p.) 1. Williams family. 2. Williams, John, ca. 1720-1783. 3. North Carolina-Genealogy. [G721].

WILLIAMS -- Watson, Ruth Lancaster Trowell. [G721]. See above: HAZELWOOD. [G308].

WILLIAMS -- Williams, Marie. *Some Genealogical Data on the Families of Williams, Eley, Whitehead, Killingsworth, Ledingham, House, Hogan, Little, and Allied Lines.* Summerton, SC, Williams, 1956. 41 leaves. [D13686].

WILLIAMS -- Williams, Robert Murphy. *Williams and Murphy Records and Related Families.* Raleigh, NC, Edwards Broughton Co., 1949. 369p. [D13690].

WILLIAMS -- Williams, Robert T. *John Sumner Williams and Helen Katherine Montgomery, Their Ancestors and Descendants, 1461-1987.* Cary, NC, R.T. Willimas, C.P. Williams, 1987. 87 leaves. 1. Williams family. 2. Montgomery family. 3. Williams, John Sumner, 1862-1943-Family. [G721].

WILLIAMSON -- Dixon, Elizabeth Williamson. *Williamson - Bethell and allied families of North Carolina.* NP, 1956. 325 leaves. [D13697].

WILLIAMSON -- Dixon, Elizabeth Williamson. *The Williamson Family of Isle of Wight County, Virginia, Southampton County, Virginia, Northampton County, North Carolina, Caswell County, North Carolina.* NP, 1958. 359 leaves. See also: The Lea Family of Virginia, North Carolina, and Mississippi: the Slade family of Caswell County, North Carolina, 1958. See also: Williamson - Bethell and allied families of North Carolina, 1956. [D13698].

WILLIS -- De Huff, Elizabeth Willis. *The Family of Robert Willis of Barnwell County, South Carolina as Far as Found, March, 1962.* Augusta, GA, De Huff, 1962. 72p. D gives underscored title. [D13705; X1034-FW].

WILLIS -- Potter, Maude. *Willises of Virginia; A Genealogical Account of the Descendants of Colonel Francis Willis of Gloucester County, Virginia, Colo. Henry Willis of Fredricksburg and William Willis of Southside Crany Creek. Rev. ed.* Mars Hill, NC, 1968. 168p. [X1034-FW].

WILMOT -- Wilmeth, James Lillard. *Wilmot - Wilmoth - Wilmeth.* Charlotte, NC, Printed by Washburn Printing Co., 1940. 374p., 1 leaf. [L18813].

WILLS -- Hoffman, Laban Miles. [G722]. See above: BEST. [G54].

WILSON -- NAS. *Wilson and Ehle Family Notes.* NP, Ruth Davidson Chapter, North Carolina DAR, G.R.C., 1986. 27 l. [DC3976].

WILSON -- Andrea, Leonardo. *Wilson - Willson Family, South Carolina.* NP, 1962. 100 leaves. [D13723].

WILSON -- De Huff, Elizabeth Willis. *The Family of the Rev. James Wilson of Barnwell County, South Carolina.* Augusta, GA, De Huff, 1963. 55p. See also: Descendants of John Willis of Richmond Co., Wirginia, 1960. (58p). [D13729].

WILSON -- Eaves, Mrs. J. B. *Sketch of Lineal Descendants of Samuel Wilson, Sr.* Rock Hill, SC, Lord Printery, 1938. 117p. [D13731].

WILSON -- Elliott, Margaret Axson. *My Aunt Louisa and Woodrow Wilson.* Chapel Hill, NC, University of North Carolina Press, 1944. vi,

302p. An account of the author's life spent in the homes of her aunt and brother-in-law. [A716].

WILSON -- Goodlett, Mildred W. *A Wilson Family Album.* Easley, SC, Southern Historical, 1986. 179p. [DC3974].

WILSON -- Konopa, Leola Wilson. *Descendants of Wilsons and Garners of Virginia.* Columbia, SC, 1970. 31 leaves. [A719; VV202].

WILSON -- McLean, Harry Herndon. *The Wilson Family.* Charlotte, NC, Observer Printing House, 1950. 102p. [D13742].

WILSON -- McQuiston, Leona B. *The "Wilson Family of South Carolina to Tennessee".* Washington, DC, 3p., iii, 39 numb. leaves. 1943. Two slips with additions inserted. Typed. [L18847].

WILSON -- Warren, Edward French. [G724]. See above: WARREN. [G701].

WILSON -- Wilson, Elbert E. *Wilsons of Western (North) Carolina.* Fort Lauderdale, FL, Bk. Bind., 1965. 78, 40p., 17 leaves of plates. [X1037-FW].

WILSON -- Wilson, George Follett. *Journal, April 27, 1828-September 30, 1830.* Winston-Salem, NC, E.H. Wilson, 1984. (Greenville, SC, A Press). xiv, 263p. 1. Wilson, George Follett, 1805-1857-Diaries. 2. North Carolina-Biography. 3. Wilson family. 4. North Carolina-Genealogy. [G724].

WILSON -- Konopa, Leona Wilson. *Wilson - Garner Family of Darlington, S.C.* Columbia, SC, 1964. 31 leaves. [L18858].

WILSON -- Wilson, Sarah S. *The Wilson Family of South Carolina...* Harrisonburg, VA, 189_. 8p. Interleaved. [X1035-LI/NY].

WILSON -- Wilson, York Lowry. *A Carolina-Virginia Genalogy*. *Wilson Family.* Aldershot, ENG, Galbe & Polden Ltd. 1962. 349p. NG gives underscored title. [NG104: VV203].

WILSON -- Wise, Frank E. [G725]. See above: CUTHBERTSON. [G171].

WILSON -- Zoellner, Leslie R. *Wilson Family of North Carolina.* Los Angeles, CA, W.P. Johnson, 1946. 51 leaves. [X1036-LA].

WINBORNE -- Winborne, Judge Benj. Brodie. *The Winborne Family.* Raleigh, NC, Presses of Edwards & Broughton, 1905. 141, 12p. [L18865].

WINBORNE -- Winborne, Benjamin B. *Winbornes of Old.* Raleigh, NC, Edwards & Broughton Prtg. Co., 1911. 5, 14-38p. [X1038-FW/NY].

WINCHESTER -- Whyte, Karel L. *Descendants of William Winchester - Rev. ed.* Aiken, SC, K.L. Whyte, 1989. 83 leaves. 1. Winchester family. 2. Winchester, William, 1710-1790-Family. [G725].

WINDHAM -- Windham, Amasa Benjamin. *The Windham Family of England, Virginia, North Carolina, South Carolina, Alabama, Mississippi, and Texas.* Sandy Springs, GA, 1982. ix, 78p. [C760; VV203].

WINGE -- Winge, Dennis R. *In Search of New Scandinavia. A Story of a Norwegian Immigrant Family.* Durham, NC, Winge, 1976. vi, 112 leaves. [X1039-MH].

WINGFIELD -- Powerscourt, Mervyn Edward Wingfield, 7th Viscount. *Muniments [sic] of the Ancient Saxon Family of Wingfield.* Durham, NC, Wingfield Family Society, 1987. viii, 88p., 58 leaves of plates. 1. Wingfield family. 2. Great Britain-Genealogy. [G728].

WISE -- Wise, Frank E. [G729]. See above: CUTHBERTSON. [G171].

WISE -- Wyse, Frederick Calhoun. *History of the Wise and Wyse Family of South Carolina; European, 1245-1750, American, 1750-1944.* Richmond, VA, W. M. Brown & Son, 1944. 4, 64, 3p. VV omits underscored part of title [L18934; VV203].

WHITHERSPOON -- DuBose, J. W. *Witherspoons of Society Hill: In Bulletin of the Pee Dee Historical Assoc., 1910.* Hartsville, SC, Hartsville Pub., 1910. 21p. [X1042-FW].

WHITHERSPOON -- Whitherspoon, David Howell. *The Witherspoons of North Carolina.* Raleigh, NC, Witherspoon, 1976. 127, 32p. [D13819].

WHITHERSPOON -- Whitherspoon, Robert. *Early Manuscripts Copy of the Witherspoon Family Chronicle. By Author in 1780 with Later Notes on Related Families; Reproduced from the Williamsburg County Historical Soc..* Columbia, SC, State Print, 1967. 39p. [X1042-MH].

WITHERSPOON -- Wardlaw, Joseph G. *Genealogy of the Witherspoon Family, with Some Account of Other Families With Which It Is Connected.* Yorkville, SC, Printed at the Enquirer Office, 3, 229p. Contains the Heathley, Donnom, Crawford, White, Dunlap, and Jones Families.
[L18954].

WITHROW -- Burlingame, Evelyn E. *Genealogy of the Withrow Family of North and South Carolina. Rawdon, Nova Scotia, Canada; Withrow, Minnesota; Stillwater, Minnesota; (and) International Falls, Minnesota, 1790-1972. Allied Families - Shannon & Mahoney.* NP, 1972. 22p. Typwritten.
[X1042-MH].

WITT -- Powers, Lee Leeper. [G730]. See above: JERNIGAN. [G349]. 2 ENTRIES.

WITTEN -- Alexander, Virginia Wood. [G731]. See above: WHIDDON. [G712].

WOLFE -- Walser, Richard Gaither. *The Wolfe Family in Raleigh.* Raleigh, NC. Wolf's Head Press, 1976. 30p. 100 copies printed. 1. Wolfe, Thomas, 1900-1938-Biography-Family. 2. Wolfe family. 3. Raleigh (N.C.)-Genealogy. 4. Novelists, American-20th century-Biography-Family. [G732].

WOMACK -- Thomas, Larry Coyle. *Womack, 1677-1987.* Sanford, NC, L.C. Thomas, 1987. vi, 168 leaves. 1. Womack family. 2. North Carolina-Genealogy. [G733].

WOOD -- Ervin, Sam J. Jr. *The Woods of Plymouth County, Massachusetts, and Randolph County, North Carolina.* NP, [between 1969 and 1972]. 60 leaves. 1. Wood family. [G733; S2756].

WOOD -- Hardin, Martha Wood. *The Ancestors of Lawrence A. Wood in Plymouth Colon, North Carolina and Indiana.* St. Louis, MO, M.W. and C.M. Hardin, 1988. xii, 216p. 1. Wood family. 2. Wood, Lawrence Anselm, 1882-1960-Family. [G733; DC4011].

WOOD -- Lyon, Josephine E. Wood. [G733]. See above: SETZER. [G598].

WOOD -- Wood, Christine. *Wood Works; Documented More Than 1100 Descendants of Wiliam Wood, Whose Will in Spartansburg District, S.C. Was Dated 22 Jan., 1787...* (Christine) Lubbock, TX, 1971. 2 vols. in 1. (iv, 221p.). [X1046-FW/NY].

WOOD -- Wood, John W. *Wood Family of Laurens County, South Carolina.* Rockhill, SC, E.M. Wood, 1967. 2 leaves, 50p. [X1046-FW].

WOOD -- Wood, William L. *Samuel Wood: His Seven Sons and Their Descendants: Virginia to North Carolina, Tennessee, Kentucky, Illinois and Beyond, 1755-1988.* Strafford, MO, W.L. Wood, 1988. xii, 320, 134p. 1. Wood family. 2. Wood, Samuel, 1737-ca. 1800-Family. [G734].

WOODIE -- Weight, Vernon F. *A Branch of the Family Tree; A Preliminary History. A Genealogy of the Woodie (Woody) Family of North Western North Carolina and Known Descendants Who Have Scattered thru out the United States. 1st ed.* Carmichael, CA, 1960. 286 leaves. [X1048-FW/IG/NY/SU].

WOODMAN -- Woodman, Helen Denny. *The Woodmans of Rhode Island: Descendants of John Woodman of Little Compton, Rhode Island* Hendersonville, NC, 1989. xvi, 382p. [DC4019].

WOODROW -- Haire, Jenny W. *Woodrow, Hyman, Wyatt, Nivens and Related Families of North and South Carolina.* NP, 1987. 59p. [NG104].

WOODWARD -- Barnwell, Joseph W. *Dr. Henry Woodward, The First English Settler in South Carolina, and Some of His Descendants.* Charleston, SC, 1907. 13p. [L19093].

WORLEY -- Worley, Mrs. George. *The Nicholas Worley Family.* Clinton, NC, Worley, 1968. 30, xvii leaves. [D13951].

WORTHINGTON -- Sims, Henry U. *The Genealogy of the Worthington Family of Alabama, South Carolina, Virginia, and Ohio, Being Descendants of Robert Worthington, Who Emigrated from Ireland to New Jersey in 1713, with an Appendix of the Symcock Family of Pennsylvania Down to 1716.* Birmingham, AL, 1937. 38(i.e.40), 10(i.e.12), 9 leaves. [X1052-NY].

WRIGHT -- Stoops, Mary De Forest W. *Descendants of Two Wright Brothers, William* *and Amos of North Carolina and Southern Indiana.* Ipava, IL, Stoops, 1944. 96p. [X1053-FW].

WRIGHT -- Stoops, Mary DeForest W. *Richard Wright of North Carolina (1730-1785) and His Descendants.* Chicago, IL, 1950. 10 leaves. Typed. [X1053-FW].

WRIGHT -- Stoops, Mary De Forest Waldrop. *Descendants of William Wright and Amos Wright of North Carolina, Kentucky and Indiana.* NP, 1959. 72, 32 leaves. [D13978].

WRIGHT -- Whitaker, C. Bruce. [G737]. See above: HARPER. [G300].

WRIGHT -- White, Lille E. W. L. *Genealogy of the Wright Family. Descendants of Richard Wright, Sr., Whose Will Was Probated in Rowan County, N. C.... 1875; In Brief Some Genealogy of the Morgan, Sears, Kutch, Hazel, and Sanders Families.* Bloomington, IN, 1943. 159p., 2 leaves. [X1053-FW].

WRIGLEY -- Harold Chandler. *Genealogy of the Wrigley Family of Saddleworth, Yorkshire, England & Their Descendants Who Emigrated to America.* Arden, NC, 1983. 216p. [NG105].

WYANT -- Young, Terry R. *Our Wyant Family.* Baltimore, MD, Gateway Press, Vale, NC, T.R. Young. 1986. vii, 351p. [G738].

WYATT -- NAS. *The Families of Joseph and Isaac Wyatt, Brothers, Who Were Sons of Zachariah ("Sacker") and Elizabeth Ripley Wyatt, of Durant's Neck, Perquimans County, North Carolina.* Washington, DC, 1950. 206p. "Compiled for private distribution". [L19176].

WYATT -- Andrea, Leonardo. *The Forty-Sixth Annual Wyatt Reunion, Combined with Reunions of ... Allied and Associated Families....*

Columbia, SC, Andrea, 1952. 48p. D gives underscored part of title. [D13996; X1054-FW/MH/OS/SP/SU].

WYATT -- Connelly, Estella Wyatt. *The Wyatts.* Easley, SC, Hucks Commercial Printers, 1975. 139p. [D13998].

WYATT -- Wyatt, Marguerite. *The Wyatts.* Easley, SC, 1975. 139p. [NG105].

WYCHE -- Allison, Charles W. *James Wyche Family History.* Charlotte, NC, Allison, 1955. 171p. [NG105: D14005].

XYZ

YODER -- Yoder, Fred Roy. *History of the Yoder Family in North Carolina.* Ann Arbor, MI, Edwards Bros., 1970. xi, 158p. [A733; D14048].

YORK -- York, Brantley. *Lineage of Brantley York of North Carolina...* NP, 1954. 5 leaves. [X1060-SU].

YORK -- York, William Alton. *A York Family in North Carolina, Tennessee, Georgia and Okalahoma and Allied Families.* Pittsburg, ?, 1984. iv, 23 leaves. [DC4055].

YOUNG -- Jenkins, F. D. *Genealogy: William Young, Sr., Holland to Orangeburg, S. C., 1735.* Ballinger, TX, 1975. 54p. [X1061-FW].

YOUNG -- Pack, Miriam Young. *Kith and Kin of James & Mary Kellough Young, South Carolina 1786 to Alabama, 1818.* North Newton, AL?, Mennonite, 1984. 243p. [DC4059].

YOUNG -- Simmons, Dessie Little. *Robert Young, Sr. Patriot and Pioneer.* Easley, SC, Southern Historical, 1984. vi, 661p. [DC4060].

YOUNG -- Young, Edward Hudson. *Our Young Family in America*. Durham, NC, Seeman Printery, 1947. xvii, 315p. [D14067].

YOUNG -- Young, Lois. *My Family, The Young - Todd Genealogy, 1754-1972*. Anderson, SC, 1972. 105p. [S2788].

YOUNTS -- Ross, Elizabeth E. *Younts and Kepley Family*. Clayton, NC, Ross, 1977. 180p. [D14079].

LIBRARY OF CONGRESS GENEALOGIES CONVERTED TO MICROFORM

A list of older genealogies in the United States Library of Congress, which have been converted to microfilm follows this brief introduction on availability of microfilms and other materials from the Library of Congress.

Where conversion to microfilm has taken place, there is usually no original volume in the Library's collection. Microfilm reels in the Library are 35mm. All listings are on 1 reel unless otherwise indicated.

The list of microfilmed genealogies in this volume can be used as a borrowing tool for librarians and those doing research on a particular family name can purchase the microfilm reels directly or paper copies made from them.

Library policy does not allow circulation of genealogy on interlibrary loan, but microfilm copies may be circulated. The Library may be able to assist in purchasing photocopies of out-of print items. The interested researcher may obtain free upon request a circular entitled Out-of-Print Materials and Reprinted Publications. Requests should be addressed to: Library of Congress, Humanities and Social Science Division, Washington, DC 20540.

Copies of microfilm listed below may be ordered from the Photoduplicating Service at the address given above at a cost of $30.00 per reel, which includes postage and handling. Requests for "Copyflow" prints on paper may also be ordered. The researcher needs to inquire regarding specific prices.

Provided there are no copyright restrictions, photocopies of any item in the

Library's genealogical collections may be obtained under the conditions specified in the order form, which may be obtained from the Library of Congress Photoduplication Service, Washington, DC 20540. As an example of the cost involved The Library indicates that the charge for preparing an unbound photocopy of a 200-page

book (page size 9" x 6") would be about $50. Note that in requesting photocopy services, the specific pages and material to be copied must be cited in the request.

The following short bibliographies on genealogical subjects are available without charge from the Library of Congress, Humanities and Social Science Services Division:

Guide to Genealogical Research, a Selected List of Publications, which tells how to trace an ancestor.

Surnames, a Selected List of References to books on family names and national origins.

Immigrant Arrivals, A Short Guide to Published Sources, of possible help in identifying ships and passenger lists.

Heraldry, a Selected List of References to books on the origins, use, design, and identification of coats of arms.

Note that there is some duplication between the works shown as being in the Library collection as those listed below as being on Microfilm. It is probable, that were duplication exists, the original work is no longer available other than in Microfilm.

The cross-index at the end of this volume includes both microfilm and paper holdings listed in the Libraries collections.

CAROLINA GENEALOGIES ON MICROFILM

AB

BAGLEY -- Bagley, E. G. *The Bagley Family, 1066-1958 [microform].* Raleigh, NC, 1958. v, 111 leaves.
MICROFILM 84/3272 (C). [G1130].

BARTON -- Barton, William Bailey. *A Genealogy Study [sic] of the Descendants of Anthony Barton [microform]: the First American Barton of This Record: An Emigrant from England to America, 1825.* Stonega, VA. W.B. Barton, 1956. 1 v. (various pagings). Cover title: The Bartons of Carolina. Half title: The Bartons of Charleston, South Carolina and Orangeburg County, South Carolina.
MICROFILM 85/631 (C). [G1133].

BEESON -- Beeson, Margaret Ailene. *A Genealogy of the Beeson Family [microform].* Greensboro, NC, 1974. 57 leaves MICROFILM 86/6083 (C) <MicRR>. [G1135].

BENNETT -- Bennett, Benjamin Hugh. *A History of the Richard Bennett Family of Westmoreland County, Virginia and Iredell County, N.C. [microform].* Washington, DC, 1960. 21 leaves. MICROFILM 86/6181 (C) <MicRR>. [G1135].

BOND -- Garrett, Samuel Bond. *Bond Genealogy [microform]: A History of the Descendants of Joseph Bond, Born 1704, in Wiltshire, England, Died 175_, in North Carolina, Also a Brief Account of Many of the Descendants of John Bond, His Brother... the Two Being Sons of Benjamin and Ann (Paradise) Bond, of Wiltshire, England.* Indianapolis, IN, W.D Pratt, 1913. 268p., 1 leaf of plates. MICROFILM 86/6711 (C) <MicRR>. [G1139].

BRANSON -- Branson, Levi, Ed. *Branson Magazine of Genealogies, Vol. 1. No. 1-2, June 1898-June 1899 [microform].* Raleigh, NC, L. Branson, 1898-1899. 57p, Title p., no. 1 reads; " The Branson Family in Europe and America. "Published Quarterly". No more published. Lib. of Congress copy imperfect: No. 1, cover (p. 1-4); and No. 2, prelim. p. between cover and p. 29 wanting.
MICROFILM 86/5105 (C) <MicRR>. [G1142].

BROWN -- Brown, Richard Lewis. *A Brown Family of Spartanburg and Greenville Counties, South Carolina [microform].* Maplewood, NJ, 1963. 35 l. 'The material was collected between 1934 and 1937 and no attempt has been made to bring it up to date.'
MICROFILM 86/5997 (C) <MicRR>. [G1144].

BRYANT -- Bryant, Lawrence Chesterfield. *A Historical and Genealogical Record of Lawrence Bryant and Pattie Sessoms' Five Other Sons of Nash County, North Carolina [microform].* Orangeburg, SC, L.C. Bryant, 1968. iv, 144p., 2 leaves of plates.
MICROFILM 87/7353 (C) <MicRR>. [G1145].

C

CALDWELL -- Weede, Fred Lewis. *The James Caldwell Family of Erie, Penna., and Chillicothe, Ill, [microform]: Geneological [i.e. Genealogical] Tabulation of Their Descendants: Including Date of Forebears, of Caldwell, Booth, Hay, Armstrong, and Other Allied Families in France, England, Scotland, Ireland, and America.* Asheville, NC, 1959. 37p, MICROFILM 86/5681 (C) <MicRR>. [G1149].

CARPENTER -- McKoy, Henry Bacon. *The Carpenter - Weir Family of Upper South Carolina and Other Ancestors Including Benson, Berry, Blassingame, Caldwell, Maxwell, Richey, Sloan, Stewart, Wilson [microform].*

Greenville, SC, Keys Print Co., 1959. 305p MICROFILM 85/7689 (C) <MicRR>. [G1150].

CASSELS -- Cassels, Louis. *An Inquiry into the Origins of the Cassels Family of Ellenton, S.C. [microform].* Bethesda, MD, 1971. 6, 4 leaves. Addendum 2 leaves in pocket. MICROFILM 86/6234 (C). [G1151].

CHANCE -- Chance, Hilda Nancy Ersula Snowberger. *Change of Ohio, Virginia, North Carolina, Georgia, Texas, Tennessee, Kentucky, Delaware, Maryland, Pennsylvania, Michigan, California, Indiana, New Jersey [microform].* Liberty, PA, H.N.E.S. Chance, 1970. 19 l. MICROFILM 86/5007 (C) <MicRR>. [G1152].

CHAPLIN -- Chaplin, Ellen Pennington. *The Chaplins and Allied Families [microform].* Neeses, SC, 1964. 124 leaves. MICROFILM 86/6307 (C) <MicRR>. [G1153].

CLAPP -- Whitsett, William Thornton. *History of Brick Church and the Clapp Family [microform].* Greensboro, NC, Harrison Print Co., 1925. 28p., 1 leaf of plates. Whitsett Historical Monographs; no. 2. MICROFILM 86/6184 (C) <MicRR>. [G1156].

CLARK -- Clark, A. Wilbur. *Ancestry and Descendants of Neill Alexander Clark (c1822/23-1864) of Cumberland County, North Carolina [microform].* __, NC, 1958. 15p. MICROFILM 84/8068 (C) <MicRR>. [G1157].

CLEVELAND -- Cleveland, James Butler. *A Genealogical Register of the Descendants of Moses Cleveland of Woburn, Mass. [microform] an Immigrant in 1635 from England with a Sketch of the Clevelands of Virginia and the Carolinas.* Albany, NY, Munsell, 1881. 48p MICROFILM 9250 (C). [G1158].

COIT -- Coit, John Eliot. *Lineage of the Descendants of John Calkins Coit of Cheraw, South Carolina, 1799-1863.* --, SC, J.E. Coit,

1945. 52p.
MICROFILM 86/5696 (C) <MicRR>. [G1160].

COOPER -- Cooper, Homer C. *Cooper, McKemy, Ferrell / Farrell, Wooddell, Gothard, Wilson, & Paton Families of Augusta & Rockbridge Counties, Virginia, York, & Adams Counties, Pennsylvania, Blount, Knox and Roane Counties, Tennessee, Pocahontas, Gilmer, & Ritchie Counties, West Virginia, Wayne County, Kentucky, Virgo & Sullivan Counties, Indiana, York County, South Carolina [microform].* Athens, GA, 1969. 7 leaves.
MICROFILM 86/6311 (C) <MicRR>. [G1162].

COSSART -- Tilley, Mary Ethel. *Cossart or Cozart [microform]: A Brief Genealogical and Historical Sketch of the Name and Family...* Rougemont, NC, 1944. 75p.
MICROFILM 85/8296 (C) <MicRR>. [G1162].

COVINGTON -- McSwain, Eleanor Pratt Covington. *My Folk [microform]: The First Three Hundred Years, 1670-1970: A Study of Many First Settlers and Founders of Old Anson and Richmond Counties, North Carolina.* Albermarle, NC, Stanly County Historical Society, 1972. 221, 12 p., 17 l. of plates.
MICROFILM 88/5270 (C). [G1163].

DEF

DANTZLER -- Dantzler, D. D. *A Genealogical Record of the Dantzler Family, from 1739 to the Present Time [microform].* Orangeburg, SC, R.L. Berry, 1899. 52, 2p. "Corrections and additions... by Wm. Zimmerman, Dantzler [sic], March 1953" (2 p. in ms.) inserted.
MICROFILM 85/5591 (C). [G1167].

DAVIDSON -- Davidson, John Mitchell. *Emigration of William Mitchell Davidson and Family from Buncombe County, North Carolina to Texas in 1844 [microform].* U.S.A. 1927.

16 leaves.
MICROFILM 85/5714 (C) <MicRR>. [G1167].

DeWALT -- McCrary, Clara Johnstone. *The DeWalt Family, Connections and Traditions [microform].* Newberry, SC, 1921, 51 leaves. Lead of addends, in ms. and a holograph letter, signed Fanny A. Johnstone inserted.
MICROFILM 86/6182 (C) <MicRR>. [G1170].

DICKINSON -- Outlaw, Lena Dickinson. *Dickinson Genealogy [microform]: circo 750 to 1977.* Winston-Salem, NC, Hunter Pub. Co., 1977. 336p.
MICROFILM 85/7867 (C) <MicRR>. [G1170].

DOBSON -- McLean, Albert S. *The Dobson Family of North Carolina [microform].* Asheville, NC, 1900. 4 leaves.
MICROFILM 85/7411 (C) <MicRR>. [G1171].

DOGGETT -- Doggett, Anna Doggett [sic]. *History of the Doggetts of Guilford County, North Carolina [microform].* Greensboro, NC, Piedmont Press, 1969. 78p.
MICROFILM 86/6593 (C) <MicRR>. [G1172].

EARLE -- Earle, Julius Richard. *Earle [microform]: Short Biographical Sketches and Family History.* Hollands, SC, J.R. Earle, 1899. 8p.
MICROFILM 84/8253 (C). [G1175].

FARMER -- Farmer, Ellery. *Descendants of Thomas Farmer Who Came to Virginia in 1616 [microform]: A Genealogy; with Sketches of Some Families Allied by Marriage to the Farmer Family.* Asheville, NC, 1956. 88p., 16p. of plates. MICROFILM 84/8544 (C). [G1179].

GHIJ

GARDNER -- Gardner, Benjamin Hard. *Genealogy of the Gardner Family [microform].*

Aiken, SC, B.H. Gardner, 1953. 25 leaves. Lib. of Congress copy imperfect: Geneal. Tbl. wanting. MICROFILM 88/5276 (C). [G1184].

HAYLANDER -- Bowen, Franklin Haylander. *Genealogy of the Haylander Family to the Fifth Generation, 1771-1887 [microform]*. Raleigh, NC, 1888. 7p.
MICROFILM 84/8371 (C) <MicRR>. [G1196].

HAYNE -- Campbell, Julia Anna Francis Courtenay. *The Hayne Family of South Carolina [microform] and Some Relatives in These Lines: Martin, Davidge, Barnwell, Courtenay, Beattie, Adams, Hazlehurst, Black, Hasekk, Davis, Foster, Houston, McIver, Woodward, Baldwin, Brevard, Trapier, Motte, Shubrick, Perry, Swinton, Splatt.* Charlottesville, VA, T. Campbell, 1956. 1 v. (various foliations). MICROFILM 83/674 (C) <MicRR>. [G1196].

HEYWARD -- Heyward, Barnwell Rhett. *Genealogical Chart [microform]: Heyward of South Carolina.* Albany, NY, 1896. 1 sheet. MICROFILM 89/3001 (C). [G1196].

JONES -- Jones, Cadwallader. *A Genealogical History [microform].* Edited by A.L. Robertson. Columbia, SC, Ye Bryan Print Co., 1900. vii, 73p., 1 leaf of plates.
MICROFILM 84/8468 (C) <MicRR>. [G1208].

KL

LANGSTON -- Langston, Carroll Spencer. *Descendants of Solomon Langston of Laurens County, South Carolina, Through His Son, Bennett [microform].* Williamsville, IL, 1942. 46 i.e. 47 leaves. Includes extra numbered leaf 41a.
MICROFILM 86/5980 (C) <MicRR>. [G1214].

LANPHERE -- Lanphere, Edward Everett. *Geneology i.e. Genealogy and History*

[microform]: Lanphear, Lamphier, Lanphere, and Related Families in America. Rev. ed. Chapel Hill, NC, 1967. 264p. Rev. ed. of History and genealogy of the Lanpheres and the Pierces / Frances Lanphere and Edward Everett Lanphere, 1958.
MICROFILM 88/5262 (C). [G1214].

LANPHERE -- Lanphere, Edward Everett. *The Lanphere and Related Families Genealogy [microform]. Rev. ed.* Chapel Hill, NC, 1970. xi, 175p. Rev. ed. of Genealogy and History, 1967. MICROFILM 88/5263 (C). [G1214].

LAWRENCE -- Lawrence, Kenan Barrett. *History of the Lawrence Family in England, Virginia and North Carolina [microform]: with Historical Sketches and Genealogical Outlines of the Lawrence Family in Connecticut, Maryland, Massachusetts, New Jersey, New York and South Carolina, also Including Genealogical Records of Other Families Converging with the Lawrence family of Virginia-North Carolina, Vaughan with Lawrence 1805, Rea with Lawrence 1836, Jordan with Darden 1825, Darden with Pruden 1844, Pruden with Lawrence 1870, Moorman with Lawrence 1901.* Bristol, VA, 1964-1965. 2 v. MICROFILM 85/9552 (C). [G1215].

MNO

McGIRT -- Love, Louis W. *The Descendants of Archibald McGirt, III and John McGirt, 1745-1969 [microform].* Wilmington, NC, 1969. 103p.
MICROFILM 86/5232 (C) <MicRR>. [G1222].

McGOWAN -- McGowan Family [sic]. *Proceedings of the Reunion of the McGowan Family Held at Liberty Springs Church (Presbyterian) [microform].* Cross Hill, SC, 1915. 51p.
MICROFILM 86/6993 (C) <MicRR>. [G1222].

McINTYRE -- McIntyre, Lucy E. *The McIntyres of Montgomery County, North Carolina [microform]*. Red Oak, NC, L.E. McIntyre, 1965. 74p. MICROFILM 84/732 (C). [G1222].

McKOY -- McKoy, Henry Bacon. *The McKoy Family of North Carolina and Other Ancestors Including Ancrum, Berry, Halling, Hasell, Usher [microform]*. Greenville, SC, Keys Printing Co., 1955. 198p.
MICROFILM 84/3204 (C). [G1223].

McLAURIN -- McLaurin, G. G. *G. G. McLaurin and Some of His Kin [microform]*. Dillon, SC, 1970. xiii, 175p., A-N leaves of plates. MICROFILM 86/6675 (C) <MicRR>. [G1223].

MARION -- Bunn, Maude Davis. *The Genealogy of the Marion - Davis Families [microform]*. Raleigh, NC, 1973. 239p., 16 pages of plates. MICROFILM 85/8417 (C) <MicRR>. [G1225].

O'CONNER -- Cox, Lula Price O'Conner. *The O'Conner - Conner - Simmons Families [microform]*. Southern Pines, NC, Wm. Edward Cox, 1941. vii, 83p., 4 leaves of plates. MICROFILM 84/3271 (C) DLC. [G1234].

OUTLAW -- Outlaw, Albert Timothy. *Outlaw Genealogy [microform]: Including English Records, Coats of Arms, Will of Edward Outlaw, dated 1713, Brief Biographical Sketches and an Account of the First Grady - Outlaw Reunion.* Wilson, NC, P.D. Gold, 1930. 71p.
[G1235].

PQR

RAVENEL -- Ravenel, William Jervey. *Ravenel Records, A-C Supplements [microform]*. Charleston, SC, W. Ravenel, 1964-1966. 3 v. Suppl. to: Ravenel Records, by Henry Edmund Ravenel, publ. in 1898.
MICROFILM 85/9656 (C) <MicRR>. [G1246].

RAVENEL -- Ravenel, William Jervey. *Ravenel Records, D Supplement [microform].* Charleston, SC, W. Ravenel, 1973. 15p., 1 folded leaf of plates. Suppl. to: Ravenel Records, by Henry Edmund Ravenel, publ. in 1898.
MICROFILM 85/9657 (C) <MicRR>. [G1246].

RAVENEL -- Ravenel, Henry Edmund. *Ravenel Records [microform]: A History and Genealogy of the Huguenot Family of Ravenel, of South Carolina: with Some Incidental Account of the Parish of St. Johns Berkeley, Which was Their Principal Location.* Atlanta, GA, Franklin Print. and Pub. Co., 1898. v, 279p., 12 leaves of plates.
MICROFILM 84/8403 (C) <MicRR>. [G1246].

ROBERTS -- Craine, Lloyd Bascombe. *The First of the Roberts and Crane Families Who Settled in Western North Carolina and Some of Their Descendants.* St. Paul, MN, Ramaley Print Co., 1955. 148p.
MICROFILM 85/6337 (C) <MicRR>. [G1249].

ROGERS -- Drummond, Josiah H. *The Rogers Family of Georgetown [S.C.?] [microform].* NP, 1897. 37p.
MICROFILM 85/5003 (C) <MicRR>. [G1250].

S

SCANLON -- Scanlon, David Howard. *Genealogy of the O'Scanlon (Scanlan, Scanlon) Family [microform].* Durham, NC, 1938. 23p.
MICROFILM 85/9459 (C) <MicRR>. [G1255].

SHULL -- Glover, Elizabeth K. *Shull: John W. and Martha Moak, Descendants [microform].* Gilbert, SC, 40p.
MICROFILM 85/8426 (C) <MicRR>. [G1256].

SELBY -- Selby, Forest T. *The House of Selby [microform].* Charlotte, NC, 1962. i, 44p.,

2 leaves of plates.
MICROFILM 86/5708 (C) <MicRR>. [G1257].

SMATHERS -- Patton, Sadie Smathers. *Smathers from Yadkin Valley to Pigeon River [microform]: Smathers and Agner Families.* Hendersonville, NC, S.S. Patton, 1954. 56p.
MICROFILM 86/6188 (C) <MicRR>. [G1264].

STURMAN -- Williams, Marguerite White. *Thomas Sturman and Ann [microform]: Col. William Hardwick and Elizabeth Sturman, Jeffrey Johnson and Margaret of Virginia, and Their Descendants of North Carolina and Knox County, Tennessee.* U.S.A., 1974. 98 i.e. 118 leaves, p. 99-110.
MICROFILM 86/6779 (C) <MicRR>. [G1274].

SULLIVAN -- Sullivan, Hazel Bird. *The Sullivan Family [microform]: William Dunklin Sullivan Line..* Enka, NC, Mrs. M.A. Sullivan, 1961. 40p., 2 leaves of plates.
MICROFILM 86/5243 (C) <MicRR>. [G1274].

TUV

TANNER -- Hussey, Marguerite Carleton. *The Family of Rev. John Tanner, Baptist Preacher [microform]: Virginia, North Carolina, Kentucky, Missouri.* Berkeley, CA, 1972. 52, 53 leaves.
MICROFILM 85/8563 (C) <MicRR>. [G1276].

TATTNALL -- Smith, D. E. Huger. *An Account of the Tattnall and Fenwick Families in South Carolina [microform].* Charleston, SC, The South Carolina Historical and Genealogical Magazine, 1913. 19p. The South Carolina Historical and Genealogical Magazine; v. 14, no. 1.
MICROFILM 86/6885 (C) <MicRR>. [G1277].

TEMPLETON -- Templeton, L. B. *The Templeton Family History [microform]: Records and Descendants of the Templetons, Who First*

Settled in what is now Laurens County, South Carolina; Together with Brief Sketches of Other Templetons, Who Settled in Other Parts of South Carolina and Other States. Union, SC, 1953. viii, 155p.
MICROFILM 86/6847 (C) <MicRR>. [G1278].

TISON -- McCormick, Sara Gray. *Forebears and Descendants of Reuben Henry Tison and Rebekah Mary McKenzie and Facts and Traditions Gleaned Through the Years... [microform].* Dillon, SC, Herald Office Supply, 1966. 74 leaves, 33 leaves of plates.
MICROFILM 85/8560 (C) <MicRR>. [G1281].

TREZEVANT -- Trezevant, John Timothèe. *The Trezevant Family in the United States [microform]: From the Date of the Arrival of Daniel Trezevant, Huguenot, at Charles Town, South Carolina, in 1686 to the Present Time .* Columbia, SC, Printed by the State Co., 1914. 122p., 2 leaves of plates.
MICROFILM 86/6890 (C) <MicRR>. [G1284].

TYNER -- Townsend, Peggy Tyner. *Tyner Family, 1704-1971 and Bruce Relations in Robeson Co., N.C. [microform].* __, NC, 1972. 30 leaves.
MICROFILM 86/6102 (C) <MicRR>. [G1286].

W

WAKEFIELD -- NAS. *The Family of Henry Wakefield [microform]: North Carolina, 1805-1950.* U.S.A. 1950. 78p.
MICROFILM 86/5244 (C) <MicRR>. [G1289].

WALKER -- Walker, Legarè. *The Walker Family, Originally of the Yeocomico River Section of Northumberland (subsequently Westmoreland) County, Virginia, Stemming from William Walker (1622/23-1657) and through One of His Descendants, Joseph Rabley Walker (1768-1816), Who Immigrated from Mecklenburg County in that State to South Carolina, circa*

1806, and Settled in Edgefieeld County, near the Town of that name [microform]: Also a Correction of certain Errors in a Chert of the Adams Family, with Which the Walkers are Connected by Marriage. Summerville, SC, 1945. vii, 60p.
MICROFILM 85/8766 (C) <MicRR>. [G1290].

WELBORN -- Wilburn, Hiram Coleman. *Welborn - Wilburn, History-Genealogy [microform]: the Families in Virginia - North Carolina and South Carolina.* Waynesville, NC, H.C. Wilburn by Miller Print. Co., 1953. 104p., 2 leaves of plates.
MICROFILM 85/8456 (C) <MicRR>. [G1296].

WHALEY -- Barton, William Baynard. *A Limited Genealogy Study [sic] of Descendants of Maj. Gen. Edward Whalley (the Regicide) [microform]: Featuring Private Thomas Whaley, Lieut. Archibald Whaley of 1776 era, Descendants Edward Charles Whaley, Joseph Whaley of Edisto Island, S.C., and Descendants of Nathaniel Whaley in Delaware, Virginia, and Maryland with Appropriate Ancestral Review, Discussion, and History, 1067-1956. 2nd ed.* Stonega, VA, W.B. Barton, 1956. 1 v. (various pagings). Cover title: Whaleys, 1066, 1660-1967. MICROFILM 85/632 (C). [G1297].

WYATT -- Wyatt, W. Carl. *Families of Joseph and Isaac Wyatt [microform]: Brothers, Who were Sons of Zachariah ("Sacker") and Elizabeth (Ripley) Wyatt of Durant's Neck, Perquimans County, North Carolina: Wyatt, Joseph (1790-1880) ZW.1, Spencer (-) ZW.2, Isaac (18-3-1885) ZW.3, Brothers...* Washington, DC, 1950. 206p.
MICROFILM 86/6845 (C) <MicRR>. [G1307].

BIBLIOGRAPHIC REFERENCES

DRAUGHTON, Wallace R. & William Perry Johnson. North Carolina Genealogical Reference. Durham, NC, 1966, v-xii, 571p.

EICHHOLZ, Alice. Ancestry's Red Book, American State, County, & Town Sources. Salt Lake City, UT, Ancestry Publishing, 1992, Rev. ed.

GRUNDSET, Eric B. & Bebe, Metz. Library Catalog, Volume Three Centennial Supplement: Acquisitions 1985-1991. Washington, DC, NATIONAL SOCIETY of the DAUGHTERS of the AMERICAN REVOLUTION, 1992.

HICKS, Theresa M. South Carolina - A Guide for Genealogists. Columbia, SC, Peppercorn Publications, Inc., 1985. 1st ed. 228p.

HOLCOMB, Brent H. Guide to South Carolina Genealogical Research and Records. Columbia, SC, 1979, Priv. Print., 29p.

KAMINKOW, Marion J. Genealogies In The Library of Congress. Baltimore, 1972. 2. v. A-J and L-Z.

KAMINKOW, Marion J. Genealogies In The Library of Congress, Supplement 1972 - 1976. Baltimore: Magna Carta Book Company, 1976.

KAMINKOW, Marion J. Genealogies In The Library of Congress, Second Supplement 1976 - 1986. Baltimore: Magna Carta Book Company, 1987.

KAMINKOW, Marion J. A Complement To Genealogies In The Library of Congress. Baltimore: Magna Carta Book Company, 1981.

LIB. OF CONGRESS STAFF — Genealogies Cataloged in the Library of Congress Since 1986. Washington, DC, Cataloging Distribution Service, Library of Congress, 1991.

LIB. OF CONGRESS STAFF — Local History & Genealogy Subject Catalog - Reference Collection - November 22, 1993. Washington, DC, Library of Congress, 1993.

NGS LIBRARY STAFF — National Genealogical Society, Library Book List, 5th Edition. Arlington, Virginia, National Genealogical Society. 1988.

NGS LIBRARY STAFF — National Genealogical Society, Library Book List, 5th Edition Supplement. Arlington, Virginia, National Genealogical Society. 1989.

MICHAELS, Carolyn Leopold and Kathryn S. Scott. Library Catalog, Volume One, Second Revised Edition, Family Histories and Genealogies. Washington, DC, National Society of the Daughters of the American Revolution, 1983.

MICHAELS, Carolyn Leopold and Kathryn S. Scott. Library Catalog, Volume One - Supplement - Family Histories and Genealogies. Washington, DC, National Society of the Daughters of the American Revolution, 1984.

VIRDIN, Donald O. Virginia Genealogies and Family Histories. Bowie, Maryland, Heritage Books, Inc., 1990.

VIRDIN, Donald O. Pennsylvania Genealogies and Family Histories. Bowie, Maryland, Heritage Books, Inc., 1992.

SUPPLEMENTAL CAROLINA FAMILY HISTORY AND GENEALOGY SOURCES

The following is a selection of Library of Congress reference material, with the Library's call numbers, related to North and South Carolina. Material cited is from the Library of Congress History & Genealogy Section Reference Collection, Author/Title Index & Shelflist, dated November 22, 1993. Similar or identical material is often available from historical society and major genealogical libraries in the Carolinas and, occasionally, in other major collections.

NORTH CAROLINA

NORTH CAROLINA -- BIBLIOGRAPHY.
Thornton, Mary Lindsay.
A bibliography of North Carolina, 1589-1956. Westport, Conn., Greenwood Press [1973, c1958]. viii, 597p. 015/.756 bi 87-6173.
Z1319 .T495 1973 LH&G

NORTH CAROLINA -- BIOGRAPHY

Cyclopedia of eminent and representative men of the Carolinas in the nineteenth century. Spartanburg, S.C. Reprint Co., [19 , c 18 2v. 920/.0756 bi 87-8207
F268 .C992 LH&G

Foote, William Henry, Sketches of North Carolina, historical and biographical, [Raleigh, N.C. , Published by J. J. Dudley for the Committee on Historical Matters of the Synod of North Carolina, Presbyterian Church in the United States, and the North Carolina Presbyterian Historical Society, 1966. a-n, 593p. 975.6 bi 87-4225
F358 .F68 1966 LH&G

Wheeler, John Hill, Reminiscences and Memories of North Carolina and eminent North Carolinians. Baltimore, Genealogical

Publishing Co. 1966. 15, lxxiv, 478p. bi 87-3951.
F253 .W56 1966 LH&G

NORTH CAROLINA--BIOGRAPHY--DICTIONARIES
Dictionary of North Carolina Bibliography / Chapel Hill, University of North Carolina Press, c1979-<1991> v. <1-4> 920/.0756 bi 87-11614.
CT252 .D5 LH&G

NORTH CAROLINA--CENSUS.
Jackson, Ronald Vern. Early North Carolina / Bountiful, Utah, Accelerated Indexing Systems, <c1981 - > v. <1, 3 > 929/.3756 19 bi 87-15187
F253 .J2 LH&G

McGrew, Ellen Z. North Carolina census records, 1787-1890, [Rev]. Raleigh, State of North Carolina, Office of Archives and History, 1972. 15p. 917/.56/03/05 s 016.312/09756 bi 87-7651
F251 .N67a no. 2 LH&G

NORTH CAROLINA--CENSUS, 1784-1787
North Carolina. State Dept. of Archives and History. State census of North Carolina, 1784-1787. ed. ed., rev. Baltimore, Genealogical Pub. Co., 1973. 233p. 919/.3756 bi 92-11946.
F258 .N9 1971a LH&G.

NORTH CAROLINA--CENSUS, 1790.
Heinegg, Paul. Free African Americans of North Carolina: Abquaiq, Saudi Arabia: Paul Heinegg, [c1991] v, 225p. 929/.3756 bi 92-11496.
E185.96 .H48 1991 LH&G.

United States, Bureau of the Census, Heads of families at the first census of the United States taken in the year 1790: [Salt Lake City]; Accelerated Indexing Systems. [1978] [64], 292p. 929/.3756 bi 87-11164.
F253 .U53 1978 LH&G.

NORTH CAROLINA--CENSUS, 1800.
See above: Heinegg, Paul.
E185.96 .H48 1991 LH&G.

NORTH CAROLINA--CENSUS, 1800--Indexes.
Bentley, Elizabeth Perry. Index to the 1800 Census of North Carolina. Baltimore, Genealogical Pub. Co., 1977. xi, 270p. 929/.3756 bi 87-8961.
F253 .B46 LH&G.

Jackson, Ronald Vern. North Carolina 1800 census index / Bountiful, Utah, Accelerated Indexing Systems, [c1974, 1977 printing] [18], 255p. 929/.3756 bi 87-11067.
F253 .J22 LH&G.

NORTH CAROLINA--CENSUS, 1810--INDEXES
Bentley, Elizabeth Perry. Index to the 1810 Census of North Carolina. Baltimore, Genealogical Pub. Co., 1978. xi, 282p. 929/.3756 bi 87-9920.
F253 .B426 LH&G.

Jackson, Ronald Vern. North Carolina 1810 census index / Bountiful, Utah, Accelerated Indexing Systems, [c1976, 1977 [20], 153p. 929/.3756 bi 87-11150.
F253 .J23 LH&G.

NORTH CAROLINA--CENSUS, 1820--INDEXES

Jackson, Ronald Vern. North Carolina 1820 census index / Bountiful, Utah, Accelerated Indexing Systems, [c1976. [20], 162p. 929/.3756 bi 87-11166. F253 .J233 LH&G.

Potter, Dorothy Williams. Index to 1820 North Carolina Census. Baltimore, Genealogical Pub. Co., 1978, c1974. 509p. 929/.3756 bi 87-10832. F253 .P67 1978 LH&G.

NORTH CAROLINA--CENSUS, 1830--INDEXES

Jackson, Ronald Vern. North Carolina 1830 census index / Bountiful, Utah, Accelerated

Indexing Systems, c1976. [29], 210p.929/.3756 bi 87-11083.
F253 .J234 LH&G.

NORTH CAROLINA--CENSUS, 1840--INDEXES

Jackson, Ronald Vern. North Carolina 1840 census index / Bountiful, Utah, Accelerated Indexing Systems, c1978. [81], 225p. 929/.3756 bi 87-11083.
F253 .J235 LH&G.

Petty, Gerald McKiney, Index of the 1840 Federal census of North Carolina. Columbus, Ohio, Petty, 1974. 273p. 929/.3756 bi 87-7025.
F253 .P47 LH&G.

NORTH CAROLINA--CENSUS, 1850.

Index of individuals born outside the United States as enumerated in the 1850 census of North Carolina. [Salt Lake City] 1972. 113 l. 929/.3756 bi 87-6746.
F258 .I52 LH&G.

NORTH CAROLINA--CENSUS, 1850--INDEXES.

Jackson, Ronald Vern. North Carolina 1850 census index / Bountiful, Utah, Accelerated Indexing Systems, c1976. [14], 342p., 1 leaf of plates. 929/.3756 bi 87-11108
F253 .J236 LH&G.

NORTH CAROLINA--CENSUS, 1870.

Steuart, Bradley W. North Carolina 1870 census index. Bountiful, Utah, Precision Indexing, c1989. 3 v. 929/.3756 bi 90-12027.
F253, .S76 1989 LH&G.

NORTH CAROLINA--CENSUS, 1890.

Almasy, Sandra Lee. North Carolina, 1890 Civil War veterans census. Joliet, Ill. Kensington Pub. c 1990. x, 316p. 929/.3756

bi 92-12621.
E494 .A494 1990 LH&G.

NORTH CAROLINA--CHURCH HISTORY--SOURCES.

Fries, Adelaide L. ed. Records of the Moravians in North Carolina. Raleigh [NC], Edwards & Broughton Print. Co., 1922-1969. 11 v. 6209p. 929/.3756 bi 87-686.
F265.M7 F75 1922 LH&G.

NORTH CAROLINA--EMIGRATION AND IMMIGRATION

Index of individuals born outside the United States as enumerated in the 1850 census of North Carolina [Salt Lake City] 1972. 113 l. 929/.3756 bi 87-6746. F258 .I52 LH&G.

NORTH CAROLINA--GAZETTEERS

Powell, William Stevens. The North Carolina gazetteer, Chapel Hill, University of North Carolina Press [1968]. xviii, 561p.
bi 87-4807
F252 .P6 MRR Alc.

NORTH CAROLINA--GENEALOGY

Bernheim, Gotthardt Dellmann. History of the German settlements and of the Lutheran Church in North and South Carolina. Spartanburg, SC, Reprint Co., 1972. xvi, 26-557p. 929.6/004/31 bi 87-9094
F265.G3 B5 1972 LH&G.

Browder, Nathaniel C. The Cherokee Indians and those who came after. Hayesville, NC, Browder, 1973, i.e. 1974, 1980 printing. 414p. 975.6/99 19 bi 87-13399.
F262.C43 B76 1974 LH&G.

Camin, Betty J. North Carolina Bastardy Bonds / Mt. Airy, N.C., B.J. and E.A. Camin, c1990. 252p. 929/.3756 20 bi 91-13596.
F253 .C32 1990 LH&G.

Camin, Betty J. North Carolina Naturalization Index, 1792-1862 / Mt. Airy, N.C., B.J. Camin, c1989. 38p. 929/.3756 20 bi 90-3045. F253 .C33 1989 LH&G.

Clemens, William Montgomery, ed. North and South Carolina marriage records from the earliest colonial days to the Civil War. Baltimore, Genealogical Pub. Co., 1973 [c1927] x, 295p. 929/.3756 bi 87-6196. F253 .C62 1973 LH&G.

Computer Index to North Carolina Marriage Bonds (number of marriages for each name). Hammond, La, Hunting for Bears, [1982] 2 v. 398p. 929/.3756 19 bi 91-2288 F253 .C73 1982 LH&G.

Cutten, George Barton. Silversmiths of North Carolina, 1696-1860 / 2d rev. ed. Raleigh, (NC) North Carolina Dept. of Cultural Resources. Division of Archives and History. 1984 xxix, 301p. 739.2/3722 b19 b1 87-20843. NK7112 .C843 1984 LH&G.

Dobson, David. Directory of Scots in the Carolinas, 1680-1830 / Baltimore Genealogical Pub. Co., 1986, ix, 322p. 929/.3/08991630756 19 bi 87-20806. F265.S3 D63 1986 LH&G.

Fisher, Primrose Watson, One dozen pre-Revolutionary War families of eastern North Carolina, and some of their descendants. New Bern, N.C., New Bern Historical Society Foundation [1958]. 629p. bi 91-19253 CS69 .F56 LH&G.

Fouts, Raymond Parker. Abstracts from newspapers of Wilmington, North Carolina / Cocoa, FL, Gen Rec Books, 1984- v. <1-2 >. 929/.375627 19 bi 87-19734. F264.W7 F68 1984 LH&G.

Fouts, Raymond Parker. Abstracts from the North Carolina gazette of New Bern, North

Carolina / Cocoa, FL, Gen Rec Books, 1982- v. <1-2 >. 929/ .3756 19 bi 87-18326.
F253 .F67 1982 LH&G.

Fouts, Raymond Parker. Abstracts from the State gazette of North Carolina / Cocoa, FL, Gen Rec Books, 1982- v. <1-3 >. 929/ .3756 19 bi 87-16641.
F 253 .F68 1982 LH&G.

Fuller, Marian Camper. Obituaries and marriage notices from the Carolina Watchman, 1832-1890. Greenville, SC, A Press 1981. 342p. 929/.3756 19 bi 87-16703.
F253 .F84 1981 LH&G.

Graves, Mae Blake. Land Grants of New Hanover County / [Wilmington, N.C.] Graves, 1980 xiii, 315p. 929/.375627 19 bi 87-=13691.
HD211.NB G7 LH&G.

Hammer, Carl, Rhinelanders on the Yadkin, 2nd ed. [rev. Salisbury, NC, 1965] 134p. 325.243097567 bi 87-3832.
F265.G3 H3 1965 LH&G.

Haun, Weynette Parks. North Carolina Revolutionary Army accounts, 1st ed. Durham, NC, W.P. Haun 1987 199p. 973.3/456 19 bi 90-7606.
E263.N8 H35 1987 LH&G.

Hofmann, Margaret M. The Granville District of North Carolina, 1748-1763. Weldon, NC, Roanoke News Co., 1986- v. <1 > 929/.3756 19 bi 87-22115. F253 .H628 1986 LH&G.

Hofmann, Margaret M. Colony of North Carolina 1735-1764. Weldon, NC, Roanoke News Co., 1986- v. <1 > 929/.3756 19 bi 87-16509.
F253 .H627 1982 LH&G.

Hofmann, Margaret M. Province of North Carolina, 1663-1729. Weldon, NC, Roanoke News Co., 1979. 384p. 929/.3756 19 bi 87-12042.
F253 .H63 1979? LH&G.

Holcomb, Brent. North Carolina Land Grants in South Carolina / Columbia, SC, Holcomb, 1980. x, 184p. 929/.3756 19 bi 87-13690.
F253 .H64 1980 LH&G.

Index of North Carolina Ancestors / Raleigh, NC, Carolina Genealogical Society, 1981-1984. 2 v, 929/.3756 19 bi 87-16565.
F253 .I53 LH&G.

Ingmire, Frances Terry,. North Carolina Marriage Records. St. Louis, MO, F.T. Ingmire, 1984- v <1-11 > 929/.3756 19 bi 87-20838.
F253 .I54 1984 LH&G.

Johnson, William Perry. Index to North Carolina Wills, 1663-1900, Raleigh, NC, 1963- v. 929/.3756 bi 87-5730.
F262.A15 J6 LH&G.

McCay, Betty L. Sources for genealogical searching in North Carolina, Indianapolis, IN, 1969. 19 leaves. 929.3 bi 87-10572.
CS47 .M33 LH&G.

Meyer, Duane Gilbert, The Highland Scots of North Carolina, 1732-1776. Chapel Hill, University of North Carolina Press, 1961. viii, 218p. 325.24109756 bi 87-2990.
F265.S3 M4 1961 LH&G.

Mitchell, Thornton W. North Carolina Wills: Raleigh, NC, T.W. Mitchell, 1987. 2 v. 929/.3756 19 bi 87-21976.
F253 .M57 1987 LH&G.

Mitchell, Thornton W. North Carolina Wills: Corrected and rev. ed., in one vol. Baltimore, Genealogical Publishing Co., 1992. xliv, 582p. 929/.3756 20 bi 93-21345.
F253 .M575 1992 LH&G.

Mitchell, Thornton W. Preliminary guide to records relating to Blacks in the North Carolina State Archives / Raleigh, NC, State

of North Carolina, Dept. of Cultural Resources, Division of Archives and History, 1980. 14p. 975.6s 016.9756/00496073 19 bi-87-13932.
F251 .N67a no. 17 LH&G.

Murray, Nicholas Russell. Computer indexed marriage records ... North Carolina / Hammond, LA, Hunting for Bears, Inc., 1981 - v. <1 >; 929/.3756 19 bi 87-15164.
F253 .M87 1981 LH&G.

North Carolina. The state records of North Carolina. New York, AMS Press, 1968-1978. 30 v. 975.6/02 19 bi 87-5944
F251 .N62 1968 LH&G.

North Carolina. Adjutant General's Dept. Muster rolls of the soldiers of the War of 1812. Baltimore, Genealogical Pub. co., 1976. 193p. 973.5/24/56 bi 87-8699.
E359.4 .N67 1976 LH&G.

North Carolina. Secretary of State. North Carolina wills and inventories, copied from original and recorded wills and inventories in the office of the Secretary of State. Baltimore, Genealogical Pub. Co., 1967. 587p. 929.3 bi87-4454.
F253 .N86115 1967 LH&G.

North Carolina. State Library, Raleigh. Marriage and death notices from Raleigh Register and North Carolina State gazette, 1799-1825. Baltimore, Genealogical Pub. Co., 1966. 178p. 929.3 bi 87-4040.
F253. N8616 LH&G.

North Carolina higher-court records. Raleigh, NC, N.C., State Dept. of Archives and History, 1968-<1981 > v. <1-5 > 929/.3756 19 bi 87-4975.
KFN917.A4 A7 1670 LH&G.

Potter, Dorothy Williams. Passport of southeastern pioneers, 1770-1823. Baltimore,

MD, Gateway Press, 1982. xi, 449p. 929/.3756 19 bi 87-16506.
F208 .P65 1982 LH&G.

Pruitt, Albert Bruce. Glasgow Land Fraud Papers, 1783-1800, North Carolina Revolutionary War, Bounty Land in Tennessee, NP, A.B. Pruitt, 1988. 1 v. (various pagings). 929/.3756 19 bi 87-24203.
F435 .P78 1988. LH&G.

Ratcliff, Clarence E. North Carolina taxpayers, 1701-1786. Baltimore, MD, Genealogical Pub. Co., 1984- v. <1 > 929/.3756 19 bi 87-19450.
F253 .R37 1984 LH&G.

Ray, Worth S. 1877 - The lost tribes of North Carolina, Austin, TX, 1947. 714p. bi 91-8245.
F253 .R38 LH&G.

Ray, Worth Stickney. The Mecklenburg signers and their neighbors. Baltimore, MD, Genealogical Pub. Co., 1966. 313-558p. 929.3 bi 87-4236.
F262 .M4 R3 1966 LH&G.

Smallwood, Marilu Burch. Some colonial and Revolutionary families of North Carolina. Washing, NC, 1964-1976. 3 v bi 87-3372
F253 .S6 LH&G.

Speidel, Frederick G. North Carolina Masons in the American Revolution. Oxford, NC, Press of Oxford Orphanage, 1975. 77p. 973.3/15/366109756 bi 87-9106.
HS537 .N82 S67 LH&G.

Spence, Wilma Cartwright. North Carolina Bible Records, 1st ed. Logan UT, Unique Print Service, 1974 c1973. 472p 929/.3756 bi 87-7448
F253 .S63 1974 LH&G.

Spence, Wilma Cartwright. Tombstones and Epitaphs of northeastern North Carolina.

Baltimore, MD, Gateway Press, 1973. 323 p. 929/.3756/1 bi 87-6548
F253 .S64 LH&G.

Steuart, Bradley W. North Carolina 1870 census index. Bountiful, UT, Precision Indexing, 1989. 3 v. 929/.3756 20 bi 90-12027.
F253 ,S76 1989 LH&G.

Topkins, Robert M. Marriage and death notices from the Western Carolinian (Salisbury, North Carolina) 1820-1842. Raleigh, NC Topkins, 1975. 255p. 929/.3756 bi 87-8273.
F261 .T66 LH&G.

United States Bureau of the Census. Heads of families at the first census of the United Stated taken in the year 1790. Salt Lake City, UT, Accelerated Indexing Systems, 1978. [64], 292p. 929/.3756 bi 87-11164.
F253 .U53 1978 LH&G.

Wheeler, John Hill. Reminiscences and memoirs of North Carolina and eminent North Carolinians. Baltimore, MD, Genealogical Pub. Co. 1966. 15, lxxiv, 478p. bi 87-3951.
F253 .W56 1966 LH&G.

NORTH CAROLINA - GENEALOGY - BIBLIOGRAPHY.

Draughton, Wallace R. North Carolina Genealogical Reference, New [i.e. 2d] ed. Durham, NC, 1966. xii, 571p. bi 87-3856.
Z5313.U6 .N63 1966 LH&G.

Schweitzer, George Keens, North Carolina genealogical research. Knoxville, TN, G.K. Schweitzer, 1991. 172p 929/.01/0720756 20 bi 93-16464.
Z1319 .S29 1991 LH&G.

NORTH CAROLINA--GENEALOGY--HANDBOOKS, ETC.

Hofmann, Margaret M. The short, short course in the use of North Carolina's early county-

level records in genealogical research. NC? M.M. Hofmann, 1988. 104p. 929/.3756 20 bi 87-907996.
F253 .H633 1988 LH&G.

Leary, Helen F. M. North Carolina research. Raleigh NC, North Carolina Genealogical Society, 1980. xxiv, 633p. 929/.3756 20 bi 87-13328.
CS49 .L4 LH&G.

NORTH CAROLINA--GENEALOGY--PERIODICALS.

North Carolina Genealogical Society. The North Carolina Genealogical Society Journal v. 1- Jan1975- Raleigh, North Carolina Genealogical Society v. 929/.11/09756 bi 87-28334.
F253 .N882a LH&G. Full set.

The North Carolina historical and genealogical register. Vol. 1, no. 1 Jan. 1900 - v 3. no. 3, July 1903. Baltimore, MD, Genealogical Pub. Co. 1970-1971. 3 v. 929/.3756 bi 90-3519.
F251 .N89112 LH&G. Full Set.

NORTH CAROLINA--GENEALOGY-PERIODICALS-INDEXES.

Hamrick, David O. Index to the North Carolina historical and genealogical register. Bradenton, FL, D.O. Hamrick, 1983. 3 v. 929/.3756 19 bi 87-23367.
F251 .N898112 Suppl. LH&G.

NORTH CAROLINA--HISTORY

Foote, William Henry. Sketches of North Carolina, historical and biographical.
Raleigh, NC, Pub. by H.J. Dudley for the Committee on Historical matters of the Synod of North Carolina, Presbyterian Church in the United States, and the North Carolina Presbyterian Historical Society, 1966. a-n, 593p. 975.6 bi 87-4225.
F258 .F68 1966 LH&G.

Reichel, Levin Theodore. The Moravians in North Carolina. Baltimore, MD, Genealogical Pub. Co. 1968. iv, 206p. 284/.6756 bi 87-4757
F265 .M8 R3 1968 LH&G.

NORTH CAROLINA--HISTORY--COLONIAL (& REVOLUTIONARY) PERIODS, CA. 1600-1783--SOURCES

North Carolina. The state records of North Carolina. New York, AMS Press, 1968-1978. 30 v. 975.6/02 19 bi 87-5944.
F251 .N62 1968 LH&G.

Daughters of the American Revolution. North Carolina. Register of soldiers from North Carolina in the American Revolution. Baltimore, MD, Genealogical Pub. Co., 1967. xii, 709 bi 91-14888.
E263 .N8 D17 1967 LH&G.

DeMond, Robert Orley. The loyalists in North Carolina during the Revolution. Hamden, CT, Archon Books, 1964, c1940 viii, 286p. bi 87-3452.
E277 .D35 1964 LH&G.

Hunter, C. L. Sketches of western North Carolina, historical and biographical. Baltimore, MD, Regional Pub. Co., 1970. xii, 379p. 976.6/7/03 bi 87-6603.
E263 .N8 H9 1970 LH&G.

NORTH CAROLINA--HISTORY--REVOLUTION, 1775-1783--REGISTERS.

Speidel, Frederick G. North Carolina Masons in the America Revolution. Oxford, NC,

Press of Oxford Orphanage, 1975. 77p. 973/.3/15/ 366109756 bi 87-9106.
HS537.N82 S67 LH&G.

Haun, Weynette Parks, North Carolina Revolutionary Army accounts, 1st ed. Durham, NC W.P. Haun, 1987. 199p.

973.3/456 19 bi 90-7606.
E263 .N8 H35 1987 LH&G.

NORTH CAROLINA--HISTORY--REVOLUTION, 1775-1783-SOURCES--BIBLIOGRAPHY--CATALOGS.

Cain, Robert J. Preliminary guide to the British records collection. Raleigh, NC, State of North Carolina, Dept. of Cultural Resources, Division of Archives and History, 1979. iv, 53p. 975.6 S 016.9756/02 19 bi 87-13927.
F251 .N67a no. 16 LH&G.

NORTH CAROLINA--HISTORY--CIVIL WAR, 1861-1865.

Histories of the several regiments and battalions from North Carolina in the Great War, 1861-'65. Wendell, NC, Broadfoot's Bookmark, 1982. 5 v. 973.7/456 19 bi 87-16725.
E573.4 .H57 1982 LH&G.

NORTH CAROLINA--HISTORY--CIVIL WAR, 1861-1865--BIBLIOGRAPHY.

Coker, Charles F. W. North Carolina Civil War Records, Rev. Raleigh, NC, State of North Carolina, Division of Archives and History, 1972. 11p. 016.91756 s 973.7 bi 87-7652.
F251 .N67a no. 4 LH&G.

North Carolina. State Dept. of Archives and History. Guide to Civil War Records in the North Carolina States Archives. Raleigh, NC, 1966. x, 128p. 016.9756/03 bi 87-4527.
Z1242 .N73 LH&G.

NORTH CAROLINA--HISTORY--BIBLIOGRAPHY.

Lefler, Hugh Talmage. A guide to the study and reading of North Carolina history. 3d ed. rev. and enl. Chapel Hill, University of North Carolina Press, 1969. viii, 280p. 016.9756 bi 87-5113
Z1319 .L42 LH&G.

Weeks, Stephen Beauregard. A bibliography of North Carolina. Cambridge, MA, Library of Harvard University, 1895. 79p. bi 87-91. Z1319 .W39 LH&G.

NORTH CAROLINA--HISTORY--MANUSCRIPTS--CATALOGS.

Cain, Barbara T. Guide to primate manuscript collections in the North Carolina State Archives, 3rd rev. ed. Raleigh, NC, North Carolina Dept. of Cultural Resources, Division of Archives and History, 1981. x, 706p. 016.9756 19 bi 87-13924.
CD3424 .C34 1981 LH&G.

NORTH CAROLINA--HISTORY--PERIODICALS--INDEXES

Hamrick, David O. Index to the North Carolina historical and genealogical register. Bradenton, FL, D.O. Hamrick, 1983. 3 v. 929/.3756 19 bi 87-23367
F251 .N89112 Suppl. LH&G.

The North Carolina historical review. Raleigh, NC, Division of Archives and History, North Carolina Dept. of Cultural Resources, 1984. 534p. 975.6/042//016 19 bi 87-19880.
F251 .N892 1984 LH&G.

NORTH CAROLINA--HISTORY--SOCIETIES, ETC.

North Carolina. State Dept. of Archives and History. Local historical societies in North Carolina. Raleigh, NC, 1958. 1 v. (unpaged) bi 92-2414. F251.M7 F75 1922 LH&G.

NORTH CAROLINA--HISTORY--LOCAL

North Carolina. State Dept. of Archives and History. The formation of the North Carolina counties, 1663-1943. Raleigh, NC, 1969.
xxix, 323p. 911/.756 bi 87-3392.
F262 .A15 N63 1969 LH&G.

Wheeler, John Hill, Historical sketches of North Carolina from 1584-1851. Baltimore, MD,

Regional Pub. Co., 1964. 2 v. in 1. bi 87-3392.
F253 .W562 1964 LH&G.

Wheeler, John Hill, Reminiscences and memoirs of North Carolina and eminent North Carolinians. Baltimore, MD, Genealogical Pub. Co., 1966. 15, lxxiv, 478p. bi 87-3951.
F253 .W56 1966 LH&G.

NORTH CAROLINA--HISTORY--LOCAL--BIBLIOGRAPHY

Powell, William Stevens. North Carolina county histories;. Chapel Hill, NC, University of North Carolina Library. 1958. 27p. bi 87-2494.
Z1319 .P6 1958 LH&G.

Stevenson, George North. Carolina local history, Raleigh, NC, North Carolina Office of Archives and History, 1972. iii, 82p. 016.91756/03 bi 87-6901.
F251 ,N67a no. 8 LH&G.

Stevenson, George North. Carolina local history, Rev. ed., Raleigh, NC, North Carolina Dept. of Cultural Resources, Division of Archives and History, 1984. v, 209p.

016.9756 19 bi 87-21199.
Z1319 .S74 1984 LH&G.

NORTH CAROLINA--HISTORY, LOCAL--SOURCES.

Leary, Helen F. M. North Carolina research. Raleigh, NC, North Carolina Genealogical Society, 1980. xxiv, 633p. 929/.1/0720756 19 bi 87-13328.
CS49 .L4 LH&G.

NORTH CAROLINA--HISTORY, LOCAL--SOURCES--BIBLIOGRAPHY--CATALOGS.

North Carolina. Division of Archives and History. Archives and Records Section. Guide to research materials in the North Carolina.

State Archives; 6th rev. ed. Raleigh, NC, Dept. of Cultural Resources, Division of Archives and History, Archives and Records Section, 1978. 267p. 2 leaves of plates. 016.9756 bi 87-11183.
CD3424 .N67 1978 LH&G.

NORTH CAROLINA--MILITIA.

Manarin, Louis H. North Carolina troops, 1861-1865. Raleigh, NC, North Carolina. State Dept. of Archives and History, 1966-<1981 > v. <1-8 > 973.7456 bi 87-6148.
E573.3 .M3 LH&G.

NORTH CAROLINA--MILITIA--REGISTERS.

North Carolina. General Assembly. Roster of North Carolina troops in the war between the states. Raleigh, NC, Ashe & Gatling, state printers, 1882. 4 v. bi 87-88.
E573.3 .N87 LH&G.

NORTH CAROLINA--POLITICS AND GOVERNMENT.

North Carolina Government, 1585-1979. An updated ed. of North Carolina Government, 1585-1974. Raleigh, NC, North Carolina Dept. of the Secretary of State, 1981. xviii, 1573p. 320.8756 19 bi 87-15398.
JK4116 .N67 1981 MRR Alc.

Powell, William Stevens. North Carolina through four centuries. Chapel Hill, NC, University of North Carolina Press, 1989. xv, 652p. 975.6 19 bi 91-119.
F253 .P63 1989 LH&G.

NORTH CAROLINA--POLITICS AND GOVERNMENT--COLONIAL PERIOD, CA. 1600-1775-SOURCES.

Records of the executive council, 1664-1734, Raleigh, NC, Dept. of Cultural Resources, Division of Archives and History, 1984. lxvii, 763p. 353.957604/09 19 bi 87-17974.
F257 .R43 1984. LH&G.

NORTH CAROLINA--POLITICS AND GOVERNMENT--REVOLUTION, 1775-1783.

Troxler, Carole Watterson. The loyalist experience in North Carolina. Raleigh, NC, North Carolina Dept. of Cultural Resources,North Carolina. Division of Archives and History, 1976. x, 69p. 320.9/756/03 bi 89-7174.
E277 .T76 LH&G.

NORTH CAROLINA -- STATISTICS--VITAL.

Historical records survey. North Carolina. Guide to vital statistics records in North Carolina. Raleigh, NC, The North Carolina Historical records survey, 1942- 1 v. bi-87-1258.
CD3421 .HS LH&G.

NORTH CAROLINA--COUNCIL--ARCHIVES.

Records of the Executive Council, 1735-1754. Raleigh, NC, Dept. of Cultural Resources and History, Division of Archives and History, 1988. lxxvii, 723p. 353 .975604/09 20 bi 91-8872.
J87 .N8b 1988 LH&G.

NORTH CAROLINA GENEALOGICAL SOCIETY.
North Carolina Genealogical Society. The North Carolina Genealogical Society journal. v. 1- Jan. 1975- Raleigh, NC, North Carolina Genealogical Society. 929/.1.3756 19 bi 87-28334.
F253 .N882a LH&G. Full Set.

NORTH CAROLINA HISTORICAL REVIEW--INDEXES.

The North Carolina Historical Review. Raleigh, NC, Division of Archives and History, North Carolina Dept. of Cultural Resources, 1984. 534p. 975.6/042/016 19 bi 87-19880.
F251 .N892 1984. LH&G.

SOUTH CAROLINA

SOUTH CAROLINA -- BIBLIOGRAPHY.

Oliphant, Mary Chevillette (Simms). The works of A. Salley. Greenville, SC, 1949. 49p bi 92-11571.
Z8779.73 .04 LH&G.

Turnbull, Robert James. Bibliography of South Carolina, 1563-1950. Charlottesville, University of Virginia Press, 1956-1960. 6 v. bi 92-11527.
Z1333 .T8 LH&G.

Biographical Directory of the South Carolina House of Representatives, 1st ed. Columbia, SC, University of South Carolina Press. 1974- <1984 > v. <1-4 >. 328.757/092/2 B bi 87-6325.
JK4278 .B56 LH&G.

Cyclopedia of eminent and representative men of the Carolinas of the nineteenth century. Spartanburg, SC,. Reprint Co. 19 , c18 2 v. 920/.0756 bi 87-8207.
F268 .C992 LH&G.

Hemphill, James Calvin, ed. Men of mark in South Carolina, Washington, DC, Men of mark publishing co., 1907-09. 4 v. bi 87-295.
F268 .H49 LH&G.

Who's Who in South Carolina. Columbia, SC, Current historical association 1935- v. bi 92-15263. F268 .W65 LH&G. Partial Set.

SOUTH CAROLINA--BIOGRAPHY--DICTIONARIES.

Cote, Richard N. Dictionary of South Carolina biography. Easley, SC, Southern Historical Press 1985- v. <1 > 920/.0757 B 19 bi 87-20707.
CT259 .C67 1985 LH&G.

SOUTH CAROLINA--CENSUS--INDEXES.

Jackson, Ronald Vern. Early South Carolina. Bountiful, UT, Accelerated Indexing Systems, 1980- v. <1 > 929/.3757 19 bi 87-15215.
F268 .J26 LH&G.

SOUTH CAROLINA--CENSUS, 1790.

United States Bureau of the Census. Heads of families at the first census of the United States taken in the year, 1790, South Carolina. Bountiful, UT, Accelerated Indexing Systems, 1978. 82, 150p, 7 leaves of plates. 929/.3757 19 bi 87-11163.
F268 .U54 1978 LH&G.

Holcomb, Brent. Index to the 1800 census of South Carolina. Baltimore, MD, Genealogical Pub. Co. 1980. vi, 264p, 929/.3757 19 bi 87-12261.
F268 .H635 LH&G.

SOUTH CAROLINA--CENSUS, 1800--INDEXES.

Jackson, Ronald Vern. South Carolina 1800 census 2d. ed. Bountiful, UT, Accelerated Indexing Systems, 1975. xxix, 148p. 929/.3757 19 bi 87-11093.
F268 .J33 1975 LH&G.

SOUTH CAROLINA--CENSUS, 1810--INDEXES.

Jackson, Ronald Vern. South Carolina 1810 census index. Bountiful, UT, Accelerated Indexing Systems, 1976. 50, xxviii, 97p. 929/.3757 19 bi 87-9901.
F268 .J332 LH&G.

SOUTH CAROLINA--CENSUS, 1820--INDEXES.

Jackson, Ronald Vern. South Carolina 1820 census index. Bountiful, UT, Accelerated Indexing Systems, 1976. 54, 156p. 929/.3757 19 bi 87-9902.
F268 .J332 LH&G.

SOUTH CAROLINA--CENSUS, 1830--INDEXES.

Jackson, Ronald Vern. South Carolina 1830 census index. Bountiful, UT, Accelerated Indexing Systems, 1976. xxviii, 115, 39p. 929/.3757 19 bi 87-11141.
F268 .J335 LH&G.

SOUTH CAROLINA--CENSUS, 1840--INDEXES.

Jackson, Ronald Vern. South Carolina 1840 census index. Bountiful, UT, Accelerated Indexing Systems, 1977. 33, xxviii, 7, 119p. 929/.3757 19 bi 87-11111.
F268 .J337 LH&G.

SOUTH CAROLINA--CENSUS, 1850--INDEXES.

Jackson, Ronald Vern. South Carolina 1850 census index. Bountiful, UT, Accelerated Indexing Systems, 1976. 33, xxiv, 174p. 929/.3757 19 bi 87-11132.
F268 .J34 LH&G.

SOUTH CAROLINA--CENSUS, 1860--INDEXES.

Arnold, Jonnie P. Index to 1860 Federal Census of South Carolina. Clarkesville, GA. J.P. Arnold, 1982. 256p. 929/.3757 19 bi 87-18295.
F268 .A76 1982 LH&G.

Arnold, Jonnie P. Index to 1860 Mortality schedule of South Carolina. Clarkesville, GA. J.P. Arnold, 1982. 32 l. 929/.3757 19 bi 87-18298.
F268 .A763 1982 LH&G.

SOUTH CAROLINA--CLAIMS

South Carolina. State Auditor. Copy of the original index book showing the revolutionary claims filed in South Carolina between August, 20, 1783 and August 31, 1776. Baltimore, MD, Genealogical Pub. Co., 1969. 387p. 929.3 bi 87-4902. E263.S7 A53 1969 LH&G.

South Carolina. Treasury. Accounts audited of revolutionary claims against South Carolina... Columbia, SC, Printed for the Historical commission of South Carolina by the State company, 1953- p. cm. bi 91-14890. E263.S7 S66 LH&G.

SOUTH CAROLINA--EMIGRATION AND IMMIGRATION.

Jones, Jack Moreland, South Carolina immigrants, 1760 to 1770. Danielsville, GA, Heritage Papers, 1988. xi, 430p. 929/.3757915 20 bi 902881.
F268 .J66 1988 LH&G.

SOUTH CAROLINA--GENEALOGY.

Abstracts of wills of Charleston District, South Carolina, and other wills recorded in the district, 1783-1800. Charleston, SC, Moore, 1974. x, 526p. 929/.3757915 20 bi 90-2881.
F279.C453 A225 LH&G.

Baldwin, Agnes Leland. First Settlers to South Carolina, 1670-1700. Easley, SC, Southern Historical Press, 1985. xii, 268p. 929/.3757 19 bi 87-20708.
F268 .B35 1985 LH&G.

Bernheim, Gotthardt Dellmann. History of the German settlements and of the Lutheran Church in North and South Carolina. Spartanburg, SC, Reprint Co., 1972. xvi, 26-557p. 975.6/004/31 bi 87-9094.
F265.G3 B5 1972 LH&G.

Berry, Faye. 1860 mortality census of upper South Carolina. Spartanburg, SC, F. Berry, 1985- v. <1 >. 929/.3757 19 bi 87-20963.
F268 .B47 1985 LH&G.

Bethea, Mary Belle Manning. Ancestral key to the Pee Dee. 1978- Columbia, SC, R.L. Bryan, v. 920/.0757/6 bi 87-10865
CT259 .B47 LH&G.

Bible Records. Greenville, SC, A Press, 1981. 203 p. 929/.3757 19 bi 87-16712. F268 .B53 1981 LH&G.

Burns, Annie Walker, Abstract of pensions of South Carolina soldiers of the Revolutionary War, War of 1812 & Indian Wars. Washington, DC, Burns 1960- v. 929/.373 bi 87-9243. E263.S7 B87 LH&G.

Charleston County, S.C. Register of Mesne Conveyance Office. In index to deeds of the Province and State of South Carolina, 1719-1785 and Charleston District, 1785-1800. Easley, SC, Southern Historical Press, 1977. 841p. 929/.3757 29 bi 87-13628. F268 .C47 1977 LH&G.

Clemens, William Montgomery, ed. North and South Carolina marriage records from the earliest colonial days to the Civil War. Baltimore, MD, Genealogical Pub. Co. 1973, 1927. x, 295p. 929/.3/756 bi 87-6196. F253 .C62 1973 LH&G.

Dobson, David. Directory of Scots in the Carolinas, 1680-1830 / Baltimore Genealogical Pub. Co., 1986, ix, 322p. 929/.3/08991630756 19 bi 87-20806. F265.S3 D63 1986 LH&G.

Draine, Tony. South Carolina tax list, 1733-1742. Columbia, SC, Congaree Publications, 1986. 100p. 929/.3757 19 bi91-2290. F268 .D72 1986 LH&G.

Fuller, Marian Camper. Obituaries and marriage notices from the Carolina Watchman, 1832-1890. Greenville, SC, A Press 1981. 342p. 929/.3756 19 bi 87-16703. F253 .F84 1981 LH&G.

Hicks, Theresa M. Compendium of South Carolina Records. Columbia, SC, Peppercorn Publications, 1985. 117p. 4p. of plates 929/.3757 19 bi 87-23293. F268 .H522 1985 LH&G.

Holcomb, Brent. A brief guide to South Carolina genealogical research and records. Columbia, SC, Holcomb, 1979. 29p. 929/.1/0720757 bi 87-12399.
F268 .H63 LH&G.

Holcomb, Brent. Index to the 1850 mortality schedule of South Carolina. Easley, SC, Southern Historical Press, 1980. 48p, 2 leaves of plates 929/.3757 19 bi 87-13349
F268 .H636 1980 LH&G.

Holcomb, Brent. Marriage and death notices from Camden, South Carolina newspapers, 1816-1865. Easley, SC, Southern Historical Press, 1978. 1, 166p 929/.375761 19 bi 13725.
F279.C2 H7 LH&G.

Holcomb, Brent. Marriage and death notices from Columbia, South Carolina newspapers, 1792-1839. Easley, SC, Southern Historical Press, 1982. v, 114p. 929/.375771 19 bi 87-16838.
F279.C7 H64 1982 LH&G.

Holcomb, Brent. Marriage and death notices from Columbia, South Carolina newspapers, 1838-1860, including legal notices from burnt counties. Columbia, SC, B.H. Holcomb, 1988. 352p. 929/.3757 19 bi 87-24344.
F268 .M19 1988 LH&G.

Holcomb, Brent. Marriage and death notices from the Charleston observer, 1827-1845. Columbia, SC, B. Holcomb, 1980. 283p. 929/.375 19 bi 92-11956.
F268 .H639 1980 LH&G.

Holcomb, Brent. Marriage and death notices from the Charleston times, 1800-1821. Baltimore, MD, Genealogical Pub. Co. 1979. 374p. 929/.3757 19 bi 87-12060.
F268 .H64 LH&G.

Holcomb, Brent. Marriage and death notices from the up-country of South Carolina as taken

from the Greenville newspapers, 1826-1863. Columbia, SC, Ordered from SCMAR, 1983. 269p. 929/.3757 19 bi 87-18257
F268 .H6418 1983 LH&G.

Holcomb, Brent. Marriage, death, and estate notices from Georgetown, S.C. newspapers, 1791-1861. Easley, SC, Southern Historical Press, 1979. 208, 20p. 929/.375789 19 bi 91-2291.
F268 .H4624 1979 LH&G.

Holcomb, Brent. North Carolina Land Grants in South Carolina. Columbia, SC, Holcomb, 1980. x, 184p. 929/.3757 19 bi 87-13626.
F253 .H64 1980 LH&G.

Holcomb, Brent. Some South Carolina county records. Easley, SC, Southern Historical Press, 1976- v. 929/.3757 bi 87-13626.
F268 .H643 LH&G.

Holcomb, Brent. South Carolina marriages. Baltimore, MD, Genealogical Pub. Co. 1980-81. 2 v. 929/.3757 19 bi 87-13480.
F268 .H645 LH&G.

Holcomb, Brent. South Carolina naturalizations, 1783-1850. Baltimore, MD, Genealogical Pub. Co. 1985. vi, 255p. 929/.3757 19 bi 87-19475.
F268 .H647 1985 LH&G.

Holcomb, Brent. Supplements to South Carolina marriages, 1688-1820. Baltimore, MD, Genealogical Pub. Co. 1984. viii, 57p. 929/.3757 19 bi 87-19488
F268 .H645 Supp01. LH&G.

Holcomb, Brent. York, South Carolina, newspapers. Spartanburg, SC, Reprint Co., 1981/ 129p. 929/.375743 19 bi 87-14425.
F279.Y67 .H64 LH&G.

Jackson, Ronald Vern. Index to South Carolina Land Grants, 1784-1800. Bountiful, UT,

Accelerated Indexing Systems, 1977. 20, 164p. 929/.3757 19 bi 87-14939.
F268 J27 LH&G.

The Keowee courier, 1849-1851, 1857-1861, and 1865-1868. Easley, SC, Southern Historical Press, 1979.
195p. 929/.375721 19 bi 87-12145.
F277.P5 K46 LH&G.

King, Susan L. History and records of the Charleston Orphan House, 1790-1860.. Easley, SC, Southern Historical Press, 1984. iii, 171p. 362.7/32/09757915 19 bi 87-19816.
HV995.C32 C44 1984 LH&G.

Langley, Clara A. South Carolina deed abstracts, 1719-1772. Easley, SC, Southern Historical Press, 1983-<1984> v. <1, 3-4 >
929/.3757 19 bi 87-19658.
F268 .L36 1983 LH&G.

Lineage charts, Greenville, SC, South Carolina Genealogical Society, 1976-<1981 >
v. <1-4 > 929/.3757 19 bi 87-15001
F268 .L56 LH&G.

Marriage and death notices from Baptist newspapers of South Carolina, 1835-1865. Spartanburg, SC, Reprint Co., 1981. 143p.
929/.3757 19 bi 87-14424.
F268 .M18 1981 LH&G.

Medlin, William F. Quaker Families of South Carolina & Georgia. Columbia, SC, Ben Franklin Press, 1982. vi, 138p. 929/.3/088286 19 bi 87-18385.
F280.F89 M43 1982 LH&G.

Moran, Alton T. Genealogical abstracts from the South Carolina gazette, 1732-1735. Bowie, MD. Heritage Books, 1987. iv, 161p 929/.3757 19 bi 90-7618. F268 .M677 1987 LH&G.

Moss, Bobby Gilmer. The patriots at the Cowpens. Blacksburg, SC, B.G. Moss, 1985.

xxiii, 261p. 973.3/457 19 bi 87-20962.
E241.C9 M67 1985 LH&G.

Parker, Elmer O. American Revolution roster, Fort Sullivan (later Fort Moultrie), 1776-1780. Battle of Fort Sullivan: events leading to first decisive victory. Charleston, SC, Fort Sullivan Chapter, Daughters of the American Revolution, 1976. viii, 311p. 929/.3/457 19 bi 87-8739.
E241.M9 jP37 1976 LH&G.

Potter, Dorothy Williams Passports of southeastern pioneers, 1770-1823. Baltimore, MD, Gateway Press, 1982. xi, 449p. 929/.375 19 bi 87-16506.
F208 .P65 1982 LH&G.

Probate records of South Carolina. Easley, SC, Southern Historical Press, 1977-<1979 > v. <1-3 >. 929/.3757 19 bi 87-12144.
KFS2315 .A545 1764[sic] LH&G.

Records of the regiments of the South Carolina line in the Revolutionary War. Baltimore, MD, Genealogical Pub. Co. 1977. 86p. 973.3/4 bi 87-9799.
E263.S7 R42 LH&G.

Revill, Janie. Some South Carolina genealogical records. Easley, SC, Southern Historical Press, 1986. v, 398p. 929/.3757 19 bi 87-22237.
F268 .R58 1944 LH&G.

Revill, Janie. South Carolina marriage records. Sumter, SC, J. Revill, 1944 88 leaves 929/.3757 19 bi 87-19732.
F268 .R48 1944 LH&G.

Salley, A. S. comp. and ed. Death notices in the South Carolina gazette, 1732-1775. Columbia, SC, South Carolina Archives Dept. 1954. 42, 39p. 929/.3757 19 bi 91-2292
F268 .S15 1954 LH&G.

Smith, Alma Spires. Patent land survey. Greenville, SC, A Press, 1978. 174p 929/.3757 19 bi 87-15022.
F268 .S58 1978 LH&G.

Some South Carolina marriages & obituaries and miscellaneous information, 1826-1854. Memphis, TN, Mrs. C.R. Barham, 1978. ix, 209p. 929/.3757 19 bi 87-15138.
F268 .S6 1978 LH&G.

South Carolina Dept. of Archives and History. The jury lists of South Carolina, 1778-1779. Bicentennial ed. Greenville, SC, Hendrix, 1975. 131p 929/.3757 19 bi 87-8236.
F268 .S64 1975 LH&G.

South Carolina Colony. Council of Safety. South Carolina Provincial troops. Baltimore, MD, Genealogical Pub. Co. 1977. 234p. 929/.3757 19 bi 87-8999
E263.S7 S74 1977 LH&G.

South Carolina genealogies. Spartanburg, SC,.Published in associated with the South Carolina Historical Society by Reprint Co., 1983. 5 v. 975.7 19 bi 87-16017.
F268 .S68 1983 LH&G.

Thomas, Betty Wood. South Carolina wills. Columbus, MS, Blewett Co., <1980-1982 > v. <2, 4 > 929/.3757 19 bi 87-16868.
F268 .T56 1980 LH&G.

Warren, Mary Bondurant. Citizens and immigrants--South Carolina, 1768. Danielsville, GA, Heritage Papers, 1980. 464p. 929/.3757 19 bi 87-13621.
F268 .W36 LH&G.

Warren, Mary Bondurant. South Carolina jury lists, 1718-1783. Danielsville, GA, Heritage Papers, 1977. 130p. 1 leaf of plates. 929/.3757 19 bi 87-10967.
F268 .W37 LH&G.

Warren, Mary Bondurant. South Carolina wills, 1670-1853 or later. Danielsville, GA, Heritage Papers, 1981. x, 157p. 929/.3757 19 bi 87-16645.
F268 .W38 LH&G.

Wilson, Teresa E. Marriage and death notices from the Southern patriot. Easley, SC, Southern Historical Press, 1982-<1986 > v. <1-2 > 929/.3757 19 bi 91-2293.
F268 .W67 1982 LH&G.

Young, Willie Pauline. A genealogical collection of South Carolina wills and records. Liberty, SC 1955-1984. 2 v. 929/.3757 19 bi 87-2086.
F268 .Y6 LH&G.

SOUTH CAROLINA--GENEALOGY--ARCHIVAL RESOURCES--DIRECTORIES.

Holcomb, Brent. A guide to South Carolina genealogical research and records. Columbia, SC, B.H. Holcomb. 1986. 62p. 929/.1/0720757 19 bi 87-23284.
F268 .H634 1986 LH&G.

SOUTH CAROLINA--GENEALOGY--ARCHIVAL RESOURCES--UNITED STATES.

Schweitzer, George Keene, South Carolina genealogical research. Knoxville, TN. G.K. Schweitzer, 1985. 192p. 929/.01/0720757 19 bi 87-20917,
Z1333 .S38 1985 LH&G.

SOUTH CAROLINA--GENEALOGY--BIBLIOGRAPHY-UNION LISTS.

Cote, Richard N. Local and family history in South Carolina. Easley, SC, Southern Historical Press, 1981. xiv, 498p. 016.9757 19 bi 86-16827.
Z1333 .C67 1981 LH&G.

SOUTH CAROLINA--GENEALOGY--HANDBOOKS, MANUALS, etc.

Bryan, Evelyn McDaniel Frazier. Hunting your ancestors in South Carolina, Rev. & enl. 2d ed. Jacksonville, FL, Florentine Press, 1974. 42p. 919/.01/09757 bi 87-8289.
F268 .B9 1974 LH&G.

Hicks, Theresa M. South Carolina, a guide for genealogists, 1st ed. Columbia, SC, Peppercorn Publications, 1985. 229p. 929/.01/0720-757 19 bi 87-21125.
F268 .H56 1985 LH&G.

SOUTH CAROLINA--GENEALOGY--INDEXES.

Cannon, Margaret H. Index to The South Carolina magazine of ancestral research, volumes I - X, 1973-1982. Spartanburg, SC, Reprint Co., 1985. iii, 388p. 929/.01/0720757 19 bi 87-20066.
CS42 .S64 Suppl. LH&G.

SOUTH CAROLINA--GENEALOGY--PERIODICALS.

South Carolina historical magazine. Charleston, SC, South Carolina Historical Society, v. bi 92-15265. Began with Vol. 53 in Jan. 1952.
F266 .S55 LH&G. Indexes only.

The South Carolina magazine of ancestral research. Columbia, SC, B. H. Holcomb v. 929/.3575 bi 87-29266. Began with issue for winter 1973. CS42 .S64 LH&G. Full Set.

SOUTH CAROLINA--GENEALOGY--SOURCES.

Moore, Caroline T., ed. Abstracts of the wills of the State of South Carolina. Charleston, SC, 1960-<69 > v. <1-3 > maps on lining paper bi 87-3013. F268 .M67 LH&G.

Revill, Janie, comp. A compilation of the original lists of Protestant immigrants to

South Carolina, 1763-1773. Baltimore, MD, Genealogical Pub. Co. 1968. 163p. 929.3 bi 87-4808.
F272 .R49 1968 LH&G.

SOUTH CAROLINA--GUIDEBOOKS.

Writers' Program, South Carolina. South Carolina. St. Clair Shores, Mich. Scholarly Press, 1976, 1941. xxvii, 514p. 32 leaves of plates 917.57/04/4 bi87-8083.
F267.3 .W74 1976 LH&G.

SOUTH CAROLINA--HISTORY.

Gregg, Alexander, Bp., History of the old Cheraws; Reprint of the enl. ed. of 1925 with addenda. Baltimore, MD, Genealogical Pub. Co. 1967. viii, 629p. 970.3 bi 87-4467.
E99.C495 G7 1967 LH&G.

Thomas, T. Gaillard pub. A contribution to the history of the Huguenots of South Carolina. Columbia, SC, R.L. Bryan, 1972. vi, 176p. 917.57 bi87-5866.
F280.H8 T4 1972 LH&G.

Writers' Program. South Carolina. Palmetto place names. Spartanburg, SC, Reprint Co., 1975. 158p. 917.57 bi 92-11955.
F267 .W7 1975 LH&G.

SOUTH CAROLINA--HISTORY--COLONIAL PERIOD, CA 1600-1775.

Hirsch, Arthur Henry. The Hugenots of colonial South Carolina. Hamden, SC, Archon Books, 1962, 1928. 338p. bi 87-3024.
F280.H8 H6 1962 LH&G.

Ivers, Larry E. Colonial forts of South Carolina, 1670-1775, 1st ed. Columbia, SC, Published for the South Carolina Tricentennial Commission, by the University of South Carolina Press, 1970. 77p. 975.7/2 bi 87-5481.
F272 .I93 LH&G.

SOUTH CAROLINA--HISTORY--COLONIAL PERIOD, CA 1600-1775--SOURCES

Esker, Katie-Prince Ward. South Carolina memorials, 1731-1776; Cottonport, SC, Polyanthos, 1973-1977 2 v. 929/.3757 bi 87-5920.
F272 .E84 LH&G.

Moore, Caroline T. Records of the secretary of the Province of South Carolina, 1692-1721. Columbia, SC, R.L. Bryan Co., xi, 457p. 929/.3757 19 bi 87-10923.
F268 .M675 LH&G.

South Carolina Colony. Governor and Council. Warrants for lands in South Carolina

Dept. of Archives and History by the University of South Carolina Press, 1973. xvi, 724p. 929/.3757 bi 87-6278.
F272 ,S69 1973 LH&G.

SOUTH CAROLINA--HISTORY-REVOLUTION, 1775-1783.

De Saussure, Wilmot Gibbes, comp. The names, as far as can be ascertained, of the officers who served in the South Carolina regiments on the continental establishment. Charleston, SC, reprinted 1894(sic). 34p. bi 87-307
P263.S7 D36 LH&G.

Society of the Cincinnati. South Carolina. The original institution of the general Society of the Cincinnati. Charleston, SC, Walker, Evans & Cogswell, printers, 1880. 126p. bi 87-163. E202.1 .S24 LH&G.

SOUTH CAROLINA--HISTORY-REVOLUTION, 1775-1783--REGISTERS.

Ervin, Sarah (Sullivan) ed. South Carolinians in the Revolution. Baltimore, MD, Genealogical Pub. Co. 1965. xiii, 217p. bi 87-3178.
E263.S7 E78 1965 LH&G.

Pruitt, Janye Conway (Garlington). Revolutionary War pension applicants who served from South Carolina. NP, 1946. 70p. bi 87-1534.
E263.S7 P78 LH&G.

South Carolina. Treasury. Stub entries to indents issued in payment of claims against Sourth Carolina growing out of the Revolution. Columbia, SC, Printed for the Historical Commission of South Carolina by the State Co., 1910- v. bi 91-14891
E263.S7 S7 LH&G.

South Carolina. Treasury. Stub entries to indents issued in payment of claims against South Carolina growing out of the Revolution. 1939- Columbia, SC, Printed for the Historical Commission of South Carolina by the State Co., v. 973.3/45/702 bi 87-9173.
E263.S7 S57 1939 LH&G.

SOUTH CAROLINA--HISTORY--CIVIL WAR, 1861-1865.

South Carolina. Archives dept. South Carolina troops in Confederate Service. Columbia, SC, The R.L. Bryan Company, 1913-1930. 3 v. bi 91-24410.
E577.3 .S72 LH&G.

SOUTH CAROLINA--HISTORY--BIBLIOGRAPHY.

Jones, Lews P. Books and articles on South Carolina History; 1st ed. Columbia, SC, Published for the South Carolina Tricentennial Commission, by the University of South Carolina Press, 1970. xiv, 104p. 016.9757 bi 87-5294. Z133 .J65 LH&G.

SOUTH CAROLINA--HISTORY--PERIODICALS.

South Carolina historical magazine. Charleston, SC, South Carolina Historical Society, v. bi 92-15265. Began with Vol. 53 in Jan. 1952.
F266 .S55 LH&G Indexes only.

SOUTH CAROLINA--HISTORY, LOCAL.

Names in South Carolina. Columbia, SC, Dept. of English, University of South Carolina, 1967. v, 271p. 975.7 bi 87-4396. F267 .N32 LH&G.

SOUTH CAROLINA--MILITIA--REGISTERS.

Moss, Bobby Gilmer. Roster of South Carolina Patriots in the American Revolution. Baltimore, MD, Genealogical Pub. Co. 1983. xxiii, 1022p. 973/.3/457 19 bi 87-16499. E263.S7 M67 1983 LH&G.

SOUTH CAROLINA--REGISTERS.

Biographical directory of the South Carolina House of Representatives, 1st ed. Columbia, SC, University of South Carolina Press, 1974- <1984 >, 328.757/092/2 B bi 87-6325. JK4278 .B56 LH&G.

SOUTH CAROLINA. GENERAL ASSEMBLY, SENATE--HISTORY.

Bailey, N. Louise. Biographical directory of the South Carolina Senate, 1776-1985, 1st ed. Columbia, SC, University of South Carolina Press, 1986. 3 v. xiv, 2235p. 328.757/0922 19 bi 87-21318. JK4276 .B35 1986 LH&G.

Reynolds, Emily Bellinger. The Senate of the State of South Carolina, 1776-1962. Columbia, SC, Senate of the General Assembly of the State of South Carolina, 1962. vii, 186p. 328.757 bi 87-1319. JK4276 .R43 LH&G.

SOUTH CAROLINA GAZETTE--ABSTRACTS.

Moran, Alton T. Genealogical abstracts from the South Carolina gazette, 1732-1735. Bowie, MD, Heritage Books, 1987. iv, 161p. 929/.3757 19 bi 90-7618. F268 .M677 1987 LH&G.

SOUTH CAROLINA MAGAZINE OF ANCESTRAL RESEARCH--INDEXES.

Cannon, Margaret H. Index to The South Carolina magazine of ancestral research. volumes I-X, 1973-1982. Spartanburg, SC,. Reprint Co., 1985. iii, 388p. 929/.1/ 0720757 19 bi 87-20066.
CS42 .S63 Suppl LH&G.

CROSS-REFERENCE TABLE OF FAMILY NAMES

This cross-reference table lists family names given in titles and accompanying descriptive statements recorded in this bibliography. Note that hyphenated names, such as FOX-JONES are, almost always, listed separately, e.g. under FOX and under JONES.